# THE PLAYS OF ŚAṄKARADEVA

# PERFORMING ARTS SERIES

*General Editor*
Kapila Vatsyayan

*Editorial Board*
Farley P. Richmond

Artists use their voices and/or their bodies in Performing Arts, often in relation to other objects, to convey artistic expression. This may include several disciplines like theatre, music and dance to be performed individually or together in front of live audiences. In India, various facets of performing arts are all pervading bringing colour and joy to numerous festivals and ceremonies, and reaffirming the faith of the people in their heritage. They are the link between the past and the present. The Series attempts to preserve and promote the vast cultural heritage of India expressed in music, dance and drama.

**12**

# THE PLAYS OF ŚAṄKARADEVA

*Introduction, Life and Works, All His Six Plays with Transliterated Text and English Translation*

YASHODHARA MEDHI

MOTILAL BANARSIDASS PUBLISHERS
PRIVATE LIMITED • DELHI

*First Edition: Delhi, 2017*



ISBN: 978-81-208-4094-2

*Also available at:*
MOTILAL BANARSIDASS
41 U.A. Bungalow Road, Jawahar Nagar, Delhi 110 007
8 Mahalaxmi Chamber, 22 Bhulabhai Desai Road, Mumbai 400 026
203 Royapettah High Road, Mylapore, Chennai 600 004
236, 9th Main III Block, Jayanagar, Bengaluru 560 011
8 Camac Street, Kolkata 700 017
Ashok Rajpath, Patna 800 004
Chowk, Varanasi 221 001

MLBD Cataloging-in-Publication Data
The Plays of Sankaradeva
by Yashodhara Medhi
ISBN : 978-81-208-4094-2
Includes 3 Appendices, Glossary, Bibliography and General and Person Index
I. Hinduism II. Vaishnavism III. Spiritualism
IV. Sankardeva V. Medhi, Yashodhara

*Published by*
Motilal Banarsidass Publishers Private Limited
*www.mlbd.com • mlbd@mlbd.com*
*Printed by* Ajanta Offset Printers

Dedicated to

the ever cherished memory

of my most beloved father

Late Professor Dr. Mukunda Madhava Sharma

## CONTENTS

**PART B**

# FOREWORD

The Neo-Vaiṣṇavite movement initiated by Śaṅkaradeva was not merely a religious movement, but it was also a cultural movement which had far-reaching impact on literature, song, dance as well as *abhinaya* and drama. He was the first dramatist of Assam who wrote a few dramas and also took active part in the performances of those dramas. The *Carit Puthis* like the *Kathā-guru-carita* and others inform us that the saint-poet had composed seven dramas, viz., the *Kāli Damana Yātrā*, the *Patnī-Prasāda*, the *Keli-Gopāla Nāṭaka,* the *Rukmiṇī Haraṇa Nāṭa,* the *Pārijāta Haraṇa Nāṭaka,* the *Kaṁsa-Vadha* or *Janma- Yātrā* (which is not found today because of many reasons) and lastly the *Śrī Rāma-Vijaya Nāṭa.*

Researchers have undertaken study in various aspects of the saint-poet Śaṅkaradeva and his literary contributions and performing art forms- art-craft-painting and so on.

But nobody had tried to render all the dramas of Śaṅkaradeva into English till now. Dr. Yashodhara Medhi took the challenge bravely and had done the Ph.D. work on the rendering of all the dramas of Śaṅkaradeva in accordance with the advice of her father late Dr. Mukunda Madhava Sharma, Ph.D., D.Litt., Professor and Head,Dept.of Sanskrit, Gauhati University and the former Vice-Chancellor, Dibrugarh University.

Professor Sharma advised her to work for her Ph.D. under the guidance of the present writer of the foreword, i.e., Dr. Nabin Chandra Sarma. Accordingly she started her Ph.D. work on the topic "A Literal English Translation of the Plays of Śaṅkaradeva with a Critical Appraisal". On the basis of that work she has already received the Ph.D. Degree in the year 2012.

The present researcher has done this great work with deep faith, profound knowledge and patience as well as great regards to the saint-poet Śaṅkaradeva.

I hope this book would be received by the readers with love and sympathy. The publisher will be benefited if this book is received with the appreciation it deserves.

Durgasarobar,
Guwahati-9
P.N.Gohain Barua Road
House No. 45
18th April,2015

Dr. Nabin Ch. Sarma
Former Professor and Head,
Dept. of Folklore Research,
and UGC Emeritus Fellow
Gauhati University

# PREFACE

Śaṅkaradeva (1449-1568), the pioneer *Vaiṣṇava* saint of Assam was also a social reformer and a great literary genius. This polymath saint translated many important original scriptures in Sanskrit with *Vaiṣṇava* faith into Assamese and *Brajāvalī* language. The six plays by him, which are called '*Aṅkīyā Nāṭa*' are the first written form of vernacular drama in India and the first formal prose in *Brajāvalī* language in Assam. The plays are faithful and bona-fide representations of the stories from authoritative Vedic texts, especially the *Rāmāyaṇa and Bhāgavata-Purāṇa* (*Śrīmad Bhāgavatam*) with a sprinkling of local flavours off course.

The performance of these plays is called '*bhāonā*', which continues to be an integral part of the Assamese culture and tradition. The entire science of composing and performing these dramas is a new genre, with unique and original techniques exclusive to these plays. As intended, the plays infuse a deep sense of religious ecstasy in the audience and as such, they were the most effective medium of propagation of the simplistic process of *Vaiṣṇava Bhakti* cult known as the *Eka Śaraṇa Nāma Dharma* among the common illiterate masses. These plays also played a great part in unifying the diverse ethnic clans and different religious groups of North Eastern India of that time introducing complete equality and democracy in religion. The *nāṭas* have greatly influenced the Assamese society and given a distinctive characteristic to the Assamese literature and culture.

Apart from the plays the saint had produced voluminous literary works which shaped the literary backbone of Assamese literature. Because of the modern and pragmatic views and secular outlook of Śaṅkaradeva, the writings of this saint of the 15th century are still very relevant today, in a strife-torn and confused world. Further, it is advised in the *Upaniṣad, dve vidye veditavye parā caivāparā ca,* which means, one should study both *parā* and *aparā vidya*, i.e., learning which teaches the reality and the true spiritual knowledge as well as learning which teaches science-technology and material wisdom that help in leading the life.[1] It seems, in the present day world, it has become very necessary to study the spiritual aspect of life as taught by our masters while studying for our material achievements side by side, to be able to lead a balanced and meaningful life.

Thus, it is obligatory to make this special genius known to the rest of the world. And the most effective way for that is to translate his literary creations into English.

English is the most widely used language in the world today. As an effect of globalization there has been much activity lately in respect of exchange of knowledge regarding socio-cultural backgrounds of different countries and also there is a growing tendency among the masses to educate through English medium. For these very reasons, original writings in Assamese are to be made available in English and other languages. There are the children of those who had to leave their motherland in search of employment and there are many people who know Assamese yet unfamiliar with *Brajāvalī*. Also there are people all over the world who are interested to study exotic literature and culture.

However, it is heartening to note that larger number of people are now realising the relevance of the teachings and philosophies of Śaṅkaradeva in the current world perspective and there is great interest for the works of Śaṅkaradeva from around the world.

But due to lack of translations, much of the world is still deprived of relishing his literary compositions. It has been felt by a concerned section that it is high time we make

1. Sharma, M. M., 'Speech of the Recipient of the Anundoram Barooah Award', *Scholar Critic Mukunda Madhava Sharma*, ABILAC, 2001, P.83.

Śaṅkaradeva's literature available for the world. But, most importantly, translation of his literary works will enrich the Assamese language and literature as it is well known that translation to and from a particular language always enriches that particular language and literature. So, translation of Śaṅkaradeva's works into English will be a great contribution not only to the Assamese literature, but will be of lasting value for all the lovers and researchers of literature of the world.

Much work has already been done in the area of the technical and critical aspects of the literary contributions of Śaṅkaradeva and many of them are in English language. But until and unless the original works are translated into English the rest of the world cannot appreciate this great genius namely Śaṅkaradeva.

In this context we can remember the famous English romantic poet John Keats as he expressed his feelings in "*On First Looking into Chapman's Homer*":

*Much have I travell'd in the realms of gold,*
*And many goodly states and kingdoms seen;*
*Round many western islands have I been*
*Which bards in fealty to Apollo hold.*
*Oft the one wide expanse had I been told*
*That deep-brow'd Homer ruled as his demesne;*
*Yet did I never breathe its pure serene*
*Till I heard Chapman speak out loud and bold:*............

Śaṅkaradeva's monumental work the *Kīrtana-Ghoṣā*, which is a valued household possession in every Assamese family worldwide, has already been translated into English. However, it is a matter of great regret that the *Aṅkīyā Nāṭas*, which are amongst the most important, original and valued creations of Śaṅkaradeva were yet to be translated and offered to the world readers for evaluation, appreciation and study.

For the past 7-8 years, I have been working on the literary works of Śaṅkaradeva particularly the *Aṅkīyā Nāṭas*. During the course of my studies it was found that among his literary creations, the six plays in consideration have an important position because of so many reasons, such as:-

a)They are the first recognized form of written drama in Assam,

b) First formal prose writing, in *Brajāvalī*, an artificially created language used for the purpose of preaching *Vaiṣṇava Bhakti* cult by the saints, poets and preachers of that time particularly in the Eastern part of India.

c)Introduction of innovative ideas leading to a new genre of art form.

Realising the significance of translating the plays of Śaṅkaradeva and being a student of English literature, having had schooling in vernacular medium and also having studied Sanskrit as a subject till graduation, I chose the task of translating the six plays and took up 'A Literal English Translation of the Plays of Śaṅkaradeva with a Critical Appraisal' as my topic for Ph.D. research and prepared a dissertation on the topic. I have already been awarded the Ph.D. degree by the Gauhati University on the basis of this thesis. It is a matter of great satisfaction for me that the work has been highly appreciated by the experts. Now, for the greater benefits of all the interested people this work needed to be published at the earliest with a little addition and omission on certain topics in places.

Within the scope of the present book, an English translation into prose of the six plays by Śaṅkaradeva has been given, and it has also been tried to give a brief critical appraisal including the various aspects of the plays along with their sources, characteristics, language and their relation with the common folk. It was felt necessary to provide the original text of the plays also side by side the translations. But as it would not be possible for the Non-Assamese readers to go through the original text in Assamese script, the transliteration of the text with Roman script along with its English translation has also been given.

For understanding the purpose of composition of the plays, the social, political and religious conditions prevalent at that time along with a short history of the life of Śaṅkaradeva, his various contributions and an introductory note on the *Vaiṣnava* Movement in Assam are given. For better assistance to the readers, the scheme of transliteration and pronunciation is given in the beginning and a glossary of mythological names and other words in *Brajāvalī* language in the texts is provided at the end.

So for all those people, Assamese or non Assamese, with the knowledge of English, who want to know Śaṅkaradeva or are engaged in studies on Indology, Religion, *Bhakti* Cult, *Bhakti* Literature, Comparative Literature, Lives of Saints or Hagiographies, Culture Studies, Studies of the North-East India and most importantly Drama and other performing art forms like Songs, Dances and tools and accessories related to them such as musical instruments, costumes and masks, etc., this book will be a valuable reference.

It is hoped that more such work like the present one, would go a long way towards making Śaṅkaradeva known and appreciated worldwide.

●●●

# ACKNOWLEDGEMENT

At the very outset, I express my sincere gratitude to my respected guide Dr. Nabin Chandra Sarma, retired Professor and Head, Department of Folk-Lore Research, Gauhati University, for his supervision, learned guidance and encouragement while preparing for my thesis for Ph.D. which is the basis for the present book. I also remain highly thankful to him for his learned foreword to this book.

I would like to take the opportunity here, to express my gratitude to Dr. Umesh Deka, Rabindranath Tagore Professor and Head of Department of M.I.L., for his advice and help from time to time.

My special thanks to my elder sister, Dr. Shrutidhara Chakravarty, Reader, Department of Sanskrit, Gauhati University, for her great help in analysing the Sanskrit *ślokas* and determining the metres and the nuances in them.

I am highly grateful to Professor Ranjit Kumar Dev Goswami, Professor, Sankaradeva Chair, Tezpur University and former Professor, Department of English, Gauhati University for his valuable guidance during the preparation of this book.

I want to offer my thanks to the staff concerned of the Bipin Chandra Barua Library, Paschim Guwahati Mahavidyalaya, Dharapur, the K.K. Handiqui Library of Gauhati University, and the Dr. S.K. Bhuyan Library, Cotton College, for their co-operation and help in finding books and materials. I also thank the library staff of Srimanta Sankardev Kalakshetra for helping me find relevant books.

My heartfelt gratitude to my respected mother-in-law Mrs. Prity Medhi and father-in-law Dr. Jyotiprasad Medhi, Retired Professor and Head, Department of Statistics, Gauhati

University, for their great encouragement and support during the whole period of time.

I want to offer my sincere thanks to my colleague brother Biswajit Sarmah for being there beside me helping me everyway possible and especially guiding me through while typing my work in the computer.

My loving gratitude to my son Riddhiman, a student of $4^{th}$ Semester M.Sc., Chemistry, Gauhati University, who has very painstakingly helped me find out references from the scriptures and do all the page-settings, bit by bit, very patiently, along with Mr. Dipen Bhuyan who has helped in the final layout.

I would also like to thank Mr. Samiran Goswami for allowing me to use some of his valuable photographs related to Śaṅkaradeva's *Satrīyā* Culture.

I also take the opportunity to thank the Secretary and the library staff of Srimanta Sankardev Kalakshetra for allowing me to take snaps of the masks at the museum and use the library. I am very much thankful to Mr. Manoranjan Mahanta of Srimanta Sankardev Kalakshetra for enlightening me regarding masks and costumes of *Bhāonā* and allowing me to use some of the photographs of the masks made by his father Sri Rebakanta Mahanta Khatpara Satra, Sivsagar, Assam.

My sincere thanks to Mr. Biswajit Sarmah again for designing the cover page.

My sincere thanks to my husband Shubhankar Medhi, who has been a constant support in every step of my work, without which I could never have completed the work.

Finally, I want to acknowledge my heartfelt gratitude to my mother Elima Sharma and father Late Dr. Mukunda Madhava Sharma, Ex-Vice Chancellor, Dibrugarh University and former Professor and Head of the Department of Sanskrit, Gauhati University, for their inspiration and trust in me, which led me to take up such a complicated topic as the present one. My father would have been the happiest to see this book published.

I offer my sincere thanks to MLBD Publishers for their great job in publishing the book and making it available for the world readers.

With great support from all the persons mentioned above, and help from friends and well wishers, seeking forgiveness for any unintentional lapses or omissions, here I am humbly presenting the book in the hands of readers and connoisseurs.

Yashodhara Medhi

# SCHEME OF TRANSLITERATION AND PRONUNCIATION

### Vowels

| | | | | | |
|---|---|---|---|---|---|
| अ a | आ ā | इ i | ई ī | उ u | ऊ ū |
| ऋ ṛ | ए e | ऐ ai | ओ o | औ au | |

### Consonants

| | | | | | |
|---|---|---|---|---|---|
| Guttarals: | क ka | ख kha | ग ga | घ gha | ङ ṅa |
| Palatals: | च ca | छ cha | ज ja | झ jha | ञ ña |
| Cerebrals: | ट ṭa | ठ ṭha | ड ḍa | ढ ḍha | ण ṇa |
| Dentals: | त ta | थ tha | द da | ध dha | न na |
| Labials: | प pa | फ pha | ब ba | भ bha | म ma |
| Semivowels: | य ya | र ra | ल la | व va | |
| Sibilants: | श śa | ष ṣa | स sa | | |
| Aspirate: | ह ha | Anusvāra: ं ṁ | | Visarga: : ḥ | |
| Compound Letters: | | क्ष kṣa | ज्ञ jña | | |

### The vowels are pronounced as follows:

**a** : as in b**u**t
**ā** : as in f**a**r but held twice as long as **a**
**i** : as in p**i**n
**ī** : as in p**i**que but held twice as long as **i**
**u** : as in p**u**sh
**ū** : as in r**u**le but held twice as long as **u**
**ṛ** : as in **ri**m
**e** : as in th**e**y
**ai** : as in l**oi**ter, and as in **ai**le in the *ślokas*
**o** : as in g**o**
**au** : as in h**ow**

### The consonants are pronounced as follows:

Gutterals :
(Pronounced from the throat)

**k** – as in **k**ite
**kh** – as in E**ckh**art
**g** – as in **g**ive
**gh** – as in di**g-h**ard
**ṅ** – as in si**ng**

Palatals :
(Pronounced with the middle of the tongue against the palate)

**c** – as in **ch**air
**ch** – as in staun**ch-h**eart
**j** – as in **j**oy
**jh** – as in he**dgeh**og
**ñ** – as in ca**ny**on

Cerebrals :
(Pronounced with the tip of the tongue against the roof of the mouth)

**ṭ** – as in **t**ub
**ṭh** – as in ligh**t-h**eart
**ḍ** – as in **d**ove
**ḍh** – as in re**d-h**ot
**ṇ** – as in bor**n**

Dentals :
(Pronounced like the cerebrals but with the tongue against the teeth)

**t** – as in **t**ub
**th** – as in ligh**t-h**eart
**d** – as in **d**ove
**dh** – as in a**dh**ere
**n** – as in **n**ut

Labials :
(pronounced with the lips)

**p** – as in **p**ine
**ph** – as in u**p-h**ill
**b** – as in **b**ird
**bh** – as in ru**b-h**ard
**m** – as in **m**other

Semivowels :

**y** – as in **y**es
**r** – as in **r**un
**l** – as in **l**ight
**v** – as in **v**ine, except when preceded in the same syllable by a consonant, the as in s**w**an

Sibilants :

**ś** – as in German word *sprechen*
**ṣ** – as in **sh**ine
**s** – as in German word i**ch**, and as in **s**un in the *ślokas*

Aspirate :

**h** – as in **h**ome

Anusvāra :

**ṁ** – a resonant nasal sound as in the French word *bon*

**ḥ** – a final h-sound: **aḥ** is pronounced like **aha**; **iḥ** like **ihi**

Compound Letters :

**kṣ** – as **khya**, and as in he**xa** in the *ślokas*

**jña** – as **gya** and as in an**ge**l in the *ślokas*

The mark ˜ over any letter indicates a nasalized sound.

# PART A

# CHAPTER I
# INTRODUCTION

The Neo-Vaiṣṇavite movement, known as *Eka Śaraṇa Nāma Dharma* was initiated by Śaṅkaradeva in the later part of the 15th century in Assam. It made him a familiar and most respected name in every household of Assam. He was not only a religious leader, but also a social reformer and a versatile and prolific writer. He brought an age of renaissance in the religious, social as well as cultural arena of the then Assam.

Saint poet Śaṅkaradeva, the pioneer *Vaiṣṇava* saint of North-East India was born (1449 A.D.) at such a time when Assam was not what it is today. It was fractioned into various small territories ruled independently by different minor rulers or kings. There were many different tribes and sects with various religious and cultural backgrounds.

Along with Śaivism and many other sectarian faiths, Śāktism was predominant and the Tantric form was the prevailing religion of the land. People in general were illiterate and they believed in whatever their religious leaders made them believe.

Śaṅkaradeva was greatly disturbed to see the general ignorance and helplessness of the masses in religious matters. So, to emancipate them from the religious and social slavery Śaṅkaradeva devised a popular and true philosophic religion, the *Eka Śaraṇa Nāma Dharma,* on the basis of the *Vedānta, Bhagavad Gītā* and the *Bhāgavata- Purāṇa*, to attain *ahiṁsā*, equality and truth.[1]

Sankaradeva's greatest achievement as a religious reformer is his success in bringing the people from various forms of Śākta Tantrism and different kinds of sectarian practices to the pure monotheism of his *Vaiṣṇava* faith. And he did not accomplish this through polemics or organized propaganda.

---

1. Medhi, K., ed. *Aṅkāvalī*, 1997, 'Introduction', p. xlvii.

Rather he thought that the best way of reforming the religious life of the people was not to attack what was evil but to present to them what was good and to make it appeal to their imagination and also to make it possible for them to get a taste of it themselves.

His cult was based on devotion to Kṛṣṇa as a personal God on the basis of the *Bhagavad Gītā* and on a firm belief in monotheism, like that of Śrī Śaṅkarācārya of the Deccan.[2] Śaṅkaradeva simplified religion bestowing utmost emphasis on *śravaṇa* and *kīrtana* and introduced democracy in religion. He strictly prohibited use of intoxicating drugs and narcotics including liquor, opium, ganja etc., among his disciples.[3] With utmost importance on *śravaṇa* and *kīrtana*, he brought religion to the masses and formed a new life-style with enhanced importance on personal purity and discipline. Thus he reformed and strengthened the backbone of what later became the Assamese society.

These new ideas and concepts attracted many people - common men and even Āhom kings alike. Many people became his disciples, both Brahmins and Non-Brahmins[4] and also people like Garo, Bhot and even Muslims.[5]

To preach his faith and reach out to the masses, Śaṅkaradeva developed a new form of drama called *nāṭa* or *bhāonā*. Śaṅkaradeva composed six full-fledged dramas by the names, i) the *Kāli Damana*, *ii)* the *Patnī-Prasāda*, *iii)* the *Keli-Gopāla*, *iv)* the *Rukmiṇī Haraṇa*, *v)* the *Pārijāta Haraṇa* and *vi)* the *Śrī Rāma-Vijaya Nāṭa*. With their audio visual effects these *nāṭas* very quickly fascinated and influenced the people.

As art and literature are strong bonding agents, so the endeavour of Śaṅkaradeva brought about a new bonding among the people of the then Assam (Asama, Kāmrūpa and Kamatā) and worked wonders in unifying them.

---

[2]. Medhi, K., ed. *Aṅkāvalī*, 1997, 'Introduction', p. xlvii.

[3]. Ibid., p. xlviii.

[4]. Ibid., p. xlvii.

[5]. Ibid., p. xlix.

However, the Neo-Vaiṣṇavism, as practised in Assam is very little known and studied outside the region and abroad. Sir Edward Gait, the eminent historian said, "...*there is, probably, no part of India regarding whose past less is generally known. In the histories of India as a whole, Assam is barely mentioned, and only ten lines are devoted to its annals in the historical portion of Hunter's Indian Empire.*"[6]

As stated above in the Introduction to the First Edition of *A History of Assam,* published in 1905 A.D., the situation remains the same even today. After more than a hundred years, very little about Assam is known yet in the other states of India and abroad. This can be inferred from the fact that even in a latest book like *The Sacred Thread, a Short History of Hinduism*, by J. L. Brockington, published by Oxford University Press, Oxford India Paperback, 2000, which is one of the most acclaimed books and considered to be quite comprehensive internationally, the *Vaiṣṇava* saint of Assam, Śaṅkaradeva and his contributions do not find a place.

Further, to quote Dr. R.K. Dasgupta, "It is indeed very curious that J.N. Farquhar's *An Outline of the Religious Literature of India* (1920), a work of 450 pages which is a sourcebook of our sacred literature, does not mention Sankaradeva either in the text or, in its long, descriptive bibliography of *Vaiṣṇava* writings. No less curious is the fact that Estlin Carpenter has no occasion to refer to him in his *Theism in Medieval India* (1921). When eight years later Ksitimohan Sen gave his lectures on medieval mysticism of India in Calcutta University, he ignored the great Assamese mystic, and there is not a word on him in the English version of the lectures published in London in 1935."[7]

This may be due to lack of information regarding Śaṅkaradeva and the region in general in the national as well as international level. As such, much room is there for work to be done in this

---

6. Gait, Sir E., *A History of Assam,* 2006, 'Introduction', p. (iv).

7. Dasgupta, R.K., 'Sankaradeva : The Founder of Assamese Vaisnavism'.

respect and various creations of Śaṅkaradeva have to be made available to the world through translations.

## 1.1. WORKS OF ŚAṄKARADEVA SO FAR TRANSLATED INTO ENGLISH:

It is a laudable effort on the part of Asom Satra Sangha and Śrīmanta Śaṅkaradeva Sangha to have come forward lately in taking the initiative of getting the *Kīrtana Ghoṣā of Śaṅkaradeva* translated into English and getting it published.

Asom Satra Sangha has published the translated version of the *Kīrtana* as *The Kirtana Ghosa English Translation* in the year 1992. The translation has been done by Chandrakanta Mahanta.

Śrīmanta Śaṅkaradeva Sangha has published the English translation of the *Kīrtana Ghoṣā* as *Srimanta* Śaṅkaradeva's *The Kīrtana- Ghoṣā (An English Verse Rendering)*. The book has been translated by Dr. Purnananda Saikia.

Moreover, Bani Mandir has published *Sree Sree Sankaradeva's Gunmālā,* rendered into English by Benudhar Rajkhowa, new edn. 2003.

Shankaradeva's *Parijata Harana Nata* was translated by eminent scholar and indologist Dr William L. Smith.[8] However, it does not contain the transliteration of the text.

The *bargīts* as the '*Great Songs*' and also the *Gunmālā* have been translated by Dr. Sanjib Kumar Borkakoti.

## 1.2. DIFFERENT COLLECTIONS OF THE PLAYS OF ŚAṄKARADEVA:

The treasure-house of the *Aṅkīyā Nāṭas* were in the form of *puthi*s and were lying scattered in obscurity and oblivion in possession of some individuals and different *satras*. The following efforts were made to compile, print and publish

---

8. William L. Smith, 'The Translation of Shankaradeva's Parijata Haraṇa Nata', in Bryant, E. F. (ed.), *Krishna. A Source Book*.

those *nāṭas* for easier availability and circulation, in *Brajāvalī* language itself:

(i) *Aṅkīyā Nāṭ* edited by Dr. Birinchi Kumar Barua, then Professor of Assamese, Gauhati University and Honorary Assistant Director of Historical and Antiquarian Studies, Assam and published by the same organization in the year 1940 was the first printed collection of the six plays of Śaṅkaradeva along with eight others by Mādhavadeva and two more by Gopāladeva. Dr. Barua took great pains to collect the manuscripts of the plays from different individuals and various *satras*. The book had attracted attention of scholars both in Assam and outside and as expressed by Professor Vidhusekhar Bhattacharya, "Srijut B.K.Barua,... has undoubtedly done a great service not only to the Assamese Language, but also to allied vernaculars of the country..."[9]

(ii) Sri Sankar Bakyamrit - Hari Narayan Dutta Baruah, Dutta & Co., Vol. 2. 2nd edn. 1964.

(iii) *Aṅkāvalī* edited by Kaliram Medhi, 1st published in 1949; later on published by the Kaliram Medhi Trust, 1st edn. 1997.

(iv) *Aṅkamālā* edited by Dr. Kesavananda Dev Goswami, published by Banalata, Dibrugarh, 1st edn.1979.

(v) *Śaṅkardevar Nāṭ* edited by Mahim Bora, published by Publication Board Assam, 1st edn.1989.

(vi) *Mahāpuruṣa Śrīmanta śaṅkaradeva Vākyāmṛta*, edited by Dr. Dharmeswar Chutia, published by Srimanta Sankaradeva Sangha, 1st edn.1998.

Amongst these, the present translation work is based on the *Aṅkāvalī* edited by Kaliram Medhi, which is considered to be one of the most authentic collections and also all the six plays are included in it.

[9]. Bhattacharya, V., *Aṅkīyā Nāṭ* ed. by Dr. B. K. Barua, 'Opinions', p. 293.

## 1.3.A BRIEF NOTE ON KALIRAM MEDHI AND THE *AṄKĀVALĪ* :

Kaliram Medhi is one of those few members of Assam Civil Service who despite of serious official responsibilities contributed substantially to the study of Assamese literature and culture during the first half of the 20th century.

Kaliram Medhi was born at Ramdia, Hajo in the district of Kamrup, Assam, in the year 1878 in an agricultural family. Though his parents were illiterate, with encouragement and concrete help from his uncle, Kaliram Medhi passed the entrance examination from Guwahati Government Seminary in 1897 securing highest marks in Sanskrit among the Assamese students and became the proud recipient of the Hem Chandra Barua and Hemadhar Barua medals. He could also obtain the Eliotee scholarship amounting to Rs 20 constituted by Charles Eliot, Chief Commissioner of Assam.

Kaliram Medhi got admitted in the City College, Calcutta and passed F.A. in 1899 and B.A. with honours in Chemistry and Physical Science in 1902. Within a year i.e. in 1903 Kaliram Medhi passed M.A. in Physics (Natural and Physical Science) and thus became the third Assamese to obtain M.A. degree from Calcutta University, the other two being Radhanath Phukan and Annada Charan Bhattacharyya who, however, belonged to educated and well to do families.

Returning home, the Government offered Kaliram Medhi the post of S.D.C. at Guwahati in 1904. After serving in various capacities like Assistant Settlement Officer of Dibrugarh, S.D.C. of Nagaon and Dhing, E.A.C. of Tura, Goalpara, Golaghat, S.D.O. (Civil) of Mangaldoi and Goalpara, Medhi became the Deputy Commissioner of Nagaon in 1936. He went on superannuation in the same year but the Government of Assam reemployed him as Special Magistrate for about ten years. He retired from active Government service on January 1, 1946. He was honoured with the Rai Bahadur title in the same year.

The eventful life of this illustrious son of Assam came to an end on January 24, 1954.

Kaliram Medhi's versatile genius has been reflected in his literary contributions both in Assamese and English languages. The onerous duties of magisterial activities could not deter his urge to work for development of Assamese language and literature which is testified by his prestigious and widely researched publications entitled *Asamiyā Vyākaraṇ Āru Bhāṣātattva* (1936), *Mahāpuruṣ Śaṅkaradevar Bāṇī* (1949) and *Aṅkāvalī* (1950) Part-I. Dr. S.N.Sarma opines that "the most painstaking scholarly work of Medhi is, no doubt, his *Asamiyā Vyākaraṇ Āru Bhāṣātattva*...In fact, the introduction itself can claim as an independent work...where the first two sections ...deal with the origin of the language and the third section which is a bit exhaustive one is entirely devoted to delineate the development of Assamese literature from the earliest times to the beginning of the modern period." To quote Dr. Sarma further "In a sense, he was the pioneer in introducing the method of textual criticism in Assamese. When early Assamese manuscripts were being published without caring a fig for the early orthography and proper reading of the texts, he was the first man to critically edit the text of *Prahlād Carit* (published in 1913 while he was serving as an E.A.C. in Tura). He followed the same method in editing *Aṅkāvalī*."[10]

Medhi contributed as many as 20 articles to various prominent periodicals of his time. Although he had a master's degree in Physics, his writings embraced arts, science, astronomy, moral science, religion, life history, history and antiquity, social evils et al. His research articles like 'The *Kalitās*' (Vol III No. 3, 1935), 'Late *Rāi Bāhādur* Kanak Lal Barua' (Vol III No. 1, 1941), *Brajāvalī* Literature of Assam (Vol III No. 4, 1941), 'Philosophic Aspects of Assam– *Brajāvalī* Literature' (Vol IX-1 and 2, 1942) and '*Brajāvalī* Literature of Assam'(Vol.IX-3 and 4, 1942) in the journal of the Assam

---

10. Sarma, S.N., cover flap, *Asamiyā Vyākaraṇ Āru Bhāṣātattva*.

Research Society evoked keen interest among the contemporary scholars.[11]

Kaliram Medhi was actively associated with various cultural organizations and institutions like the *Kāmrūp Anusandhān Samiti,* The State Museum of Assam, the *Axom Sāahitya Sabhā*', etc. He presided over the 3rd session of the prestigious literary forum of Assam the '*Axom Sahitya Sabha*' at Barpeta in the year 1918.[12]

The *Aṅkāvalī* is a collection of 21 plays by Śaṅkaradeva, Mādhavadeva, Gopāldeva, Ram Caraṇ Thākur, Dvija Bhūṣaṇa and Daityāri Thākur, where all the six plays by Śaṅkaradeva are included. Kaliram Medhi in the introduction to the collection says that to ensure correctness of texts the oldest available manuscripts had been used and the antiquated spellings as found in them were left unaltered. Justifying this stand he further says, "This is because we do not know the actual Brajāvali [sic.] spelling nor have we come across any manuscript containing the spelling adopted by the dramatists themselves....The copyists in Assam were a professional class and all the blame should not be laid at their door."[13]

## 1.4. A BRIEF WRITE-UP ON TRANSLATION

Translation has a very wide and rich history in the West. In the opinion of the researchers, writings on translation date back to the Romans. Eric Jacobson claims that translating is a Roman invention.[14] Cicero and Horace, in the first century BC, were the first theorists who distinguished between word-for-word translation and sense-for-sense translation. However, they literally cautioned against translating 'word for word' (*verbum pro verbo*)·[15] The comments on translation practice by Cicero

[11]. Sharma Thakur, G.C., 'Remembering Pundit Kaliram Medhi', The Assam Tribune, 24 January, 2009, The Editorial.

[12]. Das, M. and Goswami, J.N., ed., *Kaliram Medhi Rachanabali*, 'Introduction'.

[13]. Medhi, K., ed. *Aṅkāvalī,* 1997, 'Introduction', pp. xliii.

[14]. Zakhir M., 'The History of Translation'. *In* Zainurrahman (ed.), *The Theories of Translation: From History to Procedures,* p. 3.

[15]. Kasparek, C., 'The Translator's Endless Toil', The Polish Review, Vol. 28, No. 2 (1983), p. 84.

and Horace influenced the following generations of translation up to the twentieth century.

It is to be noted here that tradition of translating religious scriptures into various local languages have been in practice all over the world through ages.

The approach to the translation of the scriptures in the western world was greatly affected by the translation of the *Greek Septuagint Bible* into Latin by St Jerome in the fourth century CE.[16]

The history of translation in the Arab world dates back to the time of the Syrians in the first half of the second century A.D., who translated into Arabic a large heritage that belongs to the era of paganism. Syrians were influenced in their translations by the Greek ways of translation. However, the translations by the Syrians were more literal and faithful to the original.[17]

Moreover, the time of the prophet Mohamed was of paramount importance for translation in the history of translation in the Arab world. For spreading of Islam and the need to communicate with the non-Arabic speaking communities such as Jews, Romans and others learning of foreign languages and translation to and from Arabic was of utmost importance which pushed the prophet to look for translators and to encourage them.

One of the most famous translators of the time was Zaid Ibnu Thabet, who played a crucial role in translating letters sent by the prophet to foreign kings of Persia, Syria, Rome and Jews, and also letters sent by those kings to the prophet. Another era that knew significant changes in Arabic translation was related to the translation of the Holy Koran.

There have been various theories of translation over the centuries. In the eighteenth century, the translator was

---

[16]. Zakhir M., 'The History of Translation'. *In* Zainurrahman (ed.), *The Theories of Translation: From History to Procedures*, p. 3.

[17]. Ibid., p. 5.

compared to an artist with a moral duty both to the work of the original author and to the receiver.

In the nineteenth century the translator was considered as a creative genius, who enriches the literature and language into which he is translating and also performs the mechanical function of making a text or an author known (McGuire).[18]

According to Al-Jahid, one of the greatest theorists on translation in the Arab history of translation (1969), "The translator should know the structure of the speech, habits of the people and their ways of understanding each other."[19] In his two books *Al-Hayawān*(1969) and *Al-Bayān Wa Attabayyun* (1968), Al-Jahid amongst the wide range of theories also emphasised about the importance of revision after translation.

The translator's role is also very significant as a bridge for "carrying across" values between cultures. Moreover, apart from conveying knowledge between cultures and introducing ideas, they also import loanwords and calques of grammatical structures, idioms and vocabulary from the source languages, into their own languages. The role of the translator has also been compared to that of an artist.

In certain contexts many translators of literary, religious or historic texts often adhere as closely as possible to the source text and consciously seek to produce a literal translation. A translator may also adopt expressions from the source language in order to provide "local color" to the matter translated.

However, the approach to translation has undergone great changes till the recent times. Nowadays, translation research is more automatic. The invention of the internet, together with the new technological developments in communication and digital materials, has increased cultural exchanges between nations. This has led the translators to look for more practical techniques to enable them to translate quickly and larger

[18]. Zakhir M., 'The History of Translation'. *In* Zainurrahman (ed.), *The Theories of Translation: From History to Procedures*, p. 4.
[19]. Ibid p. 6.

volumes. Introduction of audiovisual translation, also called screen translation, concerned with the translation of all kinds of TV programmes, including films, series, and documentaries marks a changing era in the domain of translation. This field is based on computers and translation softwares.

In Assam there had been traditions of representing the anecdotes from different scriptures like Rāmāyaṇa, Mahābhārata and one or two Purāṇas. Prior to Śaṅkaradeva, poets like Hem Saraswati, Kaviratna Saraswati, Rudra Kandali, Haribar Vipra and Madhav Kandali rendered beautiful stories in local Kāmrūpī dialect to be understood easily by the local people. However, the translation of the seven cantos of the Ramayana by Madhav Kandali under the patronage of Mahamanikya, the *Barāha* king, as stated by Madhav Kandali himself, is an important fact as this translation of Ramayana into Assamese is considered to be the foremost amongst all the regional languages of North India[20] which according to the researchers can be no way later than fourteenth century and is a precursor to all the later translation works. Śaṅkaradeva himself acknowledges the greatness of this translator poet as 'undefeatable'[21] and might have followed his example of translating scriptures into local language which resulted into a voluminous literary treasure in Assamese.

Albeit there have been various theories on translation, yet, it must be remembered that the works of translation came first and then only the theories were formed on the basis of those works. Here it is felt to be appropriate to quote the view of Md. Ziaul Haque that the translator, at the very beginning, keeps both the source language and the target language in mind and tries to translate carefully. But it becomes very difficult for a translator to decode the whole text literally; and therefore, he takes the help of his own view and endeavours to translate accordingly.[22]

---

[20]. Sarma, S.N., *Asamīyā Sāhityar Samīkṣātmak Itibṛtta,* 2006, p. 64.

[21]. Bharali, S., *Madhav Kandalir Para Mamoni Goswamiloi,* 2004, p.2.

[22]. Haque Md. Z., 'Translating Literary Prose: Problems and Solutions', *In International Journal of English Linguistics,* Vol. 2, No. 6; 2012, p. 99.

It is quite difficult to maintain the sweetness of expression as well as to be precise in meaning while translating. It is a universal problem in respect of translation that in the process of translation, the idiomatic expressions of the original work is lost very often as every language has its own idiomatic expressions with reference to the local surrounding, customs and emotions.

While doing the present work it had to be kept in mind that it is a work involving religious sentiments of almost the whole of Assam and the essence and fervour should not be lost in the process of translation while keeping an objective attitude and obligatory detachment as a researcher.

## 1.5.THE TRANSLATOR'S NOTE

As the task of translating the plays of the great saint is a very serious one, extra caution had to be taken while doing the work. Following are some of the factors which made the work seem to be quite difficult:

• *Brajāvalī* is an artificially developed language specially for the purpose of composing the *nāṭas* and the *bargīts* and is not used otherwise.

There was also the problem of unavailability of adequate *Brajāvalī* dictionary.

• There are textual differences at certain places in different books. In the process of transliteration and translation of the plays, it has been observed that there are variations of texts in many places in different anthologies of plays by Śaṅkaradeva, edited by different persons; e.g. the *bhaṭimā* in the beginning of the play *Patnī-Prasāda* in the *Mahāpuruṣ Śrīmantaśaṅkaradeva Bākyāmṛta* published by Srimanta Sankaradeva Sangha and *Śaṅkardevar Nāṭ* edited by Mahim Bora are the same but differ from the one in the *Aṅkāvalī* edited by Kaliram Medhi and many other manuscripts as well, which is the same as in the play *Kālidamana*. There are many such instances of discrepancies in respect of words, expression and spellings in the plays. Although the present work is basically following the *Aṅkāvalī* edited by Kaliram Medhi yet, from time to time, other available texts in print such as the *Aṅkamālā* edited by Dr. Kesavananda Dev Goswami, and the *Śaṅkardevar Nāṭ* edited by Mahim Bora are also consulted to get closer to the meaning.

The probable alternative words, other than the ones found in the texts of the *Aṅkāvalī* are given in the footnotes.

• Moreover, there are many a lapse found in respect of words and letters in the Sanskrit *ślokas*, especially in case of the use of *Śloka* or *Anuṣṭubh* metre, which might have cropped up in course of repeated copying of the manuscripts and now have led to flaws in respect of metres. The metres used in the *ślokas* as well as the discrepancies found therein, are given in the footnotes.

Scholars with strong command over Sanskrit and good knowledge of prosody can do much in this respect to correct the erroneous texts.

• There are discrepancies in spelling in the different printed anthologies.It must be noted here that in respect of the spellings of texts, the *Aṅkāvalī* by Kaliram Medhi has lots of discrepancies and does not maintain any uniformity; e.g., Yaśodā is spelt with all the three types of '*sa*'s at different places.

But the important point to be noted here is that in Assamese language the difference in pronunciation of the three different types of '*sa*' and the two types of '*ca*' '*ta*' and '*na*' are not followed like in Sanskrit or many other Indian languages coming from Sanskrit. Rather, all the '*ś*', '*ṣ*' and '*s*' are pronounced similarly, and gutturally like '*ka*', '*kha*' etc., somewhat very similar to the pronunciation of '*ch*' in '*ich*'(which means 'I') in German language, and is a special characteristic feature of the language. Likewise, '*ṭ*' and '*t*' and '*ṇ*' and '*n*' are also pronounced as '*ta*' and '*na*' (dental letter) only.

Moreover, it has been observed that "ba" is put instead of "va" in many words especially in the *yuktākṣaras*. This might have happened because of inadequacies in respect of the particular computer software used in typing the texts in Assamese. It is to be noted here, that in most cases, the distinction between 'ba' and 'va' is not maintained in the manuscripts of Assam. However, using new technologies and latest updated version of software, this problem can be sorted out with some effort.

However, in this present work it has been tried to standardise the common spellings without disturbing the *Brajāvalī* words and also maintaining the original natural sweetness.

• There are also discrepancies in respect of the punctuation marks in the *Aṅkāvalī*. However, in the present work, the same punctuation marks have been retained in the transliteration of the texts as found in the *Aṅkāvalī* with whatever discrepancies they have.

• The *sūtradhāra* is the director and presenter of all the other characters and he controls all the activities on the stage till the end of the play. He is referred to as *sūtra, kathā* and sometimes as *kathā sūtra* without maintaining any discrimination among them. Hence, to differentiate and at the same time to observe uniformity, *sūtra, kathā* and *kathā sūtra* are given in the translations as 'direction', 'dialogue' and 'dialogue and direction' respectively.

• Most of the discrepancies mentioned above are due to the fact that none of the texts of the vast literary creations of Śaṅkaradeva is available in original by the creator and all the texts available now are only copies done by the followers from earlier manuscripts or by listening to performances at different times in different places. Also, the different collections edited by different scholars have their own limitations and hence suffer from inadequacies.

An important point to be noted here is that use of paper was unknown at that time and instead the people used strips of bark of the *sāci* tree, known in Bengal as *āgar(Aquilaria Agallocha)* for writing.[23] The process of preparing these writing materials was immensely long, laborious and tedious and also writing (whether in original or copying) demanded much time and patience. As such, these old manuscripts or *puthis*, as they are called, are of great value and are rare to be found easily. They were preserved carefully in *satras* or handed down as heirlooms from father to son.[24]

It will be of immense value and a great service to the Assamese language, literature and culture in general, if a group of persons, experts in their respective fields, get together and study the texts minutely with an objective view, for the greater benefit of all.

• However, to make it easier, a list of the diacritical marks used is given in the "Scheme of Transliteration".

• There are many non English words retained in the translation from the text, about which short definitions and descriptions are given in the Glossary:

(i) The different characters and mythological identities in the plays and their different names with introduction and explanatory notes;

(ii) The different local names of trees, flowers and plants with explanatory notes and scientific names for universal understanding;

(iii) Food items, dressing articles, cosmetics, ornaments, musical instruments and local social ceremonies with explanatory notes are included.

• List of the *Rāgas* and *Tālas* used in the text is given.

• A map of the then Koc-Behār, Kāmrūpa and Asama is provided for easier understanding of the places.

• A few photographs are attached to give an idea of the *Satrīyā* culture.

• Over and above the books referred to in the footnotes, names of some other works, which were consulted for developing a wider and comprehensive understanding of the topic of study, are also included in the Bibliography.

●●●

[23]. Gait, Sir E., *A History of Assam*, Appendix D.

[24]. Ibid.

# CHAPTER II

## LIFE AND WORKS OF ŚAṄKARADEVA

### 2.1. THE NEO - VAIṢNAVITE MOVEMENT:

By the 15th century, almost whole of India was swept over with the current of *Vaiṣṇava* revival and it was Śaṅkaradeva who fanned in the spirit of the movement and spearheaded the Neo-Vaiṣṇavism in the north-eastern part of India giving it distinctive indigenous characteristics yet maintaining the basic features.

Hinduism, which may also be called Vedic religion, at its earliest stage (say 5000B.C.) emphasized on sacrifice. The Vedas also recommended worship of many gods like Agni, Sūrya, Vāyu, Varuṇa, Viṣṇu, etc. However, in the same Vedas it is said that all these gods are merely different forms of only One God, and that entity is Viṣṇu. "Consequently, a religious faith evolved around Viṣṇu, which came to be known as Vaiṣṇavism, where the main element is an emotional approach. This emotional element is called *Bhakti* in the scriptures".[1]

Regarding the history of the *Bhakti* movement, J. L. Brockington says, that the *Bhakti* or devotional movement began to blossom in south India in the seventh century, although its roots may be traced back a further two centuries or so. "It was characterised by a personal relationship between the deity and the devotee, and worship became a fervent emotional experience in response to divine grace."[2] The *Vaiṣṇava Bhakti* movement was led by the Alvārs of Tamilnad and gradually the rest of India was also swept over by this *Vaiṣṇava* renaissance through the efforts of Rāmānuja and Nimbārka (11th century), Madhva (13th century), Rāmānanda

[1].Sharma, M. M., 'Introduction', in Saikia, P., *Srīmanta Śaṅkaradeva's The Kīrttana-Ghoṣā*, 2005, p. vii.

[2].Brockington, J.L., *The Sacred Thread, A Short History of Hinduism*, 2000, p.130.

(14th century), Kabīr (15th century), Caitanya and Vallabha (15th -16th century) and others at different places.

The schools of Vaiṣṇavism founded by these reformers might differ in philosophical niceties and outward religious observances, but the fundamental basis of these schools of Vaiṣṇavism did not differ very much.[3] The impact of Islam impelled the reformers of Hindu society to evolve a simpler and liberal faith that would be acceptable to all alike. The *Bhakti* cult, which started in South India and eventually spread over North India, was the most suitable answer to the need of the hour and could confront successfully even Buddhism and Jainism. As such, it was widely accepted by the reformers of different regions with certain modifications.

Though politically aloof from the rest of India till the occupation by the British, yet Assam never lost contact with the cultural events and trends of India at any time. The great *Vaiṣṇava* movement also supplied necessary ideals and inspirations to Śaṅkaradeva to initiate the *Nava-Vaiṣṇava* movement in the region.

## 2.2. LIFE OF ŚAṄKARADEVA

Śaṅkaradeva was born at Āli Pukhurī near Bardowā in the district of Nowgaon where his father, Kusumbara was the *Śiromaṇi* (chief) *Bhūñā* of the place.[4] There is much controversy about the date of Śaṅkaradeva's birth and the duration of his life. One of the earliest reliable biographers, Daityāri Thākur, clearly mentioned the date of death of Śaṅkaradeva as 1568 A.D. (1490 Śaka) but he was silent regarding the date of his birth. The later biographers recorded two dates, viz., 1449A.D. (1371 śaka) and 1463A.D. (1385 śaka) as the date of birth of Śaṅkaradeva.[5] However, the traditionally held date of his birth is Āśvina-Kārtika, 1449 A.D.( 1371 Śaka), allowing him a duration of life covering roughly 120 years.[6]

[3]. Sarma, S.N., *The Neo-Vaiṣṇavite Movement and the Satra Institution of Assam*, 1999, p.1.
[4]. Medhi, K, ed., *Aṅkāvalī*, 1997, 'Introduction', p. xliv.
[5]. See note 3 above, p.13.
[6]. Neog, M., *Śaṅkaradeva and His Times*, 1998, p. 98.

Caṇḍībara, one of the ancestors of Śaṅkaradeva, came to Assam in the 14th century from Gauḍa[7] and settled at Leṅgāmāguri.[8] However, there are many legends and various accounts regarding the *'Bāra Bhūñā'*s. According to one of them Caṇḍībara and other *Bhūñā*'s held their independent dominion at Kanaujapura and being attacked by Pāthāns or Yavanas, migrated to Gauḍeśvara's kingdom and then to Kāmarūpa as a result of a treaty concluded between Dharmanārāyaṇa of Gauḍa and Durlabhanārāyaṇa of Kāmarūpa.[9] Moreover, the term *'Bāra Bhūñā'* has got nothing to do with the number twelve as the word *'Bāra'* implies, rather it means many.[10]

Till the time of Śaṅkaradeva, the family professed Śāktism.[11]

At the age of thirteen, Śaṅkaradeva went to the *Tol*(school) of Mahendra Kandali, a *brāhmaṇa* scholar where he studied virtually all branches of Indian learning, such as, religious scriptures, grammar, lexicon and *kāvyas*. He was a devoted student and completed the course of studies within less time than was required ordinarily.[12]

After returning home, Śaṅkaradeva was given the responsibilities of *Śiromaṇi* (chief) *Bhūñā* and he performed his duties dexterously.[13] At the age of twenty one, Śaṅkaradeva married Sūryāvatī and had a daughter, Manu, by her, three years later. However, Sūryāvatī died soon after leaving behind a nine month old daughter.[14] After this incident, he became indifferent to worldly attachment and developed a strong inclination to go on pilgrimage. Accordingly, a few years later, after fulfilling his parental obligation by marrying off his

---

7. Sarma, S.N., *The Neo-Vaiṣṇavite Movement and the Satra Institution of Assam*, 1999, p.13.

8. Neog, M., *Śaṅkaradeva and His Times*, 1998, p. 65.

9. Ibid., p.50.

10. Neog, M., *Śrī Śrī Śaṅkaradeva*, 1987, p. 8.

11. Sarma, S.N., *The Neo-Vaiṣṇavite Movement and the Satra Institution of Assam*, 1999, p.13.

12. See note 8 above, p.102.

13. See note 10 above, p.30.

14. Ibid., p.32.

daughter Manu to Hari, materializing his old aspiration, he, along with seventeen other companions, set off on pilgrimage at the age of 32.[15]

Śaṅkaradeva travelled long and extensively and visited almost all the notable places in North and South India connected with the life of Rāma and Kṛṣṇa. It is fairly certain, as found from the *Carit Puthis* (hagiographies) that Śaṅkaradeva stayed at Puri for a long time and came in contact with many saints and scholars of various religious opinions.[16] From the affinity, shown by Dr. Banikanta Kakati, between the Neo-Vaiṣṇavism of Assam preached by Śaṅkaradeva and that of the south India.[17] it is evident that the sojourn had great influence on Śaṅkaradeva and inspired him to take up the task of re-orienting the religious set-up in the region.

Upon his return the grand-uncles wanted Śaṅkaradeva to take over the administrative responsibilities again. But he was more inclined towards religious pursuits only and kept himself engaged mostly in intellectual activities. However, at the great insistence of his elders and kinsfolk, Śaṅkaradeva married for the second time.

After five years, he handed over, whatever administrative duties he had, to his son-in-law Hari and shifted to Tembuvāni (Bardovā) along with some of his associate Bhūñās and his wife Kālindī and established a *Kīrtana-ghar* (prayer-hall). Congregational prayers and religious discussions were held regularly with a view to popularizing his new doctrine of *Viṣṇu Bhakti* and disseminating the concept of the new movement which was known as the *Eka Śaraṇa Nāma Dharma* (see 2.4.1.). Śaṅkaradeva also laid down certain guidelines for practising *Bhakti*.

Moreover, as a first step towards creating an atmosphere for propagating the new religious ideas among the people,

---

15. Neog, M., *Śaṅkaradeva and His Times*, 1998, p. 103.

16. Ibid., p.104.

17. Kakati, B., 'Matṛr Lagat Bibhed'. *In* Neog, M. (ed.) *Bāṇīkānta Racanāvalī*, 2003, pp. 198-202.

Śaṅkaradeva presented *Cihṇayātrā,* a dramatic performance with paintings wherein scenes of seven Vaikuṇṭhas with a presiding Viṣṇu over each one was shown.[18]

Śaṅkaradeva, along with his associates and other devotees remained at Bardovā praying to and discussing about Lord Kṛṣṇa.

But the Bhūñās had frequent skirmishes with the neighbouring Kachārīs and when the relation became strained to the utmost level, Śaṅkaradeva, along with the other Bhūñās, left Bardovā saving their lives in an emergency and crossing the river Brahmaputra, took up residence first at Rautā and then at Gāṅgmau and again at Cāṅgini Komorākaṭā. Eventually he crossed over to Dhuāhāṭā Belguri in Mājulī in the Āhom kingdom and settled down there. It was here at Belguri, that Mādhavadeva met Śaṅkaradeva for the first time and after a prolonged debate over religious and philosophical matters, Mādhavadeva accepted defeat and acknowledging Śaṅkaradeva as his spiritual master, '*guru*', renounced worshipping Śakti and embraced the new cult of *Viṣṇu Bhakti* as propagated by Śaṅkaradeva. From then on, Mādhavadeva remained the most ardent and the most inveterate disciple of Śaṅkaradeva throughout his life and succeeded him later on.[19] Belguri became the centre of great religious activity and the new *Eka Śaraṇa Nāma Dharma* spread out far and wide.

The feeling of loss of good-will and sympathy from the Āhom kingdom, continued hostility, disturbance and repeated hindrance from the *brāhmaṇas* in preaching the new cult, the execution of his son-in-law Hari in small pretext by the Āhom king, a strong desire to receive sympathy and patronage from a great scholar and pious king like Naranārāyaṇa and a desire to spread the new faith in Kāmrūpa[20] were some of the reasons which made Śaṅkaradeva decide upon leaving the Āhom

---

[18]. Sarma, S.N., *The Neo-Vaiṣṇavite Movement and the Satra Institution of Assam*, 1999, p. 16.

[19]. Ibid., p.19.

[20]. Neog, M., *Śrī Śrī Śaṅkaradeva*, 1987, pp. 74-75.

kingdom and migrating westward to the Koc kingdom. Accordingly, Śaṅkaradeva along with Mādhavadeva and other kinsmen, went downstream the Brahmaputra by boat and landed at Kāpālā in Kāmarūpa. But finding Kāpālā to be uncongenial to everyone's health, Śaṅkaradeva left the place along with all others and staying at Cūnporā, and then at Kumārkuci for some short periods of time, eventually moved to Pāṭbāusī, close to Barpeta and resided there permanently.[21]

Near about 1550 A.D., Śaṅkaradeva went out from Pāṭbāusī on his second pilgrimage with more than one hundred followers accompanying him.[22] According to the biographers, they visited Gayā, Benāras, Puri and the *matha* of Kabīr on their way,[23] and meeting several 'holy men from different parts of India, returned home after six months'.[24]

Being free from all the disturbances that were troubling him at different places so far and having found a congenial atmosphere now at Pāṭbāusī, Śaṅkaradeva engaged himself in literary activities again and the major portion of his writings were composed here itself. His teachings and preaching spread all around and a good number of followers ensued.

But this popularity of the new faith and the diminishing influence of the *brāhmaṇas* on the people made them envious of Śaṅkaradeva and they brought some false allegations against him and instigated king Naranārāyaṇa at Koc-Behār. The king ordered for immediate arrest of Śaṅkaradeva. However, Śaṅkaradeva escaped arrest somehow.[25]

After a few days, the *brāhmaṇas* reiterated their complaints to the King and the King ordered for arrest of Śaṅkaradeva again. Knowing about the impending arrest, prince Cilārai, the brother of the King and the chief of the army in the Koc

---

21. Neog, M., *Śaṅkaradeva and His Times*, 1998, p. 114.

22. Sarma, S.N., *The Neo-Vaiṣṇavite Movement and the Satra Institution of Assam*, 1999, p. 21.

23. Ibid., p. 23.

24. See note 21 above, p. 117.

25. Ibid., p.118.

kingdom, who had married Kamalpriyā, niece of Śaṅkaradeva,[26] and who was an initiated disciple of Śaṅkaradeva, intervened. Later on, however, Cilārai arranged for a visit of Śaṅkaradeva at the court of the king Naranārāyaṇa. While appearing before the king, Śaṅkaradeva entered reciting a Sanskrit hymn or *bhaṭṭimā* and then blessed the king with four other *ślokas* eulogising him. King Naranārāyaṇa was greatly impressed with his personality, erudition and dignified mien and showed him his due respect instantly. Śaṅkaradeva expounded before the king the main principles of *Eka Śaraṇa Nāma Dharma* and the king was convinced and the allegations brought by the *brāhmaṇas* were refuted. The king requested Śaṅkaradeva for a regular visit to his court and accordingly Śaṅkaradeva visited the royal court everyday during his stay at Koc-Behār. With the royal support behind them, Śaṅkaradeva and his followers felt completely secured in their movements and the Vaiṣṇava faith flourished vigorously.[27] The king held him in high esteem and Cilārai built a *satra* for him at Bhelā-ḍoṅgā near the Koc capital.[28] Śaṅkaradeva stayed there for about six months and later on kept on visiting the court. During this time, at the behest of the king, Śaṅkaradeva composed *Guṇamālā*, comprising the gist of the *Bhāgavata* in a nutshell, overnight and presented it to the King.

At the request of Cilārai, Śaṅkaradeva also composed his last play *Rāmavijaya Nāṭa* at *Bhelā-ḍoṅgā*.[29]

Śaṅkaradeva went to Pāṭbāusī for a short time and then came back to Koc-Behār and remained there till the end. On his way to Koc-Behār, Śaṅkaradeva visited Mādhavadeva at Gaṇakkuci and advised him on many topics and assigned responsibilities on him as his successor and the spiritual master designate after him. His demise took place there at Koc-Behār in the year 1568 A.D. at the age of nearly 120 years.[30]

---

26. Sarma, S.N., *The Neo-Vaiṣṇavite Movement and the Satra Institution of Assam*, 1999, p. 22.
27. Neog, M., *Śaṅkaradeva and His Times*, 1998, p. 119.
28. Ibid., p. 120.
29. Ibid., p. 120.
30. Ibid., p. 120.

## 2.3. SOCIO-POLITICAL BACKGROUND OF THE TIME:

To be able to understand the life and works of Śaṅkaradeva and to be able to appreciate the special role he played in the social life of Assam, we have to look briefly at the social and political situations prevalent at the time.

### Political Setting

Not much is known regarding the political history of Kāmarūpa during the times immediately preceding the age of Śaṅkaradeva. However, whatever can be known about the rulers of the twelfth and thirteenth centuries are only from epigraphic evidences like a few copperplates and stone inscriptions, the literary works of several pre-Śaṅkaradeva poets and of Śaṅkaradeva himself, the *Gurucaritas*, and the *Rāja-Vaṁśāvalīs* of the Koc kings of Kāmrūpa. Moreover, Muhammedan chronicles like *Tabakat-i-Naṣiri* and *Riyazu-s-Salātīn* throw some light on this point at times.[31] The *Burañjīs* i.e. the chronicles of the Āhoms, however, give a reliable account of the progress of events in the Brahmaputra valley since early thirteenth century.[32]

There have been records of repeated invasions by the rulers of Bengal in the region, and also that the western boundary of the kingdom was Karatoyā.[33]

To the east of the river Karatoyā different tribal groups like Chutiā, Barāhīs, Marāṇs, Ḍimācā Kachārīs ruled the land. There were also the petty chiefs called the '*Bāra Bhūñās*', as found in the legends of Assam.[34] On the west was the kingdom of Kāmrūpa, which later came to be known as the Kamatā kingdom ruled by the Koc.[35] Then also in the east, there were the Āhoms.[36]

---

31. Neog, M., *Śaṅkaradeva and His Times*, 1998, p. 39.
32. Gait, Sir E., *A History of Assam*, 2006, p. 38.
33. Ibid., p. 38.
34. Ibid., p. 39.
35. Ibid., p. 43.
36. Ibid., p. 38.

**Social Conditions**

All these people of different races and tribes spoke different languages, followed various religious faiths and cults and observed different customs accordingly. These different groups of people had skirmishes and fights among themselves very often which brought changes politically and also brought instabilities and insecurities among the common people. Life in those days was conditioned by the unsettled times, political turmoil, racial feuds, diseases and occasional famines following upon a state of warfare.[37]

There were many professional castes (*vṛttīyā*) in Assam and professions made an indelible mark on the caste or social positions among the people.[38] Accordingly, based on the professions people of the society were divided into various castes. The *brāhmaṇas* held an important position in the society.[39]

The common people were completely ignorant and helpless and lived in constant fear. They were afraid of the darkness, afraid of the wrath of gods and kings and also in fear of one group attacking and looting another weaker group.

**Religious Practices:**

There were many different cults among the people during those times and different religious and semi-religious activities were in practice and various rites and customs were also observed. They indulged in all sorts of elaborate pagan practices like slaughter of innocent animals, birds and also human beings in the name of religion. They even practised debaucheries.

Śaivism was the primary religion practised in ancient Assam.[40] The Koc kings were worshipers of Śiva and were

---

[37]. Neog, M., *Śaṅkaradeva And His Times*, 1998, p. 80.

[38]. Ibid., p. 77.

[39]. Ibid., p. 93.

[40]. Kakati, B., 'Purani Asamar Dharmar Dhārā', in Neog, M. (ed.) *Bāṇīkānta Racanāvalī*, p. 311.

known as "descendants of Śiva". Offerings were made following Hindu scriptures as well as tribal rites in different temples.[41]

Śāktism was the most powerful sect in Kāmarūpa by the twelfth century,[42] and the Tantric form was the prevailing religion of the land when Śaṅkaradeva was born.[43] *Kālikā-Purāṇa* and *Yoginī-Tantra* were its chief scriptures. There were descriptions of different places of worship and rituals for worshipping the Goddess[44] including comprehensive lists of objects of sacrifice in them.[45]

There were worshippers of Vāsudeva[46] and also there were other minor cults or sects like Nāthism (the Nāthas were known as Yogīs also) prevalent in some places at the time.

**Educational System**

Education seems to have been encouraged by the kings and monarchs of Kāmrūpa and poets and learned men received patronage from them.[47] In the Āhom kingdom, reading and writing in Āhom language was taught.[48] and the Āhoms were the pioneers in writing *burañjī* or history. In the Koc kingdom, educational institutions called *ṭols* or *chātra-śālis* were kept by *brāhmaṇa* scholars and copying out of religious works and the reading of them in the presence of scholars and holy men or in the temples were considered pious and "special care was bestowed on the accuracy of copies made from the original books".[49]

---

41. Neog, M., *Śaṅkaradeva And His Times*, 1998, p.80.
42. Ibid., p. 82.
43. Ibid., p. 81.
44. Kakati, B., 'Śiva-Pujār Calati', in Neog, M. (ed.) *Bāṇīkānta Racanāvalī*, 2003, p. 141.
45. See note 41 above, pp. 84-85
46. Neog, M., *Śaṅkaradeva And His Times*, 1998, p. 87.
47. Ibid., p. 95.
48. Rajkhowa, J. P., *Generalissimo Chilarai and His Times*, 2001, p.14.
49. Ibid., p. 97.

## 2.4. THE CONTRIBUTIONS OF ŚAṄKARADEVA

Śaṅkaradeva had great contributions towards the spiritual, social and literary fields of Assam. Following is a brief account:

### 2.4.1. ŚAṄKARADEVA AND HIS NEO-VAIṢṆAVITE FAITH

At the time of Śaṅkaradeva, there was distinction of castes and classes in the society and there was general ignorance and helplessness among the masses in religious matters.[50] Prāgjyotiṣa and Kāmrūpa, as the present day Assam was referred to in the earlier scriptures, was known as a land of magic and witchcraft for its tantric temple Kāmākhyā.

To bring all the indigenous people following various faiths under systematized religious codes and conduct of life, to do away with the extreme tantric observances connected with Śaivism and Śāktism, and to supply the mass with a mode of worship which would be simple and at the same time accessible to all were the pressing needs of the time. At such a juncture of time Śaṅkaradeva came forward with his neo-Vaiṣṇavite faith[51] to emancipate the common mass of people from the religious and social thraldom. He devised a popular and true philosophic religion, with *ahiṁsā*, equality and truth, based on the *Vedanta*, *Bhagavad-Gītā* and *Bhāgavata-Purāṇa.*[52] Against the dark socio-political scenario, repeated ethnic clashes and fallen moral values, Śaṅkaradeva, with his new cult of devotion or *Viṣṇu-bhakti,* brought hope and restored discipline to the trouble-torn and confused society.

***Eka Śaraṇa Nāma Dharma, Bhāgavatī-Dharma* and *Mahāpuruṣīyā-Dharma:***

Almost about the same time in the 15[th] and 16[th] century, in other parts of India also, many other saints, mystic and religious leaders tried to bring peace and morality back to the society by preaching the cult of devotion or *bhakti* among

[50]. Medhi, K., ed. *Aṅkāvalī,* 1997, 'Introduction', p. xlvii.

[51]. Sarma, S.N., *The Neo-Vaiṣṇavite Movement and the Satra Institution of Assam*, 1999, p. 11.

[52]. See note 50 above, p. xlvii.

the people. The cult Śaṅkaradeva preached among the people of Assam was called the *Eka Śaraṇa Nāma Dharma*. It was evolved after in-depth study and deep contemplation of all the important scriptures of Hinduism and observing closely the man and the society in general. The essence of this new cult was devotion to only one God, the Supreme Lord Śrī Kṛṣṇa or Lord Viṣṇu, as a personal God. The Sanskrit word '*śaraṇa*' means shelter; '*eka*' implies only one and '*nāma*' stands for the names and attributes of Lord Kṛṣṇa.[53]

As the main source book for the tenets of this *Bhakti* cult was the *Bhāgavata-Purāṇa*, this cult was also called as *Bhāgavatī-Dharma*.[54]

The cult is referred to as *Mahāpuruṣīyā-Dharma* too. One explanation of the epithet is that the term *Mahāpuruṣa* is an epithet of Lord Nārāyaṇa, as found in a few verses of the *Bhāgavata-Purāṇa*(II/1/10, XI/5/33), and as the *Vaiṣṇava* cult of Assam enjoins the worship of only Nārāyaṇa, the cult came to be known thus. However, the popular belief is that the cult is called thus because it was propagated by the '*Mahāpuruṣa*', an honorific title given to Śaṅkaradeva by his followers.[55]

## Salient Features of *Eka Śaraṇa Nāma Dharma*

The cult of Śaṅkaradeva is based on devotion to Kṛṣṇa, on the basis of the *Gītā*, as a personal God and on the firm belief in monotheism like that of Śrī Śaṅkarācārya of the Deccan.[56] Of all the manifestations of Nārāyaṇa, Kṛṣṇa is regarded as the most perfect one. As found in the *Bhāgavata-Purāṇa* (1/3/28), "*kṛṣṇastu bhagavān svayam*", Kṛṣṇa as the adorable deity of the cult, is not considered a partial manifestation but the Supreme Being himself.[57]

---

[53]. Sharma, M. M., 'Introduction', in Saikia, P., *Srīmanta Śaṅkaradeva's The Kī rttana-Ghoṣā*, ed. Das, K., 2005, pp. viii-ix.

[54]. Ibid., p. viii.

[55]. Sarma, S.N., *The Neo-Vaiṣṇavite Movement and the Satra Institution of Assam*, 1999, 'Introduction I'.

[56]. Medhi, K., ed. *Aṅkāvalī*, 1997, 'Introduction', p. xlvii.

[57]. See note 55 above, p.43.

Abolishing caste distinction that was prevalent in the society, Śaṅkaradeva welcomed people from all walks of the society including women and the lowest and had disciples from all castes and creed including even *brāhmaṇas* and Muslims.

Forsaking idol worshiping and elaborate ritualistic activities in worshiping God he propounded the doctrine of self-surrender through *dāsya-bhakti*. In his writings, Śaṅkaradeva, repeatedly and consistently, referred to himself as '*kṛṣṇara kiṅkara*' i.e., the servant of Kṛṣṇa.[58]

Śaṅkaradeva, laid down utmost emphasis on *śravaṇa* (listening) and *kīrtana* (chanting) of the prayer or *nāma*. Moreover, Śaṅkaradeva in all his writings, regarded *bhakti* as more important than *mukti*.[59]

As the character of Kṛṣṇa in the Vaiṣṇavism of Assam is based entirely on the *Bhāgavata-Purāṇa*, so the dual worship of Rādhā and Kṛṣṇa is completely absent in it.

### *Satras*

The *satras* are the *Vaiṣṇava* establishments in Assam. The word *satra* possibly meant an assembly of devotees where things about Viṣṇu or Kṛṣṇa were discussed.[60] A full-fledged *satra* included a *nām-ghar*, a *maṇikuṭ* and *hāṭis*. A *maṇikūṭ* was built when an image was installed. The central institute within a *satra* is the *nām-ghar* or *kīrtana-ghar*. The structures of the *satras* were temporary in nature made of bamboo and wood and covered with thatch on top.

Śaṅkaradeva established quite a number of *satras* in different places spreading over Assam where, inculcating communal worship with as simple a ritual as possible, he introduced complete equality and democracy among the religious brotherhood and thereby brought in an atmosphere of unity among the diverse sections of people in Assam. People from all

---

58. Sharma, M. M., 'Introduction', in Saikia, P., *Srīmanta Saṅkaradeva's The Kī rttana-Ghoṣā*, ed. Das, K., p. x.

59. Sarma, S.N., *The Neo-Vaiṣṇavite Movement and the Satra Institution of Assam*, 1999, p. 57.

60. Neog, M., *Śaṅkaradeva and His Times*, 1998, pp. 310.

walks of the society, rich or poor irrespective of their caste, creed, and religion could get together in the *satras* and *nāmghars* to take part in the community prayer and *prasaṅga*, *śravaṇa* and *kīrtana* of *Harināma* and partake of the food offered to Kṛṣṇa sitting together.

## 2.4.2. ŚAṄKARADEVA AS A SOCIAL REFORMER

To propagate the new *Bhakti* cult among the common mass of people, Śaṅkaradeva translated many important scriptures in Sanskrit with *Vaiṣṇava* faith into a poetic Assamese language that was used in literature of that time and composed *bargīts*, and six *nāṭas* in an artificially developed language called *Brajāvalī*, making it easier for the common people to know and understand the facts and philosophies of Vaiṣṇavism which were earlier the domain of only the *brāhmaṇas* and the elite class of people in the society. Henceforth, people could pray to God any time anywhere without a medium like a *brāhmaṇa* and most importantly, could communicate to God intimately with full emotions through prayers in their own language. The discrimination among the different castes was greatly removed as there was no bar for any caste in the matter of *śravaṇa* and *kīrtana* (hearing and chanting) of the holy names and attributes of the Lord.[61] Śaṅkaradeva maintained that even the lowest of the outcast is considered to be the most superior in whose tip of the tongue there is the name of the Lord and he has attained all the virtues of various religious vows.[62]

### The *Nām-ghar* or *Kīrtana-ghar*

Śaṅkaradeva set up a common prayer-hall in almost every village which were called *nām-ghar* or *kīrtana-ghar* where not only congregational prayers were held but also religious discussions were held regularly. Moreover, these *nām-ghars* (prayer-halls) also served the purpose of village courts where petty cases and matters of public interest were settled. They

61. Sharma, M. M., 'Introduction', in Saikia, P., *Srīmanta Saṅkaradeva's The Kīrtana-Ghoṣā*, ed. Das, K., p. x.

62. Saikia, P., *Srīmanta Saṅkaradeva's The Kīrtana-Ghoṣā*, ed. Das, K., sec. III, verse 111, p. 53.

were units under some central *satra.*[63] They were the public institutions for all social, intellectual and cultural activities. Śaṅkaradeva gave the people a platform for social unity where not only religion and religious practices were taught, but also instructions on different forms of art and culture and social code of conduct were given. People were taught cleanliness, health and hygiene and purity of mind as well.[64]

It is a matter of great significance that in the Assamese society the distinctions and discriminations amongst the various castes and creeds are not as strong as in most of the other places of India. This fact can very well be connected to the progressive teachings of Śaṅkaradeva which had an all pervasive influence in the society.

Thus, at a politically disturbed period of time and in an ethnically diverse place Assam, Śaṅkaradeva was not only a religious leader but also a great social reformer

### 2.4.3. LITERARY CREATIONS OF ŚAṄKARADEVA

Śaṅkaradeva's literary contributions were varied and voluminous indeed. Dr. Maheswar Neog opines that the adherence of the *Vaiṣṇava* writers to the sanction at scriptural authority amounted to limitation upon their creative abilities and a curb upon their poetic genius. Nonetheless, the literary output of Śaṅkaradeva and Mādhavadeva alone is considerable, and is characterised by a rare power of rendering the spirit of the original in unimpaired beauty and by occasional flights of creative imagination. Their literary works acted as the chief machinery of propaganda of the faith, and afforded both enlightenment and pleasure to the people.

The age of Śaṅkaradeva marks a literary and cultural resurgence in Assam. Śaṅkaradeva and Mādhavadeva themselves composed a good number of songs, dramas, verse narratives and other types of literature, wherein they expounded and elaborated the teachings of the faith they sought

63. Medhi, K., ed., *Aṅkāvalī*, 1997, 'Introduction', p. xlix.
64. Ibid., pp. xlviii-xlix.

to propagate. A host of poets, writers and scholars like Ananta Kandali, Rama Sarasvati, Vaikunthanatha Kaviratna, Sridhara Kandali, Gopaladeva of Bhavanipur, Ramacharana Thakur, Daityari Thakur, Gopalacharana Dvija, flocked under the banner of *bhakti*, and formed into a vigorous literary movement.[65]

Śaṅkaradeva, no doubt was a great literary genius and he composed many a lyrics, translated scriptures into Assamese and composed many *bargīts*, *bhaṭṭimās* and six *nāṭas* in *Brajāvalī* as a vehicle for exposition of his *Bhakti* cult. However, it is not possible yet, to give complete account and the chronologies of his literary creations as the *Carit-Puthis*, which are the main sources of information in this regard, cannot provide adequate information.[66]

Śaṅkaradeva's creative genius showed up quite early. At the *ṭol* of Mahendra Kandali, just after learning the only alphabets, Śaṅkaradeva composed a hymn using no other vowel but only '*a*' in it . It goes like this:

*Karatala kamala kamala-dala-nayana*
*Bhava dava dahana gahana vana śayana....*[67]

The verse described Lord Viṣṇu and his attributes in a beautiful and meaningful language. Later on, while still at the *ṭol*, or immediately afterwards, he also composed his first book *Hariścandra-Upākhyān*, glorifying Lord Viṣṇu and thereby laid down the foundation of the *Bhakti* cult and established the four main tenets, *guru, deva, nāma* and *bhakata* as means for pursuing *bhakti*.[68]

### The *Kīrtana Ghoṣā*

His next work was a part of the *Kīrtana Ghoṣā*, his immortal work. There are 28 sections in it and each section contains one

65. Neog, M., 'Sankaradeva and the Great Age in Literature and Fine Arts', in Chaliha, B.P. (ed.) *Mahapuruṣa Jyoti (Journal of the Srimanta Sankaradeva Sangha)*, Vol. III, 2000.
66. Medhi, K., ed., *Aṅkāvalī*, 1997, 'Introduction', p. xlix.
67. Neog, M., *Śrī Śrī Śaṅkaradeva*, 1987, p. 29.
68. Ibid., p. 30.

to 22 *kīrtanas*. Each *kīrtana* is divided into two parts, a *ghoṣā* (refrain), usually of two lines and a number of *pada* (verses) written in different metres.[69] Different portions of it were composed at different periods of time in his life and were compiled into one volume later on by Rāmacaraṇa under the supervision of Mādhavadeva.[70] Each of the chapters is complete in itself and is an independent story which deals with the glory of devotion to Lord Kṛṣṇa. Apart from the beautiful language and descriptions one can trace all the nine sentiments of literature (*Nava-Rasa, i.e. Śṛṅgāra, Hāsya, Karuṇa, Raudra, Vīra, Bhayānaka, Bībhatsa, Adbhuta* and *Śānta)* in it. The hymns of the *Kīrtana* are sung as prayers at the congregational prayers.

This was followed apparently by the *Kṛṣṇa-Uddhava Saṁbāda*. The *Daśama*, another poetical work by Śaṅkaradeva, deals with the magnificence of *Nāma Dharma* and *bhakti* and includes instructions for *Viṣṇu bhakti* and is the most popular *Vaiṣṇava* scripture.

### The *Bargīts*

According to the *caritas*, Śaṅkaradeva is said to have composed 240 *bargīts* or the noble songs.[71] But out of them only 34 are available now. Dr. Maheswar Neog says that as found from the *Caritas*, while on his first pilgrimage, Śaṅkaradeva, visited Haridvāra and Badarikāśrama; where he composed the first of the series of *bargīts*, beginning with the words, '*mana meri rāma caraṇahi lāgu*'.[72] Each of the *bargīts* is tuned to a *rāga*; however, the *tāla* is not always specified. They were composed in the artificial language called *Brajāvalī*.[73] The *bargīts* are religious in content and devotional in purpose.

[69]. Saikia, P., 'Editor's Note', in *Srīmanta Saṅkaradeva's The Kīrtana-Ghoṣā*, ed. Das, K., p. xviii.

[70]. Neog, M., *Śaṅkaradeva and His Times*, 1998, p. 167.

[71]. Kakati, B., 'Bargīt', in Neog, M. (ed.) *Bāṇīkānta Racanāvalī*, 2003, p. 45.

[72]. Neog, M., *Śrī Śrī Śaṅkaradeva*, 1987, p. 40.

[73]. Sarma , S.N., *Asamīyā Sāhityar Samīkṣātmak Itibṛtta*, 2006, p. 122.

Dr. Banikanta Kakati calls the *bargīts* as the 'Noble Numbers',[74] Kaliram Medhi and Devendranath Bezbaruah refer to them as the 'Great Songs or Songs Celestial' and the 'Holy Songs' respectively.[75] Śaṅkaradeva's songs sing of the futility of human efforts, and urge upon listeners the need for *bhakti*; some of them are prayer songs, pure and simple, and didactic verses.[76]

Another form of poetry composed by Śaṅkaradeva is the *bhaṭṭimās* or the panegyrics. It is a class of lyric, which, like the English ode is "often in the form of an address, generally dignified or exalted in subject, feeling, and style".[77] The *bhaṭṭimās* of Śaṅkaradeva are further classed into three divisions: i) *Nāṭa-bhaṭṭimā*, ii) *Rāja-bhaṭṭimā* and iii) *Deva- bhaṭṭimā.*[78]

The *Toṭaka* hymn, beginning with *'madhu dānava dāraṇa deva varaṁ...'etc.*, is written in beautiful Sanskrit and is in the *Toṭaka* metre.

**Other Lyrical Compositions**

Among his other lyrical compositions, there are the *Rukmiṇī Haraṇa Kāvya,* the *Bhakti-Pradīpa,* the *Anādi Pātana,* the *Nimi Nava-Siddha,* the *Kurukṣetra*, the *Uttarā-kāṇḍa Rāmāyaṇa* and the *Guṇamālā*. The *Bhakti-Ratnākara* is the only composition in Sanskrit by Śaṅkaradeva. It consists of 38 chapters containing the philosophy of his doctrine. The main sources of his literary creations are the *Purāṇas* and specially the *Bhāgavata Purāṇa* and other *Viṣṇuite purāṇas* and sectarian texts.[79]

---

74. Kakati, B., 'Bargīt', in Neog, M. (ed.) *Bāṇīkānta Racanāvalī*, 2003, p. 45.

75. Sarma, H. K., *Assamīyā Sāhityat Dṛṣṭipāt,* p. 95,

76. Neog, M., 'Sankaradeva and the Great Age in Literature and Fine Arts', Chaliha, B.P. (ed.) *Mahapuruṣa Jyoti*, Vol. III, 2000.

77. Neog, M., *Śaṅkaradeva and His Times,* 1998, p.195.

78. Ibid., pp. 196-97.

79. Ibid., p. 208.

Śaṅkaradeva is said to have translated eight out of the twelve cantos of the *Bhāgavata Purāṇa.*[80] In most of his renderings, Śaṅkaradeva seems to have closely followed the commentary of Śrīdhara Svāmī.[81]

For exposition of his *Bhakti* cult, *Śaṅkaradeva* composed six full fledged plays or *Nāṭa,* as he calls them, in *Brajāvalī*. They are: i)the *Kāli Damana* (at *Bardovā,* about 1518 A.D.), *ii)* the *Patnī-Prasāda* (probably at *Dhuāhāṭā,* 1521 A.D.), *iii) Keli-Gopāla,* 1540 A.D.; *iv) Rukmiṇī Haraṇa, v) Pārijāta Haraṇa* (all three at *Pāṭ-Bāusī* ) and *vi) Śrī Rāma-Vijaya* (at *Koc-behār,* as found in the colophon by the author himself, in 1490 Śaka,i.e., 1568 A.D.).[82]

**The *Cihṇa Yātrā***

However, the *Cihṇa Yātrā* was the first dramatic performance for the purpose of preaching the *Vaiṣṇava Bhakti* cult among the common people. The scenes of seven Vaikuṇṭhas with a presiding Viṣṇu over each one were shown in it.[83] Śaṅkaradeva himself took part in the performance and presided over the seventh Vaikuṇṭha. Dr. Satyendranath Sarma says that according to the hagiographies, apart from the general directions, Śaṅkaradeva not only painted all the necessary settings for the performance but also designed the costumes and masks, and arranged the music and dance in the play. Musical instruments like *khol* and *tāl* were also prepared under his supervision for the said purpose. With all the characteristics of the other later *nāṭas*, *Cihṇa Yātrā* was a full fledged play. However, there is no mention of any *vacana* or dialogues in the mouths of the characters. The performance of the play continued for seven days and seven nights at a stretch and after this, many people

---

80. Neog, M., *Śaṅkaradeva,* 2006, p. 49.

81. See note 79 above.

82. Medhi, K., ed., *Aṅkāvalī,* 1997, 'Introduction', p. L.

83. Sarma, S.N., *The Neo-Vaiṣṇavite Movement and the Satra Institution of Assam,*1999, p.16.

became attracted to the new cult. It is a matter of great regret that there is no written form of the play available now.[84]

**Paintings**

In Assam, Vaiṣnavaism brought in the practice of illuminating the holy books with small illustrative paintings. Śaṅkaradeva is believed to have been a painter himself. He is said to have painted on *tulāpāt* (paper made of cotton) all the scenes of the *'Seven Vaikuṇṭhas'* for the presentation of the *Cihṇa Yātrā* . On another occasion he painted with vermillion and yellow arsenic the picture of an elephant, and pasted it on a wooden book-case to be presented to his royal patron, Naranārāyaṇa.

Vaiṣnavaism in Assam developed a school of painting of its own and this art was later patronized by the Āhom monarchs and Koch chiefs of the 17th and 18th centuries. The conventions of angularity in figure drawing, fish-shaped eyes, arched eyebrows, pointed nose and sloping forehead, speak of an ancient tradition giving it charm and a distinctive quality.[85]

*Vṛndāvanī Vastra*

He also had a forty yard long piece of cloth woven under his guidance and regular supervision, by the weavers of Tāāntīkuci (now Barpeta), depicting the entire life of Kṛṣṇa – different incidents, from his birth at the jail of Kaṁsa to the killing of Kaṁsa,[86] woven in various colours and putting a caption to each one of them. Dr. S. N. Sarma however, gives the length of the cloth as sixty yards.[87]

It took about six months to a year to complete this *Vṛndāvanī Vastra* and upon completion of this piece of artwork, Śaṅkaradeva presented it to King Naranārāyaṇa and Prince

---

[84]. Sarma, S.N., *Asamīyā Nāṭya Sāhitya*, 2002, pp. 7-9.

[85]. Neog, M., 'Sankaradeva and the Great Age in Literature and Fine Arts', Chaliha B.P. (ed.) *Mahapuruṣa Jyoti*, Vol. III, 200.

[86]. Neog, M., *Śaṅkaradeva and His Times*, 1998, p. 120.

[87]. Sarma, S.N., *The Neo-Vaiṣṇavite Movement and the Satra Institution of Assam*, 1999, p. 23.

Cilārai, whose wish it was to have representation of the life of Kṛṣṇa in such an art form.[88] The *Vṛndāvanī Vastra* very well brings into focus the range of Sankaradeva's creative genius.

However, how and when the *Vṛndāvanī Vastra* disappeared from Koc-Behār is not known and with that, a valuable piece of history was also lost. The *Vṛndāvanī Vastra* was not heard of again for nearly another 400 years.

In 1904, Francis Younghusband, a British Army Officer serving in India, led an expedition to Tibet. Among the artifacts he took back to Britain were a few exquisitely woven 'figured silk textiles' from Tibetan monasteries. These silk tapestries were donated to the museum in Britain in 1905. For the next 85 years, despite the iconography on the textiles that was clearly *Vaiṣṇava*, far removed from the Buddhism practiced in Tibet, they remained catalogued as 'Tibetan Silk Lampas', as Tibet was their last known place of origin. Only in 1992 did a British scholar finally identify the 'Tibetan Silk Lampas' as Śaṅkaradeva's *Vṛndāvanī Vastra*.

It has come to knowledge that pieces of Vṛndāvanī Vastra are now preserved with utmost care in at least 16 museums outside India including the Victoria and Albert Museum of London and in Guimet, the national museum of Asian art in Paris[89] and the Association pour l'Etude et la Documentation des Textiles d'Asie collection at Paris, in the British Museum, Chepstow museum in UK and Gemau Museum in France.[90]

The *Vṛndāvanī Vastra* has greatly piqued the imagination of the researchers worldwide. In her write up "Vrindavani Vastra, Figured Silks from Assam" by Rosemary Crill, a curator in the Indian Department at Victoria & Albert Museum, London, says that in the *Vṛndāvanī Vastra* (Barpeta, Assam,ca.1565-1569) pictures of Silk Lampas depicting *avatārs* of Viṣṇu and scenes from the lives of Kṛṣṇa and Rāma are

88. Neog, M., *Śaṅkaradeva and His Times*, 1998, p. 120.

89. 'Majuli monks to perform unique dance drama in France, Switzerland', *The Hindu*, Guwahati: June 12, 2012.

90. 'Rare Manuscript, textile from Northeast Holed up in Museums Abroad', *The Times of India*, Guwahati: September 25, 2007.

given. The author further describes that made as an altar-cover, its[*Vṛndāvanī Vastra*] design shows the God's various incarnations (*avatārs*) including Kṛṣṇa, as well as Garuḍa, the vehicle of Viṣṇu and scenes from Rāmāyana (Rāma being the 7th incarnation of Viṣṇu).[91]

The *Vaiṣnava* Renaissance thus reached out to all fields of culture and with a unifying and glorifying vitality enriched and developed the life in Assam.

## 2.5. A LIST OF THE WORKS OF ŚAṄKARADEVA

Śaṅkaradeva was more a preacher than a literary man. Even then, his literary output is considerable and consists of a wide variety. It is also difficult to fix the chronology of the works.[92] Moreover, all the literary creations are not available now and references to some of Śaṅkaradeva's literary works are found only in the *Carit Puthis*. However, Dr. Maheswar Neog has prepared a list of the works of Śaṅkaradeva in a tentatively chronological order on the basis of certain external and internal evidences. Dividing the literary career of Śaṅkaradeva into three periods, corresponding to his stay in the *Bāra Bhūñā*, Āhom and Koc territories respectively, following is the list:

"A. Early Period : in the *Bāra Bhūyā* territories
This period is characterised by a youthful gaiety and exuberance, extends roughly up to the year 1516.

(i) Non-*Bhāgavata* group –
   1. *Hariścandra-upākhyāna (Mārkaṇḍeya-purāṇa)*
   2. *Bhakti-pradīpa (Garuḍa-purāṇa)*
   3. *Kīrtana-ghoṣā* : 'Ureṣā-varṇana' section (*Brahma-purāṇa*)

(ii) Non-*Bhāgavata* material mixed with *Bhāgavata* elements, not influenced by Śrīdhara Svāmī –
   4. *Rukmiṇī-haraṇa-kāvya (Harivaṁśa* and *Bhāgavata-purāṇa)*

91. Crill R., 'Vrindavani Vastra : Figured Silks from Assam'.
92. Neog, M., *Śaṅkaradeva and His Times*, 1998, p. 159.

(iii) Lyrics –

5. *Bargītas*

(iv) First group of *Bhāgavata* tales, taken from outside Book X –

6. *Ajāmilopākhyāna* (Book VI)
7. *Amṛta-manthana* (Book VIII)
8. *Kīrtana-ghoṣā* : 'Ajāmilopākhyāna' (Book VI), 'Prahlāda-carita' (Books III, VII), 'Haramohana', 'Bali-chalana', 'Gajendropākhyāna' (Book VIII) and 'Dhyānavarṇana' sections.

(v) 8. *Guṇamālā*, ii-vi.

It will have been seen[sic] from the names of books (from *Ajāmilopākhyāna* to *Rāma-vijaya)* that since after Śaṅkara had received a copy of the *Bhāgavata-purāṇa*, furnished with Śrīdhara Svāmī's commentary, from Purī, almost all the works of Śaṅkara are based on this purāṇa. The *Rāmāyaṇa*, Uttara-kāṇḍa, was rendered into Assamese in order to supplement Mādhava Kandali's version of the epic, and the *Rāma-vijaya* was written at the request of Cilārāya. More than three-fourths of the *ślokas* cited in the *Bhakti-ratnākara* are from the *Bhāgavata.*

B. Middle period : in the Āhom Kingdom (c. 1516—c. 1543)

This was a period of great unrest and obstruction, self-criticism, and then advance.

(i) Presentation of arguments to meet the enemy of the *bhakti* cult –

3. *Kīrtana-ghoṣā :* 'Pāṣaṇḍa-mardana' and 'Nāmāparādha' sections (*Bhāgavata-*, *Padma* and *Bṛhan-nāradīya-purāṇas*, *Viṣṇu-dharmottara* and *Suta-saṁhitā)*
9. *(Vipra-) patnī-prasāda-nāṭa (Bhāgavata-purāṇa, X).*

(ii) Tales of Kṛṣṇa's early life from the Pūrvārdha of the *Bhāgavata-purāṇa, X –*

3. *Kīrtana-ghoṣā* : 'Śiśu-līlā', 'Rāsa-Krīḍā', 'Kaṁsavadha', 'Gopī-uddhava-saṁvāda', 'Kūjīr vāñchā-pūraṇa' and 'Akrūrar vāñchā-pūraṇa' sections.

It may be added that during this period the composition of *bargītas* must have continued.

C. Final period : in the Koc kingdom (c. 1543—1568)

This period is marked by a comparative quiet in the life of Śaṅkara and the career of his order, by the fullest development of Śaṅkara's mind and art, and by the fulfilment of the mission of his life.

(i) The second group of *Bhāgavata* tales, taken from outside Book X –

*10. Bali-chalana* (Book VIII)

*11. Anādi-pātana* (Book III, *Vāmana-purāṇa)*

*(ii) Bhāgavata* tales from Book X (Uttarārdha), XI and XII –

3. *Kīrtana-ghoṣā* : 'Jarāsandha-yuddha', 'Kālayavana-vadha', 'Mucukunda-stuti', 'Syamanta-haraṇa', 'Naradar Kṛṣṇa-darśana', 'Vipra-puttra-ānayana', 'Daivakīr puttra-ānayana', 'Veda-stuti', 'Līlāmālā', 'Rukminīr prema-kalaha', 'Bhṛgu-parīkṣā', 'Śrīkṛṣṇar vaikuṇṭha-prayāṇa', 'Caturviṁśati-avatāra-varṇana' and 'Tātparya' sections.

The sections 'Rukmiṇīr prema-kalaha' and 'Bhṛgu-parīkṣā' are not generally included in manuscript copies and printed editions of the *Kīrtana-ghoṣā*. The 'Śrīkṛṣṇar vaikuṇṭha-prayāṇa' embodies three sub-sections and includes matters from Books I and III besides Book XI of the *Bhāgavata.* This group of compositions (particularly in the 'Veda-stuti', 'Caturviṁśati-avatāra-varṇana', 'Śrīkṛṣṇar vaikuṇṭha-prayāṇa', etc.) is characterized by occasional philosophical passages and may, therefore, be called 'the philosophical group'.

(iii) Renderings of the *Bhāgavata-purāṇa,* taken *skandha* by *skandha* or in the form of independent anecdotes –

12. *Bhāgavata*, X. Ādi
13. *Bhāgavata*, XI (with materials from Books I and III)
14. *Bhāgavata*, XII
15. *Bhāgavata*, I
16. *Bhāgavata*, II
17. *Bhāgavata*, IX (not available)
18. *Kurukṣetra* (Book X, Uttarārdha)
19. *Nimi-nava-siddha-saṁvāda*

8. *Guṇamālā*,

(iv) The tale of Rāma –
20. *Rāmāyaṇa*, Uttara-kāṇḍa (See also 27 below)

(v) Lyrics –
5. *Bargīta*
0. *Toṭaya*
21. *Bhaṭimā*

(vi) Doctrinal treatise –
22. *Bhakti-ratnākara*

(vii) Dramas –
23. *Kāli-damana*
24. *Keli-gopāla*
25. *Rukmiṇī-haraṇa*
26. *Pārijāta-haraṇa*
27. *Rāma-vijaya* (written in 1490 Śaka/1568 A.D.)

The songs and dramas must have been distributed all over the period.

The above list of twenty-seven independent works seems to be more or less a complete one, including all the writings of Śaṅkara so far brought to light. The *Bhāgavata*, IX, which is mentioned only in the *Kathā-guru-carita*, could not, however, be traced."[93]

●●●

[93]. Neog, M., *Śaṅkaradeva and His Times*, 1998, pp.160-1 62.

# CHAPTER III
# *AṄKĪYĀ NĀṬA* – THE PLAYS OF ŚAṄKARADEVA : AN ANALYSIS

## 3.1. A GENERAL OVERVIEW

For the purpose of exposition of his new *Vaiṣṇava* cult, Śaṅkaradeva composed his first drama, the *Cihṇa Yātrā* and the performance took place with all painted settings, perhaps for the first time, as, "in Sanskrit drama there is no reference to any use of scenery in the representation".[1]

After *Cihṇa Yātrā*, Śaṅkaradeva composed six other full-fledged dramas by the names, i) the *Kāli Damana*, ii) the *Patnī-Prasāda*, iii) the *Keli-Gopāla*, iv) the *Rukmiṇī Haraṇa*, v) the *Pārijāta Haraṇa* and vi) the *Śri Rāma-Vijaya Nāṭa*. Śaṅkaradeva himself, in the body of the dramas, referred to them as *nāṭa*, *nāṭaka*, *nṛtya* and *yātrā*. The dramatic performance of the *nāṭa* is termed in Assamese as *bhāonā*. On the other hand, 'the Assamese term "*Aṅka*" is equivalent to an English Drama; but it commonly means a book of drama'.[2]

Another epithet, *Aṅkīyā Nāṭa*, "does not occur in the body of the dramatic texts nor in the *caritas;* but is of popular application, indicating the Sankarite variety of play, as opposed to the later, decadent drama, which lack both the technical and linguistic beauty and peculiarity [sic] of the early drama".[3] This particular epithet is given to the plays also because they have only one *aṅka* in them".[4] To quote Dr. Birinchikumar Barua, "These plays, however, bear no resemblance to the

---

[1]. Medhi, K.,ed. *Aṅkāvalī*, 1997, 'Introduction', p. xxxii.

[2]. Ibid. p. i.

[3]. Neog, M., *Śaṅkaradeva and His Times,* 1998, p. 266

[4]. Sarma, H. K., *Asamīyā Sāhityat Dṛṣṭipāt*, 2005, p. 93.

*Anka* type of *Rūpakas* of Sanskrit. *Ankia Nat* is a generic term in Assamese and means dramatic compositions in a single act depicting the articles of Vaisnava faith".[5] As such this particular epithet is applied only to the plays of Śaṅkaradeva and Mādhavadeva. As such, this particular epithet is applied only to the plays of Śaṅkaradeva and Mādhavadeva.

**The First Play**

Although it is difficult to give exact dates of composition of all the *nāṭas,* yet the date of the *Śrī Rāma-Vijaya Nāṭa* can be known from the colophon given by the author himself and the other dates can be found from the *Charit Puthis* (though tentatively).

However, there is confusion as to the first play by Śaṅkaradeva. According to Kaliram Medhi, *Kāli Damana* was the first play after *Cihṇa Yātrā*. However, based on *Kathā Gurucarita* and *Śrī Śaṅkaradeva Aru Mādhavadeva* by Laksminath Bezbaroa, Dr. Maheswar Neog opines that "It is very probable that the work was done at Pāṭbāusī, as stated by Bezbaroa and the *Kathā-guru-carita*".[6] Considering the matters in the same line, Dr. Satyendra Nath Sarma also holds that there are reasons to consider *Patnī-Prasāda* and not *Kāli Damana* as the first composition of Śaṅkaradeva.[7]

Considering the amateurish handling of the play *Patnī-Prasāda,* in comparison with the other five plays composed full professionally, it can be guessed that it was composed earlier than *Kāli Damana.* Further, structurally also there are differences between the play *Patnī-Prasāda* and the other five plays; such as, the earlier one is much shorter than the other five plays and it does not have a *muktimaṅgala bhaṭimā* at the end like the other plays do. Moreover, from the reference and acknowledgement of Śrī Rāma Rāya in the *muktimaṅgala bhaṭimā* of *Kāli Damana*, it may be considered to be composed after Jagatānanda, kinsman of Śaṅkaradeva, received patronage

5. Barua, B., *Aṅkīyā Nāṭ,* 2012, 'Introduction', p. iii.
6. Neog, M., *Śaṅkaradeva and His Times,* 1998, p. 198.
7. Sarma, S. N., *Asamīyā Nāṭya Sāhitya,* 2002, p. 44.

from the Āhom king and was given the title 'Rāmrāi', sometime around their stay at Belguri. There are references and acknowledgement of Śrī Rāma Rāya in the *Kāli Damana*, the *Keli-Gopāla*, and the *Rukmiṇī Haraṇa;* however, Śrī Rāma Rāya is referred to as Jagatānanda in the *Pārijāta Haraṇa* and prince Cilārai is acknowledged as Śukladhvaja in the *Śrī Rāma-Vijaya.* But there is no particular acknowledgement to anyone in the *Patnī-Prasāda.*[8]

### Influence of Sanskrit Drama on the *Nāṭas*

The plays were the original creations of Śaṅkaradeva; albeit, the sources for them were the original *Vaiṣṇava* scriptures and the influence of the Sanskrit drama on them were great indeed. Elements like *Pūrva Raṅga, Nāndī, Prarocanā, Āmukha, Śloka, Sandhi, Rasa, Mukti-Maṅgala* and the prose, from the Sanskrit drama were there in the *nāṭas.*[9]

### Influences of Other Indigenous Folk Performances

Influences of other indigenous folk dance-forms and performances with dramatic properties, like the *Dhuliā* performance, the *Ojāpālī* performance, the *Deodhanī dance* and the *Putalā-nāc* (the puppet show) were also very much there.[10] It is difficult to ascertain the extent of influence, if any, of other forms of vernacular drama prevailing in different parts of India at that time, on the *nāṭas*. Kaliram Medhi however, opines that, "the evidence available shows unmistakably that the Assamese anka (drama) is the earliest among the regular vernacular dramatic works in India. It is an invention of Mahāpuruṣa Sankardeva [sic]. Assamese prose and drama occupy the first place among the vernacular literature of India."[11]

### Points of Differences from Sanskrit Drama

However, there were also points of differences in these plays from the Sanskrit drama.

---

8. Sarma, S. N., *Asamīyā Nātya Sāhitya,* 2002, p. 44.
9. Medhi, K., ed. *Aṅkāvalī,* 1997, 'Introduction', pp. xii-xviii.
10. Ibid., pp. ii-ix.
11. Ibid., p. xxviii.

Unlike the Sanskrit dramas, where the language was Sanskrit, the plays by Śaṅkaradeva, were composed in *Brajāvalī*. "It should not, however, be supposed that they [Śaṅkaradeva and his followers] used this language in all their religious works. They composed their lyrics and prayer-books, like the songs and lyrics of the pre-*Vaiṣnava* authors, in the classical Kāmrupī language."[12] Also, the prose in the dramas was very much poetic in nature.

There were specimens of violations of "dramatic propriety" of the Sanskrit drama in the *Brajāvalī* plays and representation of incidents like a battle, killing, marriage, amorous dalliance, bathing, anointing the body, putting on garments, eating and the like were freely shown on the stage.[13]

Unlike the Sanskrit drama, the leading figure in a *Brajāvalī* play was the *sūtradhāra* and recital of the *nāndī* was the specific function of the *sūtradhāra* in the *Aṅkīyā Nāṭas*.

In the Assamese drama there was no jester or such character as the *Viduṣaka* as in the Sanskrit drama.

Unlike the Sanskrit drama, songs in the Assamese dramatic performances were all sung by the chorus. Also, there was no division of acts and scenes in the Assamese plays; the stage was also never left vacant and the locality often changes from time to time according to the plot.

Anyway, to sum up, it can be said that Śaṅkaradeva was the father of the Assamese drama and the precursor to the regular vernacular prose which was however very much poetic in nature.[14]

**Language of the *Nāṭas***

As such, these plays can be said to be the first plays in Assamese literature and Śaṅkaradeva, the pioneer. They were composed in *Brajāvalī*, an artificial language with elements of Maithilī, old Assamese, Avadhī and Brajabhāṣā,[15] the common

---

[12]. Medhi, K., ed. *Aṅkāvalī*, 1997, 'Introduction',, p. xxii.

[13]. Ibid., pp. xviii-xxvi.

[14]. Sarma, S. N., *Asamīyā Sāhityar Samīkṣātmak Itibṛtta,* 2006, pp. 118-120.

[15]. Ibid., p.119.

language of the Kṛṣṇa Cult of Northern and Eastern India.[16] These six plays were composed during the period from 1518 A.D. to 1568 A.D. when the Assamese language was in its formative stage. As the themes of the plays were connected with Neo-Vaiṣṇavism and the activities of deities, the language used was not the language of the common people, yet easily understandable by the common people. A new literary language was created for this very special purpose catering to the need of the situation, but at the same time easily understandable both by the learned and the illiterate folk not only in Assam but also in other neighbouring states like Bengal, Bihar, Orissa and Uttar Pradesh and it was similar to the language used in those states at that time for propagating the *Vaiṣṇava Bhakti* Cult. This new literary language was called *Brajāvalī* or *Brajabuli*.

Śaṅkaradeva was very well versed in Sanskrit and prior to his pilgrimage composed books in melodious verses in Assamese. However, his use of the artificial language *Brajāvalī* in the *bargītas* and *nāṭas* might be an indication of the influence of the Maithili poets like Vidyapati and Umapati. According to Dr. Birinchikumar Barua, during the medieval time, at Mithila, the great centre of neo-Vaiṣṇavism, Maithili was the common language of the *Vaiṣṇava* literature and Vidyapati was the foremost amongst the *Vaiṣṇava* poets. A true exponent of the cult he made the language an extremely suitable and exclusive vehicle for expression for the *Vaiṣṇava* poets of his time. Soon after, a host of eminent poets, scholars, preachers from different parts of India including Kāmrūpa gathered around him and followed his example. Śaṅkaradeva, while on his pilgrimage, was also, possibly influenced by his witnessing some of the plays of the Maithili poets, such as the *Pārijāta Haraṇa* of Umapati, when he was in Bihar in the heyday of Vidyapati's fame.[17] However, as Dr. Dashrath Ojha opines[18]

[16]. Medhi, K., ed. *Aṅkāvalī*, 1997, 'Introduction', p. xx.

[17]. Barua, B.K., ed. *Aṅkīyā Nāṭ*, 2012, 'Introduction', pp. x-xi.

[18]. Ojha, D.,'The Impact of Sankaradeva's Dramas on the Literatures of Northern India', *Mahā puruṣa Jyoti*, Vol II, 1999.

that though it was Umapati of Mithilā to introduce *'Deśī Gīt'* into Sanskrit drama, namely *Pārijāta Haraṇa* yet it was Śaṅkaradeva who first composed an entire play in *'Deśī Bhāṣā'*. Moreover, as Umapati and Vidyapati did not care to write in prose no play in prose and poetry is to be found till the plays of Śaṅkaradeva.

## 3.2. THE COMPONENTS OF THE PLAYS

*Śloka, gīta, kathāsūtra* and the dialogues among the different characters, constitute the *nāṭas*. Whatever is said in the *śloka*, is presented elaborately in the exposition of the *sūtradhāra*, in the dialogues and in the songs. It will not be wrong to call them musicals with the four elements mentioned above.[19]

### The *Ślokas*

Regarding the *ślokas* in the plays, Kaliram Medhi says, "The frame-work of Śaṅkaradeva's plays (with one exception) is also in Sanskrit *ślokas*. The *ślokas* themselves form the skeleton of the plot: and, even if the songs, dialogue, recitative poetry and stage-direction are expunged, the germ (*vīja*) of the subject-matter(*vastu*) will be quite apparent from them. They supply the elements (*vindu*) of the plot for expansion and spread out in the whole drama like a drop of oil in water."[20] He further says that out of the 180 Sanskrit verses in the plays, Śaṅkaradeva had composed 179 Sanskrit verses himself and only 1 verse in the *Patnī-Prasāda* was quoted from the *Bhāgavata Purāṇa*. The metres used in them are also many.[21]

There are discrepancies found in the use of metres in quite a number of *ślokas*. However, keeping the great erudition of Śaṅkaradeva in mind, they are to be considered either as scribe's error or poetic license of the great poet.

---

[19]. Sarma, S. N., *Asamīyā Sāhityar Samīkṣātmak Itibṛtta*, 2006, p. 119.
[20]. Medhi, K., ed., *Aṅkāvalī*, 1997, 'Introduction', p. xv.
[21]. Ibid., p. xv.

### The *Gītas* or the Songs

The *nāṭas* are very much lyrical in nature and abound in songs. Including the *bhaṭimās* and *payāḍas* there are ten songs in the *Patnī-Prasāda*, sixteen songs in the *Kāli Damana*, 23 in the *Pārijāta Haraṇa*, 24 in the *Śrī Rāma-Vijaya*, 35 in the *Rukmiṇī Haraṇa* and maximum number of songs, i.e., 36 in the *Keli-Gopāla*[22] Dr. Maheswar Neog and Dr. Kesavananda Dev Goswami however, refer to the number of songs as 128[23] and 119[24] respectively. In the songs of the *nāṭas* the *rāgas* and *tālas* are always specified and there are 29 various *rāgas* used in them[25] The *satra* musicians have made assignment of *rāgas* to the different *praharas* in their own way.

### The *Bhaṭimās*

The *bhaṭimās*, in general imply eulogies and they can be divided into three wider divisions,[26] such as, *nāṭa bhaṭimā, deva bhaṭimā, and rāja bhaṭimā. nāṭa bhaṭimās*, again are of three types: eulogising Rāma or Kṛṣṇa in the beginning; praising and describing the main characters like Rāma, Kṛṣṇa, Rukmiṇī or Sītā in the main text; and lastly, seeking deliverance for the assembled audience at the end of the *nāṭa*[27] Leaving aside all other parts and taking only the songs into consideration, the story of the play can be well understood. Overall, the songs in the *nāṭas* bear exceptional poetic beauty and elegance.

No scientific treatise on the music of Assam has so far been available. A fragmentary manuscript, *Vadya-pradipa*, dealing with *tālas*, had been discovered, and was edited by Dr. Maheswar Neog.[28]

---

22. Sarma, S. N., *Asamiyā Nāṭya Sāhitya*, 2002, p. 49.
23. Neog, M., *Śaṅkaradeva and His Times*, 1998, p. 281.
24. Goswami, K. D., *Aṅkamālā*, 1999, p. 11.
25. Ibid., p. 11.
26. Ibid., p. 13.
27. Sarma, S. N., *Asamīyā Sāhityar Samīkṣātmak Itibṛtta*, 2006, p. 121.
28. Neog, M., 'Sankaradeva and the Great Age in Literature and Fine Arts', *Mahapuruṣa Jyoti*, Vol. III, 2000.

A list of the names of the *rāgas* (melody) *tālas* (time measure) and *mānas* (rhythm) as found specified in the plays is given in APPENDIX I.

### The *Sūtradhāra*

According to Kaliram Medhi, "The Sūtradhāra in an Assamese *Bhāonā* is, however, found present on the stage even after his formal exit at the conclusion of the prologue (prastāvanā). He not only sings songs in chorus with gāyana-bāyana (singers and musicians) and recites *ślokas* and *bhaṭṭimās* but also controls and directs the performance from beginning to end supplying and explaining the links of the plot as given in the *sūtras* (prose portion supplied by stage-manager).The actors take part only in dialogue, march, battle, dance and action such as the breaking of the bow, churning of curd, &c."[29] Dr. Birinchikumar Barua observes that, "In these plays songs and verses greatly preponderate and the playwrights largely use them to bring home the message inculcated in the play. Many situations and incidents are suggested by mere machinery of descriptive verses uttered by the Sūtradhāra instead of being represented through action and character."[30] The *sūtradhāra* of the Assamese drama also seems like the leader of the *ojāpāli* troupe but in a different garb.[31] Kaliram Medhi further opines that "The Sūtradhāra, like the Greek chorus, advises, directs and controls the whole performance. Thus he plays the role of the stage-manager of the Indian drama for the prologue and of the Greek chorus during the actual performance."[32]

The *sūtradhāra* is referred to as *sūtra, kathā* and sometimes as *kathā sūtra* without maintaining any discrimination among them. It is to be noted that with the novel creation of the

---

[29]. Medhi, K., ed., *Aṅkāvalī*, 1997, 'Introduction', p. xxiii.

[30]. Barua, B.K., *Aṅkīyā Nāṭ*, 2012, 'Introduction', p. iv.

[31]. See note 29 above, p. xxiv.

[32]. Ibid., p. xxv.

*sūtradhāra*, the need for dividing the play into different acts like the earlier as well as modern plays, seemed to have gone.[33]

The *sūtradhāra*, as such, is necessarily a man of great talents; he is an actor, a trained musician and an accomplished dancer with strong command over *Brajāvalī* as well as the Sanskrit language.

### *Bhakti Rasa* and Other Literary Sentiments *(Rasas)*

The main purpose of composing the plays was to arouse spiritual feelings, love and devotion to Śrī Kṛṣṇa, the Supreme Lord, in the minds of the people and to educate religion, even to the illiterate, through the performance, and while doing so, drench the audience thoroughly in pure *Bhakti Rasa*. It was not the aim of Śaṅkaradeva to evoke different literary sentiments (*rasa*) and entertain the audience through the plays. However, Śaṅkaradeva exploited many different *rasas* through thematic situations in different plays in his endeavour to bring the people to the path of devotion.[34] Although human behaviour and attributes are imposed on the characters of Śrī Kṛṣṇa and Śrī Rāma in the plays, yet Śaṅkaradeva has never forgotten to remind the audience, time and again, that they are not humans but gods. Moreover, in many of the lyrics contained in the plays, Śaṅkaradeva, mentions the word *rasa*; but that seems to point rather to the joy of devotion than to the sentiments of poetics. But the poetic sentiments are also there in the plays.[35]

It is very difficult to assess the *nāṭas* in the common platform of the nine *rasas (i.e. Śṛṅgāra, Hāsya, Karuṇa, Raudra, Vīra, Bhayānaka, Bībhatsa, Adbhuta* and *Śānta)*, like any other play. Although the dominant sentiments in the play the *Patnī-Prasāda* is *Adbhūta* (marvelous), in the *Kāli Damana* they are *Bhayānaka* (terrible) and *Karuṇa* (pathetic), in the *Keli Gopāla* it is *Śṛṅgāra*

33. Kakati, B., 'Aṅkīyā Bhāonā', Neog, M. (ed.) *Bāṇīkānta Racanāvalī*, 2003, p. 65.
34. Goswami, K. D., *Mahāpuruṣa Śaṅkaradeva*, 2007, p. 70.
35. Neog, M., *Śaṅkaradeva and His Times*, 1998, p. 255.

(erotic), in the *Rukmiṇī Haraṇa* they are *Śṛṅgāra* (erotic) and *Vīra* (heroic), in the *Pārijāta Haraṇa* and in the *Śrī Rāma-Vijaya* also it is *Vīra* (heroic) *rasa*; But they do not show automatically. Rather these evident sentiments (*rasas*) in the plays are to be accepted as manifestations of *Bhakti Rasa* only.

However, the experts in the rhetoric and poetics (*Ālaṅkārikas*) do not recognize *bhakti* as a literary sentiment (*rasa*), and they accept it to be a state of *Śānta Rasa*. Further, Abhinavagupta holds that, rather than revealing itself as an independent *rasa*, it helps in the development of another *rasa* only (it nourishes another *rasa* only). Also, as Dr. Mukunda Madhava Sharma opines, that in respect of *Bhakti Rasa*, the natural manifestation in the end is *Śānta Rasa* only.[36] However, Madhusūdana Sarasvatī remarks that "Bhakti is the real Rasa, because one can get ineffable bliss only from it and not from any other Rasa like Śṛṅgāra etc. Hence, Śṛṅgāra etc. are *kṣudrarasas*, i.e., secondary Rasas, like glow-worms in front of Bhakti, which is the *paripūrṇarasa*,i.e., the complete Rasa and like the Sun."[37] Thus, Śaṅkaradeva, through exploitation of different sentiments (*rasa*) in the plays endeavoured to give a taste of *Śānta Rasa* in the minds of the audience and thereby arouse the sense of *Bhakti* in them.

**Characterisation**:

As Śaṅkaradeva had to retain the stories in their original framework like the sources, he has not tried to develop the characters, neither has he tried to show their different facets. However, he has put human characteristics to even those characters which are gods and *asuras*. But as such, the characters in the plays are rather static and not dynamic. Also, though there are outward frictions among the characters, there is no real conflict found in the plays.[38] As the main purpose of

---

[36]. Sharma, M. M., *Dhvani Āru Rasatattva*, 1991, p. 74.

[37]. Chakravarty, S., *Studies in Sanskrit Literature Culture and Art*, 2011, pp. 63-64.

[38]. Sarma, S.N., *Asamiyā Nāṭya Sāhitya*, 2002, pp. 18-19.

these plays was to evoke *Bhakti Rasa* in the minds of the audience Śaṅkaradeva emphasized more on the principal characters like Rāma, Kṛṣṇa, Rukmiṇī and Sītā and the minor characters are drawn in bare outline only.[39]

## 3.3. PERFORMANCE OF THE PLAYS (*BHĀONĀ*)

### The *Nām-ghar* as the Theatre

Performances of the *Aṅkīyā Nāṭa* usually take place within the confines of the prayer halls or *nām-ghar*. Sometimes temporary theatre is also erected, which is called *rabhā* or *sabhā-ghar*, within the precincts of the *nām-ghar* or *Kīrtana-ghar*. The *nām-ghar,* which doubles up as a theatre-hall, is a two- roofed structure, rectangular in shape and open at the sides. At the one end of the prayer-hall is the *maṇikut* which houses the sacred throne, *guru āsana,* in which the sacred text (usually, the *Bhāgavata Purāṇa)* is placed, symbolizing the presence of the Lord and of the *guru*, his words and his teachings. It is customary to worship Kṛṣṇa before a dramatic performance is held.

About two thirds of the space between the rows of pillars in the middle of the hall is used as the stage or the *raṅgabhūmi* and it does not have a raised platform. The orchestra and the actors sit surrounding this stage. Also there is no other special arrangement on the stage except the *ārkāpor* or the white screen which is used when the musicians and the principal actors enter the stage from the *cho-ghar* or the green room. All the characters enter the stage dancing and remain seated on the stage after playing their part awaiting their next appearance to be announced by the *Sūtradhāra.* The audience consisted of all classes of people and usually, they sat on mats or on the bare ground.

A performance event usually begins in the evening and continues, sometimes, until sunrise. *Āriyās* (small torches of

[39]. Barua, B.K., ed. *Aṅkīyā Nāṭ*, 2012, p. viii.

cloth dipped in mustard oil) and *mahatas* (torches) were used for lighting the stage.

**The *Bhāwarīyā* or the Actors**

The actors in the *bhāonā* were not professionals but amateur villagers. The roles of the principal characters such as Rāma, Kṛṣṇa and their consorts were played by some handsome young men especially of the higher castes as these roles were considered to be divine and they were bowed to by the audience during the performance. Women were not allowed on the stage and female roles were performed by teen-aged youth with feminine appearance. The actors were supposed to keep a fast before the presentation of the *bhāonā*.[40] Persons of high social, religious and political status with great erudition and artistic attainments played the roles in the *bhāonā* with utmost pride and honour.

**How the Play Begins**

The performance of the *Aṅkīyā-Nāṭa* or *bhāonā* starts with a prolonged series of dances by the *gāyan-bāyan* party (*gāyan* implies the singers and the *bāyan* implies the instrumental musicians) with accompaniment of *khol* and *tāl* with the *sūtradhāra* as its leader. This is called *dhemāli* or *raṅga*.[41] The essential aim of these preliminary dances known as *saru dhemāli, bar dhemāli, deva dhemāli, ghoṣā dhemāli* and so on, is to secure the favour of God for the play to be presented. Sometimes these preliminaries continue for hours but they do not form a part of the drama proper. These preliminaries very much resemble the *pūrvaraṅga* mentioned in the *Nāṭya Śāstra*.[42]

**How the Play Proceeds:**

The *sūtradhāra* recites the *nāndī* in the beginning and then announces the subject matter of the play in a Sanskrit verse

[40]. Barua, B.K., ed. *Aṅkīyā Nāṭ*, 2012, p. xv.

[41]. Ibid., p. xii.

[42]. Ibid., p. xii.

which is invariably followed by a long *bhaṭimā*. Then follows the *prastāvanā*; the *sūtradhāra* hears a celestial sound. On this point a discussion arises and as it progresses the *sūtradhāra* announces the names of the approaching personages. At the end of this discussion the companion or *saṅgi* retires from the stage.

The *sūtradhāra*, remaining all along on the stage controls and directs the performance. He is the running commentator, introduces the characters, announces the entrances and exits of different characters, fills up the lacunae in the action of the play by song, dance and speech and also delivers brief discourses on the ethical and spiritual aspects of the plot. The role of the *sūtradhāra* is vital in a performance as the illiterate audience required explanations at every step of the development of the plot.

The play ends with a *mukti maṅgal bhaṭimā* where the *stradhāra* begs forgiveness of God for any omission or commission in the management of the play and also emphasizes upon the moral effect of the play,[43] invokes the audience to follow the path of *bhakati* (devotion) and righteousness and get engaged in the services of the 'Supreme Personality'.

The *Aṅkīyā Nāṭas* of modern times are, however, enacted on stage in the theater halls and other public places as well. Although the same (elaborate) rituals are followed, certain (minor) changes sometimes have to be incorporated in the stage-version of the plays in order to adjust to the different ambience. But, of course, the content is left untouched.

### Other Art Forms Related to Performance of the Plays (*Bhāonā*)

The performance of these plays (*bhāonā*) paved the way for development of other art forms and crafts, like singing, dancing and playing musical instruments, preparation of dress, costumes, make-up and other accessories, mask-making etc.

---

[43]. Barua B.K., ed. *Aṅkīyā Nāṭ*, 2012, Introduction, pp. vi,vii.

Śaṅkaradeva introduced the art of dancing mainly in connection with the dramatic performances, which were in most part dance and music, with prose constituting but an insignificant fraction.[44] As the *nāṭas* are lyrical in nature so all the characters move rhythmically in the form of dancing with appropriate steps, gestures and *abhinaya* postures from the beginning to the end.

Based on their characteristics the different dance forms are classified as (i)*Sūtra-bhaṅgi* or *Śūtradhāra Nāc, (ii) Kṛṣṇa-bhaṅgi* or *gosāāi-praveśar nāc, (iii) Gopī- bhaṅgi* or *Gopī- praveśar nāc, (iv)Cāli-nāc, (v)Jhumurā, (vi)Nṛtya- bhaṅgi, (vii)Rāsa-nṛtya, (viii)Yuddhar nāc* (fighting dance), *(ix)Bhāwarīyār nāc* or Dance of the general body of actors, *(xi) Dhemālir nāc* or Preliminary Dances, *(Āriyā nāc* or torch dance is a part of the *Dhemālir nāc)* and *Ojā-pāli*. Bare feet are a characteristic of these dances.[45]

"A variety of Rāgas and Tālas are used in Bhāonā performance for which, proper training in vocal and instrumental music was necessary.... Śaṅkaradeva thus established a new set of dance and music with novel thype [sic] of Rāgas and Tālas which are different from those established schools of Indian music and.... which can be termed as Śaṅkaradeva's music or loosely, the Sattriya music of Assam."[46]

The Satrīyā Dance has also been conferred the classical status by the Sangeet Natak Akademi and is listed amongst the eight recognised classical dance forms of India.

Dr. Mallika Kandali, in her doctoral thesis, "The Sattriya and the Odissi Dances: A Comparative Study" said that while other Indian classical dance forms were reconstructed through the revival of a tradition that no longer existed, *sattriyā* dance

---

[44]. Neog, M., *Śaṅkaradeva and His Times,* 1998, p. 294.

[45]. Ibid., pp. 294-300.

[46]. Goswami, K. D., *Mahāpuruṣa Śaṅkaradeva*, 2007, p. 71 .

is a living tradition, practised, preserved and performed consistently in the *satras* of Assam.[47]

*Chō* (effigies) and *mukhā* (masks) were much in use. Big-size effigies were made to present characters like Kāliya, Garuḍa, etc. To represent unusual appearances like four heads of Brahmā, the bird-like face of Garuḍa, grotesque faces of Mārīca and Subāhu masks were used. The masks are made of clay, wood or bamboo and cloth. They are painted suitably with lime, vermilion (*heṅgul*), yellow arsenic (*hāitāl*), indigo and lamp-black. The village *khanikar* was the main responsible person for preparing, maintaining and preserving these accessories.

As part of the necessary accessories, costumes suitable for each and every character was also kept in the *chō-ghar* (green-room). The *Śūtradhāra* was always dressed in white with a special turban(*pāg* or *pāguri*). Kṛṣṇa and Balarāma wore yellow and blue *dhoti* respectively with peacock feathers to a simple tiara as head-dress. The kings and warriors put on gaudy costumes and so on and so forth.

Ornaments were in profusion especially for the female characters. Weapons of battle such as sword, shield, bow, arrow, disc, club, etc. were also part of the *chō-ghar*. The paints used for make-up were generally vermilion (*heṅgul*), yellow arsenic (*hāitāl*), indigo, chalk (*dhal*), brown ochre (*gereu*), lamp-black, collyrium and mica.[48] Small tinkling bells made of brass or bell-metal were tied to the ankles of the actors.

### Mystery Plays and the *Bārecaharīā Bhāonā*

It is interesting to note that from the twelfth to the sixteenth century it was the heyday for the Miracle or Mystery plays in England. These plays were distinctly religious in character having their origin in the Bible or in the lives of the saints and, the authors were either the priests or their chosen assistants. The

---

[47]. 'Majuli Monks to Perform Unique Dance Drama in France, Switzerland'. *The Hindu*, Guwahati: June 12, 2012.

[48]. Neog, M., *Śaṅkaradeva and His Times*, 1998, p. 273.

object of these plays was to emphasize moral lessons by showing reward to the good and punishment to the evil-doer[49] and they were very much part of the religious development of all the uneducated people. The Miracles had taken strong hold upon the English people and they continued to be immensely popular until, in the sixteenth century, they were replaced by the Elizabethan drama.[50]

"Probably every important town in England had its own cycle of plays for its own guilds to perform, but nearly all have been lost. At the present day only four cycles exist ..., and these, though they furnish an interesting commentary on the times, add very little to our literature. ... It is impossible to fix either the date or the authorship of any of these plays ...."[51]

Significantly, although the *nāṭas* were so very similar to the Mystery plays in respect of time and purpose, yet contrary to the above mentioned lines, *nāṭas* are still preserved, studied, practiced and performed with utmost respect and with great religious fervour. In this respect mention must be made to the living tradition the *Bārecaharīā Bhāonā Festival* of Jamugurihat,[52] district Sonitpur, Assam.

This *bhāonā* festival has been celebrated with great solemnity and reverence for more than 200 years since 1797 in an interval of every five or six years.[53] Upholding the ideals of Śaṅkaradeva of gathering people and educating them through entertainment the local people from the villages around Jamugurihat, get together at the Pakāmūrā Paddyfield irrespective of caste creed and religion and construct theatres(called *khalā*) with locally available materials like bamboo and thatch following the

---

[49]. Long, W.J., *English Literature, its History and its Significance*, 1989, p. 116.

[50]. Ibid., p. 118.

[51]. Ibid., p. 118.

[52]. 'Bārecaharīā Bhāonā', *Asomiya Pratidin*, Feb.25, 2013, Guwahati edn., pp. 8,9.

[53]. Bhuyan, B., 'A Great Tradition', *Panorama: The Assam Tribune*, Feb.23, 2013, p. 10.

architectural pattern and artistic forms laid down by Śaṅkaradeva with provisions for twenty different troupes to perform *bhāonās* at the same time under a uniquely designed roof in an acting area shaped like a lotus in bloom. After elaborate practice for about a month, on the days of the festival, lighting lamps at the altar, singing *śloka* and *bhaṭimā*, playing the auspicious instruments like *khol, tāl* etc. performing community prayers, around 800 *bhāorīā* (the actors)offer the plays to the 'ultimate supreme personality Lord *Kṛṣṇa*'. Thousands of devotees in the form of audience throng the arena to take part in the offering.[54]

Significantly, even in present day the characteristics of the *Vaiṣṇava Bhakti* cult taught by Śaṅkaradeva like simple ways of worshipping *Kṛṣṇa*, importance of *śravaṇa* and *kīrtana* and democracy, equality and secularism in religious practices are still maintained. This fact is best substantiated by the instance of a person following Muslim faith taking part in the said *bhāonā* which is presented with great religious fervor as found from the write up by Ismail Hussain in the *Prantic* about his personal experience of taking part in the *Bārecaharīā Bhāonā*.[55]

However, point to be noted here is that the *bhāonās* performed here are not only *nāṭas* composed by Śaṅkaradeva alone but also later plays composed by the disciples of Śaṅkaradeva and later on by different senior members of the various *satras*. Regarding *Bārecaharīā Bhāonā* Dr. Madan M. Sarma and Dr. Parasmoni Dutta observed in their write up in the *Asian Theatre Journal* that "The festival offers a veritable feast of spectacle, stylized acting, classical dance, and music, all imbued with a sense of spirituality. The performance is marked by a continuous shifting between the classical and the folk, the mundane and the spiritual, providing thousands of spectators a rare aesthetic experience. The festival offers an example of a rural community's adherence to simple faith and a desire to retain the best of their cultural-

---

54. Barua, D.K., *Deobārarparā Bārecaharīā Bhāonā, Saturday Suppliment: Āmār Asam*, Feb. 23, 2013, p. 4.

55. Hussain, I., 'Bārecaharīā Bhāonāt Bhāo lovār Abhijñatā', *Prāntik*, Vol. xxvii, No. 23 1-15 November 2008.

religious tradition, and their readiness to accommodate the inevitable changes in the difficult days of globalization and cultural homogenization."[56]

## 3.4. BRIEF OUTLINES OF THE SIX PLAYS (NĀṬAS)

### The *Kāli Damana*

**Source** : Śaṅkaradeva adopts the story from *Bhāgavata Purāṇa* (x. 15-17).[57]

**The Story in Brief**: One day Kṛṣṇa along with the other cowherd boys went to the bank of lake Kālindī for grazing the cattle. Being very thirsty, the cowherd boys and the cattle drank the water from the lake not knowing that Kāli Nāga, the most venomous serpent, lived there and hence the water was strongly poisonous. As a result, all of them died. Kṛṣṇa was greatly disturbed by the event; but eventually, revived them with his immortal look (*amṛta dṛṣṭi*). Now, with an intention of punishing Kāli Nāga, Kṛṣṇa climbed up the *kadamba* tree on the bank of the lake and jumped into the water of the lake from there. With the disturbance in the water Kāli Nāga came out to the surface, and bit Kṛṣṇa with great anger and held him in the formidable clasp of his tail. Like an ordinary human being, Kṛṣṇa also lay there feigning death. Hearing the news, the parents of Kṛṣṇa along with the other cowherd boys and girls of Gokula, rushed to the lake greatly worried and seeing Kṛṣṇa lying like dead in the clasp of the terrible serpent, they became greatly afflicted. Seeing them suffering, Kṛṣṇa, after some time, freed himself with a jerk and mounting on the expanded hoods of Kāli, started a cosmic dance. Kāli was overpowered in a moment and was nearly dying. Fearing for his life, the wives of Kāli appeared before Kṛṣṇa and with folded hands, prayed for mercy. Kṛṣṇa,

---

56. Sarma, M. M, and Dutta, P., '*Bārecahariā Bhāonā:* Community Drama Festival of Assam: A Living Tradition', *Asian Theatre Journal*, 26,No.2, Nov. 2009.

57. Medhi, K., ed. *Aṅkāvalī*, 1997, 'Introduction', p. Lii.

thereupon, pleased with their prayer and devotion, spared Kāli and jumped down from his hoods. Kāli, somehow spared and still alive, fell down in the feet of Kṛṣṇa himself and prayed for his mercy. Kṛṣṇa, assuring him of his protection, ordered him to leave the lake Kālindī then and there along with his family. After that, as night approached, Kṛṣṇa, his parents and all the cowherd boys and girls with them, spent the night in the bank of Yamunā. But, at the middle of the night, a huge forest fire surrounded them all and everyone became terribly frightened. Then Kṛṣṇa, with miraculous power, swallowed in the fire and saved them all.

**Critical Analysis**: The descriptive prose in the play as comments and directions from the *sūtradhāra* reveal the expertise of Śaṅkaradeva in writing prose. However, there are very few dialogues in the play. The character of Kāli Nāga seems to be a representation of pride, ego, and cruelty in the minds which create serious disturbances in the world again and again and are the main obstructions in the path of devotion to Kṛṣṇa. The *payāḍa* by the wives of Kāli Nāga is a beautiful piece of prayer to Kṛṣṇa which establishes the supremacy and Godhead of Kṛṣṇa.[58] The character of Yaśodā is portrayed with the colour of universality in it.[59]

### The *Patnī-Prasāda*

**Source**: This is the first play by Śaṅkaradeva. It is composed on the basis of the *Bhāgavata Purāṇa* (x. 23).[60]

**The Story in Brief**: One day Kṛṣṇa and the cowherd boys were tending the cattle. The cowherd boys became very hungry and requested Kṛṣṇa to arrange for food. Kṛṣṇa directed them to go to a nearby *āśrama* (hermitage) and ask for food from the *brāhmaṇas* who were performing sacrifices there. The *brāhmaṇas*, who were very proud of their learning and the efficacy of sacrifice, however, not only refused to give them

[58]. Sarma, S. N., *Asamīyā Nāṭya Sāhitya*, 2002, p. 46.
[59]. Sharma, N. C., ed., *Kāliya Daman Nāṭ*, 1989, p. 23.
[60]. Medhi, K., ed., *Aṅkāvalī*, 1997, 'Introduction', p. Liii.

food but also passed disparaging comments on Kṛṣṇa. Then Kṛṣṇa sent the cowherd boys to the wives of the *brāhmaṇas* who were devotees of Kṛṣṇa. Hearing about the arrival of Kṛṣṇa there, the pious wives of the *brāhmaṇas* became very happy and with great excitement went out to see him with varieties of delicacies for him and the cowherd boys, resisting the strong oppositions from their husbands, brothers and sons. Coming to Kṛṣṇa, the object of their reverence, they paid their homage to him and also offered the food they had brought so lovingly. At the behest of Kṛṣṇa they returned home back and continued their devotion for him through simple prayers without rituals. Seeing their wives, eventually, the *brāhmaṇas* also realised the strength of simple prayers over great learning and elaborate ritualistic services and embraced the path of *bhakti*.

**Critical Analysis**: In this play, through contrast between the *karma-mārga* and the *bhakti-mārga*, Śaṅkaradeva tried to establish the supremacy of *bhakti-mārga* and the efficacy of *śravaṇa* and *kīrtana*. The story of the play is quite short and is devoid of dramatic qualities. There is not much action in the play and the characters are also portrayed in fractions only.[61]

### The *Keli Gopāla*

**Source**: The story occurs with slight modification in the *Viṣṇu- purāṇa (v.33), Harivaṁśa (ch.76)* and the *Bhāgavatapurāṇa* (x. 29-35). Except for the episode of Śaṅkhacūḍa, Śaṅkaradeva closely follows the last source.[62]

**The Story in Brief**: On a moonlit night of autumn, feeling like having some sport, Kṛṣṇa started playing the flute in Vṛndāvana on the bank of Yamunā. Hearing the tune, all the cowherd-women of Vraja, as if enchanted, went out ignoring their sons and husbands, to see Kṛṣṇa. There they joined him in a sportive dance. However, they became so exhilarated that they forgot themselves and being proud of the attention showed to them by Kṛṣṇa, they started showing disrespect to

---

[61]. Sarma, S. N., *Asamīyā Nāṭya Sāhitya*, 2002, p. 45.

[62]. Medhi, K., ed., *Aṅkāvalī*, 1997, 'Introduction', p. Liii.

him. Thereat, with an intention of making them realize their fault and to arouse in their minds, love and devotion for him again, Kṛṣṇa, disappeared taking along Rādhā, a maiden from amongst them. Not seeing Kṛṣṇa around, and not being able to find him in Vṛndāvana, their pride became deflated instantly and they suffered greatly from the separation and they started meditating on Kṛṣṇa and his pastime. On the other hand, receiving special care from Kṛṣṇa, Rādhā also became greatly arrogant and became disrespectful to him. Kṛṣṇa left her alone and came back to the other cowherd-women he had left behind earlier and who were now praying and entreating pitifully for his return. Kṛṣṇa started a *rāsa-maṇḍala* dance (a circular dance) with them and gave special attention to each one of them. Then they entered into the water of Yamunā and started dancing sportingly for great pleasure of all of them. Suddenly, there appeared a demon by the name Śaṅkhacūḍa, and out of lust, took away one cowherd-woman forcefully from the midst of the *rāsa-maṇḍala*. Kṛṣṇa chased threatening him, and being greatly scared, he fled leaving the maiden behind. After long hours of sporting with Kṛṣṇa, the cowherd-women became very tired and Kṛṣṇa lovingly took great care to remove their fatigue and pleased them and they also served Kṛṣṇa with great love and care. At dawn, at the request of Kṛṣṇa, the cowherd-women returned home back sadly but kept coming to the bank of Yamunā on every autumnal night and otherwise, during the day time remained at home suffering from the separation and singing the praises of Kṛṣṇa.

**Critical Analysis**: The play is very poetical in nature and also with the predominance of songs in it, can be called rather a musical. There are beautiful descriptions of the different mental states of the lovelorn cowherd-women and at times, there seems to be a resonance of the *Gīta Govinda* in the soft poetic descriptions and the songs.[63] It can be interpreted that through the description of love among Kṛṣṇa and the cowherd-

[63]. Sarma, S. N., *Asamīyā Nāṭya Sāhitya*, 2002, pp. 47-51.

women, Śaṅkaradeva tried to educate the common people about the spiritual nature of love that is there in the longing of the *ātmā* to be united with the *paramātmā* or in other words the very strong desire of the soul to get united with the supreme reality.[64] However, the emphasis laid on the portrayal of characters and composition of dialogues in the play seems to be not enough.

The name of Rādhā in the *śloka* no. 12, has led to much discussion as it is not there in any of the sources. The name of Rādhā is there in the three manuscripts consulted by Kaliram Medhi; however, there are also different manuscripts found in various *satras* which do not bear the name of Rādhā.[65] But nowhere in the vast collection of literary works of Śaṅkaradeva, there is any mention of the name of Rādhā, as dual worship of Rādhā and Kṛṣṇa is against his tenets. As such, it is probable that the name of Rādhā is only a later interpolation during the course of copying manuscript.[66]

### The *Rukmiṇī-Haraṇa*

**Source**: According to Kaliram Medhi, the story is taken from the *Harivaṁśa* (ch.116) and a few points from the *Bhāgavata-Purāṇa* (x. 52-54) as well.[67] But Dr. Satyendranath Sarma holds that the story of the play is taken from the *Bhāgavata Purāṇa* only and there is no influence of the *Harivaṁśa* in it.[68] However, the two friends, Līlāvatī and Madanamañjarī and the two *bhāṭas*, one being Vedanidhi, are the creations of Śaṅkaradeva.

**The Story in Brief**: Hearing from the *bhāṭas* (wandering minstrels) about the beauty, refinement and praises of Rukmiṇī, the daughter of King Bhīṣmaka of Kuṇḍina and the charm and qualities of Kṛṣṇa, both Rukmiṇī and Kṛṣṇa felt attracted to one another. Rukmiṇī aspired for Kṛṣṇa as her husband and

---

64. Chakravarty, S., *Studies in Sanskrit Literature Culture & Art*, 2011, p.77.
65. Bora, M., ed., *Śaṅkardevar Nāṭ*, 2003, p. 26.
66. Medhi, K., ed., *Aṅkāvalī*, 1997, 'Introduction', p. (Liv).
67. Ibid., p.(Lvi).
68. Sarma, S. N., *Asamīyā Nāṭya Sāhitya*, 2002, p. 55.

Kṛṣṇa also wanted to make her his wife. The parents of Rukmiṇī also had the same alliance in mind. But Rukma, the brother of Rukmiṇī, was determined to marry her off to Śiśupāla, the king of Cedi, and persuaded his parents and relatives accordingly. Upon invitation from prince Rukma, Śiśupāla and many other kings and princes thronged Kuṇḍina with an intention of attaining Rukmiṇī. On the other hand, coming to know about all these developments, Rukmiṇī sent her trusted priest Vedanidhi to Dvārakā, with a letter to Kṛṣṇa to come immediately and save her from Śiśupāla. As wished by her, Kṛṣṇa rushed to Kuṇḍina and entering the court and sat along with the other kings, outshining them all waiting for Rukmiṇī to enter and choose her husband from among them. When Rukmiṇī entered the court along with her friends, everyone was mesmerized by her beauty and Rukmiṇī was also greatly charmed by Kṛṣṇa and chose him as her husband in her mind. Kṛṣṇa held her by the hand and took her away from the court in his chariot then and there. Śiśupāla and the other kings chased him challenging and there was a fight among them; but, they were defeated completely. Then Rukma appeared there and attacked Kṛṣṇa with abuses and arms alike. Kṛṣṇa defeated him and brought much disgrace to him. However, at the earnest request of Rukmiṇī, Kṛṣṇa gracefully spared the life of Rukma. Then, Kṛṣṇa took along Rukmiṇī to Dwārakā and solemnized their wedding for the pleasure of everyone in the three worlds.

**Critical Analysis**: Among the six plays of Śaṅkaradeva, the *Rukmiṇī Haraṇa* is the largest in size. Though keeping himself within the framework of the original story Śaṅkaradeva has given free rein to his imagination while portraying the behaviour of the characters and the details of different situations. Though the depiction of love between Kṛṣṇa and Rukmiṇī is smeared with a sense of devotion, yet the situations are human and commonplace and even their behaviours are like ordinary young boy and girl in love. Śaṅkaradeva has also given some beautiful descriptions of the conjugal love between them. The descriptions of the wedding in the play are also completely indigenous to the core. The way Kṛṣṇa seized and forcefully took away Rukmiṇī after defeating all oppositions and then married her is similar to the custom of marriage known as *rākṣasa vivāha* which has been prevalent locally since old time.[69] Moreover, the description of Bhīṣmaka pouring water from the golden pitcher on the hair of the bride and the bride-groom put together is also reflection of folk custom in the society. Though the dominant literary sentiments *(rasa)* in the play are *Śṛṅgāra* (erotic) and *Vīra* (heroic), there are also comic interludes which give rise to *Hāsya Rasa* (laughter) as well.[70]

**The *Pārijāta Haraṇa***

**Source** : Śaṅkaradeva follows the story from the *Viṣṇu Purāṇa*(V. 29-31), but adds the episode of Satyabhāmā's wrath from the *Harivaṁśa*(ch.120-133).[71]

**The Story in Brief** : One day Nārada and the king of the gods Indra, and his wife Śacī came to Dwārakā to meet Kṛṣṇa. Kṛṣṇa and Rukmiṇī, who happened to be present there with her husband at that moment, welcomed and offered their obeisance to Nārada. Blessing them, Nārada gave a *pārijāta* flower to Kṛṣṇa and explained to them the exceptional qualities of the flower. Thereupon, Rukmiṇī besought Kṛṣṇa for that flower and Kṛṣṇa also lovingly made her wear the flower in her hair. Then, Indra, and his wife Śacī requested Kṛṣṇa for his help in controlling Narakāsura of Prāgjyotiṣa, who was creating great trouble to the gods and also requested him to rescue the maidens from heaven, the earrings of Aditi, the umbrella of Varuṇa and the *Maṇi Parbata,* all that Narakāsura had taken away forcefully. Kṛṣṇa promised to help and asked them to return to their abode in Amarāvatī. In the mean time,

---

[69]. Sarma, S. N., *Asamīyā Nāṭya Sāhitya,* 2002, pp. 55-57.

[70]. Ibid., p. 120.

[71]. Medhi, K., ed., *Aṅkāvalī,* 1997, 'Introduction', p. Lvii.

in the pretext of having a look around Dwārakā, Nārada visited Satyabhāmā, another wife of Kṛṣṇa, and reported to her about the *pārijāta* flower in such a way so as to make her greatly angry and envious of Rukmiṇī. Hearing that report from Nārada, Kṛṣṇa rushed to Satyabhāmā and tried to appease her. However, she was in no mood to listen and only when Kṛṣṇa promised to bring her the *pārijāta* tree itself from Indra's Amarāvatī, that she condescendingly calmed down, but with a condition that she would accompany him in the mission. Then Kṛṣṇa, along with Satyabhāmā went to Prāgjyotiṣa riding on the Garuḍa and after a fierce battle defeated Narakāsura there. Rescuing the things robbed by him and the 16,000 maidens abducted and kept in his palace, returned to their respective rightful places. Thereafter, they moved on to Amarāvatī. After initial pleasantries among Kṛṣṇa, Satyabhāmā, Indra and Śacī, Satyabhāmā insisted on getting the *pārijāta* flower and sent Nārada to Indra with that purpose. But, Śacī strongly refused to comply with the request saying that a heavenly flower was not meant for an ordinary woman of the earth and a war of foul words ensued between the two great women exposing the evils of the husbands of one another. And after that, when Kṛṣṇa forcefully took away the *pārijāta* uprooting the tree, a terrible war broke up between Kṛṣṇa and Indra. The latter being defeated completely, offered obeisance in the feet of Kṛṣṇa and gave the *pārijāta* tree as a gift. Returning home, as wished by Satyabhāmā, Kṛṣṇa planted the tree in front of her palace for her pride and satisfaction. But on the contrary, Rukmiṇī considered, serving Kṛṣṇa as the greatest fortune for her and became engaged in praying to him earnestly.

**Critical Analysis**: Among the plays of Śaṅkaradeva, in respect of dramatic characters, *Pārijāta Haraṇa* is considered to be the best.[72] In this play Śaṅkaradeva seems to have taken great care in composing the dialogues and portraying the

72. Sarma, H. K., *Asamīyā Sāhityat Dṛṣṭipāt*, 2005, p. 145.

characters. The freshness in the dialogues has enhanced the quality of the play and made it more enjoyable indeed. Śaṅkaradeva has extended imagination and creativity to a great extent in the play while detailing the nature of Nārada, which is reporting to one about the another in exaggeration so as to arouse jealousy and misunderstanding among the characters and thereby creating humorous situations.[73] Also while describing the pride and conceit of Satyabhāmā, the war of words between Śacī and Satyabhāmā defiling one another's husband, Śaṅkaradeva's ingenuity was at its full and all the common people, as the audience, could identify themselves with the situations so very familiar to them as a real scene next door every day. Though the dominant sentiment in the play is *Vīra Rasa* (heroic), there are many comic situations in the play and when Nārada and Satyabhāmā are the most attractive characters, Kṛṣṇa, for whose glorification the play is composed, seems to be pushed back to a less important and secondary character. Through this play Śaṅkaradeva has shown the sense of subordination and submission of the Lord in front of his devotees. Moreover, Kṛṣṇa's taking along Satyabhāmā and riding the Garuḍa to Prāgjyotiṣa has established the fact that Lord Viṣṇu and Kṛṣṇa are not different and are identical.[74] The final words of the *Sūtradhāra* and the concluding *bhaṭimā* glorify Kṛṣṇa amply and establishing his Godhead, put him in his rightful position.

### The *Śrī Rāma-Vijaya*

**Source**: The story is taken from the *Rāmāyaṇa* (I. 18-77) and *Agni Purāṇaṁ,* (ch. V).[75]

**The Story in Brief** : One day sage Viśvāmitra came to King Daśaratha at Ayodhyā and requesting him, took away his sons Rāma and Lakṣmaṇa with him, so that they can protect him and

---

73. Sarma, S. N., *Asamīyā Nāṭya Sāhitya,* 2002, pp. 51-55

74. Bora, M., *Śaṅkardevar Nāṭ*, 2003, pp. 21-22.

75. Medhi, K., ed., *Aṅkāvalī,* 1997, 'Introduction', p. lviii.

the sacrifice he was going to perform at his hermitage. On the way the sage taught them about special techniques of archery in such a way that they became experts. They killed the female demon Tāḍakā who obstructed their way. At the hermitage, the demons, Mārīca and Subāhu tried to disturb the sacrifice. Thereat, Rāma, with his arrows, pierced Subāhu to death and flung Mārīca off with his arrow, to Laṅkā. After that, free from the disturbances of the demons, the sage completed the sacrifice peacefully and then took Rāma and Lakṣmaṇa to Mithilā, where the King Janaka, was holding *svayamvara* for his beautiful and coveted daughter Sītā and kings and princes from far and wide assembled there for the purpose. The condition for the wedding was that, whoever would be able to string the huge bow of Śiva, the *Ajagava*, and put the arrow properly in it, would marry Sītā ; and that, according to Janaka, was as instructed by the divine voice (*ākāśavāṇī*). Many kings and princes, who were acclaimed as champions, tried and failed pitifully to fulfill the condition. But though very young, Rāma picked up the bow easily and while trying to string, it broke into two pieces surprising everyone. Sītā, who was aspiring to have Rāma as her husband since her earlier birth, was greatly relieved and was very happy and advancing towards Rāma, garlanded him acknowledging him as her husband. The other kings became very angry at that and a battle ensued between Rāma and the kings. After defeating the kings, Rāma chased them away. The marriage, then, was solemnized and King Daśaratha also joined in. After that, as they were returning to Ayodhyā, Paraśurāma obstructed their way, greatly angry with Rāma for breaking the bow of Śiva, his preceptor(*guru*). Abusing Rāma, uttering boastful words, Paraśurāma tried to kill him with his axe. Then, Rāma picked up his bow with an intention of punishing Paraśurāma and twanged it. Hearing the sound of the bow, Paraśurāma was greatly terrified and recognising him to be the Supreme Lord, fell down in his feet seeking mercy. Rāma forgave him and spared his life, but blocked his way to heaven forever with his arrow. Then they proceeded to Ayodhyā and entered the city amidst great fun and festivity and for the happiness of everyone.

**Critical Analysis**: This play is also known as Sītā *svayamvara* and according to the hagiographies (*carit puthi*), this is the last play by Śaṅkaradeva. He has acknowledged twice in the play, the patronage of Śrī Śukladhvaja, the great Koc general under King Naranārāyaṇa, for writing the play. It has been observed that there are many points of similarities between the plays the *Rukmiṇī Haraṇa* and the *Śrī Rāma Vijaya*; such as, (i) singing of praises of Rukmiṇī and Sītā by Vedanidhi and Viśvāmitra respectively ; (ii) obstruction to the main characters on their way of return by Rukma in the first and by Paraśurāma in the latter play; (iii) lovelorn and ludicrous conditions of the aspirant kings and princes and their pervert comments to Rukmiṇī and Sītā in their respective *svayamvaras* and subsequently the insult of the kings in the hands of the friends and companions of Rukmiṇī and Sītā; (iv) the roles of Madanamañjarī and Līlāvatī in the play the *Rukmiṇī Haraṇa* and Kanakāvatī and Madanamantharā in the *Śrī Rāma Vijaya*; (v) ridiculous conditions of Brahmā and Viśvāmitra seeing the beauties of Rukmiṇī and Sītā respectively, at the time of performing the sacrifices for their wedding; (vi) descriptions of conjugal love between Kṛṣṇa and Rukmiṇī and between Rāma and Sītā ; (v) similarities in language and style of dialogues in several places.[76]

In this play, it is noted, that Śaṅkaradeva has deviated from the original *Ādikāṇḍa Rāmāyaṇa* in respect of several particulars. In the original, Viśvāmitra took Rāma and Lakṣmaṇa to Mithilā only to show them the *Ajagava*, the huge bow of Śiva, and there was no *svayamvara* of Sītā and hence no gathering of kings and no fights as well. In the original,

[76]. Sarma, S. N., *Asamīyā Nāṭya Sāhitya*, 2002, p. 58.

while Rāma, out of curiosity, picked up the bow, it broke into pieces. Also, there was no divine voice from the sky (*ākāśavāṇī*) regarding the condition for being selected as a groom and it was only the vow made by king Janaka, to give away Sītā in marriage to him who could break the bow. In the original, Viśvāmitra did not accompany Rāma and others on their way back to Ayodhyā and hence did not fight with Paraśurāma too. There is also some variation from the original in the episode of Mārīca and Subāhu.[77]

In the play, the way characters are depicted, though within limit, and the description of situations and different emotions are such that they reveal the dexterity of the composer.

To conclude, it can be said that though initially composed for the purpose of preaching *Bhakti* cult among the common people, Śaṅkaradeva, with his plays, paved the path of development of Assamese drama in general which later helped in creating new and different genres of full-fledged dramas.

●●●

[77]. Medhi, K., ed., *Aṅkāvalī*, 1997, 'Introduction', p. Lix.

# CHAPTER IV
# CONCLUSION

In the giant task of presenting Śaṅkaradeva in the national as well as international arena for further studies, this work is only a small step forward. With the plays presented in English here, interested scholars can engage themselves in studying various aspects of the plays.

It has been observed that keeping himself within the framework of the scriptures, Śaṅkaradeva, through some very beautiful descriptions, has tried repeatedly to create an authentic and detailed image of Lord Kṛṣṇa in the minds of the people, as, for the purpose of devotional meditation, the blissful and beatific form of Nārāyaṇa has been specially recommended by Śaṅkaradeva in his *dhyāna varṇana* part of *Kīrtana Ghoṣā* (Sec. IV). The same idea may be traced back to Rāmānuja of south as well, as he too placed much stress on the inner aspect, making it clear that the worshipper must keep in mind continuously a mental picture of the deity and his activities.[1]

As the main purpose of the creation of the Vaiṣṇavite literature was propagation of the cult, hence, the main points of the faith, like the efficacy of *śravaṇa* and *kīrtana* and the supremacy of Lord Kṛṣṇa over all other gods like Brahmā, Maheśvara (*brahmā maheśvara cākara jākara...*) and subordination of the Supreme Lord near his devotees are reiterated in the plays.

In an effort to familiarise the people with the various names of Lord Kṛṣṇa, Śaṅkaradeva has mentioned different names of the Lord in the plays. For example, Acyuta, Garuḍaketu, Gopīnātha, Govinda, Gopāla, Hari, Jagannātha, Janārdana, Kānāi, Kānu, Kṛṣṇa, Keśava, Mādhava, Madhāi, Madhusūdana,

[1]. Brockington, J. L., *The Sacred Thread*, 2000, p.139.

Mohana, Murāri, Nārāyaṇa, Śāraṅgapāṇi, Banamālī, Vāsudeva, Viṣṇu, Yādava, Yadunātha are some of the names found in the plays.

With his rare genius, superior intellect and exceptionally wide knowledge, Śaṅkaradeva could have easily chosen to write in Sanskrit and be acknowledged more widely. But instead, he generously opted to shoulder the responsibilities of enlightening the illiterate common folk who were in the darkness of ignorance. With his leadership, Śaṅkaradeva not only showed proper direction to the people but also created an organised mass with them.

The strategy Śaṅkaradeva adopted in the plays was noteworthy indeed. Taking the stories from the original and authentic scriptures, Śaṅkaradeva put them in a homely and familiar setting in such a way that the audience could accept them easily. Moreover, though the main character is the Supreme Lord Kṛṣṇa, and the purpose of the plays is establishing his supremacy, yet Śaṅkaradeva portrayed the character of Kṛṣṇa as well as the other characters in such a way – talking like ordinary people, laughing, crying, quarrelling, fighting and love-making, that the common people could identify themselves in the characters and enjoy. On the other hand the characters were given such a language, which was though artificial yet similar to the language of the common people and easily understandable. However, putting Sanskrit in the mouth of the characters in between, the audience was reminded time and again of the elevated and super-human stature of the characters.

It is remarkable as to how far-stretched the audio-visual effects of the plays were. People from all walks of the society could get together to act and to watch the performances, could understand and remember the stories of the scriptures explained simply, and could memorise the beautiful prayers and *bhatimās* in the familiar language and sing them at leisure, later on with personal emotions.

The strength of a language rests on the richness of its vocabulary. Throughout his writings Śaṅkaradeva had tried to include new words denoting the same thing. In the *Amarkoṣa* (the Sanskrit lexicon) there are more than hundred words denoting a woman. cf.,

*"strī yoṣidavalā yoṣā nārī sīmantinī vadhūḥ*
*pratīpadarśinī vāmā vanitā mahilā tathā*
*viśoṣāstvaṅganā bhīruḥ kāminī vāmalocanā*
*pramadā māninī kāntā lalanā ca nitambinī...* etc."[2]

In the six plays, Śaṅkaradeva also had used about twenty – five different words which denote a girl or woman; e.g., *nārī, bālā, kanyā, Kumārī, taruṇī, gaurī, ramā, priyā, mātā, jāyā, vadhu, patnī, satī, bhāryā, strī, ramaṇī, kāminī, yoṣit, aṅganā, māninī* etc.

With his vast literary creations and through his translations of the important scriptures from Sanskrit to a language easily understandable to the uneducated common people, Śaṅkaradeva enriched the Assamese language and literature and gave it a new direction and dimension.

Most importantly, through proper guidance and motivation, Śaṅkaradeva developed a new generation of writers in his close disciples like *Mādhavadeva, Rām Sarasvatī, Ananta Kandalī, Śrīdhara Kandalī,* who, following the footsteps of their preceptor, through their continuous endeavour, carried forward the good works of their master and greatly contributed towards the enrichment of the Assamese language and literature.

Under the aegis of the *satras*, the *Vaiṣṇavite* culture and the art forms initiated by Śaṅkaradeva has been practiced and preserved with great fervour. During the last few years, performance of the *nāṭas* or *bhāonā,* as they are called, has been taking place in different countries of the world. They have received great accolade and also tickled the inquisitiveness of the connoisseurs of different parts of the world.

---

[2]. Bhattacharya, S. V., ed., *Amarkoṣa*, 1988, pp. 170-177

During the course of this study it has been deeply realised that one of the best ways to study a person and his literary works is, translating his writings; as, the work of translation demands deep study of each and every word and expression of the original works, and as such, requires in depth understanding of the ideals and philosophies of the composer.

It is hoped that, work like the present one and all other translations of different works of Śaṅkaradeva done so far, would open up new avenues for research and comparative studies in the fields of dance, music, language, prose style and other art forms like painting etc. Also, as this work is in English, it will lead to a broad scope of studies with respect to the other *Vaiṣṇava* saints of India of that time leading to new dimensions of comparative analysis.

It will be deemed greatly rewarding if this study can open up new vistas in the field of study of Assamese literature and culture among the academic circles in the national and international level.

●●●

# PART - B

# CHAPTER V

## TRANSLITERATED TEXT AND TRANSLATION OF THE PLAYS

Following are the Transliteration and Translation of the six plays :

1) *Kālidamana Yātrā*
2) *Patnī Prasāda Nāṭa*
3) *Keli-Gopāla Nāṭaka*
4) *Rukmiṇī Haraṇa Nāṭa*
5) *Pārijāta-Haraṇa Nāṭa*
6) *Śrīrāmabijaya Nāṭa*

## 5.1

### *kālidamana yātrā*

### The Play: Taming of Kāli

*namaḥ śrīkṛṣṇāya*
Obeisance to Śrī Kṛṣṇa.

*śloka* ||

*meghaśyāmala mūrtimāyata mahābāhuṁ mahoraḥ-sthalam*
*āraktāyata kañjalocana yugaṁ pitāmbaraṁ sundaram* |
*muktā hīraka - hemahāra-valayālaṅkāra kānti-dyutim*
*kṛṣṇaṁ śārada-sāndracandra-sadṛsaṁ hṛd-paṅkajeha'mbhaje* ||*1*||

Hymn[1]:

I pay my homage from my lotuslike heart to Kṛṣṇa who bears an image dark like the cloud and having wide shoulders, heavy thighs and big red lotuslike pair of eyes, wearing yellow coloured beautiful clothes and ornaments like necklace, bracelets and armlets, made of pearls, diamonds and gold and dazzling with the glow of these ornaments and pleasing like the autumnal moon.

*apica* :

*yenākāri mahāhi - darpadalanaṁ krīḍā hradinyājale*
*yenābhāji bhujaṅgabhoganikhilaṁ padbhyāṁ mudā marditam*|
*yenāmāri mahā mahāsuracamūścakraṁ paraṁ līlayā*
*tasmai śrīkaruṇāmayāya mahate kṛṣṇāya nityaṁ namaḥ* ||2||

Also[2]:

I bow down always to that same great Kṛṣṇa who is merciful and who played the sport of destroying the pride of the huge serpent in the lake and who smashed all the expanded

[1]. in *Śārdūlavikrīḍita* metre.

[2]. in *Śārdūlavikrīḍita* metre.

hoods of the snake with His feet happily, who destroyed the army of great warriors and killed them just as fun.

*kathā sūtra* :

*õhi parakāre śrīkṛṣṇaka paraṇāma kaye kahu sabhāsada lokaka sambodhi bola*

Dialogue and Direction: In this way, offering obeisance to Śrī Kṛṣṇa, addressing the audience said,

*śloka* ||

*bho bho sāmājikā yuyaṁ*[3] *śṛnudhvamadhunā vacaḥ* |
*kṛṣṇāsya kālidamanaṁ yātrāvārtaṁ nibodhata* ||3||

Hymn[4]:

Oh revered audience, now please listen to and understand properly, the story of taming of Kāli by Kṛṣṇa.

*sūtra* ||

*āhe sabhāsada loka : je parama puruṣa puruṣottama : sanātana nārāyaṇa : śrī śrīkṛṣṇa ohi sabhāmadhye : kālidamana līlā yātrā : parama kautuke karaba tāhe sāvadhāne dekhala*[5] *śunaha : nirantare hari bola hari* ||

Direction: Oh revered audience, one who is the highest, the Supreme Being, Lord Viṣṇu, the eternal Nārāyaṇa, that same honourable Śrī Kṛṣṇa is going to enact the sport of taming Kāli amongst this audience with great pleasure, watch and listen to that carefully and keep chanting the name of Hari incessantly.

*atha bhaṭimā* ||

*jaya jaya yadukula kamala prakāśaka nāśaka kaṁsaka prāṇa* |
*jaya jaya jagataka bhakataka bhīti niti karu nirajāna* ||
*jaya jaganāyaka mukuti-dāyaka sāyaka śāraṅgadhārī* |
*duṣṭa ariṣṭaka muṣṭika morḍana corḍana bandha murāri* ||1||

---

[3]. *yūyaṁ.*

[4]. in *Śloka* metre; but in the 3rd foot, the 6th and 7th letters are short instead of long.

[5]. *dekhaha.*

| | | |
|---|---|---|
| *dharu govardhana* | *bāraṇa bariṣaṇa* | *bheli indramada dūra* \| |
| *tṛbhuvana kampaka* | *kāli sarppaka* | *darppaka kayali cūra* \|\| |
| *nandaka nandana* | *bandana devaka* | *sevaka jākeri sarbba* \| |
| *gopamukhe anna* | *māgala bhāṅgala* | *dija nija karmaka garbba*\|\|2\|\| |
| *gokula jana jata* | *tāraka maraka* | *kuvalaya dhenuka- nāśi* \| |
| *putanikā tana* | *śoṣaṇa moṣaṇa* | *toṣaṇa mana brajabāsī* \|\| |
| *e dukha dāyaka*[6] | *pāvaka bhāvaka* | *pūraṇa punu manakāma* \| |
| *jagajana jāteka* | *pāteka ghāteka* | *ākeri e guṇanāma* \|\|3\|\| |
| *jāhe bhakati* | *rakati śakati* | *tāraṇa ōhi saṁsāra* \| |
| *kīṭa pataṅgama* | *jaṅgama saṅgama* | *bhakataka pāi nistāra* \|\| |
| *sohi kṛṣṇaka* | *ōhi nāṭaka* | *utpāṭaka dukhamūla* \| |
| *kalimala ānala*[7] | *jānala mānala* | *nāhi nāhi ōhi tula* \|\|4\|\| |
| *śuna saba loi* | *hoi noi* | *dekhahu bacana bicāri* \| |
| *iha saṁsāre* | *sāra āra nāhi* | *cintahu caraṇa murāri* \|\| |
| *brahmā maheśvara* | *cākara jākara* | *tākara guṇa muhe lehu*\| |
| *bāndhava mādhava* | *sādhava mukuti* | *tāhe caraṇe citta dehu* \|\|5\|\| |
| *ohi īśvara* | *tāraka maraka* | *kāraka saba saṁsāra* \| |
| *tāhe karu seva* | *deva nāhi keo* | *nāhi hari bine āra* \|\| |
| *jatae paramā* | *dharamā karamā* | *sabakahuñ rājā nāma* \| |
| *kṛṣṇaka kiṅkara* | *kiṅkara śaṅkara* | *kaha saba bola rāma rāma*\|\|6\|\| |

Here is the eulogy:

Glory to the one, who manifests as the lotus (glory) of the Yadu dynasty, and who is the annihilator of Kaṁsa.

Glory to the one who always destroys the cause of fear to the devotees.

Glory to the one who sustains the world, the one who brings forth salvation; (the one, i.e. Lord Kṛṣṇa), who holds the bow, *Śāraṅga*.

(The one) who thrashed to death with His clenched fist the villainous Ariṣṭa and Muṣṭika, and freed the world.

(The one who) holding mount Govardhana up, warded off the rain, and thus destroyed the pride of Indra.

---

6 . *dāhaka.*

7 . *anala.*

(The one who) vanquished the pride of the serpent Kāli who terrorised (the creatures of) the three worlds.

(The one who) is the son of Nanda, who is worshipped by the demigods and served by all.

(The one who) got the cowherd boys to ask for food, and (thus) destroyed the arrogance of the orthodox *brāhmaṇas*, attained through their ritualistic practices.

(The one who) protected all the people of Gokula by killing the dreaded Kuvalayapīḍa and Dhenuka.

(The one who) drew the life out of Pūtanā by sucking out her breast for the pleasure of all the inhabitants of Vraja.

(The one who) destroys all sufferings, but fulfills desires of the minds of those whose feelings are pure.

Creator of all the universe, chanting whose name and (remembering whose) attributes (*nāma-guṇa*) can destroy all the sins of the world.

By the strength of love and devotion unto Him one may get saved from this world (the circle of rebirth).

All the worms and insects and all living beings attain salvation in the association of a devotee.

This drama, which will be the cause of destruction to the root of all sufferings, is concerning that Lord Kṛṣṇa.

He (Kṛṣṇa) acts like fire in relation to the evils of Age of Kali, and it is known and accepted that there is none comparable to Him.

Please listen, all of you dear people, analyse and try to find out whether it is true or not that in this world there is nothing else more meaningful; hence concentrate in the feet of Murāri.

Even Brahmā and Maheśvara are whose mere servants, sing out His praise with your mouth; concentrate heartily on the feet of Mādhava only, who is the friend to all, and who will bring forth salvation.

He is the Lord; who creates, protects and destroys the whole world, so serve Him (the Lord Kṛṣṇa) as there is no God other than Hari.

*Nāma* (the name and attributes of Hari, Kṛṣṇa) is the Lord over all religious and ritualistic activities.
The servant of Kṛṣṇa, the servant Śaṅkara, says to all to chant "Rāma-Rāma!".

*kathā sūtra* ||
*āhe sabhāsada loka : je jagataka parama guru: parama puruṣa puruṣottama : sanātana : brahmāmaheśasevita caraṇa paṅkaja nārāyaṇa : śrīśrīkṛṣṇa : ohi sabhāmadhye kālidamana nāma līlā yātrā : kautuke karaba : tāhe sāvadhāne dekhaha śunaha nirantare hari bola hari* ||

Dialogue and Direction: Oh revered audience, the one who is the ultimate father of the world, one who is the highest, the Supreme Being, Lord Viṣṇu, the eternal Nārāyaṇa, whose lotuslike feet are worshipped by Brahmā and Maheśa, that same honourable Śrī Kṛṣṇa, is going to enact the sport of taming Kāli amongst this audience with great pleasure, watch and listen to that carefully and keep chanting the name of Hari incessantly.

*ākāśaka karṇa diyā sūtra bola* ||
*āhe saṅgi: kona bādya śunie* ||
Listening to the sky the Śūtradhāra says, "Oh dear friend, what instruments do we hear?".

*saṅgi - sakhi mṛdaṅga baṁśi dhvani śuni* ||
*āḥ milala milala* ||

Companion: "Oh dear friend, we hear the sound of the mṛdaṅga and the flute. Here they come."

*śloka* ||
*govatsān purataḥ kṛtvā gopālaḥ pālakaḥ satām* |
*praveśamakarot gopaiḥ saha veṇunninādayan* ||4||

Hymn[8]:

Taking the cows and the calves in front, Gopāla, the protector of the good, along with the cowherd boys, entered playing the flute.

*kathā sūtra:*

*āhe sāmājika loka : hāmu je kahala : sohi īśvaraśrīgopāla : batsa batsapāla sahita ethā praveśi kahuñ : jaice līlā kautuke karaba : tāhe dekhaha īunaha : nirantare hari bola ||*

Dialogue and Direction: Oh revered people, as I said, that Supreme God Śrī Gopāla, entering here along with the calves and the cowherd boys, will perform playfully with such pleasure, watch and listen to that and keep chanting the name of Hari incessantly.

*gīta || rāga sindhoḍā || ektālitālena*

Song in the *Rāga Sindhurā* with the rhythm *Ekatāli*:

*dhruṁ ||*

*āvata e kānu surabhi carāi |*
*rañjita dhenu reṇu beṇu bajāi ||*

Refrain: Here comes Kānu grazing the *surabhi* cows, covered with the dust (from their hooves) and playing the flute.

*pada ||*

*śire śikhaṇḍaka gaṇḍa kuṇḍala ḍolāye |*
*ure hemahāra hīra mañjīra jhurāe ||*
*bālaka beḍhi kheḍi kheläite jāya |*
*kahatu śaṅkara gati govinda pāya ||1||*

Verse: On the head flies a peacock feather and on the cheeks hang ear-rings; gold necklace flying and diamond anklets tinkling; surrounding Him all the boys are playing along and (they) have found the ultimate refuge in Govinda, says Śaṅkara.

---

[8]. in *Śloka* metre.

*kathā sūtra* ||

*aicana līlā kautuka nṛtya karite : gopāla sahita : śiśusaba kālindī hradaka samīpa pāvala : se biṣamaya pānī najāni : parama pipāse pīḍita hayā : sabahuñ hradaka jala : udara bhari pāna karala tatakāla durghora biṣajvālā lāgiye cetana harala : śarīra kampi kampi prāṇa cāḍi : batsa batsapālasava : kālindī tīre parala.*

Dialogue and Direction: In this way playing and dancing with great pleasure, the young boys along with Gopāla reached near the Lake Kālindī. Greatly suffering from thirst and not knowing that the water in the lake was poisonous, all of them drank the water from the lake to their fill and immediately, being affected with strong poison, the calves and the cowherd boys loosing consciousness, their bodies trembling, fell down lifeless on the bank of the Kālindī.

*śloka:*

*vatsakān bālakān kṛṣṇo vilokya mṛtakān tadā* |
*cakāra pracūraṁ khedamadbhutaṁ bhaktavatsalaḥ* ||5||

Hymn[9]: Then seeing the calves and the cowherd boys dead, Kṛṣṇa, who is very kind to his devotees, expressed much distress like never before.

*sūtra* ||

*tadanantara : batsa batsapālakasabaka : biṣa jala pāne mṛtaka dekhi : śrīkṛṣṇa hāhā ki bheli boli dhari kahu : ulaṭ-pālaṭ kariye dekhala : nirantare prāṇe marala : hāhā hāmāra bhakataka : aicana avasthā boli : se bhakatabatsala gopāla : bahuta kheda kaya kahuñ : amṛta dṛṣṭi nirekhi : tatakāla jiyāala* ||

Direction: Thereupon, seeing the calves and the cowherd boys dead drinking the poisonous water, Śrī Kṛṣṇa, saying, "Alas alas! What has happened!", examined them turning arround and finding all of them dead alike, cried, "Alas, alas! My

---

[9]. in *Śloka* metre.

devotees are in such condition!", and kind that He is to His devotees, Gopāla, lamenting greatly, bestowing His immortal glance upon them, revived them immediately.

*śloka* ||

*kṛṣṇasyāmṛtadṛṣṭyālaṁ labdhaprāṇāḥ kumārakāḥ |*
*prītāste caraṇau nemuryathā svapnāt samutthitāḥ* ||6||

Hymn[10]: Having received enough of the immortal glances from Kṛṣṇa, the cowherd boys regained life and as if rising from a dream, encircled His feet happily.

*sūtra*||

*kṛṣṇata amṛta nirikhana pāi : puṇarbbāra prāṇa āvala :*
*batsa batsapāla saba svapnara jāgi jaice uṭhi baiṭhala :*
*anyoanye kahaice* ||

Direction: Having received the immortal glance from Kṛṣṇa, they had their life back again and the calves and the cowherd boys sat down rising as if from a dream and said to one another.

*bālakasava bola* || *āhe sakhisaba : dekho õhi biṣajala pāne prāṇa cāḍi marala : kṛṣṇaka prasāde punarbbāra barttala* ||
The boys said, "Oh dear friends, look, drinking that poisonous water you lost your life and you were dead and with the blessings of Kṛṣṇa, got back (your) life again."

*sūtra*||

*ohi boli parama prīti hayā : kṛṣṇaka caraṇe praṇāma kaya bolala*||

Direction: Saying so, being very pleased, offering obeisance at the feet of Kṛṣṇa said:

10. in *Śloka* metre.

*kathā || āhe svāmi : ohi biṣa pānī piye : prāṇe marala hāmi : tohāka prasāde punarbbāra upajala ! tohāri caraṇa sevāka mahimā ki kahaba svāmi ||*

Dialogue: "Oh Lord, we died drinking that poisonous water and with your blessings we are reborn; what to say about the greatness of devotion at your feet, oh Lord."

*sūtra ||*

*śrīkṛṣṇa sabāke āliṅgi āśvāsa kayala ||*

Direction: Śrī Kṛṣṇa, embracing them all, reassured them.

*śloka:*

*tatra kāliyabhujagaṁ bhagavān bhavabhāvanaḥ |*
*dūrīkarttuṁ manaścakre hradāddaityanisūdanaḥ ||7||*

Hymn[11]: The Supreme Lord, who is the creator of this world and who is the destroyer of the demons thought of chasing away the serpent Kāli from that lake.

*sūtra||*

*duranta biṣabīrya pratāpe: pracaṇḍa kālisarppaka dami dūra karite : pravandha kaya kahu:pītabastra kaṭita mehrāvala : kadamba bṛkṣe caḍikahu : biṣamaya kālihradata jhāmpa kayala : se ananta bīryaka pracaṇḍa pratāpe : hradaka urmmi uthali:āndola milala:śrīkṛṣṇa parama kautuke jala mājhe : jaice keli kavala:tāke[12]dekhaha śunaha:nirantare hari bola hari||*

Direction: Śrī Kṛṣṇa, planning to control and chase away the fierce serpent Kali, who was indomitable on the strength of his glowing hot poison, wrapped the yellow clothing around the hips and climbing up the *kadamba* tree jumped into the poisonous Lake Kali. With the great majesty of that infinitely powerful (Śrī Kṛṣṇa), the water level of the lake heaved up to great heights and there was much turbulence. As Śrī Kṛṣṇa, with great pleasure, started

11. in *Śloka* metre.

12. *tāhe.*

playing in the water, watch and listen to that and keep chanting the name of Hari incessantly.

*gīta || rāga kānāḍā || paritāla ||*

Song in the *Rāga Kānāḍā* with the rhythm *Paritāla:*

*dhruṁ ||*

*kālindī jalamaha : khele yadurāyā |*
*bāleke beḍhi : baṁśi bajāyā ;*
*jaice nāce kānu : caraṇa calāyā ||*

Refrain:Surrounded by the boys, the son of Yadu (Kṛṣṇa) played on in the deep water of Lake Kālindī; playing the flute and moving His feet, Kānu kept on dancing.

*pada ||*

*nīla tanu tathi : pīta picori |*
*naa*[13] *ghana jaice : camaka bijori ||*
*kaustubha kaṇṭha : kauṭi naya*[14] *sura |*
*kuṇḍala jhalamala : jhanake keyūra ||*
*jala mājhe duhu bāhu āphāli |*
*krīḍā karatu bāri banamālī ||*
*urmmi uthali hrdaka lole |*
*kṛṣṇa kiṅkara śaṅkare bole ||2||*

Verse:Dark blue body and yellow clothing thereon looks as if bright lightning flashing on newly formed dark clouds.

The Kaustubha gem hanging from the neck is bright as a billion rising suns. The earrings are dazzling and the armlets are tinkling.

Spreading out His two arms in the water Vanamālī played on.

The waves rose and disturbed the water in the lake, says Śaṅkara, the servant of Kṛṣṇa.

---

[13]. *nava.*

[14]. *nava.*

*kathā sūtra:*

*śrīkṛṣṇa aicana jalakeli karite : hradaka parama āndola milala : pracaṇḍa urmika rola bahuta dūra gaila ||*

Dialogue and Direction: Śrī Kṛṣṇa, thus playing in the water, the lake water became greatly disturbed and the sound of the huge waves travelled far and wide.

*śloka ||*

*niśamya hradanirhrāda-sambādamimamadbhutam |*
*āgatya tvaritaṁ kāliḥ krodhenādaśadacyutam ||8||*

Hymn[15]: Hearing such strange news about the intense sound of the lake water, Kāli, coming immediately, stung Acyuta with great anger.

*sūtra ||*

*tadanantara : hradaka āndola kallola - rola śunie : kope kampamāna : parama darpe sarpparāja kāli kope : jaice khedi āsi kahu : marmmathāne śrīkṛṣṇaka daṁśi lāñje mehrāvala : āheloka : tāhe dekhaha śunaha : nirantare hari bola*

Direction: After that, hearing the roaring sound of the large travelling waves, as the king of the serpents, Kāli, trembling with anger, in great pride came chasing Śrī Kṛṣṇa and stung Him on his vital point and entwined Him with his tail; oh dear people, watch and listen to that and keep chanting the name of Hari incessantly.

*gīta || rāga āśovārī || paritāla ||*

Song in the *Rāga Āśovārī* with the rhythm *Paritāla:*

*dhruṁ ||*

*āve kāla kāli baliārā |*
*karatu toli pheṭa photkārā ||*

Refrain: The strong, powerful and black Kāli comes as if destruction personified, spreading wide its hood and making hissing sound.

---

[15]. in *Śloka* metre.

*pada* ||

*garaji darape sarapa biśāla* |
*pekhi nirekhae rūpa gopāla* ||

Verse: Roaring with pride the huge serpent looked on at the beauty of Gopāla.

*sūtra* ||

*ghanaśyāma pītabāsa : śrībatsa kaustubha : kirīṭi kuṇḍala : kaṅkaṇa-keyūra-rañjita gopālaka : parama kamanīya rūpa nirekhi : khaṅge jaice marmmathāne śrīkṛṣṇaka daṁśala tā dekhaha*

Direction: Looking at the charming form of Gopāla, dark like the cloud with yellow clothing, Visnu, glowing with the Kaustubha gem, the crown, the ear rings, the bacelets and the armlets, as Kāli, with great anger, stung at the most vital point of Śrī Kṛṣṇa, watch that.

*pada* ||

*kautuke karatu keli banamālī* |
*marama thāne khedi daṁśala kāli* ||
*beḍhala lāñjehi bhujaga pravandhe* |
*rahala gopāla paḍi sarppaka bandhe* ||3||

Verse: Vanamālī did it as a sport with pleasure, (when) Kāli, chasing Him, stung at the most vital spot and entrapped Him in a serpantine tie with his tail and Gopāla remained lying within the clasp of the serpent.

*sūtra* ||

*parama īśvara śrīgopāla : manuṣya-ceṣṭā daraśi : biṣa lāgi mṛtaka svabhāve : sarppaka bandhane paḍi rahala* | *tāhe pekhi : śiśusaba prāṇa antarīkṣa bhela : hā hā svāmi : ki bheli : hāmāka prāṇe jiyāi : tohõ āpune marala tohõ bine kaiche hāmu jiana rākhaba boli : kṛṣṇaka mukha nirekhi bahuta bilāpa karie : hradaka tīre rahala* ||

Direction: The Supreme Lord Śrī Gopāla, showing to make an effort like a human being, remained lying within the clasp of the serpent, as if dead, affected by poison. Seeing that, the young boys became nearly lifeless. "Alas, alas! Oh lord, what has happened, reviving us you have died yourself! Say, how we can live without you?" Thus looking at the face of Kṛṣṇa, lamenting a great deal, remained on the bank of the lake.

*śloka* ||

*tato nānādbhutaṁ dṛṣṭvā braje nandādayastadā* |
*kṛṣṇo mṛta iti matvā taṁ draṣṭuṁ yayurākulāḥ* ||9||

Hymn[16]: Then, observing many surprising events in Vraja, Nanda and others considered Kṛṣṇa to be dead and wanting to see Him, went there eagerly.

*sūtra* ||

*tadanantara : gokulata nānā bimaṅgala milala : ghana ghana bhūmikampa jāi : nirghāta paḍe : ghare ghare pheruā ārāva kare : ānābāve bṛkṣasaba ubhari pare : strīka dakṣiṇa puruṣaka bāma phande : tāhe pekhi saba loka mahābhīti bhela : yaśodāka hṛdaya kāmpe : hā hā prāṇaputra gopālaka : maraṇa milala boli : hṛdaye muṣṭi hānie kahu : śrīkṛṣṇaka dekhite : gopagopī sahita : nandayaśodā bṛndābana prabeśi jaice calali : tāhe dekhaha śunaha : nirantare hari bola* ||

Direction: After that, many misfortunes befell upon Gokula; frequent earthquakes and fall of thunderbolt occurred, jackals howled in every household, trees fell down uprooted without any wind, the right sides of the women and the left sides of the men started fluttering ominously; seeing all these all the people became very scared and Yaśodā's heart trembled, and saying, "Alas, alas! My dearest son Gopāla is dead!", and thumping blows on her chest, went to see Śrī Kṛṣṇa. As Nanda and Yaśodā, along with the other cowherd men and women, entering Vṛndāvana went to see Kṛṣṇa; watch and listen to that and keep chanting the name of Hari incessantly.

---

16. in *Śloka* metre.

*gīta* || *rāga śrīgaurī* || *paritāla* ||

Song in the *Rāga Śrīgaurī* with the rhythm *Paritāla:*

*dhruṁ* ||

*yaśovā āve ākuli śoke* |
*phokāre dukhinī*
*saṅge calali tāpe jatae gopinī* ||

Refrain: Being greatly afflicted with sorrow, poor Yaśodā, came wailing greatly, and along came all the cowherd women with great sadness.

*pada* ||

*dhvaja bajra paṅkaja dekhite dahe āgi* |
*ḍākere gopāla prāṇa gayo kāhā lāgi* |
*narahe santāpe prāṇa dekhu andhiāri* |
*kahatu śaṅkara gati mukuti murāri* ||4||

Verse: The hearts burnt as if in fire, seeing (marks of) the flag, the *vajra* and the lotus (on the ground, from the feet of Kṛṣṇa), and (they) called out aloud, "Oh Gopāla, our life, where have you gone; our life stops as you are gone; our life stops with anguish and we see darkness (all around)."; Śaṅkara says that Murāri is the way to salvation.

*sūtra* ||

*aicana parama santāpe bilāpa kari : gopālaka khojagoḍi jāhite : gopagopī sahita : nandayaśodā hradaka tīra pāvala : bidūrate dekhala : gopaśiśusaba hradaka nirekhi : ārāve krandana karaice : tāhe pekhi : parama ākula bhāye : lavaḍi jāi dekhala : ki bhayaṅkara sarppaka bandhe paḍi : śrīkṛṣṇa mṛtaka bhāye rahaiche : cakṣuta nimeṣa nāhi : daśana nispāna : nāsāta bāu khele nāhi : tāheka pekhi : gopagopīka : dhātu antarīkṣa bhela : hā kṛṣṇa hā kṛṣṇa boli : parama urmmi kaye : krandana karite lāgala : nandayaśodā mṛtaka putraka mukha nirekhi : prāṇa antarīkṣe diśadaśa āndhāri pekhi : śoka jhamake mūrccita hayā : pari rahala* ||

Direction: In this way lamenting with great sorrow, tracing the footsteps of Gopāla, Nanda and Yaśodā, along with the cowherd men and women, reached the bank of the lake; saw from a distance, the cowherd boys, looking towards the lake, were crying aloud. Seeing that, running forward very eagerly, saw Śrī Kṛṣṇa, in the clasp of a terrible serpent, lying as if dead; eyes not blinking, teeth clenching and the nose petals motionless. Seeing that, the souls of the cowherd men and women became completely empty. Saying, "Alas, oh Kṛṣṇa, alas oh Kṛṣṇa!", started crying loudly with much distress. Looking at the face of their dead son, their lives being empty, Nanda and Yaśodā saw only darkness all around and out of deep sorrow fell down lying unconsciousness.

*śloka* ||

*tatah kṛṣṇamukhaṁ vīkṣya gopyo virahakātarāḥ* |
*ruruduḥ susvarantībraṁ śokaśalyena dharṣitāḥ* ||*10*||

Hymn[17] : Then looking at the face of Kṛṣṇa, the cowherd women became greatly afflicted with the desertion and being greatly overcome with sorrow cried screaming aloud.

*kathā sūtra* ||

*tadanantara : gopīsaba kṛṣṇaka śokaśalye pīḍita hayā : prāṇa dharae napāri : prāṇagopālaka mukha nirekhite : nayanaka nīra dhāre bahi jāi : ārttarāve : māṭi loṭi : krandana kariye bolala* ||

*he prāṇa bandhu mādhava : hāmu kiṅkarīsabaka coḍi : kaice calaiche : he nātha : hāmāka saṅge niā java* ||

*toho bine jīvana nāhi dharaba : svabhāve maraba : ki nimite hāmāka cāraha : ohi cānda badana nedekhiye : kaice prāṇa rākhaba boli : kṛṣṇara mukha nirekhi jaiche bilāpa kayala tāhe dekhaha śunaha : nirantare hari bola* ||

Dialogue and Direction: After that, the cowherd women, being greatly tormented with the arrow of sorrow, unable to

[17]. in *Śloka* metre.

contain their lives any more, looking at the face of Gopāla, who was as dear as life, tears flowed from their eyes, and rolling down on the ground greatly distressed, crying aloud(they) said:
"Oh friend of our lives, Mādhava, how can you leave us, your servants behind, oh Lord, please take us along.
"We shall not live on without you, we will naturally die; why do you leave us, how can we live without seeing that (beautiful) moonlike face!"; saying thus, looking at the face of Kṛṣṇa as they lamented, watch and listen to that and keep chanting the name of Hari incessantly.

*gīta* || *rāga kau* || *paritāla* ||
Song in the *Rāga Kau* with the rhythm *Paritāla:*

*dhruṁ* ||

*dekhore dekho bandhu mādhava he*
*tuhu bine jīvana narahe* |
*teri sokānala śarīra bikala*
*bandhu birahe hṛdaya dahe re* ||

Refrain: "Look, look, oh dear friend Mādhava, we cannot stay alive without you. The body is maimed with the fire of grief for you and the heart burns in separation from a friend (you)."

*pada* ||

*gṛha moha heri saba tejiā teri*
*caraṇe śaraṇa kailo* |
*kayo saba nāśa tuhu teji jāsa*
*aba anāthinī bhailo re* ||
*baṁśī svāna śuni āsiye gopinī*
*kāheri heraba mukha* |
*kamala nayane nirekhiye kone*
*haraba hāmāra dukha re* ||
*kṛṣṇasokānala śarīra bikala*

*adhike dagadhe prāṇa*
*cetana haraya : muruci paraya :*
*kṛṣṇara kiṅkare bhāṇ*[18] *re* ||5||

Verse: "Giving a sideway glace at my household, renouncing everything, I have taken refuge in your feet; but you have ruined it all leaving us behind and now we have become forlorn.

"Coming out hearing the sound of the flute, the *gopīs* will look at whose face; looking at us with lotus like eyes, who will remove our suffering!

"The body is spiritless and the heart burns even more with the fire of sorrow for Kṛṣṇa.", and saying so, losing sense, they fell down unconscious, says Śaṅkara, the servant of Kṛṣṇa.

*sūtra* ||

*aicana parama santāpe bilāpa kaya gopīsa : kṛṣṇaka śoke : acetana hoi : murcita hayā parala* ||

Direction: In this way lamenting with great anguish from sadness for Kṛṣṇa, the cowherd women losing their sense, fell down unconscious.

*śloka* ||

*yaśodā cetanāṁ prāpya patinā saha sā bhṛśam* |
*ruroda duḥkhaśokārttā putrasya paśyantī mukham* ||*11*||

Hymn[19]: Regaining consciousness, Yaśodā, alongwith her husband, greatly afflicted with sorrow and pain, looking at the face of their son, cried very much.

*kathā sūtra* ||

*tadantara kiñcit cetana labhie : yaśodā putra sokānale : śarīra dāha kare : putramukha nirekhi bolala* ||

Dialogue and Direction: After that, regaining a little consciousness, Yaśodā, burning her body in the fire of sorrow for her son, looking at His face said.

[18]. *bhāṇa*.

[19]. in *Śloka* metre.

*kathā* ||

*āhe prāṇa bandhāi madhāi : kata tapasāyi : tohāka putra pāvalo : alpate anāthinī kaya : kāhe hāmāka tejala : dekho tohāri santāpe jīva rahe nāhi : hā hā ohi cānda badanaka : kāheka niā delō : hāmāra putraka ke niā jāi : godhūli āju baṁśī bajāi : ke brajaka jāvaba : kāheka dhūlā jhāḍi : boke bāndhi kole dharaba : kāheka gorasa pāna karāaba : ki bheli āju ai kṛṣṇa mora bāpa : kāhā gaili eḍāyeñ ōhi tohāri santāpa*

Dialogue: "Oh friend of my heart, Madhāi, we had you as our son after so much of religious austerity." After a short time the poor woman said, "Why have you abandoned us! See, our life nearly stops with grief for you. Alas, alas, how could we let go of that beautiful moonlike face. Who has taken away our son? Who would go to Vraja this evening playing the flute, shaking off the dust (from the body) who shall I be holding on to my bosom, take on my lap and feed on cows milk! Oh my dear Kṛṣṇa, what has happened to you today, where have you gone! Relieve me of this grief for you."

*sūtra* ||

*aicana putraśoke : tāpita hayā yaśodā jaicana karuṇa bilāpa kayala : tāhe dekhaha śunaha : nirantare hari bola* ||

Direction: In this way, being afflicted with grief for her son, as Yaśodā lamented pitifully, watch and listen to that and keep chanting the name of Hari incessantly.

*gīta* || *rāga kau* || *jatimāna* ||

Song in the *Rāga Kau* with the rhythm *Jatimāna:*

*dhruṁ* ||

*e suta mādhava he ki meri kapāla* |
*kahira dāruṇa sarppe teri bhaila kāla* ||

Refrain: "Oh dear son Mādhava, how unfortunate is my fate, wherefrom this ruthless serpent has come as your death incarnate?"

*pada* ||

*kāhā jāa agani jāliyā meri gāva* |
*ke nā āsi hāmāka bolaba aba māva* ||
*dhūlā jhāri kāhāka dharaba boke tuli* |
*hṛdaya dhākuḍe yaśomatī ōhi buli* ||1||
*egṛha godhana dhana sāñco kāra tare* |
*ke nā pāna karaba gorasa meri ghare* ||
*madhura adhare dhari bajāite beṇu* |
*cāraba bihāne ke nā meli meri dhenu* ||2||
*ki nā dose prāṇaputra tejali hāmāri* |
*harayī cetana diśa dekhu andhiāri* ||
*tohāri janani herā mari jāyeñ tape* |
*kahatu śaṅkara yaśomatīka santāpe* ||3||6||

Verse: "Where have you gone leaving my body burning in fire, who would come and call me mother! Dusting off who shall I hold to my bosom!", saying thus, Yaśomatī laments beating her chest. (1)
For whom shall I preserve this house and the cows; who will come to my house and drink the milk of the cows! Playing the flute holding it to the sweet lips, who will take my cows out for grazing in the mornings! (2)
Oh son, as dear as life, for what fault of us you have deserted us, loosing sense I see darkness all around! See, oh dear, your mother is dying with grief!"; says Śaṅkara about the distress of Yaśodā. (3)

*sūtra* ||

*aicana parama bilāpa kaya : yaśodā ḍāki bolala* ||

Direction: In this way, lamenting a great deal, Yaśodā called aloud.

*kathā* ||

*aye krūra pāpī sarppa : putraka prāṇa leli : āheka saṅge daṁsi hāmāka māraha* ||

Dialogue: "Oh you cruel sinner serpent, you have taken the life of my son; sting me and kill me along with him."

*sūtra* ||

*ohi boli kṛṣṇaka śoke prāṇa dharae nāhi pāri : gopagopī sahita nandayaśodā hā kṛṣṇa hā kṛṣṇa boli hradata jhāmpa dite jāi : tāhe pekhi balabhadra raha raha boli : āgabhenṭi nibāri bolala* ||

Direction: Saying so, not being able to hold onto her life any more with the grief for Kṛṣṇa, Nanda and Yaśodā, along with the other cowherd men and women, crying, "Alas Kṛṣṇa, alas Kṛṣṇa!", went to jump in the lake; seeing that, crying "Wait, wait!", Balabhadra obstructing them said,

*kathā* ||

*āhe pīta-mātṛ : gopagopī saba : ki karite cāva : raha raha kico chintā nāhi : tuhusaba kico jānaye nāhi : ohi duṣṭa sarppaka daṇḍa karie : ethā hante khedāyā śrīkṛṣṇa ei kṣaṇa āvaba : tohosaba kautuka dekhaha baiṭhi raha* ||

Dialogue: "Oh dear father, mother, cowherd boys and girls, what do you want to do? Wait, wait! There is nothing to worry; you do not know anything. Punishing that wicked serpent and chasing him away from here, Śrī Kṛṣṇa will be back right at this moment; just remain seated and watch with pleasure."

*sūtra* ||

*tadanantara : baloka bākyebraja bāsīsaba : kico śānta hayā : pariarti nijhama pariye : kṛṣṇaka mukha nirekhie rahala* ||

Direction: Thereupon, hearing the words of Bala, the dwellers of Vraja calmed down a little, returned back and waited looking at the face of Kṛṣṇa silently.

*śloka* ||

*dṛṣṭvā viṣādaṁ govindo bhaktānāṁ bhaktavatsalaḥ* |
*āsphoṭya sahasottasthau vimuktaḥ sārpabandhanāt*[20] ||12||

---

[20]. *sarpabandhanāt.*

Hymn[21] : Seeing the sadness of the devotees, Govinda, who is very kind to His devotees, stirring forcefully, arose, making Himself free from the clasp of the serpent.

*sūtra* ||

*manuṣya ceṣṭā daraśie śrīgopāla dui daṇḍa sarppaka bandhane paḍi rahala : tadanantare : gopagopīsabaka : parama biṣāda dukha dekhie : śrīkṛṣṇa ācoṭa kaya uruphāla delaha : kāli sarppa parama coṭa pāi : kṛṣṇaka cāḍi uphaḍi paḍala : hājāreka phaṇā tuli : kṛṣṇaka cāi phophāi : kope cakṣu ārakata jihbāe kavāri celekaa : nāke mukhe biṣa-bahni bariṣava pekhi śrīkṛṣṇa parama āṭope kālika hāmpholala : tāheka beḍhi : cakrākāre camatkāre : pāka phurite lāgala : se anantabīrya kāli mahā phetkāra kariye : kṛṣṇaka samukhe bharamaya : tāhe pekhi jagataka nāthe : līlāye kālika māthe : ārmbare caḍala* ||

Direction: Pretending like a human being, Śrī Gopāla remained lying in the clasp of the serpent (which was) two *daṇḍa*s long; thereafter, seeing the great sadness and suffering of the cowherd men and women, Śrī Kṛṣṇa sprang up with a jerk. Receiving the sharp pain, the serpent Kāli sprang aside releasing Kṛṣṇa, spreading out his thousand hoods, panting and hissing looking at Kṛṣṇa, eyes red with anger, licking the lips with the tongue, showering poisonous fire through his nose and mouth. Seeing that, Śrī Kṛṣṇa, with great valour struck Kāli and started moving in circles around him, surprising him. And that Kāli also, with never ending strength, started moving in front of Kṛṣṇa hissing greatly. Seeing him, the Lord of this world climbed up to the head of Kāli with much pleasure and show.

*śloka* ||

*tataḥ śirāṁsi sarpasya padbhyāmāmardya mādhavaḥ* |
*nanarta līlayā sarbakalādigururīśvaraḥ* ||*13*||

Hymn[22]: Then climbing on to the top of the heads of the serpent

[21]. in *Śloka* metre.

[22]. in *Śloka* metre.

and crushing them with His feet, Mādhava, the master of the masters in all arts, started dancing with great pleasure.

*sūtra* ||

*tadanantare kālika māthe caḍi : śrīkṛṣṇa dui pāve phanāka marddie nṛtya ārambhala : se samaye gandharbba bidyādhara saba āsi kahu : tāla karatāla ṭhuki mṛdaṅga bajāvaya : tāheka cea layā śrīkṛṣṇa jaice kotuka nṛtya kayala : tā dekhaha śunaha nirantare hari bola* •

Direction: After that, climbing onto the head of Kāli, Śrī Kṛṣṇa crushing its hood with His two feet, started dancing. At that time all the *Gandharvas* and *Vidyādharas* came and set the rhythm playing small and big cymbals and *mṛdaṅga*. Picking up the rhythm as Śrī Kṛṣṇa danced with great pleasure, watch and listen to that and keep chanting the name of Hari incessantly.

*gīta* | *rāga gaurī* || *domāni paritāla jatimāna* ||

Song in the *Rāga Gaurī* with the rhythm *Domāni Paritāla Jatimāna:*

*dhruṁ* ||

*kālā kānu nāce caraṇa calāi*
*karatu kautuka nṛtya keśava*
*aruṇa caraṇa calāya re* |
*devamuni śire sirikha barikhe*
*harikhe hariguṇa gāyare* ||

Refrain: Kānu, who is black in complexion dances moving His feet; Keśava dances with great pleasure moving His red feet and the gods and sages shower *śirīṣa* flowers on His head singing the praises of Hari with great hapiness.

*pada* ||

*kāla kālika māthe caḍi bhāḍa*
*pīḍi krīḍi kānu nāce re* |

*mṛdaṅga dimi dimi* *nāda dundubhi*
*siddhasaba bāya kācere* ||
*pāka phiri phiri* *bhiri bhiri paye*
*śira śira pāḍe ḍeo re* |
*aṅga bhaṅgima* *raṅga kautuke*
*nācata e ādideva re* ||7||

Verse: Climbing with full weight on to the head of Kāli, the death incarnate, Kānu dances, inflicting pain, as if it were a sport. All the holy sages coming nearby, play the *mṛdaṅga* and the *dundubhi* with rhythm. Swirling around again and again rhythmically on His feet, (Kṛṣṇa) steps on the heads of Kāli. The origin of all gods dances on twisting and turning His limbs making different postures and with great fun and pleasure.

*sūtra* ||

*aicana jagataka parama guru nārāyaṇa śrīgopālaka bhara sahite napāri kāli acetana bhela : parama pīḍāta ghāḍa olamala : nāke mukhe rudhira cānde : mahādukhe andhakāra dekhe : jata madagarbbadambha darppa sarppaka saba cūra bhela : bākyamukhe harala : aicana parama guruka āpada-auṣadha pāi : kālika mana nirmmala bhela : nayanara nīra nijhuraya : kṛṣṇaka parama īśvara puruṣa jāni mane śaraṇa lelaha* ||

Direction: Not being able to bear the weight of this most venerable of the world, Nārāyaṇa Śrī Gopāla, Kāli became unconscious; his neck hung out with great pain, and he vomitted out blood through the mouth and the nose and saw darkness all around in (this) great suffering. All the pride, arrogance and conceit of the serpent were crushed and he became speechless. Having found this most venerable as the remedy (for his evils) in the form of such misfortune, the mind of Kāli became purified and tears flowed down from his eyes. Knowing Kṛṣṇa to be the ultimate God he took refuge in Him within his mind.

*śloka* ||

*nāgapatnyaḥ patiṁ vīkṣya mumūrṣuṅgatacetanam |*
*tuṣṭubuḥ kṛṣṇamabhyetya bharturvirahakātarāḥ ||14||*

Hymn[23]: Seeing their husband senseless and dying, the wives of the serpent, suffering with separation from their husband, came near Kṛṣṇa and prayed to Him.

*kathāsūtra* ||

*kālika bhāryā : jata nāganārīsaba : svāmī maraya dekhi : parama santāpe ākulamati hayā : hṛdae muṣṭi hāne : nayanaka nīra jhurāe : hā svāmi hā svāmi boli : śiśusaba āga karie : jaice bilāpa karite āve : tāhe dekhaha śunaha nirantare hari bola hari bola ||*

Dialogue and Direction: Seeing their husband dying, the wives of Kāli, and all the serpent women, being very much distressed with sorrow and distraught with grief, beating their chests with their fists and tears flowing from their eyes, crying "Alas husband, alas oh husband!", and keeping the children in front, as they lamented, watch and listen to that and keep chanting the name of Hari incessantly.

*gīta* || *rāga beloāra* || *rūpakatāla* ||

Song in the *Rāga Belovāra* with the rhythm *Rūpakatāla*:

*dhruṁ* ||

*nāganārī āvayī avanata kāyī |*
*tāpita tanu manu nayana jhurāyī ||*

Refrain: The serpent women came with stooping bodies, their bodies and minds suffering and tears flowing from their eyes.

*pada* ||

*piuka santāpa tāpe prāṇa phuṭi jāi |*
*phokārayī ghana mana cetana nāi ||1||*
*parie harika āgu karu paraṇāma |*
*kahatu śaṅkara gati govinda nāma ||2||8||*

---

[23]. in *Śloka* metre.

Verse: (Their) lives nearly left (their) bodies with remorse for their husband, weeping again and again with their minds losing all sense, lying down in front of Hari offered their obeisance. Chanting the name of Govinda is the only way to salvation, says Śaṅkara.

*kathā sūtra* ||
*aicana parama santāpe : kṛṣṇaka āgu paḍi paraṇāmi nāgapatanīsaba : kara-joḍi svāmīka dukha moṣaṇa mane tuti ārambhala*||

Dialogue and Direction: In this way with great affliction, the wives of the serpent, falling down flat in front of Kṛṣṇa and offering obeisance with folded hands, started saying prayers for the relief of their husband.

*payāḍa* || *dhruṁ* ||

*ghora aparādha ācarala ohi caṇḍa* |
*bihilā ihāka hari samucita daṇḍa* ||
*purāṇa puruṣa tohõ sanātana hari* |
*āchā deva duṣṭaka daṇḍite avatari* ||1||
*ito daṇḍe svāmī õhi eḍāilā pātaka* |
*barato adhika dekhõ tohāri krodhaka* ||
*ito pādapaṅkajara pāilā dhūlācaya* |
*ki hetu ihāra hena bhaila bhāgyodaya* ||2||
*lakṣmī brahmā maheśa prabhṛti devagane* |
*ito padaraja khuji napāve jatane* ||
*tāmasika krūra krodhi kāli sarppajāti* |
*ki mate pāileka ito padadhūlā āti* ||3||
*namo namo ananta śakati nārāyaṇa* |
*kāraṇaro kāraṇa tumisi akāraṇa* ||
*nāhi ādi anta madhya paricinna jāra* |
*purṇānanda deva herā karo namaskāra* ||4||
*namo namo atarka mahimā deva hari* |
*jagatake biyāpi āpuni āchā dhari* ||

*tuhu sarbba sākhi rākhi āchā prāṇīcaya* |
*tohātese hante hove sṛṣṭi sthiti laya* ||5||
*jāhera cārio mukṣya mūrti anupāma* |
*rāma kāma aniruddha bāsudeva nāma* ||
*hena bhagavanta kṛṣṇa devatāra deva* |
*tohāri caraṇe karo lakṣa kauṭi seva* ||6||8||

Verse: Refrain: "That wrathful, performed a great crime and Hari served him with appropriate punishment. Ancient and eternal Hari, you are here oh Lord, as an incarnation, to punish the wicked. (1)

"With this punishment, oh Lord, he has become sin-free; we see, your anger to be even more valuable than your benediction. How, for what reason could he achieve such rise of fortune, that he has received the dust of these lotus feet! (2)

"Gods and goddesses such as Lakṣmī, Brahmā, Maheśa and others do not receive such (blessings) dust of these feet, even after seeking it with much endeavour. Kāli is ignorant, cruel, wicked and abusive and belongs only to the family of the serpents, how has he received then, such supreme blessings like the dust of these feet. (3)

"My repeated obeisance to Nārāyaṇa, who is infinitely powerful; you are the cause of all causes and yet you are causeless. One who does not have any beginning, middle or end, or any limitation, who is fully in bliss, oh God, kindly glance upon us; we pay our respectful obeisance unto you.(4)

"Obeisance to God Hari, whose greatness is beyond reasoning. You are all pervasive and are supporting the world all by yourself. You are the witness of all (that happens), you are preserving the animal world; the whole creation, continuation and destruction are all because of you.(5)

"Whose all the four main forms, Rāma, Kāmadeva, Aniruddha and Vāsudeva by name, are so beautiful. Such a

God, Kṛṣṇa, the God of all the Gods, we offer lacs and crores of obeisance at your feet." (6)

*sūtra :*

*aicana tuti kari kahu : nāganārīsaba sakāruṇa bhāe : kṛṣṇaka kārpaṇya karite lāgala.*

Direction: Praying in this way, in a mournful manner the serpent women started beseeching Kṛṣṇa pitifully.

*nāganārīsababola || he parama īśvara : tohāri pada prahāre : svāmī mari jāi : õhi duryane : tohāka najāni daṁśala : ihāka doṣa bāreka maraṣa gosāñiñ : tohāri āgu khudra pataṅga : āheka māri kona jasa sādhaba : dekho svāmika dhātu prāṇa rahe nāhi : jata lāge māne sāsti pāvala : he parama īśvara : śrīkṛṣṇa : aba kṛpā karu : hāmāka anātha karabi nāhi : tohāri āgu āñcola pāti : patidāna māgõ ||*

The serpent women said, "Oh Supreme God, our husband is almost dying with the kicks of your feet. Not knowing you, that wicked has bitten you; for once forgive his fault, oh God. He is an insignificant insect in front of you, what fame will you earn by killing him? See, our husband cannot contain his life anymore; he has received as much punishment as he deserved. Oh Supreme God, Śrī Kṛṣṇa, now please have mercy; please do not orphanate us. Spreading wide the fore-end of our clothing we beg of you for the life of our husband."

*sūtra ||*

*õhi bolite nayanaka nīra jhure : patika santāpe nāginīsaba : jaiche bilāpa kayala : tāhe dekhaha śunaha nirantare hari bola ||*

Direction: Saying so, tears flowing from their eyes with anguish for their husband, as the serpent women started lamenting, watch and listen to that and keep chanting the name of Hari incessantly.

*gīta* || *rāga suhāi* || *jati māna* ||

Song in the *Rāga Suhāi* with the rhythm *Jatimāna:*

*dhruṁ* ||

*abahu karunā karu kṛpāla gopāla* |
*tejavi jiana svāmīka mile kāḷa* ||

Refrain: "Now, please have pity on us, oh merciful Gopāla, now that our husband has met with his death incarnate, he will give up his life."

*pada* ||

*toho nāhi jānie daṁśala õhi caṇḍa* |
*samucita ahika kayali deva daṇḍa* ||
*tuā pāve bidita satīka pati prāṇa* |
*āñcola pātiā māgo āmi svāmīdāna* ||
*tejaya jia piu prāṇa ṭuṭi jāi* |
*pāpīka doṣasaba marasa gosāñiñ* ||
*kari kātara bilapati pari nārī* |
*kaha śaṅkara aba uddhāra murāri* ||9||

Verse: "Not knowing you, that wrathful serpent has bitten you and oh Lord, you have punished the snake rightly.

"As you know, the life of us virtuous women's husband, is under your feet. Spreading wide the fore-end of our clothing, we beg of you for the life of our husband.

"Our husband is almost dying and his life is webbing off. Please forgive the sins of this sinner, oh Lord!"

Lying flat, the good women, distressed, started lamenting. "Now, please save him, oh Murāri.", says Śaṅkara.

*kathā sūtra* ||

*nāga nārīsaba : aicana svāmīka santāpe : bilāpa kari kahuñ : kṛṣṇaka āgu pari rahala : nayanaka nīra jhure : hā svāmi boli : hṛdae muṭhi hāni : ārttarāva karie thika* ||

Dialogue and Direction: In this way lamenting with grief for their husband, the serpent women remained lying in front of Kṛṣṇa; tears flowing from the eyes, uttering "Alas, oh dear husband!", striking their chests with clenched fists, (the serpent women) continued crying aloud.

*śloka* ||

*niśamya nāganārīṇāṁ karuṇaṁ kamalekṣaṇaḥ* |
*kāliyaśirasaḥ kṛṣṇaḥ kṛpayāvatatāra saḥ* ||15||

Hymn[24]: Looking at the sad serpent women, the lotus-eyed Kṛṣṇa mercifully descended from the head of Kāliya.

*kathā sūtra* ||

*tadanantara : nāgabadhusabaka : parama santāpa pekhiye : śrīkṛṣṇaka kṛpā upajala : nāganārīsabaka sambudhi bolala* ||

Dialogue and Direction: After that, seeing the great distress of the serpent women, Śrī Kṛṣṇa felt great pity on them and addressing the serpent women said.

*śrīkṛṣṇa bola* || *āhe kālikabhāryā : nāginīsaba : santāpa coḍaha* ||

Śrī Kṛṣṇa said, "Oh you serpent women, the wives of Kāli, stop lamenting."

*sūtra* ||

*ohi buli dea : diā nāmi : sarppaka phanāhante : antara huyā rahala* ||

Direction: Saying so, Kṛṣṇa came jumping down, from the expanded hoods of the serpent and remained aside.

*śloka* ||

*tato vimurcchitaḥ kāli śanaih samprāpya cetanām* |
*tutoṣa śirasā natvā matyā kṛṣṇaṁ maheśvaram* ||16||

Hymn[25]: Then unconscious Kāli, slowly regaining consciousness, understanding Kṛṣṇa as the Supreme God, started praying with his head bowed down.

*kathā sūtra* ||

*yamapura pāi : kāli kathamkathamapi prāṇe nibarttala : mahā*

[24]. in *Śloka* metre.

[25]. in *Śloka* metre.

*pīḍā pāi : phophāata : āpada auṣadhi pāi : sarppaka darppacūra bhela : citta śānta hayā : ākhi meli : kṛṣṇaka āgu dekhi bolala : ohi kauṭi brahmaṇḍa īśvara nārāyaṇa jāni: trāhi trāhi svāmi kṛṣṇa boli : śira caraṇa paraśiye : paraṇāma kayala : paścāt jānu pāri karajoḍi : tuti ārambhala* ||

Dialogue and Direction: Nearly reaching the abode of Yama (almost dying), Kāli only somehow managed to live on and suffering with great pain started panting. Having found the remedy (for his evils) in the form of such misfortune, the pride of the serpent was destroyed. His mind calmed down, opening the eyes and seeing Kṛṣṇa in front of him, said, "I know you are Nārāyaṇa, the Supreme Lord of crores of universes, please save us oh Lord Kṛṣṇa, please save us." and saying so, touching the feet of Kṛṣṇa with his head, offered his obeisance. After that, down on his knees, with folded hands, (he) started praying.

*payāḍa* ||

*jaya jaya jagata maheśvara* |
*brahmā śaṅkara jāhe kiṅkara* ||
*jaya bhakataka bhaya-hārī* |
*namo hari caraṇa tohāri* ||*1*||
*tava pāve atae sādhi* |
*mañiñ pāpī aparādhī* ||
*daṁśala deva najāni* |
*marasa doṣa padmapāṇi* ||2||
*krūra sarppa ahaṁkārī* |
*srajanā tohāri murāri* ||
*mohala mana tuyā māyā* |
*āju kayali deva dāyā* ||3||
*garaba gucāali mora* |
*biṣaya āpada ghora* ||
*dūra kara aba moyī* |
*cinto caraṇaka toi* ||4||

*dehu hari mohi ohi śikṣā* |
*māgiye bhuñjaba bhīkṣā* ||
*bharamo tuyā guṇa gāi* |
*karahu atae karunā gosāñiñ* ||5||*10*||

Verse: "Glory to the Supreme God of the world, even Brahmā and Śaṅkara are whose servants. Glory to the one who takes away all fears from the minds of the devotees; I offer my obeisance at your feet, oh Hari. (1)
"After much worship at your feet, I am still a sinner, an offender. Not knowing you to be God, I have bitten you; please forgive my fault, oh, one who carries a lotus in his hand. (2)
"This cruel and proud serpent is (also) your creation only, oh Murāri. Your enchantment has fascinated me; oh Lord, you have shown great mercy on me today. (3)
"You have removed my pride. Also, please remove my great trouble of these worldly attachments; so that I can just meditate on your feet. (4)
"Oh Hari, please educate me in such a way that I can live only by begging. Please show me this much mercy that I can wander about singing your glories." (5)

*kathā* ||

*he parama puruṣa nārāyaṇa śrīkṛṣṇa : ohi parama āpada bişaya jañjāla dūra karaha : gale kanthā bāndhi : bhīkṣā māgi : tohāri caraṇa cinti : guṇa nāma gāi beḍāñeñ bāpa jagannātha : trāhi trāhi buli : āgu parala*

Dialogue: "Oh the Supreme Personality Nārāyaṇa Śrī Kṛṣṇa, please remove the great trouble of worldly attachment; wrapping up a piece of tattered cloth around the neck, begging around meditating on your feet and singing your praises I will roam about oh father Jagannātha, please deliver me.", and saying so, stretched out lying in front.

*śloka* ||

*vīkṣya bhaktintatastasya tuṣṭaḥ kṛṣṇo jagāda tam |*
*mābhairbhujagatīrno'si mamamāyāṁ duratyayām ||17||*

Hymn[26]: Then seeing his devotion, Kṛṣṇa became pleased and told him, "Oh serpent, do not fear, you have passed the test of my illusion, which cannot be overcome easily."

*kathā* ||

*śrīkṛṣṇa bola* || *āhe kāli sarparāja : tohō bhaya karabi nāhi : hāmāka prasāde : ōhi māyā saṁsāra tohō nistarala : sāmprata ōhi yamunāka hrada coḍi tohāri pūrva sthāna ramaṇaka dvīpa : tāheka lāgi sapariyāle calaha : ei calaha : garuḍaka kico śaṅkā karabi nāhi : hāmāra caraṇaka cihna : dhvaja bajra paṅkaja : tohāri phanāta lāgi rahala : tāhe pekhi : hāmāka bhaye : garuḍe kico karaba nāhi: bilamba coḍi : ei calaha*||

Dialogue: Śrī Kṛṣṇa said, "Oh the king of the serpents Kāli, do not be scared; with my blessings you have got rid of this world of illusion. Now, leaving this Lake Yamunā, along with your whole family go to your former place, the island of Ramaṇaka, go now. Do not worry about Garuḍa; the marks of my feet, the flag, the *Vajra*, and the lotus are imprinted on your hood and seeing those, out of fear for me, Garuḍa will not do any harm to you. Now leave this place without any delay."

*śloka* ||

*niśamya nirbhayāṁ vāṇīṁ kṛṣṇasya bhujagastadā |*
*natvā saparibāreṇa yayau ramanakaṁ mudā ||18||*

Hymn[27]: Hearing such reassuring words from Kṛṣṇa, the serpent, then, offered obeisance and along with his family left for island Ramaṇaka, happily.

*kathāsūtra* ||

*śrīkṛṣṇaka parama nirbhaya bāṇī śunie : mahā hariṣe kāli sapariāre : kṛṣṇaka praṇāma kayala : caraṇaka dhūli lelaha :*

[26]. in *Śloka* metre.
[27]. in *Śloka* metre.

*he svāmi kṛṣṇa bidāya kayala buli : preme salotaka nayane : jaiche calala : tāhe dekhaha śunaha : nirantare hari bola* ||

Dialgue and Direction: Hearing the great reassuring words of Śrī Kṛṣṇa, with great happiness, Kāli, along with his family, offered obeisance to Kṛṣṇa and took the dust of His feet. "Oh Lord Kṛṣṇa, you have bid farewell to us.", and saying so, with eyes full of tears of love, as they went, watch and listen to that and keep chanting the name of Hari incessantly.

*gīta* || *rāga kānaḍā* ||
Song in the *Rāga Kānaḍā:*

*dhruṁ* ||
*kṛṣṇaka caraṇe kariye bidāi* |
*calali kāli ramaṇaka lāi* ||

Refrain: Bidding farewell at the feet of Kṛṣṇa, Kāli set out for Ramaṇaka.

*pada* ||
*phanā maṇi jhimmika kari parakāśe* |
*nāga ramaṇī calaya laya lāse* ||*1*||
*jāhite hariṣe hariguṇa gāve* |
*kaha śaṅkara gati govinda pāve* ||2||*11*||

Verse: The stones on their hoods dazzling, the female serpents moved with poise and grace singing happily the glories of Hari; the ultimate refuge is at the feet of Govinda alone, says Śaṅkara.

*kathāsūtra* ||
*aicana parakāre : kālika damie : hrada hante dūra kari kahu : śrīkṛṣṇa kautuke kālindī tīre āvala : dekhi ānande gopīsaba jaya kṛṣṇa buli beḍhala : mukha paṅkajaka : jaiche nayana bhramare pāna karaiche : nandayaśodā bāhu meli : gale bāndhi dharala : ghane ghane śira suṅghi lotake śarīra tiyāvala: gada gada bākye bolala* ||

Dialogue and Direction: In this way, conquering Kāli and chasing him away from the lake, Śrī Kṛṣṇa came happily to the bank of Kālindī. Seeing Him, the cowherd women being very happy and exclaiming, "Glory to Kṛṣṇa!" surrounded Him, kooking at His lotuslike face, as if sucking honey with their eyes, like the black bee (sucks honey from the flower). Nanda and Yaśodā, stretched out their arms and held Him wrapping around His neck. Smelling His head again and again made His body wet with tears and in choking words said,

*yaśodā bola || āhe putā ki nimite : hradakamājhe jhāmpa delaha : aḥ hāmāka mārite cāala tohāri santāpe āju prāṇa cāḍala hoi||*
Yaśodā said, "Oh dear son, for what reason did you jump into the lake? Did you want to kill us? We would have lost our lives today out of grief for you."

*sūtra ||*

*ohi buli : mṛtaka putraka pāi : paramānande nanda-yaśodā rahala : tadanantara : kṛṣṇaka prabhāva jāni : hāsi hāsi āsi : balabhadre āliṅgi dharala : aicana parakāre : kṛṣṇaka āvari kautuke hāsite mātite : dibasa abasāna bhaila : rātṛ milala : tāhe pekhi śrīkṛṣṇa bolala ||*

Direction: Saying so, getting back their dead son, Nanda and Yaśodā became very happy. Balabhadra, knowing Kṛṣṇa's miraculous powers, came to Him laughing and embraced Him after that. In this way, surrounding Kṛṣṇa and laughing and talking with happiness the day ended and night fell; seeing which Śrī Kṛṣṇa said,

*kathā ||*

*he mātā : he pitā : he gopa gopīsaba : āju rātṛ braja jāite pāraye nāhi : jaba sabehi bhalla dekhaha : tabe ethāte rajanī bañcaha ||*

Dialogue: "Oh father, oh mother, oh dear cowherd boys and girls, tonight you will not be able to go back to Vraja. If you all find it proper, stay for the night here itself."

*sūtra* ||

*śrīkṛṣṇaka aicana bākya anumāni : jata gokulabāsīsaba : yamunākā tīre suti rahala : khudhāye tṛṣāye : hārāsāsthi hayā : nirbhara nidrā gelaha*

Direction: Following such words from Śrī Kṛṣṇa, being exhausted with hunger and thirst all the inhabitants of Gokula lay down on the bank of Yamunā and went to sleep fearlessly.

*śloka* ||

*tato lokāḥ samuttasthuḥ veṣṭitā vanavahninā |*
*cukruśuḥ kṛṣṇa kṛṣṇeti trāhi tvaṁ nijakiṅkarān ||19||*

Hymn[28]: Afterwards, all the people woke up being surrounded by wildfire and cried out "Kṛṣṇa, Kṛṣṇa, save your servants."

*kathāsutrta* ||

*tadanantara: nidrāte brajabāsīka : banāgni beḍhala : tāheka pracaṇḍa śabada śunie : nidrābhaṅga bhela : bismaya hayā jāgala : pracaṇḍa bahni pekhie śarīra : kāmpe : parama trasta hayā : trāhi trāhi kṛṣṇa boli : kolāhala karite lāgala* ||

Direction :After that, while the inhabitants of Vraja were asleep, a forest fire surrounded them. Hearing its terrible sound, their sleep was interrupted and they woke up surprised. Seeing the terrible fire, their bodies started trembling. Being greatly alarmed, they started to make great uproar crying "Kṛṣṇa, save us, save us!".

*gopa gopīsaba bola* ||

*he anāthaka nātha : he dīna dayāla svāmi kṛṣṇa : hāmāka ōhi śarīra avaśyaka paraba : ihāka cintā nāhi karaba : ōhi saṁsāra tāraka tohāri aruṇa caraṇa tāhe punarbbāra nāhi dekhaba : ōhi dukhānale hṛdaya dāha kare* ||

The cowherd boys and girls said, "Oh Lord Kṛṣṇa, protector of the helpless and kind to miserable, we are not worried

[28]. in *Śloka* metre.

that we shall need this body again. The thought that we shall not see your red feet again, oh saviour of the world, is what is burning our hearts like a fire."

*sūtra* ||

*õhi boli jaiche ārttarāve: krandana kaya lāgala | tāhe dekhaha śunaha : nirantare hari bola ||*

Direction: Saying so, as they cried expressing great distress, watch and listen to that and keep chanting the name of Hari incessantly.

*gīta || rāga śrīgāndhāra || paritāla ||*

Song in the *Rāga Śrīgāndhāra* with the rhythm *Paritāla:*

*dhruṁ* ||

*āve hari hari gopāla : prāṇa mile maraṇa hāmāru re: araṇya ānale dahe : madhāi urddhāru re ||*

Refrain: "Here comes Hari, Hari Gopāla (Hari, the cowherd boy), we are facing death, the wildfire is burning us, oh Madhāi, please save us."

*pada* ||

*nāhi õhi dukha : mohi jīva jaba jāi |*
*nācintita hāmu : ohi maraṇaka lāi ||*
*aruṇa caraṇa āra : nedekhõ tohāri |*
*ohi dukha dahe dehā : madhāi hāmāri ||1||*
*ārāye kātara kare : ai bandhu madhāi |*
*bāpa cāpa samīpa khānika thāko cāi ||*
*āju āśā dūra gela tuva darasane |*
*kahatū śaṅkara gati govinda caraṇe ||2||12||*

Verse: "The sorrow is not because my life is coming to an end; I am not at all worried about that death; that I shall not see your red feet again is the great sorrow which is burning my body, oh dear Madhāi."(1)

Crying with great grief expressing distress (they) said, "Oh dear friend Madhāi, oh dear father, please come nearer, let us look at your face for a while. Having a look at you has fulfilled all our wishes today." The ultimate refuge is at the feet of Govinda alone, says Śaṅkara. (2)

*gīta || rāga bhāṭhiāli ||*
*Song in the Rāga Bhāṭhiālī:*

*dhruṁ ||*

*trāhi trāhi hera : prāṇa nārāyaṇa :*
*harayī e bāpa : śaraṇe paśilo |*
*bana bahni dahe : narahe jīvana*
*ābese nāśilo ||*

Refrain: "Oh Nārāyaṇa, look, we are about to loose our lives, save us, please save us; we have taken shelter at your feet, oh father. The wild fire is burning us up and our lives cannot continue anymore; now we are ruined to death."

*pada ||*

*nāhi ōhi śoka : maraṇa miloka :*
*āre nācintihō hāmi |*
*tomāra aruṇa : caraṇa paṅkaja :*
*punu nedekhaba svāmi ||*
*sannihita cāpa : gopāla e bāpa*
*khānika dekhie thāko |*
*kamala nayana : e braja jīvana :*
*tore bhṛtya sabe dākō ||1||*
*rūpe madana : e cānda badana :*
*dekhite napāibo āra |*
*tohāri biyoga : āgi pīḍe prāṇa*
*adhike (aba) hāmāra ||*
*āpade magaṇa : gopagopīgaṇa :*
*ārāye kātara kare |*
*mādhava bāndhāba : uddhāra karatu :*
*kahaya kṛṣṇa kiṅkare ||2||13||*

Verse: "We do not grieve nor do we worry that we are meeting our death. But we shall not see your lotuslike red feet again, oh Lord, the lotus eyed, the life of (the people of) Vraja. We, all your servants, are calling you, please come nearer, dear Gopāla, dear father, so that we can look at you for a while. (1)

"We shall not get to see (you) again, the one who is beautiful like Madana and has a (beautiful) face like the moon. Separation from you is now greatly afflicting our lives like fire." Being plunged in danger, all the cowherd boys and girls cry with distress, "Oh friend Mādhava, please save us.", says the servant of Kṛṣṇa. (2)

*kathā sūtra* ||

*aicana bhakata sabaka ārttarāva śunie : śrīkṛṣṇaka parama karunā upajala : hṛdaya ākula bhela* ||

Dialogue and Direction: Hearing such distressed cry of the devotees, Śrī Kṛṣṇa's heart became overcome with great pity.

*śloka* ||

*tato'tibhītān bhagavān gopānāśvāsya satvaram* |
*mukhena vahnimapivat mahāyogeśvaro hariḥ* ||20||

Hymn[29]: Then reassuring the greatly scared cowherd boys and girls, Hari with his super-human power, drank up the fire with his mouth immediately.

*kathāsūtra* ||

*bhakataka bhīti pekhiye : śrīkṛṣṇa bolala* || *āhe gopagopīsaba : hāmu bidyamāna thākite : kona cintā thika : nirbhaye raha* ||

Dialogue and Direction : Seeing the fear in his devotees, Śrī Kṛṣṇa said, "Oh dear cowherd boys and girls, what is there to worry about when I am present here? Be fearless."

*ohi buli īśvara-ceṣṭā dekhāi : tatakāle se pracaṇḍa bahnika mukhe pāna kayala : durghora bahni jaice jala parie : tatakāle nirbāṇa*

[29]. in *Śloka* metre.

*gela : tāhe pekhi gopagopīsaba : jayakṛṣṇa boli jokāra pārala* ||
Saying so, exhibiting the powers of God, he immediately drank up with His mouth the terrible fire and the fierce fire, as if water was poured on it, extinguished immediately. Seeing that, the cowherd boys and girls greeted Him shouting, "Glory to Kṛṣṇa."

*śloka* ||

*śrīkṛṣṇasyādbhutaṁ karma dṛṣṭvā sarbe'pi vismitāḥ* |
*anyo'nyamiti pratyurcurna naro nandanandanaḥ* ||21||

Hymn[30]: Seeing such a miraculous deed of Kṛṣṇa, everyone became surprised and addressing one another discussed about the son of Nanda.

*kathāsūtra* ||

*śrīkṛṣṇaka ācarya mahimā dekhive : parama bismaya hayā : anyoanye sambodhi bole* ||

Dialogue and Direction: Seeing such astonishing power of Kṛṣṇa, being greatly surprised, addressing one another said,

*brajabāsī bola* || *āhe bhāisaba : dekho dekho : ohi nanda nandana mānuṣa nohe : pracaṇḍa bahnika tatakāle mukhe pāna kayala : ohi manuṣyaka kāma : aḥ jānala : je parama puruṣa puruṣottama : sanātana nārāyaṇa : se bhūmika bhāra haraṇa nimite : abatāra haye thika : ihāta kico śaṅkā nāhi : aḥ hāmāka bhāgyaka mahimā ki kahaba : ohi jagataka guru nārāyaṇa sahita : hāmāka saṅga bhela : hāmu nistarala* ||
The dwellers of Vraja said, "Oh dear brothers, look, look, this son of Nanda is not an ordinary person. The one who drank up the great fire with His mouth in a moment, this is the work of this very person. Oh we have understood, one who is the highest, the Supreme Being, Lord Viṣṇu, the eternal Nārāyaṇa, is here as incarnation, only to relieve the earth of its burden; there is no doubt about it. Oh dear, what to speak of our good fortune. We have got the association of

30. in *Śloka* metre.

that Nārāyaṇa, the father of the world. We are delivered."

*sūtra* ||

*ōhi buli śrīkṛṣṇaka praśaṁsiye : ābori gopagopīsaba : nayanabhramare mukhapaṅkajaka : preme pāna kariye rahala* ||

Direction: In this way praising Śrī Kṛṣṇa, surrounding him all around, the cowherd boys and girls, kept on looking with black bee-like eyes at the lotuslike face drinking its sweetness with love.

*śloka* ||

*govindo vādayan veṇuṁ gokulaṁ gopīgopakaiḥ* |
*sārdhaṁ yayau jagannātho harṣayan suhṛdo mudā* ||22||

Hymn[31] :Govinda, the Lord of the world, playing the flute with happiness, went to Gokula along with the cowherd boys and girls and friends with great pleasure.

*kathā sūtra* ||

*tadanantara : kālidamanabanabahnipāna : parama īśvara-līlā daraśie : śrīkṛṣṇa gopagopīsahita : dhenusaba āga kaya calaya : kṛṣṇaguṇa gāi : baṁśī śaṅkha śiṅgā bajāi : gopasaba jāi : gopīsaba parama premabhāve hariguṇagāi : kṛṣṇamukha-paṅkaja kaṭākṣe nirekhie : gokula calali : tāhe dekhaha śunaha : nirantare hari bola*||

Dialogue and Direction: Thereafter, exhibiting great sports of God such as taming of Kāli and drinking up the wildfire, Śrī Kṛṣṇa along with the cowherd boys and girls, taking the cows in front, started moving. The cowherd boys also went along praising Kṛṣṇa and playing the flute, the conch-shell and horns. The cowherd women went to Gokula singing the glories of Kṛṣṇa with great love and looking at the lotuslike face of Kṛṣṇa with sidelong glances. Watch and listen to that and keep chanting the name of Hari incessantly.

---

31. in *Śloka* metre.

*gīta || rāga kalyāṇa || kharamāna ||*
Song in the *Rāga Kalyāṇa* with the rhythm *Kharamāna:*

*dhruṁ ||*
*gokula calere murāru |*
*nīla śarīra : rañjita pīta jauti*
*ciruhīra*[32] *hemahāru ||*

Refrain: Murāri goes to Gokula with His blue body glowing bright with yellow (clothing), beautiful diamonds and a gold necklace.

*pada ||*
*bāvata beṇu :dhenu reṇu tanu :*
*kānu kautuka kaya jāi |*
*gopa śiśu saṅga : aṅga tribhaṅgima :*
*rūpe bhubana bhulāi ||*
*saṅginī raṅginī : gopinī gāve :*
*bhāve nīra jhurāve |*
*kānuka kamala amala muha heri*
*calali lahu lahu pāve ||*
*śrīrāma rāyā : hari rasa pāyā :*
*māyā karu nirajāna |*
*eku kṛṣṇaka : caraṇa parāyaṇa :*
*śaṅkara hari guṇa gāna ||14||*

Verse: Playing the flute and (covered) with dust from the cow hooves all over the body, Kānu goes along playfully with the cowherd boys, making everyone forget the world with the beauty of His form bending at three places.
Accompanying Him the happy cowherd women sang with full of love and tears flowing down from their eyes and looking at the clean and pure lotuslike face of Kānu, they walked with slow steps. Having found pleasure in the name of Hari, Śrī Rāma Rāyā had his illusion destroyed. Solely devoted to the feet of one and only Kṛṣṇa, Śaṅkara sings the praises of Hari.

---

32. *cāru hira.*

*kathā sūtra* ||

*aicana parama kautuka : keli kaya : śrīkṛṣṇa gopagopī sahita : gokula pāyi : parama ānande rahala* || *ohi gopālaka : kālidamana : banāgnipāna : līlā yātrā : jesaba loke śune bhaṇe : tāheka kṛṣṇa caraṇe : parama premabhakati bāḍhaba : ihā jāni nirantare hari bola* ||

Dialogue and Direction: In this way sporting with great pleasure, Śrī Kṛṣṇa, along with the cowherd boys and girls, reached Gokula and stayed there very happily. Those people who sing or listen to the *Kālidamana Banāgnipāna* play of this same Gopāla, their feeling of loving devotion at the feet of Kṛṣṇa will increase greatly. Knowing this, keep chanting the name of Hari incessantly.

*śloka* ||

*kṛṣṇasya kālidamanaṁ nāma yātrā cakāritā* |
*yannyunamadhikaṁ doṣaṁ kṣamatāṁ bhagavan prabhuḥ* ||23||
*namaḥ kṛṣṇāya rāmāya kāmāya mahate namaḥ* |
*namo'rabinda netrāya sadānandāya bhāsvate* ||24||

Hymn[33]: While performing the play *Kālidamana* of Kṛṣṇa, whatever fault, big or small was committed, please forgive them oh Lord. We pay our obeisance to Kṛṣṇa, Rāma and the most desirable one. Obeisance to the lotus-eyed, the (one who is) perpetually happy and the most bright and shining.

*bhaṭimā* || *muktimaṅgala* ||

Here is the eulogy which will lead to wellbeing and emancipation:

*daivaki udare : udaya johi devā : kayali bhakataka trāṇa* |
*agha baka dhenuka:keśī sabaṁśaka:kaṁsaka dhvaṁsala prāṇa*||
*birindā bipina: bihāra biśārada : śārada candra samāna* |
*sohi jagata guru : teri satate karu : mukuti maṅgala bidhāna* ||*1*||
*johi gopabadhu : bibidha bidharṣala : parirambhala bhuja meli* |
*johi yamunā jala : yāminī kāminī : mili kaya raṅga keli* ||

[33]. in *Śloka* metre.

*duṣṭa aristṣṭaka : muṣṭika moḍala : śaṅkhacūḍa lela prāṇa* |
*sohi jagataguru : teri satate karu : mukuti maṅgala bidhāna* ||2||
*johi bhūvikahuñ : bhāra uttārala : jina*[34] *jana pūrie kāma* |
*pāpī pāpaka : mūla upāḍe : ucari jākeri nāma* ||
*jāhe nāma śuni : nica svapaca muni : dohõ hove eku samāna* |
*sohi jagata guru : teri satate karu : mukuti maṅgala bidhāna* ||3||
*sohi baikuṇṭhaka kṛṣṇaka nāṭaka : utpāṭaka dukha mūla* |
*puṇyaka sañcana : kalimala dhvañcana : nāhi nāhi ohi tula* ||
*śuna sabhāsada : dekhu bicāri : bhelaha loka ekākāra* |
*dharamaka karamaka : āśā dūra kara : hari bine gati nāhi āra* ||4||
*śrīrāma rāi : hari bine nāyī : jāheri hṛdaya dhiyāna* |
*bhakatika śakati : jāheri milala : parama īśvara giāna* ||
*pāṣaṇḍa daṇḍana : maṇḍana bhakataka : hari rasa rasika sujāna* |
*kāli damana : karāvata nāṭaka : kṛṣṇa kiṅkara ohi bhāma*[35] ||5||
*śuna saba loi : bacanaka moi : sabateji bhaja hari pāva* |
*ohi bhava durgama : sāgaratarane kṛṣṇa pādapallaba nāva* ||
*devaka upari : rājā mādhava : dharamara upari nāma* |
*kauṭi kalapaka : pātaka nāśaka : ḍāki bolahu rāma rāma* ||6||

The God, who appeared in the womb of Devakī and saved the devotees, killed Agha, Baka, Dhenuka, Keśī and destroyed the life of Kaṁsa along with his family.

Roaming and sporting around in the well acquainted forests of Vṛndāvana, He looked like the autumnal moon. May He, the father of the world, constantly bestow upon you well being and salvation (1)

One who seduced the cowherd women and embraced them with open arms; one who, along with the beautiful women had amorous pastime with great pleasure in the waters of Yamunā at night.

(One who) crushed wicked Ariṣṭa and Muṣṭika and took the life of Śaṅkhacūḍa, may He, the father of the world, constantly bestow upon you well being and salvation. (2)

One who lightened the burden of the world and fulfilled

[34]. *nija.*

[35]. *bhāṇa.*

the wishes of His close ones; uttering whose name, sinners can uproot the cause of their sins.
Hearing whose name, even the lowest can become equal with the sage Svapas. May He, the father of the world, constantly bestow upon you well being and salvation. (3)
(Reading) the play regarding that same Kṛṣṇa of Vaikuṇṭha, eradicates the source of all miseries. And there is nothing comparable to it for accumulating more pious merits and destroying the impurities of the Age of Kali.
Please listen oh dear audience and consider carefully; all the people have become one; leave your hopes in ritualistic religious activities; there is no other way to salvation but the name of Hari. (4)
Śrī Rāma Rāyā, in whose heart, there is no one other than Hari to meditate upon and who, by the strength of his devotion, has acquired the knowledge of the Supreme Lord. To punish the heretics and to praise the devotees, one who is learned and knows the taste of the name of Hari, has made (us) perform this play *Kālidamana;* says thus, the servant of Kṛṣṇa. (5)
So, please listen all of you people to what I say and leaving everything else pray at the feet of Hari. For crossing this world formidable like the sea, take to the bud-like feet of Kṛṣṇa as (your) boat.
Mādhava is like the king above all the (other) gods, and above all the religious rituals is the name (of Kṛṣṇa), which destroys the sins of even one crore *kalpas*; hence, utter the name of Rāma loudly and repeatedly. (6)

*kālidamana yātrā pustaka samāpta*
Here ends the book, the play *Kālidamana.*

●●●

## 5.2

## *patnī prasāda nāṭa*

## The Play: Blessings to the Wives (of the *Brāhmaṇas*)

*śrī kṛṣṇāya namaḥ*
Obeisance to Śrī Kṛṣṇa.

*śloka* ||

*lakṣmyā oka nato nataḥ tava pade bhavabhavābhañjake*[1]
*vande nandanivāsavāsa danujaśrī-kacchidā-garvita* |
*padmāmodana sundarendu-dalitaprāya-prakāśa prabho*
*bhogavyālavalāvalepa paramākenāmṛtaṁ dehi bhoḥ* ||1||

Hymn[2]:

Abode of Lakṣmī, destroyer of all the fears of the people of this world, we bow down at your feet.
Prayer to the one who lives in the dwelling of Nanda and who is proud of destroying the super powers of the demons.
Oh Lord, you are the one who gives pleasure to Lakṣmī and you shine making the brightness of the moon looking pale.
You have forcefully controlled the expanded hood of the wicked serpent; please give us the great nectar from you, oh Lord (Viṣṇu)!

*atha bhaṭimā* 2 ||

*jaya jaya yadukula kamala prakāśaka*
*nāśaka kaṁsaka prāṇa* |
*jaya jaya jagataka bhakataka bhīti*
*niti karu nirajāna* ||
*jaya jaganāyaka mukuti dāyaka*
*sāyaka śāraṅga dhārī* ||
*duṣṭa ariṣṭaka muṣṭika moḍana*
*choḍana bandha murāri* ||

---

1. *bhaktasya bhībhañjake* is correct for metrical consideration.
2. in *Śārdūlavikrīḍita* metre.

*dharu govardhana* *bāraṇa bariṣaṇa*
*bheli indramada dūra* |
*tṛbhuvana kampaka* *kāli sarppaka*
*darppaka kayali cūra* ||
*nandaka nandana* *bandana devaka*
*sevaka jākeri sarbba* |
*gopa mukhe anna* *māgala bhāṅgala*
*dija nija karmmaka garbba* ||
*gokula jana jata* *tāraka māraka*
*kuvalaya dhenuka-nāçé* |
*putanikā tana* *śoṣaṇa moṣaṇa*
*toṣaṇa mana brajabāsī* ||
*e-dukha dāyaka*[3] *pāvaka bhāvaka*
*pūraṇa punu manakāma* |
*jagajana jāteka* *pāteka ghāteka*
*jākeri e-guṇa nāma* ||
*jāhe bhakati* *rakati śakati*
*tāraṇa ehu saṁsāra* |
*kīṭa paṭaṅgama* *jaṅgama saṅgama*
*bhakataka pāyi nistāra* ||
*sohi kṛṣṇaka* *ohi nāṭaka*
*utpāṭaka dukhamūla* |
*kalimala ānala*[4] *jānala mānala*
*nāhi nāhi ohi tula* ||
*śuna saba loyi* *hoyi noyi*
*dekhahu bacana bicāri* |
*iha saṁsāre* *sāra āora nāhi*
*cintahu caraṇa murāri* ||
*brahmā maheśvara* *cākara jākara*
*tākara guṇa nuhe lehu* |
*bāndhava mādhava* *sādhava mukuti*
*tāhe caraṇe citta dehu* ||
*ohi īśvara* *tāraka māraka*
*kāraka saba saṁsāra* |

3. *dāhaka*
4. *anala.*

*tāhe karu seva* *deva nāhi keva*
*nāhi nāhi haribine āra* ||
*jataye paramā* *dharamā karamā*
*sava kahu rājā nāma* |
*kṛṣṇaka kiṅkara* *kiṅkara śaṅkara*
*kaha saba bola rāma rāma* ||

Here is the eulogy: Glory to the one, who manifests as the lotus of the Yadu dynasty, and who is the annihilator of Kaṁsa.

Glory to the one, who always destroys the cause of fear to the devotees.

Glory to the one who sustains the world, the one who brings forth salvation; (the one) who holds the bow *Śāraṅga.*

(The one) who thrashed to death with his clenched fist the villainous Ariṣṭa and Muṣṭika, and he, Murāri, liberated the world.

(The one who) holding mount Govardhana up, warded off the rain, and thus destroyed the pride of Indra.

(The one who) vanquished the pride of the serpent Kāli who terrorised (the creatures of) the three worlds.

(The one who) is the son of Nanda, who is worshipped by the demigods and served by all.

(The one who) got the cowherd boys to ask for food, and (thus) destroyed the arrogance of the orthodox *brāhmaṇas,* attained through their ritualistic practices.

(The one who) protected all the people of Gokula by killing the dreaded Kuvalayapīḍa and Dhenuka.

(The one who) drew the life out of Pūtanā by sucking out her breast for the pleasure of all the inhabitants of Vraja.

(The one who) destroys all sufferings, but fulfills desires of the mind of those whose feelings are pure.

Creator of all the universe, chanting whose name and (remembering whose) attributes (*nāma-guṇa*) destroys all the sinners of the world.

By the strength of love and devotion unto Him one may get

saved from this world (the circle of rebirth).
All the worms and insects and all living beings attain salvation in the company of a devotee.
This drama, which will be the cause of destruction to the root of all sufferings, is concerning that Lord Kṛṣṇa.
He (Kṛṣṇa) acts like fire in relation to the evils of the Age of Kali, and it is known and accepted that there is none comparable to Him.
Please listen, all of you dear people, analyse and try to find out whether it is true or not that in this world there is nothing else more meaningful; hence concentrate in the feet of Murāri.
Do not sing the names and praises of Brahmā and Maheśvara, who are the mere servants to Him;
concentrate heartily on the feet of Mādhava only, who is the friend to all, and who will bring forth salvation.
He is the Lord; who creates, protects and destroys the whole world, so serve Him (Lord Kṛṣṇa) as there is no God other than Hari.
*Nāma* (the name and attributes of Hari, Kṛṣṇa) is the Lord over all religious and ritualistic activities.
The servant of Kṛṣṇa, the servant Śaṅkara, says to all to chant "Rāma-Rāma!".

*sūtra* ||

*āhe sāmājika loka : johi jagataka parama guru : puruṣottama : sohi nandanandana rūpe kahõ : anna-prārthanā cale : biprasarbbaka karmma garbba dūra kayala : patnīsabaka parama prasāda delaha : bālakasabaka ṣaḍarasa annabhojana karāvala : sohi patnīprasāda nāma nāṭa : ohi sabhāmadhye kautuke karaba : tāhe dekhaha śunaha : nirantare hari bola hari* ||

Direction: Oh, dear assembled people! The one who is the ultimate father of the world, the best of all the human beings, the same (he), as the son of Nanda, in the pretext of asking for food deflated the vain-glorious *brāhmaṇas* of their pride of being experts in ritualistic exercises, rewarded the wives with His greatest blessings and fed all the (cowherd) boys with sumptuous food of various tastes. That is what is enacted in the drama by the name *Patnī-Prasāda* for the pleasure of the assembled public; watch and listen to that and keep chanting the name of Hari (Kṛṣṇa).

*gīta* || *rāga kānaḍā* || *paritāla*
Song in the *Rāga Kānaḍā* with the rhythm *Paritāla:*

*dhruṁ* ||
*āvata dvijasava kau parabeśa* |
*tapa upabāse śarīra bhela kleśa* ||
Refrain: The *brahmaṇas* came entering with emaciated bodies on account of austerity and fasting.

*pada*||
*hāte gale śira rudrākṣa jhāṇṭājhoṭa* |
*bhobakāra dāri-gopha carācara phoṭa* ||
*ucārata vedamantra alpa kari hāsa* |
*cāndaka jauti daśana parakāśa* ||
*bino haribhakati biphala svargakāma* |
*harika hṛdaye dhari bola rāma rāma* ||*1*||

Verse: Bunches of rosaries of *rudrākṣa* dangling from their hands, necks and heads; their faces all covered with long moustache and beard and with big wide sacred mark covering the forehead; and chanting hymns from the *Veda*, smiling slightly, exposing their teeth bright like the moonlight. But without devotion to Hari, the aspiration for heaven is futile. Hence, keeping Hari in the heart, chant repeatedly the name of Rāma.

*sūtra* ||

*aicana prabeśa kaye biprasaba yajña karite lāgala* || *tadanantare rāmakṛṣṇa gopagaṇa sahite jaise prabeśa kayala : tā dekhaha śunaha: nirantare hari bola hari* ||

Direction: Thus entering, the *brāhmaṇas* started performing religious sacrifices; thereafter, as Rāma (Balarāma) and Kṛṣṇa, along with the cowherd boys, entered, watch and listen to that, and keep chanting the name of Hari incessantly.

*gīta : rāga : āsoāri : ekatāla*

Song in the *Rāga Āśovārī* with the rhythm *Ekatāla:*

*dhruṁ* ||

*āvata kānu beṇu bajāi* |
*calali saṅge gopa hariguṇa gāi* ||

Refrain: Here comes Kānu (Kṛṣṇa) playing the flute and the cowherd boys come along singing praises of Hari.

*pada* ||

*śyāma mūruti dīpita pītabāsa* |
*kaṇṭhe kadambamālā kayo layalāsa* ||
*hāra mukuṭa maṇi kuṇḍala ḍola* |
*kṛṣṇa kiṅkara ohi śaṅkara bola* ||2||

Verse: Dark in form, bright with yellow coloured attire, garland of *kadamba* flowers swaying gracefully from the neck, adorned with necklaces, a crown, gems, and dangling earrings; says thus Śaṅkara, the servant of Kṛṣṇa.

*sūtra* ||

*śrīkṛṣṇa aicana prabeśa kaye kahō: balabhadra sahite: aśokamūle rahala: tadanantara bālaka saba gobatsasabaka jalapāna karāvala: apunujala bhojana kayala: parama khudhātura hayā: rāmata kṛṣṇata jaice gocara kayala: tā dekhaha śunaha* ||

Direction: Entering (the scene) in this way, Śrī Kṛṣṇa along with Balabhadra stayed under the *aśoka* tree; then the cowherd boys made the calves drink water, and drank water themselves as well. Being very hungry, how they complained to Rāma (Balarāma) and Kṛṣṇa, watch and listen to that.

*kathā* ||

*bālakasaba bola : he rāma : he kṛṣṇa : tohõ hāmāra parama jīvana : āju parabhāte bhojana karaye nāhi : hāmu dadhi anna saṅge nāhi ānala :*
*kṣudhāye parama pīḍita hai āchi : ihā jāni kṣudhānibāraṇa upāya cintaha*||

Dialogue: The boys said, "Oh Rāma (Balarāma)! Oh Kṛṣṇa! You are our ultimate life; we did not have our meals this morning, and we haven't brought curd and rice with us today; we are suffering very much from hunger; knowing this, think out some way to satiate our hunger."

*sūtra* ||

*bālakasabaka bacana śuniye : śrī-kṛṣṇa bihasi bolala* ||

Direction: Listening to the words of the boys, smiling a little, Śrī Kṛṣṇa said:

*kathā* ||

*kṛṣṇa bola : āhe sakhisaba : oḥ bhallakahala : hāmo je bolõ tā śunah : ohi āśrama madhye biprasaba svargakāme yajña karitece : beda śāstrata pārgata : parama sampanna : tārāsabaka āge : dadāra hāmāra nāma dhari : anna prārthanā kara giyā* ||

Sūtradhāra says, "Kṛṣṇa said, 'Oh friends, oh you have said well; listen to what I say. In that hermitage, the *brāhmaṇas* are performing sacrifices in the hope of attaining heaven. Go to those *brāhmaṇas* who are experts in the *Veda-śāstras* and quite able; go there and in the name of elder brother (Balarāma) and me, ask for food."

*sūtra* ||

*ohi buli śrī-kṛṣṇa maune rahala : bālakasaba śrī-kṛṣṇaka ājñā śira dhari kahõ : yajñaśālā prabeśa bhela : biprasabaka dekhiye : namaskāra kari kara jori ye bolaye lagala : tā śunaha* ||

Direction: Saying thus, Śrī Kṛṣṇa remained silent. The cowherd boys, following the advice of Śrī Kṛṣṇa, entered the place of sacrifice, and seeing the *brāhmaṇas* there, greeted them with folded hands and as they spoke, listen to that.

*kathā* ||

*bālakasaba bolā : āhe gurusaba : torāsaba parama paṇḍita : yajñadāna brate parama nirmmala huyācha : ohi aśokamūle : gopagaṇa sahite rāma-kṛṣṇa : parama khudhātura hayā : anna prārpthi paṭhāvala : jebe śraddhā ācaya : anna beñjana pracura devaha : anna dāne jena puṇya : apune jānaha : ajñānaka śikṣāvaha : torāsabaka āge hāmu ki kahaba* ||

Dialogue: The boys said: "Oh respectable masters! You are the most learned; you have been purified by regular observance of the vow of performing sacrifices, offering alms and observing penances. There, under the *aśoka* tree, awaits Rāma (Balarāma) and Kṛṣṇa along with the cowherd boys, and they being very hungry have sent us here to beg for food; if you have respect for them give us plenty of rice and other foodstuffs. You know yourself the merit of giving away food (to the hungry). You are the ones who educate the ignorant; what shall we say in front of you."

*sūtra*||

*ohi boli bārambāra:gopasabe prārthanā kayala:gurusabe śunaye nāhi:o śunio gaṇaganna karaye nāhi:sohi samaye eka candrabhāratī brāhmaṇe parama krodhe je bolala:tāhe śunaha*||

Direction: Saying thus, the boys prayed again and again, but the masters did not listen to them; even hearing them, did not pay any heed. At that moment, as one *brāhmaṇa*, called Candrabhāratī, said with great anger; listen to that.

*kathā* ||

*brāhmaṇa bola* || *āhe govālasaba : hāmu bedata śāstrata parama pārgata: yajñabrata dāne parama pavitra : o hāmu bhudevatā : hāmāka sarbbaloke pujaya : nandasuta kṛṣṇa : hāmāka āge kona haya* ||

Direction: *Brāhmaṇa* said: "Oh you cowherd boys! We are great experts in the *Vedas* and all the scriptures; performing sacrifices, observing fasts and making gifts, we are absolutely pure; we are the gods in the earth; all the people worship us. Who is Kṛṣṇa, the son of Nanda, before us?"

*sūtra* ||

*ohi boli brāhmaṇa maune rahala* | *tadanantara śiśusabe anyo anye kheda karate lāgala* ||

*bālakasaba bola* || *āhe sakhisaba : ōhi biprasaba : sakala yajñamūrti devaka devatā kṛṣṇaka jānaye nāhi : ārāsaba parama murukha* ||

Direction: Saying thus, the *brāhmaṇa* remained silent. Thereafter, the boys expressed regrets to one another. The boys said, "Oh friends, see, these *brāhmaṇas* do not know Kṛṣṇa, who is the manifestation of all and is the God of all gods. They are all complete fools."

*sūtra* ||

*ohi boli śiśusabe gayā kahō : kṛṣṇaka āgu je bolaya : tā dekhaha śunaha*||

Direction: Saying so, going to Kṛṣṇa what the boys said, watch and listen to that.

*kathā* ||

*śiśusaba bola : he kṛṣṇa : tohō hāmāka badarthanā*[5] *kayala : heno abaiṣṇava thāne paṭhāvala : ārā karmmagarbbe parama dāmbhika : o tohmāra kathā gaṇaye nāhi* ||

Dialogue: The boys said, "Oh Kṛṣṇa, you have insulted us by

5. *kadarthanā.*

sending us to such a place of non-believers; they are all very proud of their performing rituals and they do not care for you at all."

*sūtra* ||

*ohi boli śiśusaba maune rahala : tadanantara śrī-kṛṣṇa śiśusabaka je bolala tāhe dekhaha śunaha : nirantare hari bola hari* ||

Direction: Saying thus, the boys remained silent. Thereafter, what Śrī Kṛṣṇa told to the cowherd boys, watch and listen to that and continue chanting the name of Hari.

*payāra* || *rāga-śrī* || *paritāla*

Verse in the *Rāga Śrī* with the rhythm *Paritāla:*

*śuniyā sidhānta pāche dilanta mādhave* |
*kona no prārthake nāhi parābhava pāve* ||
*tathāpi prārthanā neḍai śuna sakhigaṇa* |
*biprapatnī sabata māgiyo gaiyā anna* ||
*sito strīsaba mota bhakta biparīta* |
*dehā mātra gṛhata motese prāṇa cītta* ||
*tāsambāta kaiba āmi āsibāra kathā* |
*lāge māne pāibā anna beñjana sarbathā* ||
*hena śuni laḍi gaila gopagaṇa pāche* |
*dekhilā sakale dvija bhāryyā jaita āche* ||
*sabe sālaṅkṛtā sucaritā bara nārī* |
*bulibe lāgilā gopacaya jānu pāri* (||3||)

Hearing them, Mādhava offered his conclusion, "Listen, oh friends! Is there any beggar who has never faced humiliation? Even then, a beggar does not stop begging. (Hence) Go to the wives of the *brāhmaṇas*, and ask them for food; contrary to their husbands (the *brāhmaṇas*) their wives are my great devotees, who have merely their bodies at home, and their heart and soul are only with me. Tell them about my coming here, and you will get rice and other edibles as much as you want." Hearing this, the cowherd boys went running and saw where all the wives of the *brāhmaṇas* were. All the women were well-adorned with ornaments and very well behaved; (and) the cowherd boys started addressing them on their knees.

*sūtra* ||

*brāhmaṇīsabaka dekhiye : kara jori : namaskāra kaya : śiśusaba je bolala tā dekhaha śunaha* ||

Direction: Seeing the wives of the *brāhmaṇas*, bowing before them with folded hands, what the boys said, watch and listen to that.

*kathā* ||

*śiśusaba bola : he mātāsaba : ōhi rāma-kṛṣṇa : bālakasaba sahite : ohi aśoka mūle thika : parama khudhātura huyā : torāsabata anna beñjana prārthi paṭhāvala* ||

Dialogue: The children said: "Oh mothers, Rāma and Kṛṣṇa along with the boys, are waiting under the *aśoka* tree; (and) being very hungry, we have been sent to ask for rice and vegetables from you."

*sūtra* ||

*ohi śuni brāhmaṇīsaba param hariṣe ulasi uṭhala : āge bāḍhi parama sādare pucaye lāgala* ||

Direction: Hearing this, the wives of the *brāhmaṇas* became elated with great pleasure, and coming forward, started enquiring with much enthusiasm.

*kathā* ||

*brāhmaṇīsaba bola : he bālakasaba : sohi nandanandana kṛṣṇaka : hāmu ōhi cakṣuve dekhaba* ||

Dialogue: The wives of the *brāhmaṇas* said, "Oh dear boys, shall we see Kṛṣṇa, the son of Nanda, with our own eyes?".

*bālakasaba bola : he mātāsaba : ā : dekhaba* ||
The boys said: "Oh mothers, yes, you will see Him."

*sūtra* ||

*õhi śuni brāhmaṇīsaba : parama haraṣita mane : śrī-kṛṣṇaka prati:parama sugandhi ,nna beñjana : piṭhāpanā paramānna : panasa śukla cini : bahubidha ṣaḍrasa : bicitra pātrabhari laiyā kahõ : jaise calala : tā dekhaha śunaha nirantare hari bola hari* ||

Direction: Hearing this, the minds of the wives of the *brāhmaṇas* were filled with great happiness; they had bowls of different designs filled with sweet-smelling rice and vegetables, cakes and rice pudding, jackfruit, white sugar and many other varieties of food-articles of six different tastes and as they carried them for Kṛṣṇa, watch and listen to that, and keep chanting the name of Hari incessantly.

*gīta* || *rāga dhanaśrī* || *ekatāla*
Song in the *Rāga Dhanaśrī* in the rhythm *Ekatāla:*

*hāsi hāsi cale māi : haridaraśana lāyī*
*preme pulaka kāi : nayana jhurāite jāi* || *dhruṁ* ||

The women go smiling to have a glance of Hari. The body shivering with excitement out of love, they go to appease their eyes. Refrain.

*pada* ||

*jāhe nāma śuni satī : nachāḍe bhakati rati re* |
*pekhabõ kamalāpati : nāce jaicana satī* ||
*cale saba sakhigaṇa : ānande magaṇa mana re* |
*kṛṣṇa kiṅkara bhāṇa : gati meri nārāyaṇa* ||4||

Verse: Hearing whose name the virtuous women do not give up loving devotion.

The virtuous women as if dance at the prospect of seeing Kamalāpati.

All the friends go together with their minds engrossed in love,

The servant of Kṛṣṇa, (Śaṅkara) says, "The only refuge for me is Nārāyaṇa."

*sūtra* ||

*aicana prakāre brāhmaṇīsaba : śrī kṛṣṇaka dekhite calala : sohi samaye brāhmaṇasabe : jaise niṣedhala : tā dekhaha* ||

Direction: In this way, while the wives of the *brāhmaṇas* went to see Śrī Kṛṣṇa, the way the *brāhmaṇas* tried to debar them from going, watch that.

*kathā* ||

*brāhmaṇasaba bola : āhe brāhmaṇīsaba : torāsaba ki dekhala ki śunala : yajña kārya parihari govālaka pācu pācu : katī hõ jāva : hā hā torāsaba bhraṣṭā bheli* ||

Dialogue: The *brāhmaṇas* said : "Oh all the wives of *brāhmaṇas*, what have you seen and heard, leaving behind all the sacrificial rituals, why are you going after the cowherd boys; where are you going? Alas! Alas! All of you have fallen!".

*sūtra* ||

*aicana prakāre brāhmaṇasabe bahubidha bādhā kayala : pitṛputrabhātṛsabe niṣedha bolaya : haribhaktirase ākula hayā : tārāsaba śunaye nāhi | sohi samaye eka brāhmaṇa brāhmaṇīka gṛha madhye āchite jāni dvāra bandha kaya rākhala | tadanantara : kṛṣṇa daraśana āśābhaṅge : brāhmaṇī kṛṣṇaka caraṇa hṛdaye dhariye jaice prāṇa tejala : tāhe dekhaha śunaha : nirantare hari bola hari* ||

Direction: In this way, the *brāhmaṇas* hindered (them) in many different ways; their fathers, sons and brothers asked them not to go; (but) being engrossed in the deep feeling of devotion for Hari, they did not listen. At that time, one particular *brāhmaṇa*, knowing that his wife was inside the house, locked the door. Thereupon, the expectation of seeing Kṛṣṇa being thwarted, how the wife of that *brāhmaṇa*, holding the feet of Kṛṣṇa in her heart, gave up her life, watch and listen to that; and keep chanting the name of Hari incessantly.

*gīta || rāga belovāra || rūpaka tāla*
Song in the *Rāga Belovāra* with the rhythm *Rūpaka*:

*haripada pekhaye napāvali māi*
*phokāraye ghane ghana, nayana jhurāi || dhruṁ ||*
"Oh mother, (you) have failed to see the feet of Hari, and weeping again and again, your eyes are flowing tears." Refrain.

*pada ||*

*bandhu bijoga*[6] *āgi prāṇa phuṭi jāi |*
*aruṇa caraṇa mane rahali dhiyāi ||*
*choḍi parala prāṇa dhari hari pāve |*
*pāvali gati satī śaṅkare gāve ||5||*

Verse: Life (nearly) leaves (the body) in the fire of separation from a friend; meditating upon the red feet; (and) holding the red feet of Hari (in the heart), (she) fell down lifeless. Thus, the virtuous woman attained salvation, sings Śaṅkara.

*aicana prakāre brāhmaṇī prāṇa tejala : tadanantara brāhmaṇe dekhiye : hā hā buli : hṛdaye muṭhi hāni : brāhmaṇīka gale bāndhiye : guṇa barṇāi jaise kāndite lāgala tāhe dekhaha śunaha : nirantare hari bola hari bola || ikathā rahoka : tadanantara je brāhmaṇīsaba kṛṣṇadaraśana āse calacai : tārāsabaka bahubidha bādhā kaya : rākhite nāhi pārala : haribhakataka jaise bighini laṅghaye nāhi : tārāsaba parama hariṣe kṛṣṇaka samīpa pāvala ||*

In this way the wife of the *brāhmaṇa* ended her life; after that, seeing (her dead), crying "Alas! Alas!", imparting blows on his bosom and holding her onto his neck, how the *brāhmaṇa* began lamenting describing her virtues; watch

[6]. *biyoga.*

and listen to that; and keep chanting the name of Hari incessantly. Let this matter rest here. After that, those wives of the *brāhmaṇas* who went in the hope of seeing Kṛṣṇa, were prevented in many ways, but could not be stopped. As the devotees of Hari cannot be prevented by any obstacle; they reached near Kṛṣṇa with great pleasure.

*atha bhaṭimā* ||

*aśoka bana maha rahala murāri* |
*pekhala gaiyā saba dvija kumārī* ||
*śyāma śarīra basana tathi pīta* |
*navaghana jaise camake taḍita* ||
*nindi indu kauṭi bayana bikāśa* |
*banduli adhika adhara parakāśa* ||
*nāsā unnata tīlaphula bhrānti* |
*utima motima daśanaka pānti* ||
*aruṇa nayan duhõ paṅkaja pātā* |
*rucikara kara duhõ utapala rātā* ||
*māthe mayura pucca alaka kapola* |
*karṇe nava duhõ utapala ḍola* ||
*lambita bāhu duhõ ratana molāna* |
*bahala hṛdaye geru karu paridhāna* ||
*kara kaṅkaṇa keura jhātiskāra* |
*gale banamālā ratanamaya hāra* ||
*ratanaka mekhalā śohe kaṭita* |
*māṭi loṭi pāṭa dhati pīta* ||
*aruṇa caraṇa duhõ paṅkaja koṣa* |
*ratana mañjīra karaya tathi ghoṣa* ||
*māṇika ujhāi aṅgulika pānti* |
*nakhacaya cāndrakaya tathi kānti* ||
*padatala ārakata pekhi mana mohe* |
*java-paṅkaja-dhvaja-aṅkuśa śohe* ||
*tṛbhubana mohana naṭabara beśa* |
*caubhiti beḍhiyā rahu gopa niśeṣa* ||

*nīla padma phurāvata hāta |*
*pekhala dvija badhusaba sākṣāta ||*
*koṭi madana āge nuhi thiva |*
*pekhi juḍāvata tanu mana jīva ||*
*amṛta pāne jacha milala āhlāda |*
*pāvala dvijabadhu parama prasāda ||*
*kayali āgu daṇḍa paraṇāma |*
*pūrala sabahu āpona manakāma ||*
*kṛṣṇa kiṅkara kaha dharmma upāma |*
*ḍāki sabahi bolahu rāma rāma ||*

Here is the eulogy: Murāri was waiting in the *aśoka* forest, where the *brāhmaṇa* maidens went and saw Him.

Dark in body and wearing yellow clothing thereon, He looked like lightning flashing on a new cloud.

The face illuminating, surpassed millions of moon.

The lips shone belittling the beauty of *banduli* flower.

The nose pointed, gave an illusion of sesame flower.

Rows of teeth looked like the best of pearls.

The two reddish eyes looked like the petals of a lotus flower, and the two charming palms looked like red water lilies.

Peacock plumes were on the head and locks of hair fell on the forehead.

In the ears hung two fresh water lilies.

The long arms made even the (valuable) gems look pale.

The wide chest was covered with saffron clothing.

The arms were decorated with armlets and bracelets.

In the neck, a garland of wild flowers and necklaces made of different gems were hanging.

Hips were covered with a beautiful loin cloth (waist-band) made of gems, while the yellow *dhoti* made of silk trailed on ground.

Two ruddy feet looked like two lotus buds and jewelled anklets tinkled thereon.

The rows of fingers dazzled with rings of ruby, and the nails glowed with the brightness of the moon

The mind was charmed to see the rosy feet, which were adorned with barley seed, lotus, flag and an elephant hook.
In the form of a master-dancer, encircled by all the cowherd boys, enchanted the three worlds.
The wives of the *brāhmaṇas* saw Him (Kṛṣṇa) in person playing with the blue lotus in His hand.
Even millions of Madana could not equal Him.
Seeing Him, pacified the body and mind of all the living beings.
The wives of the *brāhmaṇas* obtained such excellent bliss as is obtained by drinking divine nectar.
They all paid their obeisance prostrating (on the ground) in front of Him and all had their wishes fulfilled.
The servant of Kṛṣṇa says, that this is the best of all faiths, (and hence), all of you chant aloud "Rāma-Rāma!".

*śloka* ||

*śyāmaṁ hiraṇyaparidhiṁ vanamālyavarha-*
*dhātu-pravālanaṭaveṣamanubratāṁse* |
*vinyasta hastamitareṇa dhunānamabjaṁ-*
*karṇotpalālakakapolamukhābjahāsam* ||2||

Hymn[7] : Dark blue (in complexion) with a golden halo around, decorated with garland of wild flowers, gems and corals, blue lotuses hanging from the ears, with one hand held in the pose of blessings to the devotees while waving a lotus with the other, and curls (of hair) on the cheeks and a smile in the lotuslike face, all in the form of a master dancer, appeared very charming.

*kathā* ||

*aicana rūpa pekhiye : brāhmaṇīsaba : ṣaḍarasa-anna : kṛṣṇaka āge nibedana kayala : daṇḍavate paḍi namaskāra kayala : uṭhi kahõ ānanda mūrttika nayane nirekhiye : hṛdaye āliṅgana kaye kahõ : parama premata maune rahala : tadanantara tārāsabara prema bhakati dekhiye : śrī kṛṣṇa ye bolala : tāhe śunaha*||.

[7]. in *Vasantatilakā* metre

Dialogue: Seeing such beauty, the wives of the *brāhmaṇas* offered before Kṛṣṇa, rice (and food-articles) of six different tastes; bowed to Him lying prostrate on the ground; then rising from the ground and looking at that form which gives pleasure, embraced Him in their hearts, and became speechless with deep love. Thereupon, seeing their deep love and devotion, what Kṛṣṇa said to them, listen to that.

*kathā* ||

*kṛṣṇa bola : āhe brāhmaṇīsaba : kuśale āvala : tohõsaba parama bhāgyavatī : hāmu tohāra kona kārya sādhõ : tāheka satvare kaha : pati putra suhṛdasabara bādhā nagani kahõ : hāmāka dekhite āvala : aḥ : tumisaba bhakatara henaya lakṣaṇa : parama catura mahā bibeki jārāsaba : tārāsaba hāmāka niṣkāme bhajaya : torāsabara premabhakati : hāmāka baśya kayala : idānika tumisabe : brāhmaṇasabara yajñasthāne jāva : hāmāra sanmata ohi* ||

Dialogue: Kṛṣṇa said, "Oh dear wives of *brāhmaṇas*, could you reach here safely? You all are very fortunate. Tell me quickly what I can do for you? Without heeding the resistance from your husbands, sons and well-wishers you have come to see me; these are the characteristics of devotees like you! The most intelligent and discreet ones worship me without expecting any return. But your loving devotion has conquered me. Now, you all go back to the sacrificial place of the *brāhmaṇas*. That is my advice."

*sūtra* ||

*õhi boli śrī kṛṣṇa maune rahala : tadanantara brāhmaṇīsaba : nairāśa bacana śuni : śrī kṛṣṇaka je bolala : tāhe dekhaha śunaha : nirantare hari bola hari* ||

Direction: Saying thus, Śrī Kṛṣṇa remained silent; thereafter, hearing such disheartening words, what the wives of the *brāhmaṇas* said to Śrī Kṛṣṇa, watch and listen to that; and keep chanting the name of Hari incessantly.

*gīta* || *rāga āsoāri* || *māna ekatāli*
Song in the *Rāga Aśovārī* in the rhythm *Ekatāli:*

*tohāri caraṇe mana majāilõ madhusūdana* |
*katīnā bolasi nātha : kaṭhina bacana ghana* || *dhruṁ* ||

We have engrossed our minds in your feet only, oh Madhusūdana; why do you speak such extremely harsh words, oh Lord! Refrain.

*pada* ||

*gṛha pati suta dhana : suhṛda sodara jana* |
*pekhi bikha sama mana : tejalohõ nārāyaṇa* ||
*tohāri kiṅkarī jana : punu nakarabi chana* |
*kṛṣṇa kiṅkara bhāṇa : gati meri nārāyaṇa* ||6||

Verse: Seeing the poisonous minds of our husbands, dear sons, friends and brothers at home, we have deserted them, oh Nārāyaṇa; we are your servants, please do not evade us again. The servant of Kṛṣṇa says, Nārāyaṇa is the ultimate refuge for me.

*kathā* ||

*brāhmaṇīsaba bola* || *he śrī kṛṣṇa : tohõ*[8] *bhakata batsala : beda śāstrata hāmu śunaichi : bhakatara naṣṭa nāhi : sohi bacana sāphala karaha : hāmāka tejabi nāhi : sohi patiputrasabe : hāmāka thāna nāhi devaba : hāmu gṛhe kamane bañcaba : tohāri caraṇa : nirmālya tulasī : tāheka śira dhari kahõ : dāsī huyā rahõ* ||

Dialogue: The wives of the *brāhmaṇas* said, "Oh Śrī Kṛṣṇa, you are very loving to your devotees. We have heard from the *Vedas* that (your) devotees are never lost. (Please) make that saying meaningful and do not renounce us. Those (our) husbands and sons will not allow us to stay in their homes (again). How shall we stay at home? Holding your feet on our heads, like we take a *tulasī* leaf offered to the deity, we wish to remain your servants."

---

[8]. *tohõ*

*sūtra*||

*õhi buli brāhmaṇīsaba : śrī kṛṣṇaka āge : bahubidha kātara kaya maune rahala tadanantara śrī kṛṣṇa : tārāsabaka je bolala : tāhe dekhaha śunaha* ||

Direction: In this way, beseeching Śrī Kṛṣṇa in many ways, the wives of the *brāhmaṇas*, remained silent. Thereafter, what Śrī Kṛṣṇa said to them, watch and listen to that.

*katha* ||

*kṛṣṇa bola : he brāhmaṇīsaba : torāsabaka pati putre asūyā karaba nāhi : hāmu hṛdaye thāki anumati deña : jabe pratyaya nāhi jāva: taba devatāsabaka bākye pramāṇa lava* |

Dialogue: Kṛṣṇa said, "Oh the wives of the *brāhmaṇas*, your husbands and sons will not slander you. I assure you from my heart. If you are not convinced, then take the proof from the words of the demigods."

*sūtra*||

*õhi boli śrī kṛṣṇa devatāsabaka : āniye pratyeke*[9] *jaise dekhāvala: tāhe dekhaha śunaha* ||

*devatāsaba bola* || *āhe mātāsaba : torāsabaka kāhue asūyā karaba nāhi : hāmu devatāsabe jānõ* ||

Direction: Saying so, how Śrī Kṛṣṇa brought in and showed all the demigods in person, watch and listen to that.

The Gods said, "Oh mothers, no one will be angry with you; we Gods know that."

*sūtra*||

*õhi boli devatāsaba antardhyāna bhela : brāhmaṇīsaba debaka bacane : kṛṣṇaka cāraye nāhi : punaḥ : śrī kṛṣṇa bihasi bolala* ||

Direction: Saying thus, the demigods disappeared. The wives of the *brāhmaṇas* did not leave Kṛṣṇa (even after) hearing the word of the demigods. Then again, Śrī Kṛṣṇa said smiling.

[9]. *pratyakṣe.*

*he brāhmaṇīsaba : bidūre thākiye : śravaṇa kīrtana bhaktiye : hāmāka jaise baśya karaya : nikaṭe thākite : simate bhakati karite nāhi pāraya : jaise amṛta pāna karite : mukhe rucaye nāhi : ihā jāni torāsaba sighre calaha* ||

"Oh, the wives of the *brāhmaṇas*, staying in distance (and) listening and chanting with devotion, as you have conquered me; you cannot practise the same kind of devotion staying near me, like having nectar continuously stops pleasing the palate. Hence, knowing this, all of you leave immediately."

*sūtra* ||

*ōhi boli śrīkṛṣṇa maune rahala : brāhmaṇīsaba kṛṣṇaka bacana bādhite nāhi pāri : preme krandana kaya jaice gṛhe calala : tā dekhaha śunaha : nirantare hari bola hari* ||

Direction: Saying so, Śrī Kṛṣṇa remained silent. Unable to oppose the words of Kṛṣṇa, crying out of love, how the wives of the *brāhmaṇas* went home, watch and listen to that; (and) keep chanting the name of Hari incessantly.

*gīta* || *rāga gaurī* || *jyotirmāna*

Song in the *Rāga Gaurī* with the rhythm *Jyotirmāna:*

*mohe mādhava : kayali bañchita :*
*dahe dehā saba āgiyā*|
*lahu lahu dhāyi : nayāna*[10] *jhurāyī*
*nacale cītta gṛha lāgiyā* || *dhruṁ* ||

"You have deprived us, oh Mādhava, the body burns in the fire (of leaving you). (We are) moving slowly with tears flowing from the eyes, and the mind does not want to move homewards." Refrain.

*pada* ||

*kṛṣṇa caraṇa : teji jāite : jaisana jīva jāi*
*bahuri nayana : cānda bayana : punu punu cāhe māyi* ||
*kañja locana : dukha mocana : katihu caraṇa calāyi* |
*hā hari hā hari : buliyā rahali : kṛṣṇakīṅkara gāi* ||7||

[10]. *nayana.*

Direction: Leaving the feet of Kṛṣṇa, it is as if the life stops. Turning their eyes, the mothers (women) looked at the moonlike face again and again; they moved their feet haltingly, looking at the lotus-eyed, reliever of all sorrows; they kept uttering "Oh Hari, Oh Hari!"; sings the servant of Kṛṣṇa.

*sūtra*||

*aicana prakāre brāhmaṇīsaba : gṛhe gayā kahõ : kṛṣṇaka hṛdaye dhari : anyeanye kṛṣṇaguṇa śravaṇa-kīrtana kariye rahala : tadanantara brāhmaṇasaba : patnīsabara parama premabhāva bhakati pekhiye : jaice āpunāka dhiskāra*[11] *kayala : tā dekhaha śunaha* ||

Direction: In this way the wives of the *brāhmaṇas* (after) reaching home, holding Kṛṣṇa in their hearts, remained listening and chanting the glories of Kṛṣṇa to one another. After that, seeing the great love and devotion of their wives, as the *brāhmaṇas* reproached themselves, watch and listen to that.

*kathā* ||

*biprasaba bola : he miśra, he kandali, he ācāryya, he bhāratī : ohi brāhmaṇīsaba śaucācāra hīna : beda śāstra jānaye nāhi : gurusevā paramadharmabarjjita : ārāsabara śrīkṛṣṇata parama prema bhakati bhela : āḥ ! hāmusaba strīto adhama bhelõ : karmma garbbe andha hayā : kṛṣṇaka jānite nāhi pāralõ : je kṛṣṇa sarbba yajñamūrti : bedaro udbhava bhūmi : lakṣmī jāhera caraṇa kīṅkarī : āpune nijānande purnna : sohi kṛṣṇe hāmāta anna māgi paṭhāvala : hāmusaba tāhera prārthanā bhaṅga kayalõ : hāmusaba brahmacaryya brata dhari : guruka śuśrūṣā kari : je bedasaba paḍhalõ ihāka dhiskāra rahoka : āḥ nijakarmme buddhihata bhelõ : para upadeśata paṇḍita bolachi : ihāka dhikkāra āśoka : āḥ hāmusaba brajaka jayeñ : kṛṣṇaka dekhaba : pāve dhariye : kātara kariye minati karaba : sohi bhakata batsala deva : hāmāra aparādha cāraba* ||

[11]. *dhikkāra*

Dialogue: The *brāhmaṇas* said: "Oh Miśra, oh Kandalī, oh Ācāryya, oh Bhāratī, (see) these our wives do not know the rites of purification; do not know anything about the *Vedas*; away from the noble practice of worshipping the preceptors; yet they have developed great love and devotion for Śrī Kṛṣṇa. Alas! We have fallen lower than the women. Being proud of ritualistic exercises, we became blind; we failed to realise Kṛṣṇa. That Kṛṣṇa is the form unto whom all the sacrifices are offered; the source of the *Vedas*; even Goddess Lakṣmī is a servant at whose feet; He is the one who is blissful by Himself; that same Kṛṣṇa, had sent for food from us, and we have turned down His request. Whatever *Vedas* we have learnt, observing the vow of celibacy and offering services to our teachers, let all those be condemned. Ah, we have become fools out of our own actions. We are said to be learned, giving advice to others. Let it be condemned. Ah, let us go to Vraja: we will see Kṛṣṇa; holding onto His feet we will entreat Him earnestly. He is the God, most kind and loving to his devotees; He will forgive our faults."

*sūtra* ||

*ohi buli : brāhmaṇasaba calite nicaya kayala : sohi samaye : eka bṛddha brāhmaṇa : lāṭhita bhira diye : gṛha hante bājha huyā : jaice niṣedha bolala : tā dekhaha* ||

Direction: Saying thus, the *brāhmaṇas* decided to go. At that moment an old man, leaning on a stick, came out of his house and how he prevented them, watch that.

*kathā* ||

*brāhmaṇa bola : he brāhmaṇasaba torāsaba gokule jāite cāva : torāsaba naṣṭa bhelā : rājā kaṁse ihāka jāni sahaba nāhi : torāsabaka nigrahi sarbasva āgraha kari lavaba : jāti-kula saba bhraṣṭa karaba* ||

Dialogue: *The brāhmaṇa* said, "Oh *brāhmaṇas*, you all want to go to Gokula; you are all ruined; King Kaṁsa will not tolerate knowing this. Subjugating you, he will snatch away everything from you; he will destruct your whole community and race."

*sūtra* ||

*ohi śuni brāhmaṇasaba bhīti hayā jāite nāhi pārala : kṛṣṇara caraṇe śaraṇa laiyā: karmma-garbba saba cāri : śravaṇa-kīrtana kariye: gṛhe rahala* | *tadanantara śrī kṛṣṇa bālaka sabaka : ṣaḍrasa anna : bhojāna karāvala : bhakatakāmadakṛṣṇa : āpuno bhojana kayala : tadanantara : parama kautuke gopagaṇa sahite: jaice gokule calala: tā dekhaha śunaha nirantare hari bola hari* ||

Direction: Hearing this, the *brāhmaṇas* could not go out of fear. Taking refuge at the feet of Kṛṣṇa, giving up all the pride of ritualistic practices, remained at home chanting and listening to the name of Kṛṣṇa. After that, Śrī Kṛṣṇa fed the cowherd boys with food of six different tastes. Kṛṣṇa, who fulfills all wishes of His devotees, also fed Himself. After that, being greatly pleased, how Kṛṣṇa, along with the cowherd boys, went to Gokula, watch and listen to that and keep chanting the name of Hari incessantly.

*gīta* || *rāga śyāma* || *paritāla :*

Song in the *Rāga Śyāma* with the rhythm *Paritāla:*

*gopāla cale gokula lāi* |
*bāve gopa beṇu dhenu calāyī* || *dhruṁ* ||

Gopāla moves for Gokula and the cowherd boy plays the flute while chasing the cows. Refrain.

*pada:*

*śyāmala aṅga pīta picorā* |
*nava ghana jini jaice bijurī ujorā* ||
*māthahi khanḍa śikhanḍaka lule* |
*herite hāsi bhūbana*[12] *tini bhule* ||

[12]. *bhuvana.*

*gale guñjāhāra tṛbhaṅga bhāye |*
*adhara madhura beṇu bajāite jāye ||*
*caraṇa paṅkaja maṇi mañjīra rola |*
*tāhe majoka mana śaṅkare bola ||8||*

Verse: The dark blue body with yellow clothing look like bright flashes of lightning on newly formed dark clouds. On the head, swing a plume of peacock feather. Looking at His smile, makes one forget the three worlds. A garland of *guñjā* berry hangs from the neck, and He stands with his form bending at three places; His lips play sweetly on the flute. On the lotus-like feet, jewelled anklets make soft tinkling sounds. Let the mind be engrossed in all these, says Śaṅkara.

*sūtra ||*

*āhe sāmājika loka : aicana prakāre śrī kṛṣṇa : anna prārthanā cale : biprasabaka karmma-garbba dūra kayala : patnīsabaka prasāda delaha : ohi patnīprasāda nāma nāṭa : sampūrṇa bhaila : ihāka jesaba loke : bhakti-bhāve gāve : je bhāvanā karaya : tārāsabara kṛṣṇa caraṇe : parama bhakati bāḍhaba : ihā jāni kṛṣṇa caraṇe śaraṇa sāra kaya kahõ : nirantare hari bola hari ||*

Direction: Oh revered audience, in this way, in the pretext of asking for food, Śrī Kṛṣṇa decimated the *brāhmaṇas* of their pride of ritualistic practices; blessed the wives of the *brāhmaṇas* with His favour. Thus the drama called *Patnīprasāda* is completed. Those people who recite it with deep faith and those who perform in the play, their devotion to the feet of Kṛṣṇa increase greatly. Knowing this, taking refuge at the feet of Kṛṣṇa as the ultimate essence, keep chanting the name of Hari incessantly.

## 5.3
## *keli-gopāla nāṭaka*
## The Play: Sports of Gopāla

*õ namo śrīkṛṣṇāya*
Respectful obeisance to Śrī Kṛṣṇa.

*śloka* ||
*śarat śaśāṅkakarakomalāsu*
*niśāsu śaśvat saha gopikābhiḥ* |
*cakāra kelim kalagītanṛtyaiḥ*
*sa gopamūrtirjayatīha kṛṣṇaḥ* ||*1*||

Hymn[1]:
In the soft moonlight in an autumnal night, Kṛṣṇa in the guise of a cowherd boy with the cowherd women and accompanied by songs and dance enjoyed sporting repeatedly and thereby won the hearts of the cowherds.

*apica*||
*vīkṣyendu maṇḍalamakhaṇḍamakuṇṭhabodho-*
*vṛndāvane sukalaveṇumavādayat yaḥ* |1
*sammohanāya madhuraṁ vrajasundarīṇām*
*taṁ gopaveśamaniśaṁ praṇato'smi kṛṣṇam* ||2||

Also[2]: We bow to that Kṛṣṇa, in the guise of a cowherd boy who, in the clear (bright) moonlight in Vṛndāvana, is playing (on) the flute with great pleasure, to mesmerise the beautiful women of Vraja.

*gīta* || *rāga : suhāi* || *māna ekatāli* ||
Song in the *Rāga Suhāi* in rhythm *Ekatāli:*

---

[1]. in *Upajāti* metre; apparently it is *Upendravajrā* , but in the 1st foot, the 5th letter should have been long but here it is short.

[2]. in *Vasantatilakā* metre.

*śarata śaśī niśi dhāvali adhika |*
*lahu lahu malayā pavana tathi thika ||*
*birindā bipina kusuma parakāśa |*
*pekhi karala rāsa- keli bilāsa ||*

On the autumnal night the moon was very bright and there was a soft breeze blowing slowly, the flowers in the forests of Vṛndāvana were illuminated brightly, and seeing that, Kṛṣṇa performed (His) amorous *rāsa* pastime with the cowherd women.

*dhruṁ ||*

*jaya jaya gopīnātha karu paraṇāma |*
*pūrala kaya keli gopinīka kāma ||*

Refrain: Glory to Gopīnātha, obeisance to you! (You have) fulfilled the desires of the cowherd women by performing this pastime with them.

*pada ||*

*pañcama pūri punu gāvata gīta |*
*mohita hayo brajayoṣita cita ||1||*
*harali cetana mana manasijai bāṇa |*
*kṛṣṇa kiṅkare ehu śaṅkare bhāṇa ||2||1||*

Verse: May you sing in the fifth pitch, being mesmerised like the minds of the women of Vraja, as the arrows of Manasija stole (their) mind and soul; this is what the servant of Kṛṣṇa, Śaṅkara says.

*nāndyante sūtra praveśa || alamatibistareṇa | prathamaṁ mādhavo mādhava ityuktvya hariṁ praṇamya sabhāsadjanān pratyāha ||*

After this opening benediction there enters the Sūtradhāra. That is enough. First uttering "Mādhava, Mādhava!", offering obeissance to Hari, addressing the audience, said:

*śloka* ||

*bho bho sabhāsada yuyaṁ*[3] *śṛṇuta sāvadhānataḥ* |
*keligopāla nāmedaṁ nāṭakaṁ muktisādhakam* ||3||

Hymn[4]:

Oh there audience! You please listen carefully to this drama named *Keligopāla* which will lead to emancipation.

*atha bhaṭimā* ||

Here is the eulogy:

*parama puruṣa purātana pāpī*
*pāvana īśvara deva* |
*brahmā rudra ādi digapāla*
*jāsu karata nita seva* ||
*jakṣa rakṣa bipakṣa*
*lakṣa lakṣa kṣayaṅkārī* |
*duṣṭa daitya dānava dalana*
*dīna dāridra*[5] *dukha-bhaya hārī* ||1||
*agha-baka-kubalaya dhenuka keśī*
*kaṁsanāśī banamālī* |
*gopī-pīna-payodhara dhariñaṇa*
*cañcala-kara-jugasāli* ||
*ānanda sindhu : sādhujana bandhu :*
*madhura mūruti-muranāśī* |
*birindā bipina : bihāra biśārada :*
*śārada-indu-parakāśi* ||2||
*koṭi madana-mana : mohana-rūpī :*
*paraśane paramānanda* |
*siddha munibṛnda : sādare bandita :*
*jākara e pada dvanda* ||
*pālana pralaya : srajana jagataka :*
*jāheri parama bihāra* |

---

[3]. *yūyaṁ* (which is correct both grammaticly and metrically).

[4]. in *Śloka* metre.

[5]. *daridra.*

*jāsu nāma dhari : adhamā pāpī :*
*pāvata bhava-nadī pāra* ||3||
*sohi gopālaka : keli nāṭaka :*
*ohi mukuti nidāna* |
*bho sabhāsada : sādhūjana saba*
*śuna mana kaya sāvadhāna* ||
*kalika pāpahara : nāhi ataḥpara :*
*jāni tejahu āna kāma* |
*kaha kṛṣṇa-kiṅkara : āpunu uddhara :*
*ḍāki bolahu rāma rāma* ||4||

The Supreme Person, the most powerful God, who purifies the eternal sinner; whom even gods like Brahmā, Rudra and the *digpālas*, serve every day.

Protector of the demigods and destroyer of millions of opponents (who) destroying the wicked demons, (is the) remover of all the fears and woes of the distressed and the poor. (1)

Destroyer of (demons like) Agha, Baka, Kuvalaya, Dhenuka, Keśī, and Kaṁsa, He is Vanamālī, (who is) holding the full breasts of the cowherd women joining his hands.

(The one who is) the ocean of happiness and the friend to the virtuous; beautiful in form, who killed the demon Mura. Who roams about in the well acquainted forests of Vṛndāvana looking bright like the autumnal moon.(2)

(The one who) has a form which mesmerises the minds of a million Madana, whose very touch brings great bliss. These are the two feet to which the emancipated sages pray with love.

Whose great sport is to protect, destroy and create this world. Taking whose name, even the worst of the sinners can reach the other side of this river-like world. (3)

This drama is about the pastime of that same Gopāla, the same who is the cause of liberation. Oh dear revered audience, all the good people, please listen with your mind very carefully.

To eradicate the sins of the age of Kali, there is no better way; and hence leave aside all other works, and deliver yourself by chanting aloud "Rāma, Rāma!"; says the servant of Kṛṣṇa.

*kathā* ||

*bho sabhāsada sādhujanasaba : je sakala surāsura-vandita pādapadmña : sayala saṁsāra jāhera srajanā : jāhera nāme : mahāmahā pāpīsaba saṁsāra nistare : sohi parameśvara : śrīśrī gopāla : sakala gopījana sahita : ohi sabhāmadhye : parama kautuke nṛtya karaba : tāhe sāvadhāne dekhaha śunaha : nirantare hari bola hari* ||

Dialogue: Oh, all the good people assembled here, one whose lotus feet are worshipped by the gods and the demons alike, the whole universe is whose creation, (taking) whose name rescues even the greatest of the greatest of sinners from this world; the same Supreme Godhead, honourable Śrī Gopāla (Kṛṣṇa) along with all the cowherd women, will be dancing with great pleasure amongst this audience, watch and listen to that carefully and keep chanting the name of Hari incessantly.

*punaḥ : sūtradhāra :* || *ākāśe karṇaṁ dattvā* || *saṅgi ki bādya bājaise*||

Again: Listening to the sky, the Śūtradhāra says, "Oh dear friend, what instruments are playing?".

*saṅgi - sakhi deva- dundubhi bājata : āhe deva dundubhi bājata* || *āḥ milala milala* ||

Companion: Oh friend! There plays the celestial *dundubhi*. Oh there the celestial drum *dundubhi* is playing. Oh, here He comes.

*śloka* ||

*atha praveśamakarot kṛṣṇaḥ kandarpadarpahā |*
*mohayan bādayan veṇuṁ strībhiḥ saha sakautukaḥ ||4||*

Hymn[6]:There enters Kṛṣṇa, the destroyer of the pride of Kandarpa, playing fascinating flute along with the (cow herd) women and with great pleasure.

*sūtra* ||

*bhoḥ sabhāsada : gopījana sahita śrīgopāla eāvata eāvata thika* ||

Direction: Oh dear assembled people, along with the cowherd women here comes Śrī Gopāla, here He comes.

*iti sūtraḥ niṣkrāntaḥ*||

Saying thus the Sūtradhāra exits.

*nāṭa-rāgen gītaṁ || māna ekatāli ||*

Song in the *Rāga Nāṭa* with the rhytmn *Ekatāli:*

*śyāma mūruti pīta ambara lāsa |*
*nayana paṅkaja jauti īṣata hāsa || dhruṁ ||*

(His) dark body is beautiful with yellow clothing; lotuslike eyes shining brightly, (He is) smiling a little. Refrain.

*pada* ||

*āvata govinda gopinī-piu |*
*saṅge calala gopī bhulala jiya ||*
*adhara madhura veṇu pañcama gāna |*
*kṛṣṇa kiṅkare ehu śaṅkare bhāṇa ||1||2||*

Verse: Here comes Govinda, the Lord of the cowherd women.
Along come the cowherd women as if forgetting their lives.
His lips play sweetly on the flute in the fifth pitch.
This is what Śaṅkara, the servant of Kṛṣṇa, says.

---

[6]. in *Śloka* metre, but in the 1st foot, the 6th letter is not long but short.

*ślokaǁ*

*nirīkṣya rātriṁ śaradindu śubhrām*
*tadrociṣā cāru vanaṁ vikāśam ǁ*
*gītaṁ jagau gokula-kāminīnāṁ*
*mohaṁ vitanvan nitarāṁ murāri ǁ5ǁ*

Hymn[7]: Seeing the beautiful autumnal moonlit night and the beautifully glowing forest, Murāri sang a song mesmerising the women of Gokula.

*kathā ǁ*

*śrīgopāla prabeśa die kahõ : adhare pañcama pūri : beṇu bajāite lāgala : tāhe śunie gopīsaba bimohita hayā śrīgopālaka samīpa pāvala : tāhe dekhaha śunaha : nirantare hari bola hari ǁ*

Dialogue: Entering, Śrī Gopāla started playing the flute with His lips in the fifth pitch. Hearing that, the cowherd women became mesmerised and came near Śrī Gopāla. Watch and listen to that and keep chanting the name of Hari incessantly.

*payāra śrī-rāga*[8]
Verse in the *Rāga Śrī:*

*akhaṇḍa maṇḍala śaśī śarata rātita |*
*śaśāṅke komala bṛndābana bikaśita ǁ*

In the Autumnal night the moon with its endless halo illuminated Vṛndāvana with its soft glow.

*pada ǁ*

*lahu lahu bahe manda malayā payana |*
*rāsa kṛḍā karite kṛṣṇara bhailā mana ǁ1ǁ*
*uccāyā pañcama pūri hari gāilā gīta |*
*śuni brajabālāsaba bhailā bimohita ǁ*
*patisuta tejala mayala prema sindhu |*
*hṛdaye dharala mādhavaka buli bandhu ǁ2ǁ*
*kṛṣṇaka dekhite alakhite gopajāyā |*
*cale sacakite patisuta upekhiyā ǁ*

[7]. in *Upajāti* metre.

[8]. *gīta, rāga śrīpayāra – paritāla ǁ* (Goswami, K. D., ed., *Aṅkamālā,* 3rd edn., 1999, p. 89.).

*hāthite kuṇḍala ḍoli ḍoli gaṇḍa lole |*
*kṛṣṇara caraṇa citte parsaya bhole ||3||*
*suhṛda sodara bādhe svoāmi niṣedhaya |*
*tabahu bimukhi sakhī karõ*[9] *nāhi haya ||*
*upekhiyā rādhā*[10] *dhāyā gayore gopinī |*
*bhakataka laṅghe nāhi ekave bighini ||4||*
*harika bhakati ahi parama sampada |*
*dahe doṣasava milāvaya manuratha ||*
*parama bāndhaya mādhavara guṇanāma |*
*jāniā lokāi ḍāki bolā rāma rāma ||5||3||*

Verse: A soft breeze blowing slowly, Kṛṣṇa's mind was bent on having amorous pastime with the cowherd women. (1). Hari started to sing in the fifth note and hearing that, the cowherd women became mesmerised.
Leaving their husbands and sons, plunged into the ocean of love, holding Mādhava in their hearts as their friend.(2)
To see Kṛṣṇa, the cowherd women went carefully, unobserved by anyone, ignoring their husbands and sons.
While walking, their cheeks hung and their earrings swayed, and thinking of Kṛṣṇa in their hearts, they forgot about touch.(3)
Their friends and brothers obstructed them, and their husbands forbade them; even then, they never turned back.
Ignoring opposition, the cowherd women went running. The devotees cannot be prevented by any obstacles. (4)
Devotion to Hari, is the most valuable asset. It burns out all sins and fulfills all the wishes of the mind.
Knowing that the name and praise of Mādhava is the best friend, oh dear people, call out loudly "Rāma, Rāma!". (5)

*śloka* ||

*yā gopyaḥ pārśvamaprāptā niruddhāḥ patidevaraiḥ |*
*hṛdi govindacaraṇaṁ vicintya vijahuḥ tanūḥ ||6||*

Hymn[11]: Those cowherd women (who) being debarred by

---

9. *kabõ.*
10. *bādhā*
11. in *Śloka* metre, but in 3rd foot, the 6th and 7th lettes are short, not long.

their husbands and brothers-in-law, could not be near Kṛṣṇa, sacrificed their lives meditating upon the feet of Kṛṣṇa in their hearts.

*kathā* ||

*āhe sāmājika loka : je gopīsaba : kṛṣṇaka dekhite napāvala : svāmīdevare dvāra bandha kaya rākhala : sesaba birahatāpe tāpita hayā : hṛdiprāṇamādhavaka nibiḍa dhyāne āliṅgi kahõ : jaice pṛyatama tanu cārala : tā dekhaha śunaha : nirantare hari bola hari* ||

Dialogue: Oh dear assembled people! Those cowherd women who could not see Kṛṣṇa, as their husbands and brothers-in-law kept them within locked doors, burning out of anguish caused by separation, embracing Mādhava, who is dear as life, in their hearts in deep meditation, how they left their bodies, which is so dear, watch and listen to that and keep chanting the name of Hari incessantly.

*gīta* || *rāga kedāra* || *tāla jyoti* ||

Song in the *Rāga Kedāra* with the rhythm *Jyoti:*

*dhruṁ* ||

*hariko gopinī pekhaye napāi :*
*adhike milala moha biraha dahanu :*
*dahe tanu dharanu najāi* ||

Refrain: Not being able to see Hari, the cowherd women pined even more for Him; separation burning them so much that it became difficult to live on.

*pada* ||

*ghana ghana svāsa : phokāre bara bālā*
*hariko rahali dhiāi* |
*eku mane premabhakati bhāvai :*
*hṛdi pada paṅkaja : dharaye jhurae nīra*
*prema pulaka bheli kāi* ||1||

*bhakati karama-bandha kayo kṣinā*
*kaha śaṅkara paramānā* |
*birahe mudi rahu duho nayanā* |
*kṛṣṇara caraṇa cinti : pāye paramagati :*
*chori parala gopīprāṇā* ||2||4||

Verse : Breathing deeply and quickly, the beautiful women remained meditating on Hari concetrating wholeheartedly with love and devotion; holding the lotuslike feet in their hearts, tears flowing from their eyes, their bodies shivered with excitement out of love. Devotion destroys the entanglement of *karma,* it is proved, says Śaṅkara. Keeping both the eyes closed in separation (from Kṛṣṇa) meditating on the feet of Kṛṣṇa, the cowherd women fell down lifeless and met with the ultimate emancipation.

*kathā* ||

*ahe lokāi : pekhu pekhu ajñānī anācārī gopīsaba : kāmabhāve kevale kṛṣṇara caraṇa cinti : tatakāle parama gati pāvala : hari bhakatika mahimā ki kahaba : ihā jāni nirantare hari bola hari* ||

Dialogue: Oh dear people! See, see, the cowherd women who do not have any (spiritual) knowledge and do not know any ritual; just by meditating on the feet of Kṛṣṇa with lust, attained the final emancipation immediately. What to say about the greatness of devotion to Hari; knowing this, keep chanting the name of Hari incessantly.

*tadanantara : je gopīsabaka : bandhubāndhave rākhaye nāhi pārala : bṛndābane gaiā kahon : sakala surāsureśvara-śira-śikhara-cūḍāmaṇi : birājita pāda-paṅkaja parameśvara śrīśrīgopālaka samīpa pāvala : tāheka bṛtānta śunaha* | *sesabaka hari parihāse svabhāve pucaye lāgala* ||

After that, those cowherd women who could not be stopped by their friends, went to Vṛndāvana and reached near the one, whose lotuslike feet adorn like a jewel the crown of all the gods and demons alike, the Supreme God, honourable Śrī Gopāla. Listen to that account. (Then) Hari, in a joking manner, started asking them (the cowherd women).

*he sakhīsaba : kamana utapāta gokule milala : ki nimite rajanī lavari kahõ banamadhye ihā āvala ||*
"Oh friends, what calamity has befallen upon Gokula that you have come running at such hour of night to this jungle?"

*saba gopī kaha : he parameśvara : nāhi nāhi kico śaṅkā ||*
All the cowherd women said (together): "Oh Almighty, there is nothing to worry."

*punaḥ hari bihasi bola || he sakhīsaba : kuśale āvala : hāmāta kamana prayojana thika : satya kahu : tā sādho ||*
Again Hari said smiling, "Oh friends, have you reached here well? Tell me exactly how I am needed; tell me the truth, so that I can fulfill that."

*śuni gopīsabe: parama lajjita huyā | heṭhamātha kaya rahala*
Hearing that, all the cowherd women became greatly ashamed and remained there with their heads lowered.

*punaḥ hari bihasi bola || torāra patiputra pitāmātāsaba : tohāka bhenṭa napāi : parama cintita huyāce : tāsambāra āti satvare dukha dūra kara giyā : bilambaka yogya nohe : ai cala ai cala ||*
Again Hari said smiling, "Being unable to find you, your husbands, sons and parents are very much worried; go back to them immediately and remove their grief. It is not proper to delay. Get going, get going."

*gopīsaba parihāsa nāhi bujhala : kṛṣṇaka kaṭākṣe kope nirekhiye : garyaya lāgala ||*

The cowherd women could not understand the joke and throwing sideways glances at Kṛṣṇa with anger started reproaching.

*he sakhīsaba : śrīkṛṣṇa ki kahaice : unikara citta bujhaye nāhi pāri* ||
"Oh friends, we cannot understand Kṛṣṇa's mind from what he says."

*punaḥ hari bihasi bola* ||
Again Hari said smiling:

*śloka* ||
*dṛṣṭaṁ vanaṁ vikaśitaṁ śītalāṁ śaśiśobhitam* |
*yamunā- jala- bātena pratiyāta vanāt drutam* ||7||
Hymn[12]: "You have seen Vṛndāvana illuminated with the cool moon-light. There might be tide of water and storm in the Yamunā, hence go back from here immediately."

*kathā* ||
*he sakhīsaba : bṛndābana jadi dekhite āvala : bikaśita bṛndābana*
*dekhala: aba satvare cala : ei cala* ||
Dialogue: "Oh dear friends, if you had come to see Vṛndāvana, you have seen Vṛndāvana fully flourishing, now leave quickly, leave."

*gīta* || *rāga śrī gāndhāra* || *ekatāli* ||
Song in the *Rāga Śrī Gāndhāra* with the rhythm *Ekatāli:*

*e sakhī calahu bahuri gori : gokula goāri :*
*karabinā kāminī : kalaṅka hāmāri :*
*nāhi paraśõ paranārī* || *dhruṁ* ||
"Oh friends, oh fair cowherd women of Gokula, go back. Oh beautiful women, do not put me to disrepute, I do not touch the wives of other people." Refrain.

---

12 . in *Śloka* metre; but in 1st foot ,the 6th and 7th lettes are short, not long.

*pada*||

*ākulamati pati : suta sodara he :*
*cāhe cakita diśa pāśā |*
*hoi kulakāminī : yāminī kaice :*
*tejala nija piu pāśā ||1||*
*svāmī jānaye java : milaba maraṇa tava*
*calahu pātakamati cori |*
*kṛṣna kiṅkara kaha : śaṅkara hariko :*
*aicana bacana cāturī ||2||5||*

Verse: "Being restless, your husbands, sons and brothers are looking around apprehensively. Being the beautiful women of the family how could you leave the side of your husbands at such an hour of the night.(1)

"When your husbands will come to know, you will be dead! So go quickly, giving up this unholy thought." Such were the clever words of Hari, says the servant of Kṛṣna.(2)

*kathā* ||

*śrīkṛṣṇaka parama bipṛya bāṇī śuni kahõ : gopīsaba duranta cintā pāvala : parama dukha bhara-pāi : heṭhamātha kayala : ghana ghana niśvāsa phokārite adhara śukhāvala : mukha malina bhela : jaise śiśira pari padma saṅkocita bhela : hṛdaye marama caḍala ||*

Dialogue: Hearing such extremely unpleasant words from Śrī Kṛṣṇa, the cowherd women became very much worried. Heavy with sorrow, they lowered their heads, heaving sighs, their lips became dry, their faces became gloomy, as when dew falls, the lotus flower closes (its petals). And their distress in the heart increased.

*gīta || rāga belayāra : rūpakatāli ||*

Song in the *Rāga Belovār* with the rhythm *Rūpaka*:

*cintita gopinī : pekhae nairāśā :*

*lambita ānana : phokāre nisvāśā || dhruṁ ||*

The worried cowherd women saw only hopelessness; their faces became long drawn and they sighed heavily. Refrain.

*pada ||*

*tanu mana jhāmari nayane jhure bāri |*
*padanakha khite lekhu dekho āndhiāri ||1||*
*kucaduhu kuṅkuma lepita lole |*
*tāpita brajabadhu śaṅkare bole ||2||6||*

Verse: Being morose both in body and mind, tears flowed from the eyes. Scratching on the ground with the nails of the feet, (they) saw only darkness all around. And the flowing tears washed away the *kuṁkum* from the breasts of the suffering wives of Vraja, says Śaṅkara.

*kathā ||*

*tadunantara : kathaṅkathamapi śokaka tambhāi kahõ : āñcole ākhimukha mucala : āśāceḍa dukhe dīrgha niśvāsa cāḍala : preme kope bākya gadagada : kaṣṭakaṭākṣe kṛṣṇaka nirekhi : bolala se gopīsava : tāhe dekhaha śunaha ||*

Dialogue: After that, somehow containing the sorrow, the cowherd women wiped (away) the eyes and face with the fore-end of their clothing; out of sorrow, losing all hope, breathed heavily. Looking at Kṛṣṇa with sideway glances and in great pain, stammered out of great love; watch and listen to that.

*gīta || rāga suhāi || jautimāna ||*

Song in *Rāga Suhāi* with the rhythm *Jautimān*:

*harihe bujhalo tuho bara nidaā |*
*nikaruṇa bāṇī : bāṇa mārala hāni*
*dārala hāmākeri hṛdayā || dhruṁ ||*

"Oh Hari, we have understood that you are very pityless, you have thrown at us arrows of unkind words which have pierced our hearts." Refrain.

*pada* ||

*pati suta saba aba : cori parala nātha :*
*tuā padapaṅkaja āga* |
*bhakata kṛpāla : gopāla teri kaiche :*
*ṭuṭala nava anurāga* ||
*tuhu bine mādhava : dehā nāhi rākhaba :*
*birahiṇī coraba prāṇa* |
*nakarahu nairāśā : toho jagatabāsā :*
*kṛṣṇa kiṅkare ehu bhāṇa* ||1||7||

Verse : "Leaving husband and son and everyone else we have now come and surrendered ourselves at your lotus like feet. Oh Gopāla, merciful to the devotees, how has your newly found affection abated! Without you, oh Mādhava, I shall not live anymore and shall die lovelorn. Oh the one pervading throughout the whole universe, please do not disappoint us.", describes the servant of Kṛṣṇa.

*kathā* ||

*he svāmi : tohāri gīte mohita huyā : patisutasaba coḍi : tatsu pada samīpa pāvala : toho dāruṇa bākya bolaica : he parameśvara : tatsu mukha paṅkaja coḍi : hāmāra cakṣu āna pekhaye nāhi : tuyā kathā coḍi karṇe : āna punu kico śunaya nāhi : tatsu caraṇa coḍi : hāmāra pāva khojeko calaya nāhi : braja gaiyā ki karaba svāmi | je lakṣmī gosānī : hṛdaye thāna labhi kahõ : tathāpi ohi padapaṅkaja reṇu āśā karaice : ohi caraṇa seyā karite : dharma artha kāma mokṣa cāri padārasa sukhe pāi : aicana tava padapaṅkaja: ihā cārite hāmāka prāṇa chuṭi jāi : he parameśvara svāmi : taba padapaṅkaja tejaya nāhi pārie : nāhi pārie :*

Dialogue: "Oh Lord, being mesmerised by your song, leaving behind (our) husband, son and everyone else we have reached near your feet and you have spoken such ruthless words. Oh the Supreme Lord, leaving your lotuslike face our eyes see nothing else; other than your words, our ears hear nothing else; away from your feet; our feet are unable to take steps; going back to Vraja what shall we do oh Lord! Goddess Lakṣmī, even after having received a place in your heart, still aspires for the dust of your lotus feet; serving those same feet one can easily get *dharma*, *artha*, *kāma* and *mokṣa*, the four prime objects of human life – such are your lotus feet; leaving these feet we almost lose our lives. Oh the Supreme Lord (the God of gods) we cannot leave your lotus feet, we cannot."

*śloka* :

*na pārayāmastava pādapaṅkajaṁ*
*vayaṁ vihātuṁ navakañjalocana* |
*svanena te mohita mānasā bhṛśaṁ*
*tyajasva mā mādhava naḥ kṛpāṁ kuru* ||8||

Hymn[13]: "We cannot leave your lotus feet, oh you who have eyes like newly blooming lotus. The sound of your flute has greatly attracted our minds, please do not leave us, oh Mādhava have mercy on us."

*gīta* || *rāga śrīgāndhāra* || *jauti māna* ||
Song in the *Rāga Śrī Gāndhāra* with the rhythm *Jautimāna:*

*nāhi pāraa :* *pāya paṅkaja :*
*tejaya jādaya rāi :*
*lo hari hari :*
*kusuma dhanu manu :*
*mohana mūruti :*
*pekhite mukuti milāi* || *dhruṁ* ||

(We) cannot leave your lotus feet, oh Hari, cannot leave the king of the Yadu dynasty, whose form can mesmerise

[13]. in *Vaṁśasthavila* metre; but the last letters of the 2nd and 4th feet are short which should be long in normal course. However, by the rule *tathā pādāntago'pi vā* these two letters should be considered as long letters.

the mind of even the god with arrows of flower (Cupid), seeing which one can attain salvation. Refrain.

*pada* ||

*hāmu anucarī : caraṇa anusari :*
*parama prema rase āśa* |
*kaṭhina bacane : harasi cetana*
*kaice karasi nairāśa* ||1||
*mohana baṁśīra : svāna śuni kahu :*
*jīvana dhāraṇa najāye* |
*rākhare prāṇa : bandhu mādhava :*
*madhura adhara suāi* ||2||
*biraha dahanu : tāve tanu manu :*
*dūra karu tāhe hāsi* |
*kṛṣṇakiṅkara : kahaya śaṅkara :*
*charaṇa reṇu abhilāsī* ||3||8||

Verse: "We are your servants, following your footsteps in expectation of receiving ultimate love. Robbing us out of minds with your harsh words why do you disappoint us. Hearing your mesmerising flute (our) lives cannot be sustained any more. Please maintain our lives, oh friend Mādhava, with the nectar of your lips. The body and the mind are burning with the feeling of longing. Drive it away (the suffering) with a smile." Expecting to receive the dust of (Kṛṣṇa's) feet, Śaṅkara, the servant of Kṛṣṇa, says thus:

*kathā* ||

*gopīsabaka aicana kārunya bilāpa śuni kahō : śrīkṛṣṇaka sneharase ākula kayala : kamalalocana duhu lotake pūrala : tattakāle uthi kahō : gāve gāve gopīka : ākhi mukha āpune pītabastre muci kahō :prabodha kavala* ||

Dialogue: Hearing the cowherd women lament so pathetically, Śrī Kṛṣṇa became overwhelmed with love. His lotuslike eyes filled with tears. Rising immediately, wiped the eyes and face of each of the cowherd women, with His yellow clothing and consoled them thus:

*he sakhīsaba : kahõsaba parama bhakata : hāmāra prāṇato adhika : hāmu parihāsa keli kautuka kavala : tāhe nāhi bujhala : dukha coḍaha : dukha coḍaha : torāsabaka mano ratha pūri : kṛḍā- kautuka karaba | prāṇasakhīsaba uṭhaha uṭhaha||*
*aicana āśvāsa śuni : gopīsaba kṛṣṇara bākyāmṛte : biraha-tāpa tattakāle dūra kavala : jaice banāgni bṛṣṭijale nirbāṇa bhela : parama utsuke uṭhi kahõ : kṛṣṇaka ābari kṛḍā kaya lāgala || tadanantara śrīgopāla : parameśvara gopīsabaka kāma baḍāi kaho : keli kaya lāgala ||*
"Oh friends, you all are great devotees, dearer than my life to me. I said fun making jokes, that you could not understand. Give up this sadness. Give up this sadness for fulfilling your wish we shall sport and have fun. My dear beloved friends, get up, get up."
Hearing such reassuring words, such nectar like sweet words from Kṛṣṇa, immediately drove away all the cowherd women's suffering from unattained love, as if a wild fire was extinguished by rain water. Rising with great anticipation, surrounding Kṛṣṇa, started playing. After that Śrī Gopāla, the supreme God, to increase the longing of the cowherd women started sporting with them.

*gīta || rāga śrīgāndhāra ||*
Song in the *Rāga Śrīgāndhāra*:

*dhruṁ||*
*dekho sakhī aicana nikaruṇa kāna |*
*payodhara adhara daśana nakha hāna ||*
Refrain: Look, oh friends, how pityless is Kānu (Kṛṣṇa), biting and scratching the breasts and lips with teeth and nails.

*pada* ||

*khakhāila keśapāśa : ṭuṭālo hāra* |
*phoḍala kāchuā kucaka hāmāra* ||*1*||
*kayala āliṅgana ghana ghana bāhu* |
*jaice cāndaka garasī raha rāhu* ||2||
*harika suruti-rase nārahe giāna* |
*kṛṣṇa- kiṅkara ehu śaṅkare bhāṇa* ||3||32||

Verse: The hair-knots (of the cowherd women) loosened, necklace broke, the blouse covering the breasts torn, arms entangled in close embrace as if Rāhu was devouring the moon. Hari was out of senses being deeply engrossed in love, that is what Śaṅkara, the servant of Kṛṣṇa says.

*śloka* ||

*athāpi tā svayā bācā svāśvāsya snehayantritaḥ* |
*gopīnāṁ bardhayan kāmaṁ ramayāmāsa keśavaḥ* ||9||

Hymn[14]: After that, encouraging the cowherd women with loving reassuring words, increasing their longing, Keśava made love to them.

*gīta* || *rāga suhāi* || *paritāla* ||
Song in the *Rāga Suhāi* with the rhythm *Paritāla:*

*dhruṁ* ||

*keśaya*[15] *karata keli : gopinī saṅge raṅge* |
*gobinda karata keli : kāhāku heraye hāsi :*
*ākhi bhṛṅge lo rāma* ||

Refrain: Keśava started playing with the cowherd women with enjoyment; Govinda started sporting with them, looking at some of them with a smile and some others with sideway glance of his eyes, oh Rāma.

*pada* ||

*kāhāku cūmbai banamālī lāgi mukha* |

---

[14]. in *Śloka* metre.

[15]. *keśava.*

*āliṅgane gopīka milata rati-sukha* ||
*uccha kucha karo khata nakhera paraśi* |
*gopālaka keli kṛṣṇa kiṅkara kahasi* ||1||9||

Verse: Vanamāli kissed some of them and they had the pleasure of love from his embraces. Made marks on their breasts touching them with his nails, those were the pastimes of Kṛṣṇa, says the servant of Kṛṣṇa.

*kathā* ||

*evambidha nānā khelā : śrīgopāle kayala* | *gopīsaba manoratha pūri : ānande mana magna hayāche* | *se samae kuberaka eka anucara : eka jakṣa tanikara nāma śaṅkhacuḍa* | *se pāpī kāmātura hayā : gopīka hari nibāka prati : prabeśa kavala : tāhe dekhaha śunaha : nirantare hari bola* ||

Dialogue: In this way Śrī Gopāla played different games (sports). The cowherd women, with their desires fulfilled, were minds engrossed in bliss. At that time a servant of Kuvera, a demon whose name was Śaṅkhacuḍa, a wrong doer, being love-sick, and with an evil intention of kidnapping a cowherd woman entered there, watch and listen to that and keep chanting the name of Hari continuously.

*śloka :*

*atha praveśamakarot yakṣo rakṣa ivāparaḥ* |
*śaṅkhacūḍa itikhyāto nāmnā gopībhayaṅkaraḥ* ||10||

Hymn[16]: Then like a terrifying devil, scaring the cowherd women, entered a demon, who was known as Śaṅkhacuḍa.

*gīta : rāga kānaḍā* || *tāla – chuṭā* ||

Song in the *Rāga Kānāḍā* with the rhythm *Cuṭā*:

*āvata śaṅkhacūḍa uḍi bāhu* |
*jaice cānda garasite milala rāhu* || *dhruṁ* ||

Śaṅkhacuḍa came with his arms open, as if Rāhu has come to devour the moon. Refrain.

---

16. in *Śloka* metre; but 6th and 7th lettes in the 1st foot are short, not long.

*pada* ||

*kāyā thula śūla tuli hāte* |
*kampita medanī caraṇa-āghāte* ||
*ārakata ākhi cāhe diśa-pāśa* |
*śaṅkara kaha ohi keśava dāsa* ||*1*||*10*||

Verse: With a huge body carrying the spear in his hand, shaking the earth with the blow of his steps, (Śaṅkhacūḍa) looked around with his blood-shot (red) eyes, this is what Śaṅkara, the servant of Keśava, says.

*kathā* ||

*se śaṅkhacūḍa : gopīsabaka bhaya jani kahõ : bibhasya rasa bhāvanā kaya thika : bhayaṅkara rūpa jakṣaka pekhie : gopīsaba bhaye kampaye lāgala* | *trāhi kṛṣṇa : trāhi kṛṣṇa : ghana ghana jampata : tāhe pekhie bhakataka bhayahārī hari : gopīsabaka āśvāsa āliṅgana kavala : bikrama daraśiye jakṣaka khedāvala : tāhe dekhaha ityādi* ||

Translation: This same Śaṅkhacūḍa, frightening the cowherd women, behaved unpleasantly and acted in a disgusting manner; seing this terrible looking demon, the cowherd women started trembling with fear and chanted repeatedly "Oh Kṛṣṇa, save us, Oh Kṛṣṇa, save us." Seeing them, Hari, the one who steals all fears of the devotees, comforted the cowherd women by embracing them. Showing much valour (he) chased away the demon. Watch that and others.

*gīta* || *rāga śyāma* ||
Song in the *Rāga Śyāma*:

*dhruṁ* ||

*ramāyā kā karu madana khelā* |
*khele saṅge raṅge goparamaṇī melā* ||

Refrain: What a love game Śrī Kṛṣṇa plays, and along with him play the group of cowherd women with great pleasure.

*pada* ||

*kāhāku hari hāsi karu māna* |
*kāhāku cumbana carccana dāna* ||
*kāñcuri chari kucha parakāśa* |
*hāte ghori gaurī karata hāsa* ||*1*||
*kāhāku lelā hari ambari curi* |
*rahala lāje gopī aṅga muri* ||
*sabahu bekata guputa aṅga* |
*bachana charapati baḍhāyā ḍhaṅga* ||2||
*jākeri sevā kayo surāsure* |
*so hari gopī manuratha pure* ||
*bhakata bāndhaya mādhava prāṇa* |
*kṛṣṇara kiṅkare kahaya paramāṇa* ||3||*11*||

Verse: Hari showed respect to some (cowherd women) with a smile, some others with a kiss and chewed betel. Tearing the chest cover (blouse) exposed the breasts and covering themselves with their hands the cowherd women laughed. Hari (Kṛṣṇa) took some of them stealing their clothes and the cowherd women remained in a twisted pose out of shame. Everyone's secret parts became exposed and Kṛṣṇa with his teasing wordplay increased their body twists (embarrassment). Hari, whom the gods and demons serve and worship with devotion, is now busy fulfilling the wishes of the cowherd women. Friends of the devotees, Mādhava is like the (source of) life; here is the proof, says the servant of Kṛṣṇa.

*kathā* ||

*je parameśvara śrīkṛṣṇa : brahmarudrādidevatā : jāheri padapaṅkaja sadāye sevata : aicana jagata-guruka : banacarī anācārī gopanārī : kāma- bhakatiye baśya kayala : hari-bhakatika mahimā ki kahaba : āhe lokāi : pekhu pekhu hari-guṇa- nāma śravaṇa-kīrtana : bine kalita gati nāhi nāhi : jāni nirantare hari bola hari* ||

Translation: Śrī Kṛṣṇa the the Supreme God, Brahmā, Rudra and all other demigods always worship whose lotus feet, that Lord of the whole universe, has been won over by the wayfaring and unethical cowherd women by their devotion, though stinted by lust. Oh, what to say about the power of devotion! Oh, revered assembly there! See, there is no way except the listening and chanting the name and atributes of Hari for attaining salvation in the age of Kali. Knowing this, chant the name of Hari incessantly.

*śloka* ||

*gopyo govinda-sanmāna-mada- mohitacetasaḥ* |
*garbbeṇa kharbbavākyena cakrustā harihelanam* ||11||

Hymn[17]: Receiving respect from Govinda, pride developed in the minds of the cowherd women, and fed with this vanity and pride, (they) started neglecting Hari.

*kathā* ||

*tadanantara : strīka duryanya bhāva śunaha : je pūrnānanda śrīkṛṣṇa: tanikara kucitta biṣaya-sukhe : kona abhilāṣa thika : nāhi nāhi : jaice kāmadhenubṛnda adhikārīka : cāgalita ki prayojana thika : gopīsabe tāhe nāhi jānave : mādhavata mahāmāna pāi kahõ : buddhi andha bhela : kṛṣṇaka avhelā kaya lāgala : anyo anye kahai* ||

*he sakhīsaba : hāmāra rūpa jauvana pekhi : śrīkṛṣṇa bholala : hāmāra kola cāḍaya nāhi : bākya bādhaya nāhi* |

Dialogue: After that, listen to the evil nature of women. Śrī Kṛṣṇa, who fully in bliss, what interest he might have in the mean material happiness! No, not at all. Like the one who owns a herd of *kāmadhenu* cows, what need he has for a goat. The cowherd women do not know that. Receiving great attention from Mādhava, they were blinded of intelligence, and started neglecting Kṛṣṇa and started talking to one another:

[17]. in *Śloka* metre.

"Oh dear friends, seeing our beauty and youth, Śrī Kṛṣṇa has became mesmerized and does not leave our laps and does not refute our words."

*ohi buli bāhu lāḍi : madagarbbe bhramae lāgala : śrīkṛṣṇa tāhe dekhie : pācu pācu cāṭu buli calaice* ||
Saying thus shaking their arms started moving about with pride. Seeing that, Śrī Kṛṣṇa, saying flattering words, followed them about.

*he sakhīsaba : hāmāka kaice prya sambhāṣaṇa nāhi karata : hāmu kona aparādha kavala : prāṇa gopīsaba : prema kaṭākṣe nirekhi hāmāka : āśvāsa karaha* ||
"Oh dear friends, why do you not greet me with love; what wrong have I done; oh my life, dear cowherd women, giving a loving sideway glance, reassure me."

*gopīsaba parama garbbe piṭhi diye kahõ calaya : kico śunaye nāhi : tāhe dekhi śrīkṛṣṇa hāsi hāsi līlāye : prema kaya lāgala : tāhe dekhaha śunaha : nirantare hari bola hari* ||
The cowherd women being very proud showed their backs to him and moved away not listening to him at all. Seeing that Śrī Kṛṣṇa started laughing and to have fun started making love to them. Watch and listen to that and keep chanting the name of Hari incessantly.

*gīta* || *rāga suhāi* ||
Song in the *Rāga Suhāi:*

*dhruṁ* ||
*e sakhī katanu kayālo hāmu dukha rukha cora* |
*dehu dahe kāma āṅgi āliṅgana kora* ||
Refrain: "Oh friend, how much I have requested (you) to forgive my fault and leave this arrogance. My body burns with desire like fire, take me in an embrace."

*pada* ||

*naya premarasa bicuraṇa kaiche hoi* |
*baṅkima nayane herahu hāsi moi* ||
*dharaye napāri mana manamatha bhole* |
*hariko caritra kṛṣṇa kiṅkare bole* ||1||12||

Verse: How could you forget the newly found taste of love; look at me with a sidelong glance and give me a smile; Madana has mesmerized my mind and I cannot hold it within control. Such is the nature of Kṛṣṇa, says the servant of Kṛṣṇa.

*kathā* ||

*he prāṇa gopīsaba : kona aparādhe hāmāka prema coḍala : tohāka nimitta hāmāra mana madane marddaya jāni preme nirekhi āliṅgaha* ||
*kṛṣṇaka bākya gopīkā karṇapathe jāye nāhi : adhina kṛṣṇa buli gaṇaye nāhi : jaice seḍuyā svāmīka : peḍāpātraka jhīva kaṭākṣe gaṇaye nāhi : bāhu lāḍi kahõ : līlāye bharamaya lāgala* ||

Translation: "Oh my life, the cowherd women, why, for which fault of mine have you forsaken my love? My mind is assaulted by Madana for you. Knowing this, embrace me with a loving glance."
What Kṛṣṇa said did not enter through the ears of the cowherd women. Thinking Kṛṣṇa to be under their spell (the cowherd women) did not consider him, as henpecked husbands are not given importance by the wives who are the daughters of King's ministers. And shrugging their shoulders moved about having fun.

*śloka* ||

*niśamya garbaṁ govindo gopīnāṁ premabṛddhaye* |
*rādhāṁ vidhāya hṛdaye tatyāja brajayoṣitaḥ* ||12||

Hymn[18]: Listening to the vain words of the cowherd women, Govinda (Kṛṣṇa), to increase the sense of devotion in the minds of the cowherd women, took one cowherd woman, Rādhā, along and left leaving behind other cowherd women.

*kathā* ||

*tadanantara : śrīkṛṣṇa gopīsabara : āti garbba-bhāva nāhi sahala : hāhā ki bhela : gopīsaba hāmāka gaṇaya nāhi : ārāsaba hāmāka napāi : prema- bhakati hauka buli kahõ : rādhā nāma eka gopīka : hṛdaye bāndhi kahõ : tathāye antardhyāna bhaila*||

Dialogue: After that Śrī Kṛṣṇa did not tolerate the extreme arrogance of the cowherd women. "Alas, alas, what has happened!" The cowherd women do not care for me any more. Not having me with them their love and devotion would increase; thinking that, holding a cowherd woman by the name of Radhā close to heart, (Kṛṣṇa) vanished.

*śloka* ||

*tatra kṛṣṇamapaśyantyo rajanyāṁ brajayoṣitaḥ* |
*ruruduḥ susvaraṁ bhītā harervirahavihbalāḥ* ||13||

Hymn[19]: Then not seeing Kṛṣṇa (around) the cowherd women, being very scared at night and lovelorn for Hari started crying very loudly.

*kathā* ||

*tadanantara : gopīsaba āgupācu cāi : kṛṣṇaka dekhaye nāhi : bṛndābane bicāri napāi : tattakāle garaba cūra bhela : biraha-kātari huyā : kṛṣṇadaraśana prārthaya saba* ||

Dialogue: After that, the cowherd women looking around here and there, unable to find Kṛṣṇa in Vṛndāvana, their pride

---

[18]. in *Śloka* metre; but the 5th letter in the 1st foot is long, not short, and the 6th and 7th letters in the 3rd foot are short, not long.

[19]. in *Śloka* metre.

became shattered immediately. Being distressed in love, they all prayed for a glimpse of Kṛṣṇa.

*he svāmi kṛṣṇa : svabhābe cañcala strīka doṣa dharabi nāhi : hāmu kiṅkarī tohāka : ihā jāni daraśana dehu ||*
*aneka pravandhe kṛṣṇaka bheṭa napāi : parama ākula huyā : jaice krandana kae lāgala bālāsaba : tā dekhaha śunaha : nirantare hari bola hari ||*
"Oh Lord Kṛṣṇa, please do not take offence on the women who are by nature fickle minded. We are your servants; knowing that, please give us a glimpse of you."
Not being able to see Kṛṣṇa after much effort, being very disturbed, how the girls started crying, watch and listen to that and keep chanting the name of Hari without stopping.

*gīta : rāga kalyāṇa || jautitāla ||*
Song in the *Rāga Kalyāṇa* in the rhythm *Jauti:*

*dhruṁ ||*

*kāhe gayo kāhe gayo re hāmāri bandhu madhāi |*
*phokāre niśvāsa : jhuraye nīra nayanā :*
*bayanā hāta charāi ||*

Refrain: "Why have you gone, why have you gone, oh friend Mādhava!" Sighing deeply, tears flowing from the eyes, they (the cowherd women) covered their faces with their hands.

*pada||*

*hā hari hā hari : karaye kāminī mili :*
*birindā bipina bicāri |*
*ghana ghana mūruchi : paraye barabālā*
*diśa daśa dekhu āndhiāri ||1||*
*prāṇa-gopāla piu : bine nāhi raha jīu :*
*biraha dahanu dahe prāṇa |*
*karata bilāpa : gopāla guṇa gāve :*

*kṛṣṇa kiṅkara guṇagāna* ||2||*13*||

Verse: All the women looked around Vṛndāvana together saying, "Oh Hari, alas Hari!". And seeing darkness all around the beautiful young women fainted again and again. "Without our Lord, dear like life Gopāla, our life may not continue, our hearts burn with separation." Thus lamenting, singing praises of Gopāla, the servant of Kṛṣṇa started singing the glories of Kṛṣṇa.

*kathā* ||

*he kamalalocana : dukha-bimocana svāmi : hāmu pāpinīsaba : tohāta garaba kavala : bara aparādha ācarala : se doṣasaba marasa svāmi : hāmu kiṅkarīka darasana dehu*||

Dialogue: "Oh lotus-eyed, the reliever of all the sorrows, we the sinners showed pride in front of you, we have committed great offence; please forgive our faults, oh Lord. Please give a glimpse to us, your servants."

*sūtra* ||

*ohi buli ārttarāve krandana kae lāgala* ||

Direction : Saying thus, (they) started crying aloud in distress.

*śloka* ||

*tathālapantyo gopyastā alabdhā mādhavaṁ dhavam* |
*mattāḥ praviśya bipinaṁ papracchustarurājiṣu* ||14||

Hymn[20]: Not having found Lord Mādhava, lamenting, being distressed, the cowherd women asked the groves and thickets regarding Kṛṣṇa.

*kathā* ||

*aicana kṛṣṇa guṇa gāi : kāndite gopīka prema bhakati upajala: śarīra pulakita : netraka nīra jhuraye : matta huyā katihõ : kṛṣṇa ceṣṭā kavala : katihõ kṛṣṇara kṛḍā sumari : mane maḍama caḍala : hā kṛṣṇa hā kṛṣṇa buli : ḍhalie paḍala : katihõ unmatta mane : bṛndābana paśie : punu kṛṣṇa kṛṣṇa buli : bicāra kave*

20. in *Śloka* metre; but the 5th letter in the 1st foot is long, not short, and the 6th and 7th letters in the 3rd foot are short, not long.

*lāgala : je śrīkṛṣṇa jagataka bāhire bhitare thika : se kṛṣṇaka birikha samīpa cāpie puchave lāgala : tā śunaha* ||

Dialogue: Thus crying, singing praises of Kṛṣṇa the cowherd women developed love (for Kṛṣṇa), and their bodies became excited with love. Tears flowing down from the eyes, they became intoxicated. Some of them enacted Kṛṣṇa, some of them remembered Kṛṣṇa's sports and their love increased in their minds. Uttering "Oh Kṛṣṇa, oh Kṛṣṇa", they collapsed. Being frantic some of them enterd Vṛndāvana, and uttering "Kṛṣṇa" again and again, started searching for him. Going near the trees, they (the cowherd women) started asking about Kṛṣṇa, that same Kṛṣṇa, who is present inside and outside (all the things of) this world,

*gīta* || *rāga gaurī* || *jautimāna* ||

Song in the *Rāga Gaurī* with the rhythm *Jautimāna:*

*dhruṁ* ||

*puchatahõ mādhava : bāndhava madhusodana :*
*katinā rahali hari : gopinī jīvana* ||

Refrain: (The cowherd women) asked Mādhava, "Oh friend Madhusūdana, life of the cowherd women, where are you?".

*pada* ||

*bakula kadamba banduli baka tulasī :*
*tuhu saba para upakārī* |
*kaha kāheā gelo bandhu madhāi hāmāri* |
*birahiṇī jīvana dharaye nāpāri* ||
*campaka cuta āncora pāti māgu :*
*prāṇabandhu deha dekhāi* |
*pahubine tanu manu : dharaye najāi :*
*rahai na prāṇa kṛṣṇa : kiṅkare gāi* ||1||14||

Verse: "*Bakula, kadamba, banduli, baka, tulasī*, you all benevolent to others, please tell us where our friend

Mādhava has gone. Being separated (from Kṛṣṇa), cannot hold on to our lives. Oh *campaka*, oh mango tree, (we) beg of you (humbly) with our clothes spread out in front of you, please show us where our friend, who is as dear as our lives, is. Without the lord and master, we cannot bear this life and mind anymore; oh Kṛṣṇa, we cannot live any more." Thus sings the servant of Kṛṣṇa.

*kathā* ||

*aicana parakāre tarusabata kṛṣṇaka guṇa gāi gopī pucite : parama prema upajala : śarīra bicūrala : abiceda dhārāve : nayanaka nīra nigaḍe : kṛṣṇara caraṇa hṛdaye dhari kahō : ānande magana mana : katiho mauna huyā thika : bhakatika mahimāye : kṛṣṇamaya dekhae : hāmu kṛṣṇa māni preme matta huyā : kṛṣṇa-ceṣṭā kaye lāgala* ||

Dialogue: In this way singing the praise of Kṛṣṇa, asking around the trees, great love developed in the minds of the cowherd women. They forgot their own self and tears flowed in torrents. Keeping Kṛṣṇa's feet in their hearts their minds became absorbed in happiness. Some of them remained silent. Realising the greatness of devotion they saw everything pervaded with Kṛṣṇa only and considering themselves as Kṛṣṇa incarnate, being intoxicated in love, started enacting as Kṛṣṇa.

*śloka* ||

*bhaktyā pramattāstā gopyo matvātmānaṁ hi mādhavam* |
*anyo'nyamabhisambhāṣya vicakruḥ kṛṣṇaceṣṭitam* ||15||

Hymn[21]: Being engrossed in devotion, thinking themselves as Kṛṣṇa and greeting one another (the cowherd women) tried enacting Kṛṣṇa.

*kathā* ||

*kṛṣṇa-bhakati-matta hayā kahō : saba śoka bicūrala : anyo anye sambhāṣiyā : kṛṣṇa-līlā āpune kava lāgala gopīsaba : tāhe ~~dekhaha~~ śunaha* ||

[21]. in *Śloka* metre; but the 5th letter in the 1st foot is long, not short.

Dialogue: Being intoxicated in devotion for Kṛṣṇa (they) forgot all the sorrows. Greeting one another, all the cowherd women started enacting the pastimes of Kṛṣṇa, watch and listen to that.

*payāra* || *rāga - kānarā* || *paritāla* ||
Song in *Rāga Kānārā* with the rhythm *Paritāla:*

*mañi kṛṣṇa buli kare bhāvanā* |
*tanapāne susi māre putanā* ||
They considered themselves as Kṛṣṇa, (and enacted like Him) and killed Pūtanā sucking out her breast.

*pada*||

*hāmu kṛṣṇa buli jhaṅkāre buka* |
*māre agha baka batsa dhenuka* ||*1*||
*kāhu bole hāmu gopinī nātha* |
*marddaye kālika caḍiyā mātha* ||
*ohi hrada coḍa are durācāra* |
*duṣṭaka daṇḍite hāmu avatāra* ||2||
*nāhi bhaya kāhu gopinī buli* |
*eka hāte dhare mandara tuli* ||
*cāpa gopa-gopī hāmāra pāśa* |
*indraka garbba kailo saba nāśa* ||3||
*hāmuse kṛṣṇa dekha kehõ bole* |
*gopinī deho āliṅgana kole* ||
*abahu nāhi paricaya bālā* |
*dekhahõ pītabastra banamālā* ||4||
*bolaya kāhu āilõ hāmu hari* |
*beṇu bajāvata adhare dhari* ||
*gopinī kaṇṭhe kāhu bāhu meli* |
*kare līlā-gati darase keli* ||5||
*kāhu bole bilāi dadhika mora* |
*dharilõ kṛṣṇaka lavanu cora* ||

*toi māthā khāibo bolaya bāṇī |*
*gopīka bāndhava*[22] *urale ṭāni ||6||*
*bhakati pramatta gopa- aṅganā |*
*aicana karatu hari bhāvanā ||*
*kṛṣṇara kiṅkara śaṅkare bole |*
*pavitra kara hari hari bole ||7||15||*

Verse: Beating their breasts said "I am Kṛṣṇa.", and killed Agha, Baka and the calf Dhenuka.(1)

Some said "I am the lord of the cowherd women" and crushed Kāli climbing on to his head (and said), "Leave this lake, oh you wicked one, I am here as the incarnation (of Viṣṇu) to punish the wicked." (2)

"You have nothing to fear", saying thus some cowherd women (paused as if) picking up the Mandara (mountain) with only one hand and said, "Come closer to me all the cowherd boys and girls, I have vanquished all the pride of Indra."(3)

Some said, look, "I am Kṛṣṇa; oh cowherd women, come near, and embrace me. I am no more a woman now, look at my yellow clothing and the *vanamālā*."(4)

Some other said, "Here I come as Hari!", and started playing the flute holding it to the lips. Some extended their hands and embracing the cowherd women sported playfully showing (Kṛṣṇa's) pastime.(5)

Some said, "Look at the plight of my butter, here I have caught Kṛṣṇa, the thief of my butter. I shall chew away your head!" Saying thus, tied up the friend of the cowherd women to a grinding mortar tightly. (6)

Being engrossed in love, the cowherd women engaged themselves thus in the thought of Kṛṣṇa. The servant of Kṛṣṇa, Śaṅkara says, "Make yourself pure by chanting the name of Hari repeatedly".(7)

*kathā ||*

---

22. *bāndhala.*

*parama bhāgyavatī gopīsaba : hari-bhakatika mahodaya milāvala| aicana kṛṣṇa bhāvanā kari kahõ : matta hayā rahala : jo gopī kṛṣṇaka saṅge jāi : tanikara duryana bhāva śunaha : śrīkṛṣṇa se gopīka : katihu uruta baisāi : kusume lāsa karāvala : katihu kṛḍā kautuka karite jāi | tadanantara : śrīkṛṣṇaka se gopī bolala ||*

Dialogue: The cowherd women were very lucky; they have found the greatness of devotion to Kṛṣṇa and having found such devotion to Kṛṣṇa remained intoxicated. Listen to the wicked thinking of that cowherd woman who went with Kṛṣṇa. Śrī Kṛṣṇa, sometimes took that woman on his lap and adorned her with flowers, some other time played and had fun with her. After that, the cowherd woman said to Śrī Kṛṣṇa,

*he svāmi kṛṣṇa : hāmāka padatale kaṇṭake bedhala : calaye nāhi pāri ||*
"Oh Lord Kṛṣṇa, my foot has been pierced by a thorn; I cannot walk any further."

*kṛṣṇa bola* || *he prāṇa rādhe : hāmāka boke caḍasiyā* ||
Kṛṣṇa said: "Oh my life, my love Rādhā, come, climb on my back."

*ohi buli gopīka boke tuli : śrīkṛṣṇa bahaya lāgala || tā dekhaha śunaha : nirantare hari bola hari ||*
Saying thus, Śrī Kṛṣṇa started carrying the cowherd woman on his back; watch and listen to that and keep chanting the name of Hari incessantly.

*gīta || rāga suhāi ||*
Song in the *Rāga Suhāi*:

*dhruṁ||*

*gopīnātha līlā jānaba koi |*
*biparīta kautuka toi ||*

Refrain: "Oh Gopīnātha, can anyone understand your pastimes! Your pleasures are of opposite (strange) nature."

*pada||*

*caudhaya bhubana adhikārī |*
*so boke bahe gopanārī ||*
*jo rahe garuḍa āsane |*
*so hari gopinī bāhane ||*
*bhakata bāndhava ki nā bheli |*
*śaṅkara kaha kṛṣṇa keli ||3||16||*

Verse: Owner of the fourteen worlds, and he carries a cowherd woman on His back. One who sits on the throne of Garuḍa, that same Hari is now the carrier of the cowherd woman. Oh the friend of the devotees what has not become of you! Śaṅkara says such is the sport of Kṛṣṇa.

*kathā ||*

*aicana kṛḍā kaya kṛṣṇe : kāmātura puruṣaka dukha dekhāvala : strī bhaila rājā : kāmātura tanikara dāsa : strīka ājñā pāli sarbbathā thika : ihā jānaba ||*

Dialogue: Sporting thus, Kṛṣṇa showed the plight of the lovesick man. Woman is the ruler and the love-sick man is her servant. He is always obedient to the wishes of his woman, know that for sure.

*śloka ||*

*kṛṣṇena saha sā yāti gopī tanmāna darpitā |*
*kṛṣṇasya skandhamaroḍhuṁ gatā sā duḥsvabhāvataḥ ||16||*

Hymn[23]: The cowherd woman who went with Kṛṣṇa became proud having received the respect of Kṛṣṇa and because of her depraved and vile nature went to climb on the back of Kṛṣṇa.

*kathā* ||

*tadanantara : se strīka duryanya-bhāva śunaha : bokā hante kṛṣṇe namāvala : rādhā hāṇṭhiye cale | kṛṣṇaka sanmāne garbba upajala : bole saba gopī teji hāmāka ānala : aḥ mohi sama kona sobhāginī thika : darpe ṭhes kave baiṭhala : tāhe pekhi śrīkṛṣṇa bola* ||

Dialogue: After that, listen to the evil nature of that woman. Kṛṣṇa put her down from his back and Rādhā (the cowherd woman) started walking. She became proud of Kṛṣṇa's attention towards her and said that "Leaving all the other cowherd women, Kṛṣṇa has brought me along. Oh there is no one as lucky as me.", and sat down stubbornly with pride. Seeing that Kṛṣṇa said,

*he prāṇa rādhe* || *tuhun ki nimite rahala* ||

Kṛṣṇa said: "Oh my life, my love Rādhā, why have you stopped?".

*rādhā bola* || *he kṛṣṇa : tuhu baḍa dāruṇa puruṣa : hāmu bhūmi-pāve calaici : tohō dekhaye nāhi : aba calaye nāhi pāri : jeman kaye niyā java* ||

Rādhā said, "Oh Kṛṣṇa, you are a very heartless man. I am walking on the ground, can't you see? I cannot walk any more. Now carry me anyhow."

*svabhāve cañcalā strī : lāi pāi : īśvara kṛṣṇaka gaṇaya nāhi* | *śuni śrīkṛṣṇa bola* ||

Women are by nature fickle minded; receiving such favour, she did not care for even Lord Kṛṣṇa. Hearing her, Kṛṣṇa said:

*he prāṇa rādhe : atakṣaṇa kene nāhi kaha : jadi calaye nāhi para : hāmāka kāndhe caḍasiyā*||

"Oh my life, my love Rādhā, why have you not told me before? If you cannot walk, come and climb on my shoulder."

[23]. in *Śloka* metre.

*gopī kaṭākṣa nāhi bujhala : bastra kāci kāndhe caḍite range calala : tāhe pekhi kṛṣṇa antardhyāna bhela | gopī kṛṣṇaka nāhi pekhi : bhaya-bihbala huyā : hā kṛṣṇa hā kṛṣṇa buli : jaiche daraśana prārthala : tā śunaha ||*

The cowherd woman could not understand the indirect words and rearranging her clothes, moved on happily to climb onto the shoulder (of Kṛṣṇa). Seeing that, Kṛṣṇa disappeared. Not seeing Kṛṣṇa around, the cowherd woman became greatly scared and uttering "Oh Kṛṣṇa, oh Kṛṣṇa!", as she prayed for his appearance, listen to that.

*gīta || rāga suhāi || māna jauti ||*

Song in the *Rāga Suhāi* with the rhythm *Jauti.*

*dhruṁ||*

*daraśana dehu daāla : meri bandhu madhāi |*
*kaiche karase dāsīka roṣa re :*
*doṣa maraṣa gosāi ||*

Refrain: "Oh merciful, please appear before me, oh dear friend Mādhava. How can you be so angry with your maid servant. Oh God, forgive my faults."

*pada ||*

*niśi ekeśvarī : nārī anāthinī :*
*karo karunā murāri |*
*tuhu bine pāraya : jīvana rahai nā :*
*dahe hṛdaya hāmāri ||1||*
*karala garbba : nātha toi :*
*hāmu pāpinī āndhā |*
*kaha śankara : nara hari bola re :*
*chora biṣayaka dhāndā ||2||17||*

Verse: "Oh merciful Murāri, have mercy on this helpless poor woman in this night. Without you, life cannot continue and my heart is burning. The sinner that I am, I became blind and showed pride to you." Says Śaṅkara, "All of you, oh people, take the name of Hari and leave all material interests."

*kathā* ||

*aicana ārttanāda kave rahala bālā | je gopīsaba kṛṣṇa-bhāvanā kave thika : punu prāṇa kṛṣṇaka sumari : tāpita huyā : bṛndābana pasi bicārala : tadanantara : kṛṣṇaka khoja pekhi kahõ : kāhõ gopī sakhīsabaka je bolala : tā śunaha : nirantare hari bola hari* ||

Dialogue: The cowherd woman continued crying in distress in this way. Those cowherd women who were meditating on Kṛṣṇa remembered, dear like life Kṛṣṇa, again and being aggrieved entered Vṛndāvana and started looking around for Him. After that, seeing footprints, as some of the cowherd women told to their friends, listen to that and keep chanting the name of Hari incessantly.

*gīta : rāga śrīgāndhāra* || *māna* || *ekatāli* ||
Song in the *Rāga Śrīgāndhāra* with the rhythm *Ekatāli:*

*dhruṁ*||

*õre sakhī pekhare : hāmāra jīvana kānu :*
*ohi pathe gaila līlāi* |
*dhaja baja paṅkaja : khoja heralõ re :*
*kamana ramaṇī saṅge jāi* ||

Refrain: "Oh friends, see our life Kānu has gone playing this way, I can see His footsteps along with the signs of His flag, His weapon *vajra* and the lotus. What type of woman is that who is accompanying Him!".

*pada* ||

*satinīra khoja dekhi : hṛdaye nasahe re :*
*ādhiko milala dukha mora* |

*saba gopinīka dhana : bandhu-adhara-madhu*
*piye ekuśvarī kari cora ||1||*
*dekho sakhī satinīka : kole kariyā re :*
*kusume karāyali lāsā |*
*bahe gopinīka kānu : boke tuliā re :*
*kahatu śaṅkara kṛṣṇadāsā ||2||18||*

Verse: Seeing the footsteps of rival mistress the heart cannot endure any more and my sorrows increased even more. Valued object of affection for all the cowherd women is the honey of the lips of their friend (Kṛṣṇa) and it is being drunk by a lone thief. (1)
See, oh friends, taking our rival mistress on His lap, (He) adorns her with flowers, and Kānu carries the cowherd woman on His back, says Śaṅkara, the servant of Kṛṣṇa.

*kathā ||*

*aicana khoja guṭi jāite : gopīsaba se satinīka : krandana śuniyā : bege āsi kahō : rādhāka beḍiyā bāta pucata ||*

Dialogue: In this way following the footsteps, the cowherd women heard the other rival woman crying and moving towards her very fast, encircled Rādhā and asked her about the matter.

*he sakhī : ki bhela ki bhela : prāṇakṛṣṇa kona bhiti gela : satvare kaha ||*

"Oh friend, what has happened, what has happened? In which direction has our life, our love Kṛṣṇa gone, tell us quickly."

*rādhā ākhimukha muci : niśvāsa teji kahō kahala || sakhīsaba : kī pucaha : hāmu abhāginī svāmī kṛṣṇata kona māna nāhi sādhalu : kṛṣṇe boke bāndhi hāmāka phurāvala : se garbbe andha bh[illegible]ilō : kṛṣṇaka kāndha bagāite bhailo : se aparādhe bāndh[illegible]a kṛṣṇa : kona bhiti bhela : ihā nāhi jāno||*

The cowherd woman, wiping out her mouth and eyes and sighing deeply said: "Oh dear friends, what do you ask? I am the unfortunate one, did not show proper respect to my Lord Kṛṣṇa; carrying me on His back, Kṛṣṇa took me around. I became blind with pride about it and dared to climb onto the shoulder of Kṛṣṇa. For that offence of mine, our friend Kṛṣṇa, has gone away in which direction that I do not know."

*ohi buli krandana kave lāgala bālā* ||
Saying thus, the girl started crying.

*śloka* ||

*niśamya tadvaco gopyo nirāśāḥ kṛṣṇa darśane* |
*punaḥ pulinamāgatya jagurgovinda ceṣṭitam* ||17||

Hymn[24]: Listening to her words, the cowherd women became disappointed of having a glance of Kṛṣṇa and returned to the sandy bank (of Yamunā) and singing prayers to Kṛṣṇa tried to get back Govinda.

*kathā* ||

*tāhe śuniye : kṛṣṇa darasane nirāśā bhela : gopīsabe rādhāka saṅge laiyā kaho : jamunāka bāli nāmive : kṛṣṇaka prārthi krandana kave: jaice hariguṇa gāvala : tāhe śunaha* ||

Dialogue: Listening to that, the cowherd women became disappointed of not seeing Kṛṣṇa and taking Rādhā along went down to the sandy bank of the Yamunā and started crying seeking Kṛṣṇa and how they sang the praises of Kṛṣṇa, listen to that.

*gīta : rāga āśovārī* || *ekatāli* ||
Song in the *Rāga Āśovārī* in the rhythm *Ekatāli:*

*dhruṁ*||

*gopinīka kaiche keśava jīva le* |

[24].in *Śloka* metre.

*avahu bāhuri nātha daraśana de* ||

Refrain : Why did Keśava revive the cowherd women, now please come again and appear before us.

*pada* ||

*tuā padapaṅkaja jīvana ādhāru* |
*tāhe nāheri hari rahaye nāpāru* ||
*darasa sarasa mukha- kamala madhāi* |
*karahu karunā kṛṣṇa- kiṅkare gāi* ||1||19||

Verse: Your lotuslike feet are the support for sustaining our lives. Oh Hari, we cannot stay without seeing those (the feet). Show us your fresh lotuslike face, oh Madhāi! Please have mercy on us, sings the servant of Kṛṣṇa.

*kathā* ||

*he bandhu mādhava : tohāri janama nimitte : gokula adhika sampūrṇa bhela : sarbbaloka sukhe rahaici : hāmāka kaice madanaka hāte mārayata thika | he sakhi : tohō yasodānandana naha : jagata rākhite brahmāve prārthala : se nimitte tohō sarbba antaryāmī : śrīkṛṣṇa bekata huyāca : āmarāsabaka : aghabaka batsa putanā bṛṣṭi bahni hante rakṣā karaica : akhana ki nimitte rajanī kahō : banamadhye hāmāka tejala svāmi | je īśvara nārāyaṇa tumi : aicana bhakataka tyāga : tohāka ucita nahe | he nātha : je bhakataka manuratha pure : se hastapadma hāmāra māthe thayosiyā svāmi | jāhera smaraṇe jagataka pāpa hare : sohi padapaṅkaja : hāmāra stana upare arpaha nātha | dekho dekho : tohāri kiṅkarī mari jāña : adharāmṛte jivāvāsiyā svāmi* ||

Dialogue: "Oh dear friend Mādhava, because of your birth Gokula has become more complete. Everyone is living happily and why are you making us die in the hands of Madana. Oh friend, you are not the son of Yaśodā. To maintain this world Brahmā prayed (to you) and that is why you being the omniscient, have appeared as Śrī Kṛṣṇa. You are protecting us all from (the demons like) Agha, Baka, Vatsāsura and Pūtanā, and also saving us from rain and fire. Now, oh Lord, for what reason have you abandoned us in this forest at such hour of the night? You are the Lord Nārāyaṇa, to desert your devotees like this does not suit you. Oh Lord, the hand which fulfills the wishes of the devotees, place that same lotuslike hand on our heads. The feet, remembering which, the sins of this world are washed away, place those same lotuslike feet on our breasts. Look, look, your servants are dying. Bring them to life with the nectar of your lips, oh Lord."

*ohi buli punu jaice krandana kaye prārthala : tāhe dekhaha||*
Saying thus, how they started crying again, look at that.

*gīta : rāga māura || jauti māna ||*
Song in the *Rāga Māura* with the rhythm *Jauti Māna:*

*dhruṁ ||*

*karunā sindhu : jīvana lehu kati lāi :*
*mohana baṁśīra sāne : niśi bipina āni :*
*kaiche tejali madhāi ||*

Refrain: "Oh the ocean of mercy, why do you take our lives? With the sound of the tempting flute, alluring and bringing us to the forest at night, how can you abandon us, oh Madhāi."

*pada||*

*patisuta saba teji : teri kiṅkarī hayo :*
*hāmu mugudhi gopanārī |*
*tuhõ kapaṭa kaya : kaiche nā desi he*
*daraśana meri murāri ||1||*
*tohõ parama dhana : gopinī jīvana :*
*jāni kayalu taju āśā |*
*tohõ daāla : dīnajana bāndhaya :*
*kahatu śaṅkara haridāsā ||2||20||*

Verse: "Leaving our husbands and children, we mesmerised cowherd women, have become your servants, why are you playing tricks on us and not appear before us, oh Murāri? You are very precious and the source of life for the cowherd women; knowing that, we had hoped (to see) you. You are so merciful and friend to the poor people", says Śaṅkara, the servant of Hari.

*kathā* ||

*he svāmi kṛṣṇa : tohāra je caraṇa paṅkaja : kaṭhina tana upare : hāmu lāse lāse thañō gosāñi : sesukomala pāve kaice kaṇṭaka bane beḍāva : ihāka sumarite : prāṇabandhu hāmāra prāṇa phuṭi jāi* ||

Dialogue: "Oh Lord Kṛṣṇa, we would place your lotuslike feet on our hard breasts very softly oh God; with those soft feet how are you moving in a forest full of thorny bushes. Thinking about that, oh friend dearer than life, we almost loose our lives."

*ohi bulite prema upajala : lotaka jhuri māṭi luṭi paḍala : atisaya marama caḍala : dīrgha niśvāsa teji ḍāki bolala* ||

Saying thus, their love increased, tears flowed down to the earth, great love emerged. Sighing long they said aloud.

*he svāmi : tohāri dāsīsaba : marie jāñō : nātha daraśana dehu*||

"Oh Lord, we, your servants, are dying; oh master, please appear before us."

*ohi buli hā kṛṣṇa hā kṛṣṇa ghana ghana jampie : ārttarāye krandana kaya lāgala gopīsaba : se krandanaka urmmi gagana maṇḍala beḍala* ||

Saying thus, uttering "Oh Kṛṣṇa, oh Kṛṣṇa" the cowherd women started wailing repeatedly. The sound wave of that crying crossed even the horizon of the sky.

*śloka* ||

*gopīpremākulaḥ kṛṣṇo vāripūrita locanaḥ* |
*āvirvabhūva tanmadhye sākṣānmadanamohana* ||18||

Hymn[25]: Being engrossed in love for the cowherd women, Kṛṣṇa, eyes filled with tears, appeared before them as if the mesmerising Madana himself.

*kathā* ||

*tadanantara : gopīka prema-bhāvanā dekhiye : śrīkṛṣṇa parama byākula bhaila : hṛdaya drabila : tatakāle gopīsaba madhye : koṭi kandarpa-darppa-dalanu rūpe : jaice bekata bhela : ta dekhaha śunaha : nirantare hari bola hari* ||

Dialogue: After that, seeing the feeling of love of the cowherd women, Śrī Kṛṣṇa became very restless and His heart melted. Immediately, as He (Kṛṣṇa), like the one who destroys the beauty and charm of one crore of Kandarpa, appeared among the cowherd women; watch and listen to that and continue chanting the name of Hari incessantly.

*gīta : rāga dhanaśrī* ||
Song in the *Rāga Dhanaśrī:*

*dhruṁ* ||

*bekata bhela murāri* ||
*gopinī prema-sudhā rase ākula :*
*kamala nayane jhure bāri* ||

Refrain : Being overwhelmed with the flow of the nectar of love, and with tears flowing from the lotus like eyes, Murāri appeared.

*pada* ||

[25]. in *Śloka* metre.

*hāra mukuṭa maṇi : kuṇḍale maṇḍita :*
*śyāma rucira pītabāse* |
*manamatha kauṭi : mathana mana mūruti :*
*indu kauṭi parakāśe* ||1||
*adhara madhura beṇu bāyata āvata :*
*kaṇṭhe kadamba mālā dole* |
*padajuga mañjīra : juraye śaṅkare kaya :*
*ehu rūpe tṛbhubana bhole* ||2||21||

Verse: With necklace, crown and earrings of percious stones, Śyāma, in His yellow clothing was very much attractive. The idol of the mind subdues even crores of Manmatha, and shines like one crore of moons.(1)
Playing the flute sweetly with His lips, He comes with a garland of *kadamba* flowers dangling from His neck and His feet adorned with anklets; with such beauty, makes one forget the three worlds, says Śaṅkara.(2)

*kathā* ||
*aicana koṭi indu parakāśa : kṛṣṇa rūpa pekhie : gopīka tāpa tatkāle dūra gaila : aḥ pāvala pāvala buli : āti satvare uṭhi kahõ : prāṇa mādhavaka beḍi dharala gopīsaba* ||

Dialogue: Seeing the beauty of Kṛṣṇa as if a crore of moons were shining together, all the pains and sufferings of the cowherd women vanished instantly. "Oh, we have found Him, we have found Him!", saying thus (they) got up immediately and all the cowherd women encircled Mādhava, their life.

*śloka* ||
*indriyānāṁ yathā prāṇamāyāntaṁ vīkṣya gopikāḥ* |
*jagṛhuḥ sahasotthāya kṛṣṇaṁ prema rasākulam* ||19||

Hymn[26]: As if life has come back to the sense organs, the cowherd women having found Kṛṣṇa, who is full of love, getting up instantly surrounded Him.

*kathā* ||

*gopīsaba kāhuñ kṛṣṇaka āliṅgi dharala : kāhu padapaṅkaja : kāhu bāhu kāndhe layā suṅghaya : tadanantara prāṇabandhu mādhavaka sanmāna kaye : añcora pāti baisāyā : parama bhakati kave lāgala : kāhuñ dhari hastapāva marddaya : kāhõ tāmbula jogāvaya : kāhõ añcore biñci kahõ : praṇaya kope je bolala : tā śunaha* ||

Dialogue: Some of the cowherd women embraced Him, some taking the lotus like feet, and some, taking His arms on their shoulders smelt it (lovingly), after that, showing respect to friend Mādhava, precious like life, made Him sit spreading out the hanging fore-end of their clothing, started to serve Him with great respect. Some massaged His hands and feet, some supplied Him with areca nut and betel leaf, some fanned Him with their fore-ends of upper clothing and with anger out of love, what they said, listen to that.

*gīta : rāga gaurī* ||

Song in the *Rāga Gaurī*:

*dhruṁ* ||

*jānalu re : prāṇapiu re : teri jaichana rīta* |
*nāi ekutila teri tirībadha bhīta* ||

Refrain: "Now we know, oh dear lord of our lives, your way of doing things. You do not have even a little bit of fear for killing us women."

*pada* ||

*prāṇa ṭuṭata teri caraṇa nā heri* |
*kaiche nā desi daraśana eti beri* ||

---

26. in *Śloka* metre.

*ataye kaṭhina kaicana chitta toi |*
*śaṅkara kaha hari bine gati koi* ||1||22||

Verse: "Life nearly snapped not seeing your feet.
"How can you not appear before us for so long?
"How come your heart is so hard?"
Śaṅkara says there is no other way but Hari.

*kathā* ||

*he svāmi : tohõ kapaṭa kaya : niśi hāmāka banamadhye tejala*||
*ohi bulite nayanaka nīra jhurāi: heṭhamātha kayala gopīsaba* ||

Dialogue: "Oh Lord, you have tricked us and abandoned us in the forest at night." Saying so, tears flowing from their eyes, the cowherd women remained with downcast heads.

*śloka* ||

*nirīkṣya karuṇaṁ kṛṣṇo gopināṁ pītavāsasā* |
*mārjayanmukhamāśvāsya provāca sāśrulocanaḥ* ||20||

Hymn[27]: Seeing the sadness of the cowherd women, Kṛṣṇa with tearful eyes consoled them, wiping away the tears from their face with His yellow clothing.

*kathā* ||

*gopīka karuṇa pekhiye : ṣrīkṛṣṇa sajala nayana bhelā tatkāle uṭhikahõ : pītabastre sakhīsabaka mukha muci kahõ : prabodha kayala* ||

Dialogue: Seeing the sadness of the cowherd women Śrī Kṛṣṇa's eyes became moist, and rising immediately, wiping away their faces with His yellow clothing, consoled them.

*he sakhīsaba : tomrāsabaka aicana prema-bhakatita : hāmu parama ākula : ataye kaṭhina bacana nāhi bolaba* | *hāmāka nimite bilāpa coḍaha : hāmu bacaneka bolo : tā śunaha* ||

"Oh friends, I am very much touched with such love and devotion of you all. Please do not speak such harsh words.

27. in *Śloka* metre

Please stop lamenting for me. I shall say something, listen to that."

*gīta : rāga kedāra*||
Song in the *Rāga Kedāra:*

*dhruṁ* ||
*sakhīsaba aichana bacana nā bola* |
*tohāri parama prema pekhi bhakati :*
*sahaje nā sahe hṛdi mora* ||

Refrain: "Oh dear friends, please do not speak such words. My heart cannot bear your deep love and devotion that I have seen."

*pada* ||
*tohāka bhakati : sujhae nāhi pāru*
*rahala dhāra mohe gopinī* |
*śuna sakhī svarūpa kaho bāṇī* ||
*aba jaba dāya : sundarīsaba āpuna :*
*corabaha taba arini* ||1||
*tohōsaba bine : nāhi bandhu hāmāri*
*prāṇa adhika pṛva māni :*
*aba sakhī bilāpa tāpa tejahu :*
*bhakatabatsala moka jāni :*
*bhakataka dukha dekhi : hṛdi sahe nāhi :*
*śaṅkara kaha hari bāṇī* ||2||23||

Verse: "I cannot repay back your love and devotion, I remain indebted to all of you, oh dear cowherd women, listen oh dear friends, I am telling the truth. Now, when all of you beautiful women will forgive me on your own for all my faults, then only, I shall become free from my debts to you. I have no other friends than you all and I consider you dearer than my life. Now that you know how I love my devotees, oh friends, please stop lamenting, give up this sadness. Seeing the suffering of the devotees, the heart cannot tolerate any more.", Śaṅkara says the words of Hari.

*kathā* ||

*śrīgopāla bola || he sakhīsaba : bilāpa coḍaha : torāsaba je prema bhakati kayala : tāhe sujhaye nāhi pāri : hāmu ṛiṇi hayā rahala : ohi satyabāṇī jāni asūyā coḍaha : hāmāka śapata uṭhaha uṭhaha : parama utsuke hrāsa-keli*[28] *karasiyā* ||

Dialogue: Śrī Gopāla said: "Oh friends, please stop lamenting; the way you have showed love and devotion, I cannot repay you back. I shall remain indebted to you. Knowing that as true, leave your anger. Upon my honour, get up, get up. With great pleasure let us do the sportive dance."

*ohi boli hāte dhari tuli kahõ : jamunāka bāli nāmi : rāsa-kṛḍā ārambhala | gopīsaba biraha-tāpa tejiye : kṛṣṇa bākyāmṛte : tṛpiti hayā : parama ucchuke kṛḍāka prabeśala* ||

Saying thus, holding them by their hands to help them stand up, going down the sands of Yamunā, started the sportive dance. The cowherd women also leaving the pangs of separation and being fully satisfied by the nectar like sweet words of Kṛṣṇa, entered sports with great enthusiasm.

*hari kāhuka cumbaya : kāhāku hāsye nirikhaya : kāhāku nakhe tana paraśaya : kāhāku āliṅgaya : ebambidha anaṅga-khelāye : gopīka citta rañji: śrīgopāle kṛḍā kayala | gopīsaba kṛṣṇaka : sanmāna pāi : jaice parama utsuke keli kayala : tā dekhaha śunaha* ||

Hari kissed some cowherd women, glanced at some others with a smile, touched some others on their breasts with His nails, embraced some others. In this way, with such sports of Anaṅga, entertaining the minds of the cowherd women Śrī Gopala had His pastime.

28. *rāsa keli.*

The cowherd women also, receiving honour from Kṛṣṇa, how they took part in the play with great eagerness, look and listen to that.

*gīta : rāga māura* ||
Song in the *Rāga Māura:*

*braja ramaṇī saṅge : khelata gopāla :*
*ānande mana magane* |
*hariko makara : kuṇḍala lelā kāhuñ*
*bihasi hāsi badane* || *dhruṁ* ||

Gopāla played with the women of Vraja with His mind fully engrossed in happiness; some (women) took away the spider shaped earrings with a widely smiling face. Refrain

*pada* ||

*kāhu karu-kaṅkaṇa kāḍhi lelā kāhuñ*
*hāsi bāśī lelā gori* |
*pīta-ambaru bara : bālā lelā hasi :*
*kāhu karaya kara-mori* ||*1*||
*kāhuñ kadambamāla*[29] *bālā lelā hasi :*
*kaṇṭha kaustubha kāhu lelā* |
*ramaṇīka bināye : ramayā mage :*
*śaṅkara kaha hari- khelā* ||2||24||

Verse: Some took away the bracelets from His wrists; some other beautiful women smilingly took away the flute. Some other smiling beautiful girls took away the yellow clothing and some squeezed His hands. (1)

Some other girls laughing, took away the garland of *kadamba* flowers, some others took away the *kaustubha* gem from (Kṛṣṇa's) neck. One who bestows pleasure (Kṛṣṇa), asks them back from the women with great modesty; such is the game of Hari, says Śaṅkara.

---

[29]. *kadambamālā.*

*kathā* ||

*gopīsaba śrīkṛṣṇaka beḍi dhari kahõ : kāhu basana : kāhu baṁśī : kāhu kaṅkaṇa : kāḍhi leleha | kṛṣṇe binaye khujite : hāsi hāsi punu pindhāvala | āhe lokāi : pekho pekho : jāhera caraṇa brahmārudrādi dhyāne dharaya : sohi parameśvara : ajñānī anācārī : gopanārī : sesaba sahite : kāma-keli kaya thika : hari bhakatika aicana mahimā : ihā jāni nirantare hari bola hari* ||

Dialogue: Encircling Śrī Kṛṣṇa, some of the cowherd women snatched away His clothes, some others His flute, some others took away His bracelet. When Kṛṣṇa asked them modestly, they put them back on. Oh dear people, look look, whose feet, even Gods like Brahmā and Rudra meditate upon, that same Supreme God, played love game with the ignorant cowherd women who do not follow customs. Such is the greatness of devotion to Kṛṣṇa; knowing this, utter the name of Hari incessantly.

*śloka* ||

*tato'ti kautukodrekaṁ niśamya braja yoṣitām* |
*gopībhirbhagavān kāmakrīḍāmārabhatācyutaḥ* ||21||

Hymn[30]: Then seeing the rising desire of the women of Braja, Achyuta started sporting love games with the cowherd women.

*kathā* ||

*tadanantara : śrīkṛṣṇa saṅge niyā : raṅge anaṅga-keli karate : jamunāka bāli nāmi : rāsa maṇḍala kayala : jata gopī tata mūruti huyā : bāhu meli gopīka kaṇṭha āliṅgi kaho : jaicana kṛḍā kayala : tā dekhaha śunaha* ||

Dialogue: After that, Śrī Kṛṣṇa, taking them along, playing amorous sports with great happiness, going down to the sandy bank of Yamunā, formed a circle for sportive dance, and taking as many forms as there were cowherd women,

[30]. in *Śloka* metre.

spreading out His hands and embracing them by their necks as He sported with them, watch and listen to that.

*gīta : rāga gaurī* ||
Song in the *Rāga Gaurī:*

*dhruṁ*||

*bhubana bhulāi : ānande gobinda nāche :*
*prabhu nāchata caraṇa calāi* |
*bhuja meli keli : karata kaṇṭha ālāṅgi :*
*raṅginī gopī milāi* ||

Refrain :Forgetting the world Govinda dances with bliss, the lord dances moving his steps. Outstretching His arms and holding them by the neck in an embrace, (Govinda) starts sporting, gathering together the playful cowherd women.

*pada* ||

*jata gopī tata : mūruti mādhava :*
*calali laya lāse hāse* |
*joiche hemamaṇi : mājhe mājhe :*
*maṇimarakata parakāśe* ||*1*||
*karaite nṛtya : kaṅkaṇa jhanakita:*
*mañjīra runjhuna role* |
*kaha śaṅkara keli : hariko herata:*
*sura-ramaṇī para bhole* ||2||25||

Verse: As many cowherd women, so were the forms of Mādhava, moving in slow rhythmic movement with a smile, as if gold intermittent with dazzling emeralds. (1)
While dancing, the bangles jingled and the anklets tinkled. Śaṅkara says that seeing Hari dance, even the goddesses forgot everything else.(2)

*kāthā* ||

*aicana kṛṣṇasame nānā kṛḍā karite gopīsaba : ānanda samudre mana magna hayā : sabahi bole : hāmāka mātra kṛṣṇe ālāṅgi rahe : ohi boli kautuka keli kaya thika | sohi samaye punaḥ : śaṅkhacūḍa jakṣa : gopīka bhaya janite āvala : tāhe pekhiye : trāhi trāhi buli gopīsaba : kṛṣṇata śaraṇa lela : bikrama dekhāyā kṛṣṇe jakṣaka khedāyala | tadanantara : punaḥ kṛḍā kaya lāgala : śrīkṛṣṇa gopīgaṇa same jaice : tā dekhaha śunaha ||*

Dialogue: In this way playing many games with Kṛṣṇa, the cowherd women became absorbed in the ocean of happiness and everyone said, "Let Kṛṣṇa embrace only me.", and saying thus continued sporting.

At that time, a demon named Śaṅkhacuḍa arrived there again to scare the women. Seeing that, the cowherd women saying "Save us, save us!", took refuge under Kṛṣṇa. Showing much valour, Kṛṣṇa chased the demon away.

After that, as Kṛṣṇa started sporting again with the cowherd women, watch and listen to that.

*gīta : rāga nāṭa |*

Song in the *Rāga Nāṭa:*

*dhruṁ ||*

*khele madhura madhāi re :*
*saṅge gopinī nāce re*
*jaiche tarita jaḍita mehu :*
*maṇḍalī prakāśe re ||*

Refrain: Sweet Madhāi plays and dances on along with the cowherd women and looking as bright as if lightning illuminating the dark cloud.

*pada ||*

*calite cumbayi bālā : gāye gīta nika re |*
*gopī gopālaka keli : milala adhika re ||1||*
*dharata gopinī kaṇṭhe : bāhu meli keli re |*
*bhuli śaśadhara ratha : tambhita bheli re ||2||*
*heraye sura-ramaṇī : mūruchita bheli re |*
*gobinda karata keli : śaṅkara bola re ||3||26||*

Verse : Kissing the beautiful women while moving and singing melodious songs, Gopāla and the cowherd women had more fun in their amorous sports. (1)
While sporting, Kṛṣṇa embraced the cowherd women by their necks. Seeing that, the chariot of the moon stopped with amazement.
Seeing (the wonderful sight), even the goddesses fainted, Govinda played (such) amorous sports, says Śaṅkara.

*śloka* ||

*surasebita śrīkṛṣṇa -krīḍāpīḍāturā bhṛśam* |
*śarīraṁ nāpi uddhartuṁ śekurgokulayoṣitaḥ* ||22||

Hymn[31]: The women of Vraja became very much dishevelled with the amorous sports of Śrī Kṛṣṇa, who is worshipped even by the gods, and they became unable to hold their bodies upright.

*kathā* ||

*śrīkṛṣṇaka kṛḍāye pīḍita hayā : se gokulakāminīsaba ākula bhela : keśa beśa khacala : bastra sambaraye nāhi : kaṇṭhaka sātesari ciṇḍi paḍala : kaṭika mekhalā śithila bhela : kucaku kāñculi phāṭi paḍala : saba sarire gharmma bahaya : mukhe svāsa phokāre : kṛṣṇaka dhari kahõ : mahā śrānta huyā rahala* | *śrīkṛṣṇa gopīsabaka : jaice śrama dūra kayala : tā dekhaha śunaha : nirantare hari bola hari* ||

Dialogue: Being tormented by Śrī Kṛṣṇa with His amorous sports, the women of Gokula became overcome with fatigue; their hairdo loosened, clothes became dishevelled, their necklace fell apart torn, the waist clothing loosened, the blouse, covering the breasts tore, sweat flowed throughout the body, taking deep breaths and being very exhausted, they remained holding onto Kṛṣṇa. How Śrī Kṛṣṇa removed their fatigue, watch and listen to that and keep chanting the name of Hari without stopping.

---

[31]. in *Śloka* metre.

*gīta : rāga gaurī* ||

Song in the *Rāga Gaurī:*

*dhruṁ* ||

*karata surata-keli : gopī durabali bheli* |
*dhari harikaṇṭha rahatava bāhu meli* ||

Refrain: Playing amorous game, the cowherd women become weak, and spreading out their arms remained holding onto Kṛṣṇa's neck.

*pada* ||

*sutala kāminī kāhuñ hariko kole* |
*kānu gopīka pīta ambaru ḍole* ||1||
*śramajalabindu indubadana birāje* |
*hari kāhuka*[32] *karapaṅkaje jala māje*||2||
*kāhuka keśa keśava bāndhe hate* |
*śaṅkara kaha khele gopinī nāthe* ||3||27||

Verse: Some women slept down on the lap of Hari and Kānu fanned them with His yellow clothing. (1)
(As) sweat covered their moon-like faces, Hari wiped off some of their sweat with His lotus like hands. (2)
(He) tidied up the hair of some others with His own hands. This is how the lord of the cowherd women played, says Śaṅkara. (3)

*kathā* ||

*śrīgopāle kāhu gopīka keśa bāndhala : kāhuka gāve āgara-candana ghasala: karpūra tāmbula sāji yogāvala : eyambidha nānā khelāna kaye kaho : gopī sabaka śrama dūra kayala | āhe lokāi : pekho pekho : kauṭi kauṭi brahmāṇḍaka īśvara śrīkṛṣṇa : kaire anācārī gopī : tāhe kṛpāe śrama dūra kavala : hari- bhakatika mahimā ki kahaba : ihā jāni nirantare hari bola hari* ||

Dialogue : Śrī Gopāla tied up the hair of some of the cowherd women: smeared perfumes like *āgar* and sandal on some of

32. *kāhāku.*

their bodies, offered some with camphor and betel nut, well decorated and beautifully prepared. In this way playing many different games, (He) removed the tiredness of the cowherd women.

Oh dear people, look look, Śrī Kṛṣṇa, the master of crores and crores of universes, removed the tiredness of unknown indecorous cowherd women with mercy. What to say about the greatness of devotion to Hari! Knowing that, keep chanting the name of Hari incessantly.

*śloka* ||

*tataḥ āgatya tarasā gopāle kṛtakautuke* |
*jahāra yakṣo gopināmekāṁ kāmabimohitaḥ* ||23||

Hymn[33]: While Gopāla was having fun, suddenly a *yakṣa* arrived there and being lustful, carried away one of the cowherd women.

*kathā* ||

*gopīsaba sahite : nānā bidha kautuka keli kave : śrīgopāla tathi thika* | *tadanantara : parama kāmātura haya : jakṣa śaṅkhacūḍa : kāle garasala : hrāsa maṇḍala hante : eka gopīka dhari kaho : kole kari bege kaho lavaḍa dela* | *tāhe pekhi saba gopī tarāse kāmpaya : trāhi kṛṣṇa jampaya* | *jo gopīka jakṣe layā jāi : se bālā trāhi kṛṣṇa trāhi kṛṣṇasvāmi : anāthaka bandhu buli : ārttarāya kaye jāi* | *anantare bhakataka dukha dekhi kope gopala : sāla bṛkṣa utpāṭi kaho : tāhe tuli : jakṣaka tatkāle dhāyā calala : are pāpī : kāhā jāvaba : raha raha buli ḍāka cāḍala* ||

Dialogue: Śrī Gopāla was there playing many different games with the cowherd women. After that, being very lusty, demon Śaṅkhacūḍa was (as if) seized by his death incarnate. Clasping one cowherd woman from among the circular dance, and taking her on his lap, ran away fast. Seeing that, all the cowherd women trembled with fear and chanted

33. in *Śloka* metre, but in the 1st foot , the 6th and 7th letters are short instead of long and in the 3rd foot, the 5th letter is long instead of short and the 7th letter is short instead of long.

the name of Kṛṣṇa, praying for safety. That cowherd woman who was taken away by the demon cried aloud calling "Save me Kṛṣṇa, oh Lord Kṛṣṇa save me, save me oh the friend of the helpless." After that seeing the anguish of His devotee, Gopāla became very angry and uprooting a *sāl* tree, and carrying it, chased after the demon. "Oh you sinner, where will you go? Wait, wait!", saying so called at the demon.

*payāḍa* ||

*coḍa coḍa pāpī gopī hāmārā* |
*garajaya jakṣaka nanda-kumārā* ||

Refrain : "Oh you sinner, let go of my cowherd woman!", roared the son of Nanda (Kṛṣṇa), to the demon.

*pada* ||

*trāhi trāhi kṛṣṇa gopinī rāye* |
*pācu pācu tacu mādhave dhāve* ||*1*||
*nāhi nāhi bhaya bole gopāla* |
*jakṣaka khede dhari taru sāla* ||
*re re śaṅkhacūḍa tirī- cora* |
*moḍaba ghāḍa coḍa gopī mora* ||2||
*śuni tarāse jīu gaila uḍi* |
*pāpī palāvata gopinī eḍi* ||
*begahi jāi jani sarbatrāsa* |
*jakṣaka khede deva diṣapāṣa* ||3||
*rahi kope dānta kāmuḍi khāi* |
*khepala śūla mādhavaka lāi* ||
*pekhi tahe hari kari āsphāla* |
*bhāṅgala śūla hāni taru sāla* ||4||
*lavaḍe śaṅkhacūḍa uḍi prāṇa* |
*dhāve pācu pācu puruṣa purāṇa* ||
*bāghaka āgu palāya jaca cāga* |
*dharala gopāla pāi tacu lāga* ||5||
*mārala kope muṣṭi gopīnātha* |

*paḍala jakṣaka ciṇḍikaho mātha* ||
*tāheka ratna cūḍāmaṇi āni* |
*gopīka abhaya bulila bāṇī* ||6||
*tāhe pekhi gopī dānta prakāśi* |
*sādhu sādhu kaya pujaya hāsi* ||
*mārala śaṅkhacuḍa durācāra* |
*milala raṅga- ḍhaṅga gopikāra* ||7||
*śirata kānura kusuma siñce* |
*beḍhi kāhu kāhu āñcore biñce* ||
*moce śramajala kato gopinī* |
*katoho gāyata gīta āpuni* ||8||
*kṛṣṇaka bhakati mokṣa nidāna* |
*śuna saba loka beda pramāṇa* ||
*kṛṣṇaka kiṅkara śaṅkare bole* |
*pabitra karā hari hari bole* ||9||

Verse: "Oh Kṛṣṇa, save me, save me!", cried the cowherd woman and behind her, Mādhava ran following. (1)
Saying, "There is nothing to fear", Gopāla chased the demon holding the *sāl* tree. "Oh you, thief of woman, leave alone my cowherd woman or I shall strangle your neck." (2)
Hearing Him Śaṅkhacūḍa's heart nearly failed and the sinner fled leaving the cowherd woman behind. Going fast, creating fear in the minds of everyone, the God chased the demon in all directions. (3)
Being angry, (the demon) started to chew his own teeth and hurled the spear towards Mādhava. Seeing that, Hari attacked and throwing the *sāl* tree broke the spear. (4)
Saving his life, Śaṅkhacūḍa started running, like goats fleeing from tigers, and behind him ran chasing the Etermal Person. Gopāla reaching near, caught hold of the demon. (5)
With great anger, Gopīnātha planted a heavy blow and the demon fell down with his head severed from his body. Bringing that to the cowherd woman the Supreme Person assured her of safety.(6)

Seeing that, the cowherd woman smiled widely showing her teeth and saying "Well done, well done!", worshipped Him with a smile. Śaṅkhacūḍa, the evil, was killed and the cowherd women became elated. (7)
Some cowherd women sprinkled flowers on the head of Kānu and encircling Him, some others fanned Him with the hanging fore-end of their clothing. Some cowherd women wiped away His sweat and some others sang songs (of praises) themselves. (8)
Devotion to Kṛṣṇa is the way of achieving salvation. Oh all of you dear people, listen to that as even the Vedas prove that. Śaṅkara, the servant of Kṛṣṇa, says, "Purify everything, uttering 'Hari! Hari!' " (9)

*śloka* ||

*nihatya gopī- harttāraṁ yakṣaṁ strībhistuto hariḥ*
*jala krīḍāṁ samārebhe praviśya yamunājalam.* ||24||

Hymn[34]: Killing the abductor of the cowherd woman, Hari then, entering the water of Yamunā, along with the women, started playing in water.

*kathā* ||

*tadanantara : śaṅkhacūḍa jakṣa mārikaho : parama pṛya gopīgaṇa sahita : jamunāka jala praveśi : ati kautuke jala-kṛḍā ārambhala | mattamātaṅga jaice : hastinisaba sahite : līlāye khelāvata : saba gopī beḍikaho : śrīkṛṣṇa jaice jala-līlā kavala : tāhe dekhaha śunaha : nirantare hari bola hari* ||

Dialogue: After that, killing demon Śaṅkhacūḍa, Kṛṣṇa with His most beloved cowherd women, entering the water of river Yamunā, started playing in water with great fun. As elephants in rut play sportively with the female elephants, how Kṛṣṇa, encircled by the cowherd women, enjoyed playing in the water, watch and listen to that and keep chanting the name of Hari.

---

[34]. in *Śloka* metre, but in the 1st foot, the 5th letter is not short but long.

*gīta : rāga gaurī* ||
Song in the *Rāga Gaurī:*

*dhruṁ*||

*karata gopāla jala-keli*
*caubhiti gopinī : pānī sechata hasi*
*ramayāke muha nehāri* ||

Refrain: Gopāla was having fun in the water and all around, the cowherd women splashed water laughing and looking at the face of their charming lover (Kṛṣṇa).

*pada* ||

*kāhuka ambaru : choḍi lelā hari :*
*kāhuka āliṅgana dāna* |
*kahuka bhore : kore kari cumbñana:*
*kāhuka kaca nakhe hāna* ||*1*||
*matta gaja jaichana: jala maha khelatu :*
*taruṇī karani saba saṅge* |
*līlā gopāla : pekhi sura- sundarī :*
*dārala hṛdaya anaṅge* ||2||
*jāheri caraṇa : surāsura sevata :*
*so hari gopinīka piu* |
*śaṅkara kaha hari : caraṇa śira dhari :*
*tāru tāru jagajīu*||3||29||

Verse: Hari stole away the clothing of some of the cowherd women and offered some others with His embrace; being agitated, took some of them on the lap and kissed them; scratched some others on the breasts with His nails. (1)
Like an elephant in rut plays in the water with the female elephants, seeing such amorous games of Gopāla, the hearts of the goddesses were pricked by Anaṅga. (2)
Whose feet are worshipped even by gods and demons, that same Hari is the master of all the cowherd women. Śaṅkara says "Oh Hari, I take your feet on my head, oh the life of the world, please save us, protect us." (3)

*kathā* ||

*ebambidha nānā khelanā kave : jalakeli samāpala | tadanantara : gopīsaba kṛṣṇaka sebā kaya lāgala : kāho pītabastra paridhāna karāye : kāho gandha- candana gāye carḍāye : kāho kadambñamālā gānthi gale pindhāve : kāho tāmbñula sāji jogāve : kāho āñcore biñce : kāho surabhi kusuma siñce : kāho kṛṣṇa-mukha-paṅkaja nayana-bhṛṅge pivata : kāho kāho bālā : beḍi govindara guṇa gāvata : kāhuka prema-raṣe śarīra pulakita : nayanaka nīra dhārāye bariṣe : bhāgyavatī gopīsaba mahodaya pāvala | āhe lokāi : pekho pekho : parama anācārī gopanārī : kāmabhāve hariguṇa gāi : parama gati pāvala : hari bhakatika aicana mahimā : ācārī anācārī bāchaye nāhi : ihā jāni nirantare hari bola hari* ||

Dialogue: In this way, playing different games concluded the water sports. After that, the cowherd women started offering their services to Kṛṣṇa. Some clothed Him in yellow clothing, some smeared Him with perfumed sandal on His body. Some strung garlands of *kadamba* flowers and put them around His neck. Some prepared the betel and offered to Him, some fanned Him with the long hanging fore-ends of their clothing, some others sprinkled Him with fragrant flowers. Some others drank the (nectar of) beauty of the lotus like face of Kṛṣṇa with their eyes like the big black bees. Some of the cowherd girls, surrounding Him, sang the praises of Govinda. Bodies of some others shivered out of excitement of love and tears started flowing down their eyes. The fortunate cowherd women received great fortune. Oh dear people, look, look, the cowherd women, who didn't follow customs, singing the praises of Hari with an amorous feeling have achieved salvation. Such is the greatness of devotion to Hari. He does not discriminate between the good and the depraved; knowing that, keep chanting the name of Hari incessantly.

*śloka* ||

*ebaṁ bṛndāvane tasmin byatītāṁ krīḍayā niśām |*
*nirīkṣya bhagavānāha brajaṁ yātāvalādrutam* ||25||

Hymn[35]: In this way having fun, the night ended and observing that, God told the women of Vraja to go home back immediately.

*kathā* ||

*nirbhara kṛdā karite sakala niśi samāpala : pekhi śṛīkṛṣṇa bola*||

Dialogue : Beeing deeply engrossed in playing, the night nearly ended and seeing that, Śrī Kṛṣṇa said:

*he sakhīsaba : jābata prasanna nāhi hove : tāve satvare ājū brāja jāva: bilambña parihara* ||

"Oh dear friends, when it is yet to be morning, go back to Vraja immediately for today and avoid any delay."

*aicana bāṇī śuni : gopīsakalaka māthe : jaice kalasa bhāṅgala : niśvāsa phokāri mukhe bacana harala : tabadha nayane heṭha mātha kavala* ||

Hearing such words, the cowherd women as if had an urn broken on their heads. Releasing deep sighs, at a loss for words, and with eyes fixed, stayed with downcast heads.

*punaḥ kṛṣṇa bola* || *he sakhīsaba* || *jāve nāhi prabhāta haya : loke nāhi jānata : tāve satvare gṛhaka cala | hāmāka yadi rākhaba : bege java*||

Kṛṣṇa said again, "Oh dear friends, when it is not morning yet, people will not know, so go home quickly. If you want to keep me with you, go quickly."

*gopīsaba śuni : niśvāsa phokāri : kṛṣṇara caraṇa-reṇu : māthe mākhi : parama maune braja calala : jaice rajanīka gāri dei : kukurāku śapaya : tā dekhaha śunaha : nirantare hari bola hari* ||

35. in *Śloka* metre.

Hearing that, sighing deeply, smearing the dust of His feet on the head quietly, the cowherd women returned back to Vraja, and how they scolded the night and cursed the cock, watch and listen to that and keep chanting the name of Hari incessantly.

*gīta : rāga ahira*
Song in the *Rāga Ahira:*

*dhruṁ*||
*bahuri gaurī gopāla prāṇa nehāri* |
*phokāre nisvāśā : calaye nāhi caraṇā :*
*nayanā pūrita bāri*||

Refrain: Looking back at Gopāla who was dear like life, and sighing deeply and their feet not wanting to move, the eyes of the young girls became full of tears.

*pada*||
*kukurā rāve : jāni rayanī śeṣa :*
*tāku śapaya putamāthe* |
*āju bairī niśi : nimiṣe puhāvali :*
*hāmāku tejala prāṇanāthe* ||1||
*bhari pāñca sāta : calite tanu tāpita :*
*hari bine dekho āndhiāri* |
*prema paraśe punu : paraye parani luṭi :*
*śaṅkara udhāra murāri* ||2||30||

Verse: The cock crows knowing that the night ended, even he is cursed in the name of their (the cowherd women's) son. The night is like an enemy today, (passed very fast) and the day broke in a blink of an eye; and so the lord of our lives has deserted us. (1)

Even to move five to seven steps with our feet, the body suffers and we see darkness all around without Hari. Again with His loving touch, men crumple down crushing to the ground. Oh Murāri, please deliver Śaṅkara. (2)

*kathā* ||

*śrīkṛṣṇaka tejite jaice prāṇa cuṭe : māṭi loṭi krandana karaye bālāsaba : tāhe pekhi śrīkṛṣṇa prabodhi bolala* ||

Dialogue : To leave behind Kṛṣṇa as if they loose their lives; rolling on the ground, the young girls started crying. Seeing that, consoling them, Kṛṣṇa said:

*sakhīsaba : ucita nohe : āju gṛhe jāva : prāṇasakhīsaba : hāmāku bacana rākhaha : uṭhaha uṭhaha* ||

*gopīsaba śuni : ākhimukha muci : śrīkṛṣṇaka praṇāmi : punaḥ calala : bhari āgaku bāḍhaye nāhi : kathaṅkathamapi brajajāi : kico kṛtya karaye nāhi pārie : kevala kṛṣṇacaraṇa cinti rahala : kṛṣṇaka birahe saba dehā dahaye : ekathāna huyā: kṛṣṇaguṇa gai : jaice dibasa bañcala : ta śunaha : nirantare haribola hari* ||

"Oh dear friends, it is not proper, go home today, oh my life, oh dear friends, please obey my words and please get up, get up."

Listening to Him, the cowherd women wiping clean their eyes and face and offering obeisance to Kṛṣṇa moved again. Their feet did not move forward, and somehow only reached Vraja. But not being able to do any work, remained thinking of Kṛṣṇa only. Their whole body burned from the pain of separation from Kṛṣṇa. Gathering together, singing the praises of Kṛṣṇa, how they spent the day, listen to that and keep chanting the name of Hari incessantly.

*gīta : rāga tathā* || *ekatāli* ||[36]

Song in the *Rāga Tathā* with the rhythm *Ekatāli:*

*dhruṁ :*

*māyi māi : harika bicuri kata rahari*[37]*:*
*jāhe nehāri sura : ramaṇī mūruchi pare :*
*tāhe biraha kata sahari*[38]||

[36]. *Rāga- Ahira, Jauti Tāla* (Goswami, K. D., *Aṅkamālā,* 1999, p. 115).

[37]. *rahabi.*

[38]. *sahabi.*

Refrain: "Alas, oh dear mother, being separated from Hari where will you stay? Seeing whom, even the celestial damsels faint out, how can you bear separation from Him?"

*pada* ||

*bāma bāhuta bāma* : *kapole milāya keli:*
*kadambñaka mūle beṇu bāi* |
*śuni beṇu dhenu* : *dharata tṛṇa daśanu* :
*rahi*[39] *nīra nayana jurāi* ||*1*||
*śuniā mohana dhuni* *tambhita taraṅginī* :
*pulaka kamalakula dole* |
*hariṇi harāyata* : *cetana etanu* :
*bichuri rahata rasa bhole* ||2||
*nīla tanu pītapaṭa* : *pekhi gagana ghana* :
*boli suruja karo māna* |
*chāyā chatra dharata* : *karata madhura dhuni*
*kṛṣṇa kiṅkare rasa bhāṇa* ||3||*31*||

Verse: Placing the left arm on the left forehead plays the flute under the *keli-kadamba* tree. Hearing the sound of the flute the cows stop, holding the grass between their teeth and tears flow. (1)
Hearing such sweet mesmerising tune, the river (Yamunā) stops flowing and all the flowers like lotus move with the rhythm. The deer gets engrossed by its (tune's) charm and as if senseless, forgets about its own existance. (2)
Seeing His (Kṛṣṇa's) deep blue figure with yellow clothing, the dark cloud asked the sun to show respect to Him and, as if holding an umbrella shaded Him and He (Kṛṣṇa) created sweet melodious sounds; this is how Śaṅkara, the servant of Kṛṣṇa, describes about the enjoyment.(3)

*kathā* ||

*he sakhīsaba : jekhane śrīkṛṣṇa : bāma bāhu bāma kapole thāpi : komala aṅgulicaya cāli : beṇu bajāvaya : tā śuni sura-sundarīsaba : muruci paraya : dhenusaba tṛṇa dante nayanaka*

[39].*bahi*.

*nīra jhure : hariṇīsaba cetana harāvata : nadīsaba kāme kampaye raha : pekhu pekhu birikha-paśu : se sabo kṛṣṇa-gīte mohita haya : se prāṇabandhu birahe hāmu kaice jīva rākhaba* ||

Dialogue: Oh dear friends, when Kṛṣṇa, placing His left arm on His forehead, moving His soft fingers plays the flute, listening to that tune even the beautiful celestial women faint out. The cows remain holding the blade of grass in their teeth and tears flow from their eyes. The deers loose consciousness and the rivers keep trembling with desire. Look, look, the trees and animals as well become mesmerised with the music by Kṛṣṇa. How can we live being separated from such a friend, who is dear like life.

*aicana bevahāre : kṛṣṇa guṇa gāi : biraha bilāpa kaya: dinasaba bañcaya : sandhyā samaye : purbbavate bṛndābane gaiyā kahu : punupṛānakṛṣṇa sahita : samasta śarat rātṛ : hrāsakṛḍā kaya rahata gopīsaba : śrīkṛṣṇa evambidha nānā khelanā kaya gopīsabaka manoratha pūrala | ohi kāmajaya : keligopāla nāma nāṭaka sampūrṇa bhela | āhe lokāi : ohi bhārata barikhe : naratanu koṭi kalapa antaro jīve nāhi pāi| biśeṣata kalijuge : kṛṣṇa-guṇanāma śravaṇa kīrtana bine gati nāhi : ihā jāni nirantare haribola hari* ||

Behaving in this way, the cowherd women, singing the praises of Kṛṣṇa, lamenting for the separation from Him, spent the days somehow. In the evenings, going to Vṛndāvana like before, (they) spent the whole autumn nights having amorous fun with Kṛṣṇa, who was dear like their lives. In this way, playing different games, Śrī Kṛṣṇa, fulfilled the wishes of the cowherd women.

That is the victory of love and here the drama by the name Keligopāla is completed.

Oh dear people, in this land of Bhāratavarṣa, a soul does not get a chance to have birth as human being even after crores of *kalpas*.

Especially in this age of Kali, there is no other way for salvation but listening to and chanting the name of Hari. Knowing that, keep chanting the name of Hari incessantly.

*tadanantara : capaya chande : maṅgala bola* ||
After that, in the *Capaya* metre, here is the benediction.

*bhaṭimā* |
*mīna rūpe pralaya payasi*
*satyabrata jo tārile* |
*kuruma rūpe : khīra sāgara :*
*mathane mandara dhārile* ||
*śukara rūpe : hiraṇya bidāri :*
*deva bhaya kayo trāṇa* |
*sohi hari teri : karatu nitya :*
*mukuti maṅgala bidhāna* ||*1*||
*narasiṁha rūpa : prakaṭi āṭope :*
*hiraṇyakasipu dārile* |
*bāmana mūruti : bali chali kahõ :*
*indra johi tārile* ||
*paraśurāma : nāme avatari :*
*kṣatra kaya nirajāna* |
*sohi hari teri : karatu nitya :*
*mukuti maṅgala bidhāna* ||2||
*dāśarathi rāma : rūpa dhari kahõ :*
*jaladhi bāndhala setu* |
*sītā uddhārala :badhala bairī :*
*e daśaskandha dhumaketu* ||
*rāma haladhara : rūpe dhenuka :*
*dibidha kara nirajāna* |
*sohi hari teri : karatu nitya :*
*mukuti maṅgala bidhāna* ||3||
*bodha mūruti : jagata mohiye :*
*kayala pāṣaṇḍa rita* |

*dharama dūra gela : bhela malamati :*
*loka sakala kalita ||*
*kalaki rūpe: bhakataka tāri :*
*karabi mleca uchāna |*
*sohi hari teri: karatu nitya :*
*mukuti maṅgala bidhāna||4||*
*kṛṣṇa rūpe : parama īśvara :*
*bheli līlā avatāra |*
*jāsu nāma guṇa : śravaṇa-kīrtana :*
*karata jagata udhāra ||*
*johi agha baka : kaṁsa kubalaya :*
*kayala māri nirajāna |*
*sohi hari teri : karatu nitya :*
*mukuti maṅgala bidhāna ||5||*
*jāhe mahimā : brahmā śaṅkara :*
*kabahu anta napāi |*
*jāsu nāma dhari : munibara pāmara :*
*duhō eka gati pāi ||*
*jahe bhakatika : śakatika aicana :*
*nigama saba paramāṇa |*
*sohi hari teri : karatu nitya:*
*mukuti maṅgala bidhāna ||6||*
*śrīrāma rāyā : hariko paramā :*
*bhakati rasika sujāna |*
*keli gopāla : karāvata nāṭaka :*
*kṛṣṇa- kiṅkara ohi bhāṇa ||*
*śunaha budhajana : nāhi nindaba :*
*mohi nāhi doṣa bakhāna |*
*johi sohi bāṇī : hari guṇa miśrita :*
*mukuti milāvata jāna ||7||*
*devaka durllabha : bhārate naratanu :*
*hari bine biphalehi jāi |*
*ohi janama : cintāmaṇi kaice :*
*becahu kācaku lāi ||*

*ohi saṁsāra : sāra nāhi heraba :*
*hariko bino guṇanāma* |
*nistara nistara : loka nirantara :*
*ḍāki bolahu rāma rāma* ||8||

Eulogy: Taking the form of a big fish one who rescued Satyavrata from amidst the deep waters of dissolution. In the form of a tortoise holding the weight of the Mount Mandara helped in the churning of the ocean of milk. In the form of a huge boar, ripping up Hiraṇyākṣa, saved the gods from their fear. To that same Hari, we pray every day asking for well-being and salvation. (1)

Appearing in the form of Narasiṁha tore apart Hiraṇyakaśipu with great prowess. In the form of Vāmana outwitted Bali and saved Indra. In His incarnation as Paraśurāma, (He) annihilated the *kṣatriyas*. To that same Hari, we pray every day asking for well-being and salvation.(2)

Taking the form of Rāma, the son of Daśaratha, constructed a bridge on the sea, and rescued Sītā killing the enemy, the ten-headed meteor (Rāvaṇa). In the form of Rāma, the Lord with a plough, annihilated the demons Dhenuka and Dvividha. To that same Hari, we pray every day asking for well-being and salvation.(3)

In the form of Buddha mesmerised the whole world and transformed the wicked and sinners into well behaved human beings. So in the age of Kali religion forsook the people and they became shallow in their minds. In the form of Kalki, you will protect the devotees and you will destroy the wicked persons. To that same Hari, we pray every day asking for well-being and salvation. (4)

The incaration of the Supreme God in the form of Kṛṣṇa was His ultimate pastime, chanting and listening to whose name and praises, saves the whole world. The same who killed demons like Agha, Baka, Kaṁsa and Kuvalaya. To that same Hari, we pray every day asking for well-being and salvation. (5)

Whose greatness even Brahmā and Śaṅkara cannot finish talking about, taking whose name both sages and fallen sinner alike, attain the same salvation. All the Vedas can prove the strength of devotion to Him. To that same Hari, we pray every day asking for well-being and salvation. (6) Śrī Rāma Rāyā, the great devotee of Hari and a knowledgable person has made Śaṅkara do this drama namely *Keli Gopāla*, the servant of Kṛṣṇa says thus. Please listen, oh dear wise people, please do not blame me. Whatever is there about Him, those same words mixed with the praises of Hari can give salvation. (7)

Unattainable even by gods, is the birth in the form of human being in this country Bhārata (India); life is in vain without Hari (Kṛṣṇa). How can a wise man sell such a life like the jewel *cintāmaṇi* in exchange for glass (jewellery). In this world one cannot find any essence other than the name and praises of Hari. So call aloud the name of Rāma repeatedly, to save and protect all the people all the time.(8)

*keli-gopāla nāmedaṁ nāṭakaṁ samāptam.*

Here ends the play by the name *Keli Gopāla.*

●●●

## 5.4
## *rukmiṇī haraṇa nāṭa*
## The Play : Abduction of Rukmiṇī

*namaḥ śrīkṛṣṇāya* ||
Obeisance to Śrī Kṛṣṇa.

*śloka* ||
*yat pādapaṅkajarajaḥ śirasā sureśāḥ*
*śarbādayo diviṣado'ti mododbahanti* |
*yat kīrtanāt kalimalaṁ manujāḥ tyajanti*
*kṛṣṇasya tasya caraṇaṁ śaraṇaṁ brajema* ||*1*||

Hymn[1]: Whose dust of the feet, even Śiva, Indra and all other gods take with pleasure on their heads, by chanting whose name people can get rid of all the sins in this Age of Kali, I take refuge in those feet of Kṛṣṇa.

*apica:*
*caidyādīn nṛpatīn pramathya tarasā yenāhṛtā rukmiṇī*
*yenājau vinijītya durjayaripuḥ rukmībirūpaḥ kṛtaḥ* |
*vaidarbhīṁ vidhivat bivāhamakarot yo dvāravatyāṁ mudā*
*tasmai śrīparamātmane bhagavate kṛṣṇāya kurmo namaḥ* ||2||

Also[2]:
That person, who at once carried off Rukmiṇī defeating the king of Cedi (Śiśupāla) and all others, and who, offending him, overpowered the formidable enemy Rukmī and He who married the daughter of Vidarbha in Dwārakā amidst great pomp and happiness, to that Supreme Personality of Godhead Kṛṣṇa, we offer our respectful reverential salutation.

---

1 . in *Vasantatilaka* metre.
2 . in *Śārdūlavikrīḍita* metre.

*nāndīgīta* || *rāga suhāi* || *māna ekatāli* ||
Benediction in *Rāga Suhāi* with the rhythm *Ekatāli:*

*jaya jaya jagajīvana murāru* |
*pāve paraṇāma hāmāru* || *dhruṁ* ||

Glory to Murāri, the life of the world, we pay our obeisance on your feet. Refrain.

*pada :*

*pañca muhe jāhe tuti buli* |
*śira hara dharu padadhūli* ||
*jāhe surāsura karu sevā* |
*sohi mohi gati deva devā* ||*1*||
*ripu nṛpasaba johi jini* |
*harala harakhe rukaminī* ||
*karala hari bibidha bilāsā* |
*kahatu śaṅkara haridāsā* ||2||

Verse: The five-headed (Lord Śiva) says whose prayer and Hara takes on his head the dust of whose feet, whom both the gods and demons serve; He is the one, the God of gods, the ultimate end for me.(1)

Conquering the enemies and the kings, who with great pleasure abducted Rukmiṇī, and (that same) Hari, had different pleasures and merriments and luxuries; says Śaṅkara, the servant of Hari, (about it).(2)

*nāndyante sūtradhāraḥ* || *alamati vistareṇa* || *prathamaṁ mādhavo mādhava ityuktvā natvā nārāyaṇaṁ sabhāsadaḥ sambodhyāha* ||

At the end of the benediction the Sūtradhāra says that there is no need for any further elaboration. And at first, uttering the name of Mādhava and bowing to Nārāyaṇa, addressed the assembled audience.

*śloka* ||

*bho bhoḥ sabhāsadaḥ yūyaṁ sṛnudhvaṁ śrddhayādhunā* |
*rukminīharaṇaṁ nāma nāṭakaṁ muktisādhakam* ||3||

Hymn[3]: Oh dear audience, you all now listen with great devotion, here will be presented before you a play by the name *Rukmiṇī-haraṇaṁ*, which will deliver you all.

*atha bhaṭṭimā* ||

*jaya jaya yādava deva* |
*ādi anta napāvata keva* ||
*jākeri caraṇa saroruha brahmā :*
*śaṅkara karu nitya seva* || *1*||
*johi bhayo avatāra* |
*harali bhūmikeri bhāra* ||
*kayali narasiṁha mūruti dāruṇa :*
*hiraṇyaka hṛdaya bidāra* ||2||
*niramie sayala saṁsāra*|
*karata bibidha bihāra* ||
*yo brahmāṇḍabhāṇḍa bhedala :*
*padanakha paraśa prahāra* ||3||
*kalimala- mocana citra* |
*jākeri parama caritra* ||
*pada- paṅkaja raja paraśini gaṅgā :*
*sura- nara karaya pavitra* ||4||
*aghabaka dhenuka māri* |
*kaṁsa keśī antakārī* ||
*madhu mura naraka nibāraṇa bāraṇa :*
*kubalaya jīvana hārī* ||5||
*indra-darapa karu cūra* |
*brajajana bhaya bheli dūra* ||
*hrāsa- bilāsa hāsa parirambhala :*
*gopī manoratha pūra* ||6||

---

[3]. in *Śloka* metre.

*marddiye biṣadhara kāli |*
*yamuna hrada nikāli ||*
*kubujā kāma manoratha pūrala :*
*barada barada banamālī ||7||*
*jākeri e guṇa nāma |*
*jagajana pūrala kāma ||*
*pāpī pāpa parābhava bhirjei*
*jo muhe lehi avirāma ||8||*
*sohi kṛṣṇaka nāṭaka |*
*pāpamūla utapātaka ||*
*śunā sādhujana jākeri icā :*
*jāhite baikuṇṭha bāṭaka ||9||*
*kṛṣṇa caritra āti sāra |*
*rukuni haraṇa bihāra ||*
*tāhe śunite bhaṇite pāvata :*
*papa- payonidhi- pāra ||10||*
*bho bho sādhu sabhāsada |*
*āve maraṇa mahāpada ||*
*jānahu kṛṣṇara caritra mṛtyu tāraka :*
*kāraka mukuti sampada ||11||*
*dharamaka rājā nāma |*
*jāni nakara birāma ||*
*kṛṣṇaka kiṅkara śaṅkara kahai :*
*ḍāki bolahu rāma rāma ||12||*

Glory to Lord Yādava, whose dimension one cannot asess, whose lotus feet are worshipped by Brahmā and Śaṅkara every day. (1)

Who appeared as incarnation of God and removed the burden of the earth. As Narasiṁha, with fierce appearance tore apart the chest of Hiraṇyakaśipu. (2)

Creating this whole world He has enjoyed various pastimes. Who broke the universe, which is like a pot, with a knock of His toe nail.(3)

Who eradicated the various sins of the Age of Kali, and that is his special characteristic. Touching the dust of His

lotus feet, Gaṅgā purifies the gods and human alike. (4)
Killing Agha, Baka and Dhenuka, finished off Kaṁsa and Keśī, warded off and restrained Madhu, Mura and Naraka and took away the life of Kuvalaya.(5)
Shattered the arrogance of Indra and warded off the fears of the people of Vraja. Having amorous games with the cowherd women and embracing them, fulfilled their wishes.(6)
Crushing poisonous Kāli chased him away from the lake Yamunā. He who wears a garland of wood flowers, bestows boon even upon the bestower of boons, fulfilled the amorous wishes of the hunchback maid.(7)
In whose names are these songs of praise, He fulfills the wishes of everyone in this world. The sins of all the sinners are destroyed whoever takes His name continuously.(8)
(This) play (is) about this same Kṛṣṇa, who is the destroyer of all the sources of evil; listen to that all the wise people, whoever wants to take the path to Vaikuṇṭha.(9)
The tales of Kṛṣṇa are extremely essential; listening to His sport of abduction of Rukmiṇī, and speaking about it, one can reach the other side of the wide sea of sin.(10)
Oh wise audience, death comes as the ultimate disaster; and know, that, remembering the activities of Kṛṣṇa can save one from death and it can also lead to achievement of the great wealth of salvation.(11)
The best of religious practices is (chanting) the name (of Kṛṣṇa); knowing that don't take rest from chanting. The servant of Kṛṣṇa, Śaṅkara says, "Sing aloud Rāma-Rāma!". (12)

*sūtra* ||

*bho bho sabhāsada : sādhujana : je jagataka parama guru : nārāyaṇa : jāheri aṁśa avatari : bārambāra bhūmika bhāra haraya : sohi bhagavanta śrīkṛṣṇa : sākṣāte āpune avatari : ōhi sabhā madhye rukmiṇī haraṇa : bihāra nṛtya : parama kautuke karaba : tāhe sābadhāne dekhaha śunaha | prathame uddhava sahita : śrīkṛṣṇaka prabeśa : tadanantara sakhīsaba sahita : rukamiṇīka prabeśa | iti jñātvā sarbbe sāvadhāne sthīyatām||*

Direction: Oh dear audience, oh good people, one who is the father of this whole world, Nārāyaṇa is whose part; and appearing as the incarnation, relieves the world of its burdens again and again, that same God Śrī Kṛṣṇa, incarnating Himself in person, is going to perform the abduction of Rukmiṇī, alongwith playful dance, with great fun and enjoyment, amidst this assembled audience; watch and listen to that carefully. At first, Śrī Kṛṣṇa enters with Uddhava, after that, along with friends enters Rukmiṇī; knowing this everyone should remain carefully.

*punaḥ sūtradhāraḥ || ākaśe karṇaṁ dattvā – saṅgika bola || āhe saṅgi : ki bādya śunie ||*

The *sūtradhāra* again, listening to the sky, says to the companion, "Oh friend, which instrument do we hear?".

*saṅgi bola || sakhi : devadundubhi bājata : āhe deva dundubhi bājata ||*

The companion says, "Oh friend, the divine drum is playing; oh, there plays the divine kettle drum."

*sūtra||*

*āḥ, se parama īśvara śrīkṛṣṇa milala milala||*

Direction: The Supreme God Śrī Kṛṣṇa comes, here He comes.

*śloka ||*

*praveśamakarot kṛṣṇaḥ svakāntyā kāmakoṭijit |*
*jagatāṁ janako dhātā soddhavaḥ sādhuvāndavaḥ*[4] ||4||

Hymn[5]: Surpassing the beauty of crores of Kāmadeva with His own brilliance and loveliness, the creator and the protector

[4] . *sādhuvāndhavaḥ*.

[5] . in *Śloka* metre.

of the whole world, the friend of the virtuous men, Śrī Kṛṣṇa entered along with Uddhava.

*sūtra* ||

*āhe sabhāsada loka : jākara kathā kahaici : sohi śrīkṛṣṇa uddhava sahite e āvata* ||

*iti sūtraḥ niṣkrāntaḥ* ||

Direction: Oh dear audience, about whom we are speaking, that same Kṛṣṇa comes this way along with Uddhava. Saying so, the Sūtradhāra exits.

*gīta* || *rāga sindhuḍā* || *ekatāli* ||

Song in the *Rāga Sindhuḍā* with the rhythm *Ekatāli*:

*āve jagata guru kaya paraveśa* |
*jinie kamakauṭi naṭabara beśa* || *dhruṁ* ||

Here comes and enters the Lord of the universe, the most expert and best of dancers, defeating a crore of Kāmadeva.

*pada:*

*śyāmala tanu pīta ambaru lāsā* |
*badana indu ruci īṣata hāsā* ||
*nayana paṅkaja bhuja lambita jānu* |
*kaṇṭhe kaustubha nava śobhita bhānu* ||*1*||
*hāra mukuṭa maṇi kuṇḍala ḍole* |
*caraṇapaṅkaja maha mañjīra role* ||
*śaśadhara kauṭi kānti parakāśā* |
*śaṅkara kaha ōhi keśava dāsā* ||2||

Verse: The bluish-black body is adorned with yellow clothing. The face, beautiful like the moon, is smiling slightly. The eyes look like lotus and the hands are stretched out to the knee. The *kaustubha* gem is on the neck, dazzling like a newly rising sun. (1)

Necklace and earrings made of pearl are also dangling. In between the lotus like feet the anklets are making sounds, and He is radiating brightness like a crore of moons, says Śaṅkara, the servant of Keśava.(2)

*kathā sūtra* ||

*õhi prakāre : śrīkṛṣṇa prabeśa kae kahu : eka pāśa huyā rahala : tadanantara rukamiṇīka prabeśa śunaha* ||

Dialogue and Direction: In this way after entering, Kṛṣṇa remained in one side. After that, listen to the entering of Rukmiṇī.

*saṅgi ki bādya bājaya* ||

Oh friend, what instrument plays there?

*saṅgī bola* || *ae devabādya bājata* ||

The companion says, "Oh, here plays the celestial drum."

*sūtra* ||

*āḥ se gosānī rukamiṇī : milala milala : ae loka dekhaha* ||

Direction: Oh, there is goddess Rukmiṇī, here she comes, here she comes, oh people, look.

*śloka*||

*rukminīṁ kārayāmāsa praveśaṁ sakhīsaṁyutām* |
*mohayan harṣayan cāru rūpalāvaṇya kāntibhiḥ* ||5||

Hymn[6]: Fascinating the audience with her beauty and charm, Rukmiṇī was made to enter along with her friends.

*sūtra* ||

*sakhīsaba sahita : se rukamiṇī jaice praveśa kayala : tāhe dekhaha śunaha : nirantare hari bola* ||2||

Direction: As Rukmiṇī enters along with her friends, watch and listen to that and keep chanting the name of Hari incessantly.

---

6 . in *Śloka* metre, but in the 2nd foot, the 5th letter is long and not short.

*gīta || rāga suhāi || ekatāli ||*
Song in the *rāga Suhāi* with the rhythm *Ekatāli*:

*dhruṁ ||*

*āvata rukamiṇī kaya parasāra |*
*sakhīsaba saṅge raṅge karata bihāra ||*

Refrain: Here comes Rukmiṇī, entering along with her friends moving with fun and great pleasure.

*pada ||*

*īṣata hasita mukha cānda ujora |*
*daśana motima jaca nayana cakora ||*
*māṇika mukuṭa kuṇḍala gaṇḍa ḍola |*
*kanaka putali tanu nīla nicola ||*
*kara kaṅkaṇa kejura jhankāra |*
*māṇika kāñci racita hemahāra ||*
*calāite caraṇa mañjīra karu rola |*
*rūpe bhuvana bhole śaṅkara bola ||3||*

Verse: The moonlike face is bright with a smile. The teeth look like pearls and the eyes are like the *cakora* bird. Earrings made of pearls and gems are dangling on the cheeks. The body is like a golden doll and is (covered) in blue clothing. The bracelets and armlets jingle; a girdle with rubies, gold necklaces and the anklets tinkle as she walks. Her beauty makes all forget the world, says Śaṅkara.

*sūtra ||*

*āhe lokāi : se gosānī devī rukamiṇī : aicana praveśa kaye kahu : nṛtya kaye : ekapāśa huyā rahala | āhe sāmājika loka : tadanantara prastuta kathā śunaha : surabhi nāma eka bhikṣuka bhāṭa : kuṇḍina nagarī hante : kṛṣṇaka bheṭa pāvala : tāhe dekhi śrīkṛṣṇa bāta pucata ||*

Direction: Oh dear people, that goddess, respectable Rukmiṇī, entering in this way, dancing, remained on one side. Oh dear assembled people, now please listen to the present context. A messenger beggar by the name Surabhī, coming from the city of Kuṇḍina met Kṛṣṇa; seeing him, Śrī Kṛṣṇa asked him about his well being.

*kathā* ||

*ae bhikṣuka : tuhu ke kathā hante ethā āvali thika !*

Dialogue: "Oh dear mendicant, for what reason you have come here?"

*śloka* ||

*kastvaṁ kasmādihāgataḥ pṛṣṭaḥ kṛṣṇena bhikṣukaḥ* |
*prāhāhaṁ kuṇḍinānnātha tvāṁ didṛkṣurihāgataḥ* ||6||

Hymn[7]: "Who are you, what have you come here for?" the mendicant was asked by Kṛṣṇa. The mendicant said, "I have come here from Kuṇḍina to have a glimpse of you."

*bhikṣuka bola* || *hāmo surabhi nāma bhāṭa : kuṇḍinahante tohāka daraśana nimite : āvala thika : āḥ tohāka aparūpa rūpa sampattika mahiṁa kī kahaba : he svāmi kṛṣṇa : hāmāra rājanandanī rukamiṇī : jaba tohāra gṛhiṇī hae : tabe tohāra gṛhabāsa saba : sāphala hae : se rukamiṇīka rūpaguṇa kico kahaba tā śunaha* ||

The mendicant said: "I am a messenger and my name is Surabhī. I have come from Kuṇḍina with an intention of seeing you. What to tell you, of the greatness of the wealth of incomparable beauty. Oh Lord Kṛṣṇa, when our Princess Rukmiṇī becomes your wife, then your home life will be fruitful. I shall say a little about the beauty and quality of Rukmiṇī, please listen to that."

*bhaṭṭimā* ||

*paḍhi punu bhāṭa capaya kaha bāṇī* |
*kṛṣṇaka āgu rūpa bakhāni* ||
*jaya yadunandana devaku deva* |

---

7 . in *Śloka* metre, but in the 1st foot, the 7th letter is short and not long.

*tohāri caraṇe karahu bahu seva ||1||*
*tohi mahimā kahatu nāhi anta |*
*pūrala paramā kiriṭī diganta ||*
*tuhu sama puruṣa katihu nāhi pāi |*
*śuna aba bacaneka bolohõ gosñāi ||2||*
*hāmāku kuṇḍina nagarī anupāma |*
*ache kanyā eka rukamiṇī nāma ||*
*bhīṣmaka rājanandanī barabālā |*
*bāḍhaya nava joni cāndaka kālā ||3||*
*ki kahaba ramaṇīka rūpa pracura |*
*bayanaka pekhi cānda bheli dūra ||*
*nayanaka pekhi pāi bāḍi lāja |*
*kayala jhāmpa kamala jalamājha ||4||*
*banduli adhika adhara karu kānti |*
*otima motima daśanaka pānti ||*
*suvalita bhujajuga ratana molāna |*
*uru karikara kaṭi ḍambaruka ṭhāna ||5||*
*nava pallava ruci padajuga śohe |*
*pekhite sura-nara-muni-mana mohe ||*
*bāṇī āmiyā rasa gune nohe hīna |*
*rājakumārīka bayasa navina ||6||*
*katanu jatane bidhi kae niramāṇa |*
*se kanyā have prabhu tohāri samāna ||*
*kahalu svarūpa aba bacana bicāri |*
*hovaya gṛhiṇī, jaba rukamiṇī nārī ||7||*
*taba gṛhabāsa sāphala hove nātha |*
*kahalu bhāṭa upara tuli hāta ||*
*kṛṣṇara kiṅkara ohi śaṅkara bola |*
*karu ava narasaba hari hari bola ||8||*

Here is the eulogy: Again the messenger started reciting, in the metre *Capaya*, praising the beauty (of Rukmiṇī) in front of Kṛṣṇa. "Glory to the son of Yadu, the God of all gods; I pay lots of obeisance at your feet. (1)

"There is no end talking about your greatness. Your great glory has pervaded till the horizon. There is no one else like you anywhere; now oh God, please listen to what I say. (2)

"There is no other country comparable to our Kuṇḍina. There lives a girl by the name Rukmiṇī. The princess of King Bhīṣmaka, a very beautiful girl,(she) is growing up like the ever increasing digits of the newly visible moon. (3)

"What to speak of the abundant beauty of the lovely young woman! Looking at her face, even the moon shies away with shame. Looking at her eyes, even the lotus, out of great shame, jumps deep into the water. (4)

"Her lips are more beautiful than the red *banduli* flower; and the set of teeth are also like the best quality pearls. The arms are so beautiful that they make even the gems and jewels fade away. The thighs are like the trunks of elephants and the hips look like the hour-glass shaped small drum (5).

"The pair of feet is beautiful like fresh buds or newly sprung sprouts, and seeing those, the minds of even gods, men and sages are fascinated. Her voice is sweet like nectar and there is no lack of wit and humour in her words. The princess is young in age. (6)

"God has created her with so much endeavour and she is only fit for you, oh Lord! I have spoken the truth after much consideration that, when this girl Rukmiṇī becomes your wife, (7)

"Your family life will be successful, oh Lord. Here I am speaking with raised hands (as blessings)." Says Śaṅkara, the servant of Kṛṣṇa, "Oh dear people, now please utter the name of Hari." (8)

*kathā sūtra* ||

*tadanantara : rukamiṇīka rūpa guṇa śunie śrīkṛṣṇa heṭhamāṭha kaya : niśvāsa phokāri : ghana ghana rukamiṇīka mātra : dhyāna kaye rahala : śrīkṛṣṇa uddhavaka bolala || he sakhi : ohi bhalla bhāṭa : unikara mana pūrie : bahuta prasāda dehu* ||

Dialogue and Direction: After that, hearing about the beauty and qualities of Rukmiṇī, Śrī Kṛṣṇa, with bowed head and sighing deeply, repeatedly kept thinking only about Rukmiṇī. Śrī Kṛṣṇa said to Uddhava, "Oh dear friend, here is this good messenger, offer him gifts enough to his heart's content."

*tadanantara : kṛṣṇaka ādeśe: uddhave bahuta dhana : bhāṭaka delaha | śrīkṛṣṇaka prasāda pāyā : cirañjīva cirañjīva gosāñi buli : surabhi santoṣe : nija deśe gela* ||

After that, as instructed by Kṛṣṇa, Uddhava paid lots of money to the messenger. Receiving the gifts from Kṛṣṇa, uttering, "Oh Lord, may you live long, live long!", Surabhī (the messenger), with much satisfaction, went back to his own country.

*śloka* ||

*śrutvā bhikṣumukhāt kṛṣṇo rukmiṇyā rūpamadbhutam* |
*tvāmeva satataṁ dhyāyan tasthāvākulamānasaḥ* ||7||

Hymn[8]: Hearing from the mendicant about the exceptional beauty of Rukmiṇī, Śrī Kṛṣṇa, thinking about her constantly, remained in a restless state.

*kathā sūtra* ||

*bhikṣuka mukhe rukunika rūpa guṇa śunie : śrīkṛṣṇa āna cintā saba choḍi : rātri divase : rukamiṇīka mātra dhyāna kae rahala : tāhe dekhaha śunaha : nirantare hari bola hari* ||

Dialogue and Direction: Hearing about the beauty and qualities of Rukmiṇī from the messenger, Kṛṣṇa, giving up all other thoughts, meditated only about Rukmiṇī day and night. Watch and listen to that and keep chanting the name of Hari incessantly.

---

8 . in *Śloka* metre.

*gīta || rāga- dhanaśrī || ekatāli ||*
Song in the *Rāga Dhanaśrī* with the rhythm *Ekatāli:*

*priyākeri kāhinī : śunie murāri |*
*birahe dahanu cita : ākula kiñcita :*
*mānasa madana bigāri || dhruṁ||*

Hearing the stories about his beloved, Murāri remained restless with His heart burning out of separation and Màdana afflicting His mind. Refrain.

*pada ||*

*jagata nibāsa : svāsa ghana phorāre :*
*cintite rukamiṇī nārī |*
*kamana upāya pāi : punu paraśana :*
*daraśana rājakumārī ||1||*
*gunite kāminī : yāminī jāi :*
*nayane ninda nāhi āi |*
*divasa rayanī hari : rahali dhiyāi :*
*kṛṣṇa kiṅkara rasa gāi ||2||*

Verse: The whole world is whose abode, sighs repeatedly thinking of the beautiful woman Rukmiṇī, and thinking how to find means to have a glimpse and touch of the princess. (1) Thinking about the woman, the night passes by and sleep does not descend upon the eyes. Hari remained meditating this way day and night; the servant of Kṛṣṇa sings about this love. (2)

*sūtra ||*

*ohi parakāre śrīkṛṣṇa : pṛyāka birahānale : ākula hayā : hā rukminī hā rukminī : mātra bākya phokāri kahu : rukunimaya mātra dekhiye : sarbbathā rahala : kṛṣṇaka dukha ki kahaba| āhe loka : tadanantara : rukamiṇīka bṛtānta śunaha : dvārikā hante haridāsa nāma : eka bhikṣuka bhāṭa kuṇḍina gaiyā :*

*rājanandanī rukamiṇīka : daraśana bhela : tāhe dekhie bāta puchata || aye bhikṣuka : tuhuke : kathā hante ethāvali thika||*

Direction: In this way Śrī Kṛṣṇa, suffering from the fire of separation from the beloved, being restless, shouting only one sentence, "Oh Rukmiṇī, oh Rukmiṇī!", remained seeing only Rukmiṇī all around. What to speak of the grief of Kṛṣṇa. Oh dear people, after that, listen to the account of Rukmiṇī. A beggar messenger by the name Haridāsa went to Kuṇḍina from Dwārakā and met Princess Rukmiṇī. Seeing him, Rukmiṇī asked him, "Oh there, oh beggar, wherefrom have you come here?"

*śloka* ||

*ko bhavāniha samprāptaḥ pṛṣṭo bhikṣurabhāṣata|*
*dvārakānagarāt prāptaḥ prārthako'haṁ nṛpātmaje ||8||*

Hymn[9]: "Who are you, who have arrived here?" Being asked in this way, the mendicant said, "Oh Princess, I am a beggar, I have come here from the city of Dwarakā."

*kathā* ||

*bhikṣuka bola || aḥ : hāmu dvārika nibāsī : haridāsa nāma bhikṣuka bhāṭa : hāmāra sudivasa : tohāka daraśana bhelu : aḥ tohāka aparūpa sampattika : mahimā ki kahaba : hāmāra dvārikānātha śrīkṛṣṇa : se jebe tohāka svāmī hae : tebe e rūpa jaubana : sāphala hae hā hā he rājanandanī : se śrīkṛṣṇaka rūpa guṇa kico kahu : tā śunaha||*

Dialogue: The mendicant said, "Oh, I live in Dwārakā, my name is Haridāsa, and I am a beggar messenger. It is a lucky day for me that I have met you. Oh, what to speak about the greatness of your wealth of incomparable beauty! When our king of Dwārakā, Śrī Kṛṣṇa, becomes your husband, only then, such beauty and youth of you will be successful. Oh there Princess, let me say about some of the beauties and qualities of Śrī Kṛṣṇa, please listen to that."

9 . in *Śloka* metre.

*bhaṭṭimā* ||

*śuna śuna rukaminī māi* |
*hari guṇa kahana najāi* ||
*mukha indu kauṭi parakāśa* |
*daśana motima manda hāsa* ||1||
*nayana paṅkaja navapātā* |
*karatala utapala rātā* ||
*madanaka dhanu bhruva bhaṅga* |
*bhuja juga balita bhujaṅga* ||2||
*bahala bakṣasthala siṁha bandha* |
*tribali balita kaṭi kandha* ||
*uru karikara ava bhāsa* |
*mṛdu padapaṅkaja bikāśa* ||3||
*nakhacaya cāndaka pānti* |
*padatala alakata bhānti* ||
*dhvaja java paṅkaja śohe* |
*pekhite tribhubana mohe* ||4||
*abhinava taruṇa mūruti* |
*ki kahaba rūpaka bibhūti* ||
*gati gambhīra mṛgarāja* |
*kauṭi madana heri lāja* ||5|
*tuhuñ nava taruṇī pradhāna* |
*so hari navina juvāna* ||
*duhu eka bayasa samāna* |
*kayali bidhi niramāṇa* ||6||
*bhubana niropama rūpa* |
*śuna dhaṇi bacana svarūpa* ||
*jaba tuvā pati sohi hoi* |
*sāphala janama taba toi* ||7||
*kahalu bhikṣuka aba jāni* |
*kṛṣṇa kiṅkara bola bāṇī* ||
*teju sāmājika kāma* |
*ḍāki bolahu rāma rāma* || 8||

The eulogy:"Listen oh listen, dear girl Rukmiṇī, (nobody) can speak enough of the qualities of Hari. The face is bright like a crore of moons shining, the set of teeth look like pearls when He smiles lightly. (1)

"The eyes are like newly blooming petals of lotus and the palms are red like water lilies. The curves of His eyebrows are like the bows of Madana. The arms are like long serpents. (2)

"The chest is wide and well-built like a lion. His tummy and neck have the (beautifying) three folds on them, and the thighs resemble the fore trunk of an elephant. The feet are like the blooming lotus and are very soft. (3)

"The toes look like rows of moons and the soles of the feet are bright with redness. The feet are decorated with the symbols of a flag, a maize and the lotus, and seeing that, all the three worlds are fascinated. (4)

"Fresh and young is His body, what to speak of the splendour of His beauty. His gait is dignified like that of a tiger; seeing that even a crore of Madana become ashamed. (5)

"You are the best young girl, and this Hari is a freashly youthful man. And the creator has created both of you of the same age. (6)

"There is none to compare His beauty with, in this world; oh young girl, listen to these true words. When He becomes your husband, your life will become successful. (7)

"I am a beggar and knowing everything, I have told you." The servant of Kṛṣṇa says, "Oh dear assembled audience, leave all other work and call out aloud Rāma, Rāma!". (8)

*kathā sūtra* ||

*tadanantara : bhikṣuka mukhe : kṛṣṇaka guṇarūpa śunie : rukamiṇīka mane parama ānanda milala : āti hariṣe sakhīka sambodhi bolola* ||

Dialogue and direction: After that, hearing about the charm and qualities of Kṛṣṇa from the beggar, Rukmiṇī became very happy and with great joy, addressing her friend said:

*he sakhī madana mañjarī : ohi bhalla bhāṭa : unikara mana pūrie : bahu bidha prasāda deha* ||
"Oh dear friend Madana Mañjarī, here is the good bard, give him various gifts to satisfy his mind."

*devīka ādeśa śuni kahõ : madana mañjarī bahutara rajata subarṇa āni : bhāṭaka delaha : cirañjīva cirañjīva māi boli : utsuke bhikṣu bhāṭa : nija deśe gela : rukamiṇī bhikṣuka mukhe : kathā śunie : mohita hayā : śrīkṛṣṇaka svāmī bhāve barala : kṛṣṇa grahe hṛdaye dharala : kṛṣṇaka caraṇa cintie : mātra sarbbathā rahala : āna cintā saba chāḍala* ||
Hearing, the instruction of the lady, Madana Mañjarī brought lots of gold and silver and gave them to the bard. "Long live, long live, oh dear girl!", saying thus, with great enthusiasm the beggar bard left for his country. Hearing from the beggar about all the things, Rukmiṇī became fascinated and selected Śrī Kṛṣṇa as her husband with great eagerness and keeping Kṛṣṇa in her heart, remained meditating only on His feet all the time and gave up all other thoughts.

*śloka* ||

*kṛṣṇasya rūpalāvaṇyaśravaṇena bimohitā* |
*dadhau taccaraṇāmbhojaṁ bhajanīyaṁ satāṁ satī* ||9||

Hymn[10]: Hearing about the beauty and charm of Śrī Kṛṣṇa, being fascinated, the virtuous woman Rukmiṇī, started meditating on the lotus feet of the one honoured and worshipped by all.

*sūtra* ||

*se rājakumārī rukamiṇī : kṛṣṇaka rūpalāvaṇya śunie : mohita hayā : jaice kṛṣṇaka caraṇa cintie rahala : āhe loka : tāhe dekhaha śunaha : nirantare hari bola* ||

Direction: Hearing about the beauty and charm of Kṛṣṇa, that Princess Rukmiṇī, became mesmerised and remained

[10] . in *Śloka* metre.

mediatating on the feet of Kṛṣṇa. Oh dear people, watch and listen to that and keep chanting the name of Hari incessantly.

*gīta || rāga- āśoāri || jautimāna ||*

Song in the *Rāga Āśovārī* with the rhythm *Jautimāna:*

*kaicana keśava daraśana hoi |*
*hari bine biphala janama aba moi || dhruṁ ||*

How can I see Keśava! My life is now useless without Hari. Refrain.

*pada ||*

*basati digantara nātha hāmāru |*
*bheṭa kamane hui svāmī murāru ||*
*hāmu kiṅkarī hari nātha hāmāra |*
*kaha śaṅkara rukunika bevahāra ||5||*

Verse: He is our master, pervading all across the horizon, how can we meet the Lord Murāri, we are the servants and Hari is our master, that is how Śaṅkara describes the behaviour of Rukmiṇī.

*sūtra :*

*āhe loka : dekhu dekhu : rukamiṇī aicana kṛṣṇa caraṇa cintie rahala | tadanantararukamiṇīka pitā : bṛddha rājā bhīṣmaka : pātramantrījñātisabaka āni kahu : je bolala tā dekhaha śunaha||*

Direction: Oh dear people, look look, this is how Rukmiṇī remained thinking of Kṛṣṇa. After that, as the father of Rukmiṇī, the old King Bhīṣmaka, assembling the ministers and the relatives, said to them, watch and listen to that.

*bhīṣmaka bola || āhe pātramantrījñātisaba : hāmāra duhitā rukamiṇī : bibāhaka jogya bhela : kanyāka sadṛśa bara kona thāne thika : sabahi bimariṣa kaye bola | hāmu jānu eka*

*daivakīnandana bine : kanyāka samāna bara nāhi : jaba sabahi bhalla dekhaha : tabe svahaste kṛṣṇaka kanyā dāna karu* ||
Bhīṣmaka said, "Oh there, dear ministers and relatives, our daughter Rukmiṇī has come to a marriageable age. Where to find a suitable groom for the girl, all of you please advise after deliberation. I know that except the son of Devakī, there is no one else fit for her. It you all find it proper, then I will give away the girl to Kṛṣṇa with my own hands."

*jñātisaba bola* || *dhanya dhanya rājā : aḥ tohāka uttama mati thika : apekṣā nāhi karaba : parama puruṣa śrīkṛṣṇaka kanyā dāna karaha : puruṣa uddhāra hauka*|
Relatives said, "Very good, excellent! You are great oh dear King, yours is the best judgement. Do not wait, give away the girl in marriage to the Supreme Personality Śrī Kṛṣṇa, and let this generation be rescued."

*sūtra* ||
*se rājamahiṣī śaśīprabhā : tāhu svāmīka bolala* ||
Direction: The Queen's consort Śaśīprabhā said to her husband.

*śaśīprabhā bola* || *parama īśvara śrīkṛṣṇaka : kathā śunie : hāmāro ohi sanmata* | *se yadunandanaka ānie : satvare kanyā dāna karaha* ||
Śaśīprabhā said, "Hearing about the Supreme Godhead Śrī Kṛṣṇa, I agree with what you have said. Inviting Him, the son of Yadu, give away our daughter to Him in marriage."

*sūtra* ||
*śrīkṛṣṇaka bibāha dite : sabahi niścaya kayala* ||
Direction: Everyone decided to marry her (Rukmiṇī) off to Śrī Kṛṣṇa.

*śloka* ||

*śrutvā sakhīmukhāt sākṣādvārtāmānanditā satī |*
*rukmiṇī krīrḍayāmāsa spṛṣṭvā haripadaṁ hṛdi ||10||*

Hymn[11]: Receiving the exact information from her friend, Rukmiṇī became very happy and meditating on the feet of Hari in her mind, became excited.

*kathā ||*

*samasta bṛtānta śuni kahu : sakhī līlāvati : rukamiṇīta kahala || he sakhī : tohāka manoratha sāphala bhela | śrīkṛṣṇaka bibāha dite niścaya kayala : svarūpa jānalu|| tāhe śuni rukamiṇī : ānande jaice nācae lāgala || āhe loka : tāhe dekhaha śunaha : nirantare hari bola ||*

Dialogue: Hearing all the details, friend Līlāvatī said to Rukmiṇī, "Oh dear friend, your wishes have been fulfilled. It has been decided upon to marry you off to Śrī Kṛṣṇa, I have come to know for sure."

Hearing that, how Rukmiṇī started dancing with happiness, oh dear people, watch and listen to that and keep chanting the name of Hari incessantly.

*gīta || rāga- śrīgāndhāra || paritāla ||*

Song in the *Rāga Śrīgāndhāra* with the rhythm *Paritāla:*

*dhruṁ ||*

*sakhī he sudina bhayo ri ||*
*nāce jaicana sakhī saṅge raṅge gori |*

Refrain: "Oh dear friend, good days are here!" The maiden as if danced with her friend with great happiness.

*pada ||*

*parama puruṣa piu bheli murāru |*
*janama saphala sakhī abahu hāmāru ||*
*nāhi mohe sama sobhāginī śuna sai |*
*rukunika raṅga kṛṣṇa kiṅkara kahayī ||6||*

---

[11] . in *Śloka* metre.

Verse: "The Supreme Personality Murāri has become my beloved. Oh dear friend, now my life has become fulfilled. Listen, oh dear friend, there is no one else as fortunate as I am!" This is how the servant of Kṛṣṇa describes the happiness of Rukmiṇī.

*kathā* ||

*aḥ īśvara śrīkṛṣṇaka svāmī pāvalu : sakhī hāmāka sama sobhāginī kona thika* ||

Dialogue : "Oh, I have found Lord Kṛṣṇa as my husband. Oh friend, is there another one as fortunate as me!"

*sūtra* ||

*ohi buli rukamiṇī parama utsuke : jaice nācae rahala thika* ||

Direction: Saying so, Rukmiṇī, with great enthusiasm, remained dancing thus.

*śloka* ||

*tato rukmī sabhāṁ gatvā garhayitvātha mādhavam* |
*garbeṇa kharbbavākyena kanyāṁ dātuṁ nyavārayat* ||*11*||

Hymn[12]: Then Rukmī going to the (royal) court, reproached Mādhava and with great pride stopped with vile language to give away the maiden to Him.

*kathā* ||

*tadanantara : se sabhāmadhye āsi kahu : rukamiṇīka jyeṣṭhabhrātā : rukmi nāma mandamati : se pāpī parama darppa kaye bolala* ||

Dialogue: After that, coming to the court, the elder brother of Rukmiṇī, Rukmī by name, foolish and sinner, said with great pride:

*rukmi bola* || *aḥ hāmāra bhaginī rukamiṇīka : kāhāka śakati kṛṣṇaka bibāha devaba* | *se yādava anācāra : gobadha : strībadha : mātulabadha : katapāpa kaya thika* | *se hāmāra*

12 . in *Śloka* metre.

*sambandhaka : jogya hae nuhi | ae bṛddharājā : tuhu kichu bujhaye nāhi : je mahārājāsiṁha śiśupāla : se rukamiṇīka jogya bara haya : niṣṭe tāheka bibāha devaba : hāmu aṅgīkāra kaye bolalu ||*

Rukmī said, "Ah, who dares to marry off my sister to Kṛṣṇa. He, who is a Yādava, is an immoral person. He has committed all sorts of sins like killing cows and woman and maternal uncle and what not. He is not fit to establish our relationship with. Oh you old King, you do not understand anything. The king of kings and powerful like the lion, Śiśupāla is proper as the groom for Rukmiṇī. For sure, we will marry her off to him, I say with a promise."

*kathā ||*

*tanikara bola bādhaye nāhipāri : bhīṣmaka je bolala || aye putā : bibāhaka nimite : śiśupālaka satvare ānaha || rukmi tāhe śunie : kautuke dūta pāñcikahõ : śiśupāla pramukhye : rājāsabaka ānāvala : tāhe dekhaha śunaha ||*

Dialogue: Not being able to oppose his words, Bhīṣmaka said, "Oh dear son, bring in Śiśupāla immediately for marriage." Hearing that, Rukmī, with great pleasure, sending messenger to Śiśupāla and other kings, brought them in; watch and listen to that.

*śloka ||*

*niśamya rukminyudbāhaṁ śiśupālādayo nṛpāḥ |*
*gṛhītvā ca śaraṁ cāpamāyayuḥ kuṇḍinaṁ prati ||12||*

Hymn[13]: Knowing about the wedding of Rukmiṇī, Śiśupāla and the other kings, bearing bows and arrows in their hands started towards Kuṇḍina.

*kathā :*

*rukunika bibāha karae lāgi : rājāsaba sahite : jaice śiśupāla āvala: tāhe dekhaha śunaha : nirantare haribola ||*

---

[13] . in *Śloka* metre.

Dialogue : How Śiśupāla, along with the other kings came to marry Rukmiṇī, watch and listen to that, and keep chanting the name of Hari incessantly.

*gīta* || *rāga- kānaḍā* || *paritāla* ||

Song in the *rāga Kānaḍā* with the rhythm *Paritāla:*

*āve rājā siṁha śiśupāla* |
*hāte tīra dhanu bīra biśāla* || *dhruṁ*||

Here comes King Śiśupāla, who is like a lion, holding bow and arrow in his hands as a great hero. Refrain.

*pada* ||

*kaye ārambara bājanā bāje* |
*cale saṅge sāji rāja samāje* ||
*karata*[14] *kirīṭi kuṇḍala parakāśa* |
*kahatu śaṅkara kṛṣṇaka dāsa* ||7||

Verse: The musical instruments played with much splendour and the kings came along into the society nicely dressed, and the earrings in the ears and the crowns shone brightly, says thus, Śaṅkara, the servant of Kṛṣṇa.

*kathā :*

*se rājāsabaka : bhīṣmake sanmāna kaya kahõ bāsāghara diye rākhala* | *tadanantara : rukamiṇīka sakhī : madana mañjarī esaba bṛttānta jāni āti satvare rukamiṇīka samīpe gayā kahu : jānāvala* ||

Dialogue: Bhīṣmaka, showing respect to those kings, received them, offering lodgings. After that, the friend of Rukmiṇī, Madana Mañjarī, coming to know about all the details, went to Rukmiṇī immediately and informed about it.

14. *karṇata kuṇḍala kiriṭi* .

*madanamañjarī bola || āhe prāṇasakhī : biṣama bipāka milala : tā śunaha | tohāri jeṣṭhabhrātā : rukmikumāra : se pāpī tohāka : śrīkṛṣṇaka bibāha dite niṣedhala : tohāka nimite śiśupāla nṛpatika bara anāvala : ihāka niṣṭe jāni hāmu jānāvalu | sakhī je jogya tā karaha | hā hā prāṇasakhī śrīkṛṣṇaka : svāmī bañcita bheli : hā hā bidhika biḍambana ki bheli ||*

Madana Mañjarī said, "Oh my friend, dear as my life, great calamity has befallen, listen to that. Your eldest brother, Prince Rukmī, the sinner, has forbidden to marry you off to Śrī Kṛṣṇa. He has brought King Śiśupāla as your bridegroom, knowing it for certain, I have informed you. Oh dear friend, do whatever you think proper. Oh alas, dear friend, you have become deprived of having Śrī Kṛṣṇa as your husband; oh alas, what great misfortune has befallen!".

*śloka ||*

*niśamya vipriyaṁ bālā bhītā bhūmau papāta sā |*
*ruroda hṛdaye dhyāyan kṛṣṇasya caraṇaṁ ciram ||13||*

Hymn[15]: Hearing such unpleasant words, being very scared Rukmiṇī fell down on the ground and meditating on the feet of Śrī Kṛṣṇa started crying a lot.

*sūtra : tadanantara parama vipriya bāṇī śunie : rājanandanīka māthe jaice kalasa bhāṅgala : śrīkṛṣṇaka nairāśā śunie : diśa daśa āndhiāri dekhie : murcchita hayā tattakāle parala : jaice kadalika bāte upāḍala | śrīkṛṣṇaka birahatāpe : rukamiṇīka jaice avasthā milala : tāhe dekhaha śunaha : nirantare hari bola ||*

Direction: After that, hearing the most unpleasant words, as if a pot had broken on the head of the princess. Being despaired of ever having Śrī Kṛṣṇa, saw darkness in all the ten directions and fell down unconscious then and there, as if the wind has uprooted a banana tree. In the fire of

---

[15] . in *Śloka* metre.

separation from Kṛṣṇa, what condition befell to Rukmiṇī, watch and listen to that, and keep chanting the name of Hari incessantly.

*gīta* || *rāga – gaurī* || *jautimāna* ||
Song in the *Rāga Gaurī* with the rhythm *Jautimāna*:

*haribine ramaṇī : dekhata andhivāri* |
*rahaye nā dehā biraha karu nārī* || *dhruṁ*||
Without Hari, the maiden sees only darkness and because of this separation the body cannot carry on living. Refrain.

*pada*:

*ghana ghana muruci parae baranārī* |
*kokāraye svāsa nayane jhure bāri* ||
*kṛṣṇaka caraṇa cintiye citta lāi* |
*ghana yadunātha jampaye punu māi* ||
*harika nairāse hrāsa bheli dehā* |
*śaṅkara kaha ramaṇīka nava nehā* ||8||

Verse: The beautiful woman fell down unconscious again and again, taking deep breaths and tears flowing from the eyes. To meditate on the feet of Kṛṣṇa, the young girl chanted the name of Yadunātha frequently. Being disappointed of (not getting) Hari (as her husband), her body thinned out. This is how Śaṅkara describes the new love of the girl.

*kathā* ||

*tadanantara : kṛṣṇaka biraha tāpe : tāpita hayā : rukamiṇī ghana ghana kṛṣṇaguṇa jampae : diśa daśa āndhāri dekhie : murcchita hayā parala | tāhe dekhiye : sakhī madana mañjarī : sakhī līlāvati : hāhākāra kae : āti satvare : bāhu meli dharala : śira jala siñcala : āñcore biñci kahu : āśvāsa bolala* ||

*he prāṇasakhī : se pāpī śiśupāla : tohāka nāhi pāve : ki nimitta ākula bheli : se bhakata bāndhava mādhava : tohāka avaśyaka rakṣā karaba : ihā jāni prāṇa sakhī : svastha hava* ||

Dialogue: After that, being burnt in the fire of separation from Kṛṣṇa, Rukmiṇī, repeatedly chanting the praises of Kṛṣṇa, and seeing darkness in all the ten directions, fell down unconscious. Seeing that, her friends Madana Mañjarī and Līlāvatī, raising a hue and cry, supported her immediately with open arms, sprinkled water on the head, fanned her with the fore-end of their clothing and consoled her.

"Oh dear friend, that sinner Śiśupāla will not have you; why do you become restless? That Mādhava, who is a friend to his devotees, will definitely save you. Knowing that, oh dear friend, compose yourself."

*śloka* ||

*lapantī kṛṣṇa kṛṣṇeti harervirahakātarā* |
*ruroda rājaduhitā sakhībhiḥ sahitā satī* ||14||

Hymn[16]: Afflicted with separation from Kṛṣṇa, the princess calling out, "Kṛṣṇa, Kṛṣṇa!" again and again, started crying along with her friends.

*kathā* ||

*tadanantara : rājanandanī : cetana labhiye : hā kṛṣṇa hā kṛṣṇa buli dīrgha niśvāsa phokāri : rukmika gāri dei* ||

Dialogue: After that, the princess, having regained consciousness and releasing long sighs, saying "Oh Kṛṣṇa, oh Kṛṣṇa!" started scolding Rukmī.

*he pāpī sodara : tuhu sāta śatruto adhika bheli : prāṇakṛṣṇa sahita kaice hāmāka bañcita kayali : tuhu janami ki nimitta nāhi marali* ||

[16]. in *Śloka* metre, but in the 3rd foot, the 6th and 7th letters are short and not long.

*ohi buli rukamiṇī : sakhī duhu sahita jaice : śrīkṛṣṇaka bilāpa kayali : tā śunaha* ||

"Oh you sinner brother, you have become worse than the worst enemy. How you have deprived me of the company of my beloved Śrī Kṛṣṇa! Why have you not died immediately after your birth!"

Saying so, as Rukmiṇī, along with her two friends, lamented for Śrī Kṛṣṇa, listen to that.

*gīta* || *rāga – śrīgāndhāra* || *jautimāna* ||

Song in the *Rāga Śrīgāndhāra* with the rhythm *Jautimāna:*

*hari hari hāmāra karama kinā bheli* |
*prāṇa piu āśa kaicana dūra geli* || *dhruṁ* ||

Oh Hari what fate befell to me; how all the hope for the lord of my life has gone away. Refrain.

*pada* ||

*pāpī sodara tuhu nāhi bheli nāśa* |
*durllabha ballabha kṛṣṇa kayali nairāśa* ||
*jagajana tāraṇa caraṇa jāhāru* |
*bañcala kaicana kṛṣṇa ballabha hāmāru* ||*1*||
*kṛṣṇara caraṇa cira johi kayo kāma* |
*dūra gela sohi mohi bihi bheli bāma* ||
*nāhi nāhi dharabahu hari bine prāṇa* |
*bikali rukuni kṛṣṇa kiṅkara bhāṇa* ||2||9||

Verse : "Oh, wicked brother, why have you not perished. You have disappointed me in having Kṛṣṇa, who is so difficult to attain, as my husband. One who redeemes all the people of this world who take to His feet; how you have deprived me of having Kṛṣṇa as my beloved husband! (1)

"My only wish forever has been to be under the feet of Kṛṣṇa, but now He has gone away from me and my fate is rather averted from me. I shall not hold on to my life without

Hari." Thus, Rukmiṇī became very disturbed, says the servant of Kṛṣṇa. (2)

*kathā* ||

*aicana bilāpa kaya : rājakumārī : murcchita hayā parala : sakhīsabe bodha dite : svastha hayā : āñcore ākhi mukha muci kahõ : niśvāsa phokāri bolaye lāgala* ||

Dialogue: Lamenting in this way, the princess fell down unconscious. When the friends reasoned with her, she felt a little better and wiping away her eyes and face with the fore-end of her clothing, sighing deeply, started saying.

*ae pāpī śiśupāla : tuhu hāmāka bibāha karite āvala : hā hā jaice siṁhaka bhāryāka : śṛgāla abhilāṣa kaya thika | hā hā kṛṣṇa bine : hāmu prāṇa rākhaba : tabe hāmāri jīvana dhika dhika | he prāṇa svāmi śrīkṛṣṇa : toho isaba bṛtānta nāhi jānaha : tohāka samīpa kāheka pathāñu* ||

"Oh you sinner Śiśupāla, you have come over here to marry me like a jackal wishing to have the wife of a lion. Oh alas! (If) I still hold onto my life without Kṛṣṇa, my life will be condemned! Oh Śrī Kṛṣṇa, the lord of my life, you do not know about all these details. Who shall I send near you!"

*ohi buli bālā heṭha mātha kaye cintite : eka mitra brāhmaṇaka mane pāvala : sotsāhe sakhī līlāvatika bola*||

Saying thus, the young girl with her head bowed down, started thinking and remembering a *brāhmaṇa* friend, said enthusiastically to her friend Līlāvatī.

*he sakhī līlāvati : tuhu satvare jāva : hāmāra mahāmitra bedanidhika ānagiyā* ||

"Oh dear friend Līlāvatī, you please go quickly and fetch my great friend Vedanidhi."

*śuni līlāvati tattakāle cali jāi : kumārīka kathā brāhmaṇaka janāvala* ||
Hearing that, Līlāvatī left immediately and informed the *brāhmaṇa* about the princess.

*śloka* ||

*niśamya tvaritaṁ prāgādvākyaṁ devyāḥ dvijottamaḥ* |
*nāmnā bedanidhiḥ khyāto rukmiṇyāḥ priyakṛtadā* ||*15*||

Hymn[17]: Hearing the words of the lady, the best of the *brāhmaṇas* known by the name Vedanidhi, presented himself immediately to perform the desired task.

*sūtra* ||

*rājanandanīka bāṇī śuni kahu : jaice bedanidhi āvala : tāhe dekhaha śunaha : nirantare hari bola* ||

Direction: Hearing the words of the princess, as Vedanidhi came, watch and listen to that and keep chanting the name of Hari incessantly.

*gīta* || *rāga kānaḍā* || *māna paritāla* ||
Song in the *Rāga Kānaḍā* with the rhythm *Paritāla:*

*āvata bedanidhi dvijarāja* |
*sādhite rājakumārīka kāja* || *dhruṁ*||

Vedanidhi, the chief of the *brāhmaṇas*, comes to perform the task for the princess.

*pada* ||

*rañje tilaka kapālaka chāni* |
*dhautabāsa kuśa śobhita pāṇi* ||
*cāndaka pānti daśana parakāśa* |
*śaṅkara kaha ohi keśava dāsa* ||*10*||

Verse: The sandal wood mark covered and beautified the whole forehead, clean clothes enhanced his beauty and holy

---

17 . in *Śloka* metre; but in the 4th foot, the 6th letter is short and not long.

*kuśa* grass adorned his hand. His teeth glowed like a row of moon. This is how the servant of Keśava looked, says Śaṅkara.

*kathā* ||

*tadanantara : se rājakumāra*[18] *heṭha māthe krandana kayethika : nayanaka nīra dhāre bahi jāi | tāhe dekhie brāhmaṇa bola ||*

*he maī rājanandanī : ki apamāna milala : kona nimitta krandana kae thika : hā hā hāmāka śapata jaba satvara nāhi kaha | hāmo thākite tohāra ki mana dukha thika : he mātā : tāpa cāḍaha ||*

Dialogue: After that, with her head hanging down, the princess kept crying, tears flowing down from the eyes. Seeing that, the *brāhmaṇa* said, "Oh dear Princess, what disgrace has befallen, why are you crying, oh, upon my honour, if you do not speak up immediately. How can you be so unhappy when I am here. Oh mother, stop being sad."

*śloka* ||

*niśamya tadbaco bālā viniḥśvasya punaḥ punaḥ |*
*viprasya caraṇau śirṣā spṛṣṭvā śokākulābravīt ||16||*

Hymn[19]: Hearing his words, sighing again and again and touching the feet of the *brāhmaṇa* with her head, the young girl started speaking very sadly.

*kathā* ||

*tadanantara : rukamiṇī āñcore ākhi mukha muci : bipraka jānupāri : praṇāma kae kahu : bolaye lāgala ||*

*he guru : hāmu māri jāñu : hāmāta ki bāta puchaha : je śrīkṛṣṇa svāmīta : cirakāla āśā kaye chilo : hā hā tāheka hāmāra pāpī sodare dūra kayala : hāmāka dite śiśupāla bara ānāvala : se pāpīka dekhite jīu jāi | he guru bāpa : ki kahaba : tuhu jaba dvārakāpure gaiyā : kṛṣṇaka ānite pāraha : tabe hāmāka prāṇa dāna devaba ||*

---

[18]. *rājakumārī.*

[19]. in *Śloka* metre.

Dialogue: After that, wiping off her eyes and face with the fore-end of her clothing, Rukmiṇī offered obeisance to the *brāhmaṇa* on her knees, and started talking.

"Oh father, here I am dying, what do you want to know from me? Śrī Kṛṣṇa, whom I have always been wishing to have as my husband, my wicked brother has finished that hope of mine. He has brought in Śiśupāla, as the bridegroom to marry me off. Even to see him makes me die. Oh great father, what to say, if you can go to the city of Dwārakā and fetch Kṛṣṇa here, then only, you will be giving me back my life again."

*śloka* ||

*niśamya tadbaco vipro vihasyovāca rukmiṇīm* |
*kumārī kuru mā śokaṁ kā cintā te sthite mayi* ||17||

Hymn[20]: Hearing her words, the *brāhmaṇa* said to Rukmiṇī smiling, "Oh Princess, don't grieve, what is there to worry for you, when I am here."

*kathā* ||

*tāhe śuni bedanidhi : bihasi bola* ||
*āḥ he māi rukamiṇī : kṛṣṇaka ānite kona cintā thika : tapaka mahimāe : ākāśaka candra anite pāru : hāmu dvārakā ei calalu : je bāta thika : tā kaha* ||

Dialogue: Hearing that, Vedanidhi said smiling, "Oh dear girl Rukmiṇī, there is nothing to worry about bringing in Kṛṣṇa here. With the great power of penance, I can bring down here even the moon from the sky. Here I am leaving for Dwārakā; what is to be told there, say that."

*tāhe śunie : kumārī kico svastha hayā bola* |
Hearing that, the Princess felt a little better and said.

*he guru : śrīkṛṣṇa svāmīka caraṇe : prathame hāmāra praṇāma kahabi : tadanantara : hāmāka dukha nibedaba : tohāri kiṅkarī*

[20]. in *Śloka* metre; but in the 1st foot, the 7th letter is short and not long.

*rukamiṇī : aicana bolala || he svāmi kṛṣṇa : bhikṣuka mukhe tohāka rūpaguṇa śunie : hāmu kāyabākyamane : tohāka patibhāve baraici : tathi śiśupāla pāpiṣṭhe hāmāka nite cāhe : jāni prāṇanātha satvare āsi : hāmāka rakṣā karaha : tohoka cāḍi hāmāra gati nāhi gati nāhi ||*

"Oh preceptor, first convey my obeisance at the feet of my Lord Śrī Kṛṣṇa. After that, tell Him about my sorrows, 'Your servant Rukmiṇī says thus, oh dear Lord Kṛṣṇa, hearing about your beauty and qualities from the beggar bard, I have chosen you with all my body, mind and words, as my husband. And here the sinner Śiśupāla wants to take me away (as wife). Knowing all these, oh the lord of my life, come quickly and save me; leaving you, there is no other way out for me, no other way out for me.'

*gīta || rāga- ahira || jautimāna ||*

Song in the *rāga Ahira* with the rhythm *Jautimāna:*

*dhurā ||*

*keśava he : hāmākeri rākhabi prāṇa |*
*nija kiṅkarīka jīvana dehu dāna |*

Refrain: "Oh Keśava, save my life, give life to your servant."

*pada ||*

*tuyā padapaṅkaja : jīvana jagabāsa |*
*kavalu kamalanayana cira āśa ||*
*bipada payonidhi : paralu murāru |*
*dīna bāndhava deva uddhāra hāmāru ||1||*
*pāpī śiśupāla kāla bhelo meri |*
*tohāri caraṇe śaraṇa lelu hari ||*
*gati govinda bine nāhi nāhi āna |*
*rukmiṇī karunā karu śaṅkara bhāṇa ||2||11||*

Verse : "Your lotus-like feet are my life, oh omnipresent. I have hoped for the lotuslike eyes forever. I have fallen into the sea of danger, oh Murāri. Oh God, the friend of the poor, please save me. The sinner Śiśupāla has become my destiny. I have taken refuge at your feet oh Hari. There is no other way but (to take refuge in the feet of) Govinda." Please show mercy on Rukmiṇī, says Śaṅkara.

*kathā* ||

*he svāmi kṛṣṇa : śiśupāla pāpita hante : nija dāsīka rakṣā kari nevasiyā* ||

Dialogue: "Oh Lord Kṛṣṇa, please rescue and take away your servant from the sinner Śiśupāla."

*bipraka bola* || *he guru : hāmāra eka gāci kheḍa : kṛṣṇaka āgu diyā : kātara kae : satvare ānaha : jaba bilamba haya : kṛṣṇaka prāṇa sampie : hāmu maraba* | *aḥ bistara ki kahaba : eka patiā lekhi deñu : tāhe loyā jāva : jaba bistara bilamba hae : tebe hāmu maraba* ||

(Rukmiṇī) said to the *brāhmaṇa*, "Oh preceptor, offering a blade of grass to Kṛṣṇa on my behalf and requesting Him in earnest, bring Him here immediately. If you are delayed, dedicating my life to Kṛṣṇa I shall die. What more shall I say. Let me write a letter. Take it along. If you delay any more, then surely I shall die."

*ohi buli rukamiṇī : svahaste patra lekhi : brāhmaṇaka hāte delaha* | *bedanidhi hāta pāti lelaha* | *rājakumārīka prabodha buliye bipra calala* ||

Saying so, Rukmiṇī wrote a letter with her own hands and gave it to the *brāhmaṇa*. Vedanidhi took it extending his hands and consoling the princess, the *brāhmaṇa* left.

*bedanidhi bola* || *he rājanandanī : kico cintā nāhi karabi : eka tile kṛṣṇaka ānabu tuhu sukhe raha* ||

*ohi buli bipra dvārakā calala : tāhe dekhaha śunaha : nirantare hari bola* ||

Vedanidhi said, "Oh Princess, do not worry at all. I shall bring Kṛṣṇa in a moment, be happy."
Saying so, the *brāhmaṇa* started for Dwārakā. Watch and listen to that and keep chanting the name of Hari incessantly.

*payāḍa* || *rāga- śrī* || *māna paritāla* ||
Verse in the *Rāga Śrī* with the rhythm *Paritāla:*

*kumārīka āśvāsa bulie bacana* |
*dvija dvārikāka lāgi karala gamana* ||
Thus uttering consoling words to the princess, the *brāhmaṇa* started on his way to Dwārakā.

*pada* ||
*cāḍala nagara giri araṇya āśeṣa* |
*bhela dvāraati pūri bipra parabeśa* ||*1*||
*manohara nagara sāgara maha thika* |
*karu parakāśa surapurīka adhika* ||
*jagata bibhūti tathi bheli ekuthāna* |
*haripurī dekhala kanaka niramāṇa* ||2||
*dvāri dvārapālaka bola pāi lāga* |
*kuṇḍinaka dvija hāmu kaha kṛṣṇa āga* ||
*kṛṣṇata hāmāra thika gopya prayojana* |
*rāma rāma bolahu hariṣe sarbbajana* ||3||*12*||
Verse: Leaving many towns and cities, mountains and forests, the *brāhmaṇa* entered the city with many doors. (1)
The beautiful city is situated in the midst of the sea and it was brighter even than the city of the gods. All the wealth of the world is accumulated there and the *brāhmaṇa* saw the city of Hari to be made of gold. (2)
Meeting the door-keeper on the doorway he said, "Go and tell Kṛṣṇa that I am a *brāhmaṇa* coming from Kuṇḍina and I have some serious and secret matter with Him. And everyone utter 'Rāma, Rāma' with pleasure."(3)

*kathā* ||

*tadanantara : dvārapālasaba gayā : kṛṣṇaka praṇāma kaya bolala* ||

Dialogue: Thereupon, the door-keepers going to Kṛṣṇa, and offering obeisance said.

*he svāmi : kuṇḍina hante : eka biśiṣṭa bipra hāmāra dvāre rahaye thika : ki ādeśa haya nātha* ||

"Oh Lord, there is an eminent *brāhmaṇa* from Kuṇḍina, waiting at our door. Now, what is your command?"

*ōhi śuni śrīkṛṣṇa tattakāle uṭhi kahu : gaurave gaiyā brāhmaṇaka praṇāmi : āliṅgi dharie : abhyantara prabeśa karāvala : svahaste pāva pakhālie pañcāmṛta bhuñjāvala : tadanantara bipra suvarṇṇa khātata sutala : śrīkṛṣṇa nija haste pāva marddie : śrama dūra kaya kahu : bāta pucata* ||

Hearing that, Śrī Kṛṣṇa got up immediately and going to the *brāhmaṇa*, bowed with honour and then embracing him took him to the inner chamber. Washing his feet with His own hands fed him (the *brāhmaṇa*) with *pañcāmṛta*. After that, the *brāhmaṇa* took a nap on a golden bed. Śrī Kṛṣṇa, after removing his tiredness by rubbing and massaging the legs and feet of the *brāhmaṇa* with His own hands himself, asked him about the matter.

*śloka* ||

*kuśalaṁ tava viprendra kimarthamihāgataḥ* |
*pavitraṁ kṛtamasmākaṁ tadpādarajasā gṛham* ||*18*||

Hymn[21]: "Oh noblest *brāhmaṇa*, may you be well; why have you come here? With the dust of your feet you have purified our home."

*kathā* ||

---

[21]. in *Śloka* metre; but in the 2nd foot, the 5th letter is long and not short.

*he guru : toho kuśale āvala : tohāri pāda- reṇue gṛhasaba pavitra bhela : tohāri bhīṣmaka rājā : kukhale thika : svadharmme ki prajā pālaya : hāmu kona prayojana sādhu : tā ājñā karaha ||*

Dialogue: "Oh preceptor, have you come safely? With the dust of your feet our entire home has become pure. Is your King Bhīṣmaka well? Is he protecting his subjects well with his own judgement? How can I be of any use, order me."

*śloka ||*

*ebaṁ sabhājito vipro niśamyeśvarabhāṣitam |*
*prītyā pratyāha prahasan mādhavaṁ sādhuvāndhavaṁ ||19||*

Hymn[22]: Hearing the lord speak in this way, the *brāhmaṇa*, who mesmerises the assembly, being very happy started saying to Mādhava, the friend of all the good people.

*kathā ||*

*tāhe śunie bedanidhi bihasi bola ||*

*he svāmi śrīkṛṣṇa : tuhu jagataka parama īśvara : tohāka e ākhie dekhalu : ataḥpara hāmāra kamana kukhala thika | tuhu daivakī putra : sohi nahi : brahmā maheśa sevita : śrīnārāyaṇa : se tuhu bhūmika bhāra haraṇa nimitta avatāra bheli thika : aḥ tohoka mahimā ki kahaba | hāmu jadarthe āvalu tā śunaha : hāmāra bidarbharājanandanī rukamiṇī : bhikṣuka mukhe tohāri guṇarūpa śunie : mane svāmī bhāve barala : se kainyāka bibāha karite : pāpī śiśupāla āvala : tāhe dekhie rājakumārī maraice | aḥ hāmu ki kahaba : eka patiā lekhi paṭhāvala thika : tāheka dekhaha ||*

Dialogue : Hearing that, Vedanidhi said smiling, "Oh Lord Śrī Kṛṣṇa, you are the Supreme Lord of this world; I have seen you with these eyes of mine; what good can I achieve beyond this? You are not (only) the son of Devakī; worshipped by Brahmā and Maheśa, you are Śrī Nārāyaṇa and you have incarnated only to relieve the earth of its

---

22 . in *Śloka* metre; but in the 3rd foot , the 5th letter is long instead of short and the 6th and 7th letters are short instead of long.

burdens. Oh, what to speak of your greatness! Now listen, for what reason I have come here. Our princess of the kingdom of Bidarbha, Rukmiṇī, hearing about your charm and qualities from a beggar bard, has chosen you as her husband. To marry this girl, sinner Śiśupāla has come. Seeing that, the princess is dying. Oh, what shall I say; here she has written a letter and sent it through me. Have a look at that".

*ohi buli rukamiṇīka patra : kṛṣṇaka hāte delaha : śrīkṛṣṇa sādare dharie : muda bhāṅgala : se bipraka bola* ||
Saying so, (the *brāhmaṇa*) gave the letter from Rukmiṇī, in Kṛṣṇa's hands. Śrī Kṛṣṇa received it eagerly and uncovered it. He said to the *brāhmaṇa*,

*he guru : tuhu pāṭha karaha : hāmu śunie raho* ||
"Oh preceptor, you please read it aloud and I shall listen."

*bipre patra loyā paḍhaite lāgala : śrīkṛṣṇa ekacite śunie thika*| *āheloka : tāhe dekhaha śunaha : nirantare hari bola* ||
The *brāhmaṇa* took the letter and started reading aloud and Śrī Kṛṣṇa listened to it attentively. Oh dear people, watch and listen to that and keep chanting the name of Hari incessantly.

*svasti śrīparameśvara : sakala surāsura bandita pādapadmña: prapannajanatāraṇa nārāyaṇa : śrī śrī kṛṣṇacaraṇasaroruheṣu* | *rukmiṇyā : sahasrapraṇāma-likhanaṁ : kāryaṅka : śivamiha nivedanañca* ||
"May you be well, oh honourable Supreme Lord. One whose lotuslike feet are worshipped by gods and demons alike, who rescues those who seek refuge, who is Nārāyaṇa himself, offering thousands of obeisance to the lotus feet of that Kṛṣṇa, Rukmiṇī writes, also that may he have well being."

*he svāmi : bhikṣuka mukhe tuyā guṇa rūpa śunie: kāyabākyamane tohāka patibhāve baraici | tathi pāpī śiśupāla | hāmāka bibāha karite āvala thika : jaice siṁhaka bhāryā nite : śṛgāla cumpi rahaya thika | tāhe dekhi bhaye daṇḍe juga jāi : jāni hāmi nija dāsīka : satvare nevasiyā svāmi | jaba bola tuhu anteṣapure raha : kuna parakāre bhenṭa pāñu : tatocita upāya kahu : henātha tā śunaha : bibāhaka purbba divase : bhavānīka maṭhe calaba : se samaye hāmāka hari niyā jāya | jebe tuhu helā kaye nāhi nevaba : tebe tohāta badha diye : hāmu prāṇa cāḍaba | pāpī śiśupālaka : chāyāka hāmu kabahu pāve nāhi parakṣu | ohi jāni dīna dāsīka : he nātha : uddhara uddhara | taba caraṇasaroruhe kiṁ bahu lekhyamiti patramidam |*

"Oh Lord, hearing about your charm and qualities from the mendicant, I have chosen you as my husband with my body, mind and words. And here the sinner Śiśupāla has come to marry me, like a jackal, hiding, expecting to take away the wife of the lion with him. Seeing him, out of fear, a moment passes like an age. Knowing all these, take away your own servant immediately, oh my Lord. If you agree to stay at the inner apartments of the palace, then we can meet somehow. Then, here I say the proper way, oh Lord, listen to that. On the day prior to the marriage I shall go to the temple of Bhavānī. At that time abduct and take me away. If you neglect to take me away, then leaving you responsible, I shall end my life. I shall never ever touch, even with my feet, the shadow of wicked Śiśupāla. Knowing that, oh Lord, save this poor servant, save her. What more to write to be offered in your lotus feet, so here ends the letter."

*śloka* ||

*nirīkṣya karuṇaṁ patraṁ patnyāḥ paramapuruṣaḥ |*
*premāśrulocanastasthau mlānanetramukhāmbujaḥ ||20||*

Hymn[23]: Looking at the sorrowful letter of his wife, the eyes of the Supreme Personality became full with tears of love and His eyes and lotuslike face became wearied.

*sūtra* ||

*tadanantara : rukamiṇīka sakāruṇa patra dekhie : kṛṣṇaka hṛdaye tāpa upajala : kamala nayanaka nīra jhuraye lāgala : jaicana bilāpa kayala : tāhe dekhaha śunaha : nirantare hari bola* ||

Direction : After that, seeing Rukmiṇī's sad letter, afflication arose in Kṛṣṇa's heart and tears started flowing down from the lotuslike eyes and as He lamented, watch and listen to that and keep chanting the name of Hari incessantly.

*gīta* || *rāga- gaurī* || *rūpaka tāla* ||

Song in the *rāga Gaurī* with the rhythm *Rūpaka:*

*dhruṁ* ||

*hari hari kinā bheli rājakumārī* |
*kamalanayana pūri : bāri jhurāvata :*
*ghana ghana phokāre murāri* ||

Refrain : Oh Hari what has happened to the princess? Tears filled the lotuslike eyes of Murāri and He sighed deeply again and again.

*pada* ||

*karata katanu teri : nārī nikāru :*
*mohe biraha dahe āgi* |
*toho jaba jīvana : bālā coḍaha :*
*hañuñ taba tuyā badha bhāgī* ||*1*||
*terā daraśana : kaicana hoi :*
*sumarite tanumana tāve* |
*milala adhikahu : hariko ākula :*

[23]. in *Śloka* metre; but in the 2nd foot, the 6th letter is short instead of long.

*kṛṣṇa kiṅkara rasa gāve ||13||*

Verse: "Oh woman, you are suffering so much and I am suffering from the fire of separation. Oh girl, if you give up your life, I shall be responsible for your death. (1)

"How shall I be able to see you, thinking that (my) body and mind suffer." And Hari became more and more restless, sings the servant of Kṛṣṇa with pleasure.

*kathā* ||

*kṛṣṇa bola || he bedanidhi : tuhu kahibāra pātra | jo divase se pṛyāka guṇa-rūpa śunalu : sehante rukamiṇīka : mātra dhiyāna kaya hāmāra mana thika : se prāṇa pṛyāka : avasthā kathā śunie : kaice jīvana dharu | aye dāruka : satvare ratha ānaha : kuṇḍinaka cali kahu etikṣaṇe jañe : se pṛyāka dukha śunie : prāṇa rahaye nāhi ||*

Dialogue: Kṛṣṇa said, "Oh Vedanidhi you are fit to be spoken to. From the day I heard about the beauty and qualities of my beloved, since then my mind has been fixed in meditation of Rukmiṇī. Now hearing about the condition of my beloved, how can I live on! Oh Dāruka, bring the chariot immediately. Let us move for Kuṇḍina right at this moment; knowing about the plight of my beloved I cannot live any more."

*śloka* ||

*atha rathamadhiruhya keśavo'sau*
*sapadi sārathinoddhavena yuktaḥ |*
*karakṛtadhanurīśvaraḥ priyāyā*
*premākulaḥ kuṇḍinamojasvān yayau ||21||*

Hymn[24]: Then Lord Kṛṣṇa, being very much restless with love for His beloved, riding the chariot along with the charioteer Uddhava and holding the bow and arrows in His hands started towards Kuṇḍina very fast.

*sūtra* ||

[24]. in *Puṭa* metre, a variety of *Jagatī* metre.

*tāhe śuni : dāruka tattakāle ratha jogāvala : pekhi śrīkṛṣṇa brāhmaṇaka hāte dharie : ratha upare tuli : hāte śaracāpa dhari kahu : uddhava sahite : tathi caḍala : dāruka mahābege ratha ḍakāvala : śrīkṛṣṇa jaice calali : tāhe dekhaha śunaha : nirantare hari bola* ||

Direction: Hearing Him, Dāruka immediately arranged for the chariot. Seeing that, Śrī Kṛṣṇa helped the *brāhmaṇa* by hand to climb onto the chariot and holding bow and arrows in His hands climbed onto the chariot along with Uddhava. Dāruka drove the chariot with great speed and as Śrī Kṛṣṇa went, watch and listen to that and keep chanting the name of Hari incessantly.

*gīta* || *rāga- māhura dhanaśrī* || *paritāla* ||

Song in the *Rāga Māhura Dhanaśrī* with the rhythm *Paritāla:*

*kuṇḍinaku āvata mohana murāru* |
*kauṭi indunindi : badana birāju :*
*kara śāraṅga śara dhāru* || *dhruṁ* ||

Here comes Mohana Murāru to Kuṇḍina with His face glowing, defeating even a crore of moons, and holding the *Śāraṅga* bow in His hand. Refrain.

*pada* ||

*śyāma mūruti pīta : ambaru ambuda :*
*taḍita jaḍita jaca śohe* |
*ratana mukuṭa maṇi : kuṇḍala ḍolita :*
*hāsi jagata jana mohe* || *1*||
*bhujajuga kejura kaṅkaṇa āṅguli* ||
*āṅguri ratana bikāśa* |
*mañjīra rañjita : caraṇa saroruha :*
*śaṅkara kaha hari dāsa* ||2||*13*||*14*||

Verse: Bluish-black in body, with yellow clothing, shining like the quick flash of lightning in the cloud. The crown with precious stones and earrings made of gems and jewels dangling and His smile charming all the people of this world.(1)

Armbands on the arms and bracelets in the hands and gems in the rings brighten the fingers. The lotuslike feet glow with the anklets, says Śaṅkara, the servant of Hari.(2)

*kathā* ||

*ohi parakāre : kṛṣṇaka ratha bāu bege cale : tathi ālolya brāhmaṇa : bedanidhi rathabege śrutibhaṅga huyā parala : hātapāva thira bhela : peṭa uphandala : nāsāta niśvāsa nāhi niḥsare : jaice mṛtaka : tadvat acetana bhela : tāhe pekhie śrīkṛṣṇa : hā hā buli śira jala siñcie : phuṅki phuṅki dhātu ānala* ||

Dialogue: In this way, the chariot of Kṛṣṇa moved as fast as the wind. Vedanidhi, the delicate *brāhmaṇa,* fainted at the high speed of the chariot. His hands and feet stiffened, his stomach puffed up, and his breaths stopped coming out of his nostrils, and he became unconscious like a dead man. Seeing that, Śrī Kṛṣṇa crying, "Alas, alas!", sprinkled water on his head and blowing breath into him brought his life back.

*kṛṣṇa bola* || *he bedanidhi : svastha hava svastha hava* ||
Kṛṣṇa said: "Oh Vedanidhi, get well, get better."

*kṛṣṇaka āśvāsa śunie : kico cetana pāi : bipra bola* ||
*he bāpu : tuhu bā ke : hāmu bā kuna : kinimitta ethā āvalu thika* || *śrīkṛṣṇa bihasi bola* || *hāmu dvārakāra kṛṣṇa : tuhu bedamini*[25] *: rukamiṇī paṭhāvala : tannimitta tuhu hāmu kuṇḍine calaici* ||
Hearing Kṛṣṇa's assurance, having regained some sense, the *brāhmaṇa* said, "Oh father, who are you and who am I? Why have we come here?" Śrī Kṛṣṇa said smiling, "I am Kṛṣṇa

[25]. *vedanidhi.*

from Dwārakā and you are Vedanidhi sent by Rukmiṇī. For her, you and I are going to Kuṇḍina."

*sūtra* ||

*tāhe śunie : bipra bāhu meli kṛṣṇaka dharala ||*
*bipra bola || hā hā bāpa barttalu : hāmu kṣaṇeke mari jāñōñ : tohāka nimite punu upajalo |*

Direction : Hearing that, the *brāhmaṇa*, extending his arms, held Kṛṣṇa. The *brāhmaṇa* said, "Oh father I am alive, I died for a moment and only because of you, I am born again."

*sūtra* ||

*brāhmaṇa kampaya dekhi : śrīkṛṣṇa āśvāsa buli svastha kayala* ||

Direction: Seeing the *brāhmaṇa* trembling, Śrī Kṛṣṇa, uttering consoling words, made him feel better.

*śloka* ||

*tato vipraṁ prabhuḥ prāha gaccha tvaṁ satvaraṁ guro |*
*madāgamanamākhyāsi priyāyāḥ prītimābahan* ||22||

Hymn[26]: Then (Kṛṣṇa) said to the *brāhmaṇa*, "Oh preceptor, please go quickly, and to increase the love of my beloved towards me and to tell her about my arrival."

*kathā* ||

*tadanantara : śrīkṛṣṇa kuṇḍina samīpa pāi : bipraka bola ||*
*he guru : toho āgu hayā calaha : se prāṇapṛyā nairāśā dekhiye : prāṇa chāḍaba : hāmāra āgamana rukamiṇīta kaha giyā ||*
*bipra śuniye kṛṣṇaka āśīrbbāda kaya kaho : āgu huyā calala |*
*i kathā rahoka | rukamiṇīka bṛtānta śunaha ||*

Dialogue : After that, nearing Kuṇḍina, Śrī Kṛṣṇa said to the *brāhmaṇa*, "Oh preceptor, you please proceed in advance.

---

26 . in *Śloka* metre.

That beloved of mine, being hopeless will give up her life, so please go and tell Rukmiṇī about my arrival."

Hearing that, blessing Kṛṣṇa, the *brāhmaṇa* proceeded in advance. Let this topic rest here. Listen to the account of Rukmiṇī.

*śloka* ||

*vilambaṁ vīkṣya viprasya rukmiṇī rājanandinī* |
*cintāṁ durantāmāsādya*[27] *ruroda sakhīsannidhau*[28] ||23||

Hymn[29]: Seeing that, the *brāhmaṇa* is delayed, Princess Rukmiṇī became greatly worried and drowned in deep worry, started crying near her friends.

*kathā*||

*tadanantara : bipraka bilamba dekhi : rukamiṇīka mane cintā milala || madanamañjarīka bola || he sakhī : hāmāra parama anartha milala : āju adhibāsa : kāli bibāhaka divasa : se bedanidhi : kṛṣṇaka ānae nāhi pāri : lajjāye nāvala : hā hā aba svāmīka āśā cheda bhela ||*

*ohi buli kumārī : jaice krandana kayala : tāhe dekhaha śunaha : nirantare hari bola*||

Dialogue: After that, seeing that the *brāhmaṇa* is delayed, Rukmiṇī became very worried and said to Madana Mañjarī, "Oh dear friend, I am very unfortunate. Today it is *adhivāsa*, and tomorrow it is the wedding day. Not being able to bring Kṛṣṇa with him, out of shame, Vedanidhi has not come. Oh alas, now all my hopes for my lord are shattered!"

Saying so, how the princess started crying, watch and listen to that and keep chanting the name of Hari without stopping.

*gīta* || *rāga- gaurī* || *biṣama tāla* ||

Song in the *Rāga Gaurī* with the rhythm *Viṣama:*

[27]. *durantamāsādya.*

[28]. *sakhisannidhau.*

[29]. in *Śloka* metre; but in the 3rd and 4th feet, the 5th letters are long instead of short.

*māyi mādhava aba kayali meri nairāśa |*
*pantha nehāri : rājakumārī : phokāre ghane niśvāsa ||*
*dhruṁ||*

Oh friend(Madana Mañjarī), Mādhava has disappointed me. Looking towards the road, the princess released deep sighs again and again. Refrain.

*pada ||*

*parama puruṣa : keśava bino :*
*biphala janama moi |*
*milala maraṇa : kṛṣṇa caraṇa :*
*daraśana nāhi hoi ||*
*hāmu abhāgī : lāgi jānalu :*
*jīvana nātha nave |*
*nuruci paḍala : cetana harala :*
*ramaṇī śaṅkare gāve ||2||15||*

Verse: Without that Supreme Personality Keśava, my life is vain. I shall have to die if I cannot have a glimpse of the feet of Kṛṣṇa.

Now I know, the master of my life will not come for an unfortunate like me. The lovely young woman fell down and lost consciousness. Thus sings Śaṅkara. (2)

*kathā :*

*aicana krandana kae bālā : murcita hayā parala : sakhī saba dekhiye : hā ḥā buli bāhu meli dhari kaho prabodha bolala || sakhī madana mañjarī bola || he sakhī : svastha hava : svastha hava : se śrīkṛṣṇa tohāka nimite : avaśye āvaba : jākeri nāma mātre : mahā mahā pāpīsabo saṁsāra nistare : se bhakataka bāndhava mādhava : tohāka nāhi rakṣā karaba : prāṇasakhī : õhi śaṅkā chāḍaha : hāmāka śapata uṭhaha uṭhaha ||*

Dialogue: Crying in this way, the young girl fell down fainting. Seeing that, all her friends crying, "Alas, alas!", held her with extended arms and consoled her.

Friend Madana Mañjarī said, "Oh dear friend, get well, and get better. Śrī Kṛṣṇa will definitely come for you. Just by (uttering) whose name, even the worst of the sinners are saved from this world. He is the friend to His devotees, Mādhava, and will He not save you? Oh friend, dear as life, give up this doubt. Upon my name, get up, get up."

*śloka* ||

*tataḥ utthāya sā bālā viniḥsvasya punaḥ puna* |
*ruroda karuṇaṁ bālā smṛtvā kṛṣṇapadāmbujam* ||24||

Hymn[30]: Then the young girl (Rukmiṇī) sat down rising and sighing again and again frequently, remembering the lotus feet of Kṛṣṇa, distressed, started crying pathetically.

*kathā* ||

*kumārī cetana labhi kahu : niśvāsa phokāri : hāte badana caḍāi baiṭhala : sakhīsavaka bola* ||
*he madana mañjarī : he sakhī līlāvati : hāmāra bihi baṅka bhela : bedanidhi gaiyā kahu bāhuri nāvala : prāṇakṛṣṇaka bātrā kico nāhi pāvalu : hā hā ohi janame se svāmīka caraṇa : daraśana dullabha bhela* ||
*ohi buli punu jaice krandana kayala bālā : tāhe dekhaha śunaha : nirantare hari bola* ||

Dialogue: The young girl, regaining consciousness, heaving sighs, sat down supporting her face with her hands and said to her friends, "Oh dear Madana Mañjarī, oh dear friend Līlāvatī, my fate has become adverse to me. Vedanidhi went, but has not come back. I did not get any message from Kṛṣṇa, who is as dear as life to me. Oh alas, alas, to get a glimpse of the feet of my master has become scarce in this life."

Saying so, how she started crying again, watch and listen to that and keep chanting the name of Hari incessantly.

*gīta* || *rāga- gaurī* || *jautimāna* ||

30 . in *Śloka* metre.

Song in the *Rāga Gaurī* with the rhythm *Jautimāna:*

*mādhava meri bichuri aba nāvala |*
*hari birahānale cetana gori ||*
*nāvala avahu : bāhuri dvijanandana |*
*kaha kaicana sakhī jīvana dhari || dhruṁ ||*

"Forgetting me, Mādhava has not come. The fire of separation from Hari has devoured the senses. The son of the *brāhmaṇa* also has not returned yet. Tell me oh dear friends, how can I live on!" Refrain.

*pada* ||

*ōhi śiśupāla kālā bheli meri |*
*heri harata cetana tanu khīṇa ||*
*hāmu abhāgī bihi baṅkima hāmāri |*
*prāṇa piu kaicana kayali bihīna ||*
*karabi kamana upāya punu pāi :*
*abadhi bibāha rayanī maha thika |*
*heraba-āvari hariko nāhi caraṇā |*
*kaha śaṅkara jhure ramaṇī adhika ||2||16||*

Verse: "That Śiśupāla has become my death incarnate; only one look from him makes my thin body lose consciousness. I am very unfortunate and my fate is adverse to me. Oh my life, my Lord, how could you abandon me.

"Find some way so that I can get you back again. Only the night remains between now and the wedding. I shall not see the feet of Hari any more." Śaṅkara says, more tears started flowing from the (eyes of the) young girl.(2)

*kathā* ||

*aicana bilāpa kaye bālā : haraki birahe murccita hayā parala : dekhi sakhīsaba hā hā boli : śira jala siñciye : āñcore biñcaya : kāhu āṅkovāli tuli baiṭhāi : madhura bāṇī bola ||*

*he prāṇasakhī : āju divasa nāhi jāi : aicana tāpa kaicana karasi : se kṛpāmaya mādhava : tohāka manoratha niścaye pūraba : duranta cintā chāḍaha ||*

*tāhe śunie : kumārī heṭhamāthe rahala thika | sohi samaye rukamiṇīka : bāma ūru kara ākhi phāndie gela : tāhe dekhie hariṣe bola ||*

*āhe sakhīsaba : hāmāra bāma aṅga phānde : kuna subha bāta kahe : ihā nāhi jānu ||*

*ōhi buli kumārī rahala thika ||*

Dialogue : Lamenting in this way, being separated from Hari, the young girl fell down unconscious. Seeing that, all the friends, crying "Alas, alas!", sprinkled water on her head, fanned her with the extended fore-end of their clothing, some others, embracing her, made her sit down and spoke pleasant words to her.

"Oh friend, dear like my life, this day is not finished yet. Why are you lamenting in this way? That merciful Mādhava will definitely fulfill your wishes. Give up such terrible thought."

Hearing them, the princess remained with downcast head. Just then the left thigh, left hand and left eye of Rukmiṇī started fluttering. Seeing that, the princess spoke happily. "Oh dear friends, my left limbs are fluttering, what good news is implied, that I do not know." Saying so, the princess waited.

*śloka* ||

*sāthitārtho*[31] *dvijaḥ prāgāt prītyutphullabilocanaḥ* |
*nāpatat caraṇau tasya dharaṇyāṁ harṣabegataḥ* ||25||

Hymn[32]: Having successfully completed his mission, the *brāhmaṇa* has come back. Being happy, his eyes are filled with tears. Out of happiness and enthusiasm, he walked with his feet as if not even touching the ground.

*kathā* ||

*tadanantara : devī dekhala : āti ānande bedanidhi : hariṣa bege āvala : māṭita pāva parae nāhi | bipraka mukha pekhi jānala :*

---

31 . *sādhitārtho.*

32 . in *Śloka* metre.

*aḥ hāmāra prāṇa piu āvala āvala : bhari pāñca – sāta āga bāḍhi giyā : bipraka praṇāma kayala ||*

Dialogue: After that, the lady saw Vedanidhi coming very fast with great happiness, with his feet, as if not even touching the ground. Looking at the face of the *brāhmaṇa* she came to know, "Oh my life, my Lord has come, He has come!" and advancing a few steps forward, offered her obeisance to the *brāhmaṇa*.

*bedanidhi bola || he rājanandanī : tuhu cirañjīva cirañjīva : tohāka prayojana saba sādhalu | se yadunandana tohāka nimite : annapāna saba chāḍala : niśi nidrā karata nāhi : he mātā : kṛṣṇaka dukha ki kahaba : kevala tuhāka mātra : dhiyāna kaya raha : aba õhi nagara prabeśa kayala | toho satvare dṛḍha huyā raha : saba manoratha āju śrīkṛṣṇa pūraba ||*

*ohi śuni devīka ānande lotaka jhure : bipraka praṇāma kaye bola ||*

*he pitā : bāpe upajāila mātra : tuhu prāṇadāna devala : tohāka guṇa sujaye nāhi pāru : ki prasāda deñuñ ||*

Vedanidhi said, "Oh Princess, may you live long, live long! I have fulfilled all your needs. The son of Yadu has given up eating and drinking in your name; does not even sleep at night. Oh dear mother, what to speak of the suffering of Kṛṣṇa. He keeps meditating only upon you. Now, He has entered the city. You become firm quickly. Śrī Kṛṣṇa will fulfill all your wishes today."

Hearing that, out of happiness, tears flowed from the eyes of the lady. Bowing to the *brāhmaṇa*, she said.

"Oh dear father, my father has given birth only. You have given life to me. I can never repay back your favour. What gift shall I give to you!"

*bedanidhi bola || he mātā : hāmāra āsirbāde śrīkṛṣṇa sahita : tohāka subasati hoka : taba hāmāra sakala prasāda bhela ||*

*ohi buli bipra nija bāḍi calala | tadanantara : rukamiṇīka jyeṣṭhabhrātā : rukmikumāra : se āsi kahu : bolala ||*

*āhe bhaginī : tuhu āti satvare bhūṣita hayā : sakhīsaba sahite : bhavānīka maṭhe calaha : āju adhibāsa : kāli bibāhaka divasa : devīka pujā kara giyā : āti satvare calaha ai calaha* ||

Vedanidhi said, "Oh mother, with my blessings may you live well with Śrī Kṛṣṇa , then I will get everything." Saying so, the *brāhmaṇa* went to his home. After that, Rukmī Kumara, the elder brother of Rukmiṇī , entered and said. "Oh dear sister, you dress up very quickly and along with your friends, go to the temple of Bhavānī. Today is *adhivāsa* and tomorrow it is the day of the wedding. Go and pray to the goddess. Go quickly, go quickly."

*śloka* ||

*niśamya vacanaṁ bhrātur bhūṣayitvātha bhūsaṇaiḥ* |
*jagāma sakhibhiḥ sākamātmānamambikālayaṁ* ||26||

Hymn[33]: Hearing the words of the brother, being adorned with ornaments, (the dear girl) along with her friends, went to the temple of Ambikā.

*kathā* ||

*bhrātāka bākya śuni kahu : kumārī sakhīsaba sahita : bhūṣita hayā jaicana calali : tāhe dekhaha śunaha : nirantare hari bola hari* ||

Dialogue : Hearing the words of her brother, how the princess went, dressed and ornamented and along with her friends, watch and listen to that and keep chanting the name of Hari incessantly.

*gīta* || *rāga – māura* || *paritāla* ||

Song in the *rāga Māhura* with the rhythm *Paritāla:*

*dhruṁ* ||

*raṅginī sakhī saṅginī bālā* |

---

[33] . in *Śloka* metre.

*calali jaice cāndakeri kālā* ||

Refrain: Along with the merry friends, the young girl went like the new digit of the moon.

*pada:*

*pahrie paṭṭāmbara lahu lahu dhāi* |
*matta gajagāminī kāminī māi* ||
*otima mautima mālā lule* |
*herite hāsi tubana*[34] *mana bhule* ||
*harikahu caraṇa cintie cali jāi* |
*kṛṣṇa kiṅkara ohi śaṅkara gāi* ||17||

Verse: Wearing silk clothing, excited, the lovely woman walks slowly in a stately elephant like gait. Garlands made of the best of the pearls hang (on her body). Seeing her smile, the whole world forgets everything. Thinking only of the feet of Hari, she walks on. The servant of Kṛṣṇa sings in this way.

*kathā* ||

*tadanantara : se rājakumārī : sakhīsaba sahita : bhavānīka maṭha pāi kahu : pāva pakhālie : nānābidha naibedya die : devīka pujā kayala : tutinati karie : bara sādhala : devīka āgu parie bola* ||

*he mātā bhavānī : svāmī śrīkṛṣṇa hāmāka : abighinie nehantoka : tohāka caraṇe ataye sādho* ||

*ohi bara prārthie : kumārī tathi rahala thika* ||

Dialogue: After that, the princess along with her friends, reaching the temple of Bhavānī, washing the feet, offering varieties of edibles, prayed and worshipped the goddess and asked for a boon. Prostrating in front of the goddess (Rukmiṇī) said,

"Oh mother Bhavānī, let my Śrī Kṛṣṇa be able to carry me off without any obstacle, I seek for that much only at your feet."

Praying for that boon, the princess remained there.

---

[34] . *bhubana.*

*śloka* ||

*kṛṣṇaḥ kuṇḍinamāgatya vipraṁ prasthāpya sādaram* |
*dārukoddhavasaṁyuktaḥ praviveśa vibhuḥ sabhām* ||27||

Hymn[35]: Coming to Kuṇḍina, sending the *brāhmaṇa* ahead with honour, being accompanied by Dāruka and Uddhava, Kṛṣṇa entered the court.

*sūtra* ||

*tadanantara : śrīkṛṣṇa bipraka āgu paṭhāi kahu : dāruka uddhava sahite : jaice sabhā madhye prabeśa kayala : tāhe dekhaha śunaha : nirantare nirantare hari bola hari* ||

Direction : After that, Śrī Kṛṣṇa, sending the *brāhmaṇa* in advance, entered the court along with Dāruka and Uddhava, watch and listen to that and keep chanting the name of Hari incessantly.

*gīta* || *rāga-gaurī* || *ekatāli* ||

Song in the *Rāga Gaurī* with the rhythm *Ekatāli:*

*dhurā* ||

*meri madhāi āvata ānanda mane*
*pekhi bhulala rūpa mana paurajane* ||

Refrain: Here comes my Mādhava, happily and seeing His beauty, the citizens forget their minds.

*pada* ||

*paṅkaja bayana nayane karu pāna* |
*heri hṛdaye mane milala dhiāna* ||
*śyāma rucira tanu pīta picorā* |
*nava nirada jaca bijurī ujorā* ||
*caraṇa rañjita maṇi nupura bikāśa* ||
*kaha śaṅkara haridāsaku dāsa* ||18||

---

[35] . in *Śloka* metre.

Verse: The eyes feed on the lotuslike face, seeing which, both heart and mind start concentrating on Him. The bluish-black body with yellow clothing looks bright like the flashing lightning on the newly formed cloud. The feet are decorated and brightened with anklets of gems, says Śaṅkara, the servant of Kṛṣṇa.

*kathā* ||

*śrīkṛṣṇa aicana prabeśa kaya : rājamaṇḍalī madhye baiṭhala: jaicana nakṣatra mājhe punnimāka cānda : parakāśa kaye thika* | *śrīkṛṣṇaka rūpa sampatti pekhie : sabaloka bhulala : mukhapaṅkajaka jaice nayane pāna karata* | *bipakṣa nṛpasaba : trailokya camatkāra : birapratāpa dekhie : parama bhaya bhela : anyo anye karṇe karṇe kahe* ||

Dialogue: Entering in this way, Śrī Kṛṣṇa sat amongst the host of kings, looking bright like the full moon among the stars. Seeing the wealth of beauty of Śrī Kṛṣṇa, everyone forgot themselves and as if fed their eyes on His lotuslike face. The rival kings, seeing such heroic glory which attracted the admiration of the three worlds, became very scared and whispered in the ears of one another.

*ohi kṛṣṇaka yuddha karite : śiśupāla āśā karie thika : aḥ unikara saṅge sabahi maraba : oe bhāisaba : uṭhaha uṭhaha : jāvata yuddha nāhi haya : āgu deśe jāñu* ||

"Śiśupāla has been waiting expecting to fight with this same Kṛṣṇa. So everyone will die along with him. Oh dear brothers, get up, get up, before the war breaks up, let us go back in advance to our countries."

*tadanantara : jarāsandhe dekhala : rājāsaba kṛṣṇaka bhaye kampita bhela : hāta nisāne niṣedhi bolala* ||

After that, Jarāsandha saw that all the other kings were trembling out of fear for Kṛṣṇa; forbidding them to go, with a gesture of his hand, said:

*oḥ hāmu bidyamāna thākite : kāheka bhaya thika : he rājāsaba : kṣetriyara bevahāra nohe : nirbhaye raha nirbhaye raha* ||
"Why do you fear, when I still exist? Oh kings, this does not fit the behaviour of a *kshatriya*, remain fearless, remain fearless."

*tanikara garihā śunie : nṛpasaba antargata bhaye : heṭhamāthe rahala* ||
Hearing his reproach, the kings with hidden fear in their minds remained with hanging heads.

e *kathā rahoka : rukamiṇīka bṛtānta śunaha* |
Let this topic rest, now listen to the account of Rukmiṇī.

*śloka* ||
*sakhībhiḥ saha baidarbhī kṛṣṇadarśanalālasā* |
*lalitā līlayā gatyā jagāmāthāmbikālayāt* ||28||
Hymn[36]: With an intention of seeing Kṛṣṇa, the Princess of Bidarbha, along with her friends went out with ease from the temple of Ambikā.

*sūtra* ||
*tadanantara : rājanandanī rukamiṇī : sakhīsaba sahite : karppūra- tāmbula bhojana kaya : eka sakhīka hāte dharie kahu : kṛṣṇa daraśana nimittte : parama ākula cite : līlāgati karie : rājasabhā samīpe calala : tāhe dekhaha śunaha : nirantare haribola* ||
Direction : After that, Princess Rukmiṇī, along with her friends, chewing camphor and areca nut, holding the hand of one of her friends, with a restless mind, to have a glimpse of

[36]. in *Śloka* metre.

Kṛṣṇa, went near the court playfully; watch and listen to that and keep chanting the name of Hari incessantly.

*gīta || rāga – māura dhanaśrī || domani-jatitāla ||*
Song in the *rāga Māhura Dhanaśrī* with the rhythm *Domāni Jatitāla:*

*cāndamukhi pekhite madhāi |*
*calali līlāgati bhubana bhulāi ||dhruṁ||*
To see the moon-like face of Madhāi, here goes Rukmiṇī playfully, forgetting the whole world. Refrain.

*pada ||*

*kaṅkaṇa kiṅkiṇī dhvani : bāṇake* [37] *mañjīra maṇi:*
*dole hṛdaye hemamālā |*
*cañcala locana mana: heraya ramaṇī ghana :*
*hari bayana barabālā ||1||*
*sakhīsaba saṅge khele: jaicana nakṣatra mele :*
*sucānda cāndaka kālāśohe |*
*rūpa rukamiṇīkeri : rāja samāje heri :*
*parala sabahi mana mohe ||2||19||*

Verse: The golden anklets made sound, the gems of the anklets tinkled and the golden garland hung on the chest of the lady. With restless eyes and mind, the lovely lady looked around frequently searching for the face of Hari. (1) Playing along with the friends, she looked as if in the fair of stars the digit of the beautiful noon was shining. Seeing the beauty of Rukmiṇī in the assembly, all the kings were mesmerised. (2)

*kathā ||*

*tadanantara : rukamiṇīka navina jaubana rūpa dekhie : jata rājāsaba kāmabāṇe murccita hayā : āsana hante ḍhali ḍhali parala | bihbala bhāve kāhu karajorḍi bola ||*

---

[37]. *jhanake*

Dialogue : After that, seeing the fresh youthful beauty of Rukmiṇī all the kings, became unconscious with (the attack of) the shaft of love and fell down fainting from their seats. Agitated and distressed some of them said with folded hands.

*he prāṇeśvarī : kāmasāgare nistāra karaha || kāhu āṅguli mukhe layā bola ||*
"Oh beloved, save us from the deep sea of desire." Some of them said with fingers in their mouth.

*he prāṇa-pṛye : madane mana marddaya : hāmāka hāsya nirīkṣaṇa karaha || kāhu dante kheḍa kāmuḍie bola ||*
"Oh beloved, Madana is crushing our minds, please give us a smiling glance." Some others, chewing a blade of grass with their teeth, said:

*he rājakumārī : tohāka nimite : kāma-bāṇe phuṭi prāṇa chuṭi jāi : caraṇaka dāsa bhelu : hāte paraśi hāmāka jīvāva : saba mahādeika dāsī kari deñu ||*
"Oh dear Princess, we are almost loosing our life for you (being pierced) with the shaft of love. We are servants at your feet. Revive us with a touch of your hand, we shall give all the other queens as your maids."

*kāme matta hayā : ityādi nānā bibhatsa bhāvanā kayala rājāsaba : pekhi rukamiṇīka sakhīsaba kāhuka ṭheṅganā dei : kāhuta goḍe māri bharcaya : tathāpi rājāsaba : kāmātura huyā : kumārīka kātara kaye thika | āhe loka : haribhakati bihīna : kāmāturaka dukha dekhaha | ihā jāni harika caraṇa cintie : haribola hari ||*
Mad with love, the kings expressed many such depraved thoughts. Seeing that, the friends of Rukmiṇī pushed aside some and rebuked some others with a kick. Even then, the kings, being lovesick, continued entreating the princess. Oh dear people, look at the suffering of those lovelorn

people who are without devotion for Hari. Knowing all this, thinking of the feet of Hari, chant the name of Hari.

*śloka* ||

*kṛṣṇo'pi kṣubhitaṁ cittaṁ sthiraṁ kṛtvā jahāra tām |*
*īkṣatāṁ dviṣatāṁ madhyāt mṛgāṇāṁ keśarī yathā* ||29||

Hymn[38]: Kṛṣṇa too, who was like a lion among a herd of animals, controlling His excited mind, abducted her, from among the on looking enemy kings.

*sūtra* ||

*tadanantara : śrīkṛṣṇa rukamiṇīka : rūpalāvaṇya dekhie : mohita huyā : kathaṁkathamapi citta śānta kayala | rukamiṇī sakhīsaba sahite : līlāye calite : kṛṣṇaka dekhala : bhāṭaka mukhe jaicana guṇa rūpa śunala : tāhāto adhika sākṣāte dekhala : õhi kṛṣṇa svāmī boli mane praṇāma kayala : lajjā hāsya karie : adhomukhi huyā rahala | śrīkṛṣṇa tattakāle uṭhi kahu : rājasabhāmadhya hante : rukamiṇīka hari layā : āpuna samīpa kayala | jaicana mṛgajutha madhya hante : siṁhe nija bhāga laiyā jāi : tadvat : kumārīka hāte dharie : āpuna rathe tulie : rukamiṇī sahita : śrīkṛṣṇa jaice līlāe calala : āhe loka : tāhe dekhaha śunaha : nirantare haribola* ||

Direction: After that, seeing the beauty and charm of Rukmiṇī, Śrī Kṛṣṇa became mesmerised and only somehow controlled His mind. Rukmiṇī, along with her friends, walking briskly, saw Kṛṣṇa. The beauty and quality of Kṛṣṇa, as she found in actual, was even more than what she had heard from the bard. Accepting Kṛṣṇa as her husband, offered obeisance within her mind and smiling bashfully, remained with downcast face. Śrī Kṛṣṇa, rising quickly, abducted Rukmiṇī from amidst the royal court and brought her close to Him. As the lion snatches away His share from among the herd of deers, so Śrī Kṛṣṇa also, holding the hand of the princess, and lifting her onto His chariot, as He went away quickly,

[38] . in *Śloka* metre.

along with Rukmiṇī, oh dear people, watch and listen to that and keep chanting the name of Hari incessantly.

*gīta || rāga – māura dhanaśrī || ekatāli||*
Song in the *rāga Māhura Dhanaśrī* with the rhythm *Ekatāli*:

*lahu lahu gati dhāi : priyā saṅge raṅge jāi |*
*hari hasi hasi cāi : jaice matta siṁha rāi || dhruṁ||*
Moving slowly, going with the beloved one happily, Hari looks on smiling like an excited lion king. Refrain.

*pada ||*
*rūpe bhubana jini : sakhī same rukamiṇī |*
*cale bāmā madhya khini : jhanake mañjīra maṇi ||*
*piu mukha beri beri : lajjita nayane heri |*
*kaha śaṅkarakeri : gati govinda meri ||20||*
Verse: Conquering the whole world with her beauty, the lovely woman with narrow waist, moved along with her companion. The jewels in her anklets tinkled, as she looked at the face of her husband again and again with shy eyes. Says Śaṅkara playfully, "Govinda is the ultimate refuge for me."

*kathā ||*
*tadanantara : śrīkṛṣṇa rukamiṇīka hāte dharie : hasi hasi priyāka mukha nirekhie : līlāgati cali jāi : jaicana matta siṁha calaice | se rājanandanī : śrīkṛṣṇaka svāmī labhie : lajjita nayane ghana ghana svāmīmukha nirekhiye : parama ānande cali jāi | tadanantara : śiśupāla prabhṛti jata rājā bipakṣa : cetana labhi kahu : dekhala : śrīkṛṣṇa rukamiṇī kanyāka : hari liyā jāi ||*
Dialogue: After that, holding Rukmiṇī by the hand, smiling and looking at the face of His beloved, Śrī Kṛṣṇa moved on quickly as if an excited lion was moving. And that princess, having found Kṛṣṇa as her husband, looking at the face of

her husband again and again with shy eyes, moved on with great bliss. Thereupon Śiśupāla and all the rival kings, regaining consciousness, saw Śrī Kṛṣṇa taking away the bride Rukmiṇī.

*śiśupāla bola || aḥ hāmāka jīvana dhika dhika : hāmu bidyamāna thākite : hāmāra bibāhaka kanyā : kathāka yādave liyā jāi ||*

Śiśupāla said, "Shame on my life! When I am still there, wherefrom does this Yādava take away my bride".

*ohi buli parama darppa kari kahu : hāte śara dhanu dharie : śrīkṛṣṇaka pācu pācu jaice khedi jāi : tāhe dekhaha śunaha : nirantare haribola ||*

Saying thus, with great arrogance, carrying bow and arrow in his hand, as he chased behind Śrī Kṛṣṇa, watch and listen to that and keep chanting the name of Hari incessantly.

*gīta || rāga-kānaḍā || payāḍa || paritāla ||*

Song in the *Rāga Kānaḍā* with the rhythm *Paritāla*:

*kope nṛpasaba kāmāḍe bāhu |*
*cāndaka khedi jāi jaca rāhu ||*

The kings bit their own arms out of anger and chased Him as if demon Rāhu chasing the moon.

*pada ||*

*hāte śaradhanu dhari sava dhāve |*
*kampita medinī e pada ghāve ||1||*
*bāhu darape karae ṭaṅkāra |*
*bolae ḍāki ḍāki ahaṅkāra ||*
*re re yādava pārae gāri |*
*choḍa choḍa ava rukamiṇī nārī ||2||*

*āra kati jāsi pāvalu lāga* |
*kope garajaya jaicana bāgha* ||
*raha raha buli pāre ghane rāva* |
*śaṅkara kaha gati govinda pāva* ||3||21||

Verse: Holding bows and arrows in their hands everyone ran and the earth trembled being hurt by their footsteps. Twanging the bowstring with great pride on the strength of their arms, started shouting boastfully. Shouting, "Oh you Yādava there!", started abusing Him, (saying) "Leave alone that lady Rukmiṇī now; where do you flee, now that we have found you!", and as a tiger roars in anger, shouted "Wait, wait!", again and again; says Śaṅkara that the ultimate way is at the feet of Govinda alone.

*śloka* ||
*rājñāmāṭopaṭaṅkārakallolaṁ rukmiṇī sate* |
*niśamya bepitā bhītā manasyevamacintayat* ||30||

Hymn[39]: Hearing the loud arrogant boasting of the kings, Rukmiṇī became very scared and trembling, started thinking in her mind.

*kathā* ||
*rājāsabaka āṭopa ṭaṅkāra : dekhie śunie : mahābhaye devī rukamiṇīka : hṛdaye kampa milala : mukha malina bhela : svāmī śrīkṛṣṇaka nimite cintita huyā : nayane nīra nigare : niśvāsa phokāri mane bola* ||

Dialogue: Seeing and hearing the boastful twanging of the (bows of the) kings, Rukmiṇī became very scared and her heart trembled with fear, her face became pale. Worrying for her husband Śrī Kṛṣṇa, tears flowed from her eyes, and sighing deeply said within her mind.

*hā hā daiva : abhāgī rukamiṇīka kapāle ki bhela : bighinika upare bighini milala : ohi pāpī rājāsaba bahuta : svāmīka saṅge : sahāya kehu nāhi : hāmāka kona gati haya : ihā kāhi*[40] *jānu*

---

39 . in *Śloka* metre.
40 . *nāhi*.

*: hā hā sonāka putali : śrīkṛṣṇa svāmīka : hāmu pāpinī kauce anāvalu : jono kācaka cāhite māṇika harāi ||*

"Alas, alas, oh God, what has happened to the fate of unfortunate Rukmiṇī, facing obstacles over and above the already existing obstacles! Those wicked kings are many in number, and my Lord has no one to help Him. What will happen to me, that I do not know. Alas, alas, why have I, the wicked me, made my (most beloved) golden doll, my Lord Śrī Kṛṣṇa come here; lest, seeking after some glassware, the gem gets lost."

*ohi buli rukamiṇī : jauce bilāpa kayala : āhe loka : tā dekhaha śunaha : nirantare hari bola ||*

Saying so, as Rukmiṇī lamented, oh dear people, watch and listen to that and keep chanting the name of Hari incessantly.

*gīta || rāga – śrīgāndhāra || jauti tāla ||*

Song in the *Rāga Śrīgāndhāra* with the rhythm *Jautitāla*:

*dhruṁ ||*

*hari hari kino bihi lihili lalāṭe |*
*abahu milala meri maraṇaka bāṭe ||*

Refrain : "Oh Hari, what fate have you written down on my forehead! Now I am faced with the way to death."

*pada ||*

*pāvalu pahu bahu puṇye hāsu raṅka |*
*hāte haraya nidhi bidhi bhela baṅka ||*
*āvala kaicana nātha abhāgīka lāi |*
*kācaka cāhite junu māṇika harāi ||*
*bihika birambana kinu meri bhela |*
*prāṇapiu pāśa āśa dūra gela ||*
*heṭha bayane nayane jhure lora |*
*śaṅkara kaha gati govinda mora ||22||*

Verse: "Poor me, I smiled, having found the Lord after much pious deeds, but then my fate was adverse, and I have lost the treasure from my own hands. How my master had come for me, the unfortunate one. Now, as if seeking after some glassware, the gem is about to be lost. How fate has made a mockery of me. My hope to be near my beloved is gone.", and she waited with her face downcast and tears flowing down from her eyes. Śaṅkara says, "Govinda is the ultimate way for me."

*śloka* ||

*bhayabepitacittāyāḥ rukmiṇyāḥ rodnaṁ drutaṁ* |
*nirīkṣya dṛḍhamāliṅgya sāntvayāmāsa keśavaḥ* ||31||

Hymn[41]: Seeing Rukmiṇī crying with a trembling heart out of fear, Śrī Keśava immediately embracing her deeply, started consoling her.

*kathā* ||

*tadanantara : kṛṣṇaka nimite : bilāpa karite rukamiṇī : ghanaghana niśvāsa phokāre : nayanaka nīra bahi jāi : tāhe dekhi bhakata bāndhava mādhava : āti satvara bāhu meli : āliṅgi dhari kahu : āśvāsa bola* ||

Dialogue: Thereafter, crying for Kṛṣṇa, Rukmiṇī sighed deeply again and again and tears flowed down from her eyes. Seeing that, Mādhava, the friend to the devotees, immediately stretched out His arms and holding her in an embrace, said to her consoling.

*āhe prāṇa-pṛye : ki nimitte krandana karaica : hāmu bidyamāna thākite : tohāka kona cintā : kāheka bhaya thika* || *ohi buli śrīkṛṣṇa rukamiṇīka : jaice prabodha kayala : āhe loka : tāhe dekhaha śunaha : nirantare haribola* ||

"Oh my love, why do you cry? Why do you worry, when I am here, what are you afraid of?"

---

[41] . in *Śloka* metre.

In this way, as Śrī Kṛṣṇa consoled Rukmiṇī, oh dear people, watch and listen to that and keep chanting the name of Hari incessantly.

*gīta* || *rāga belovāra* || *paritāla* ||
Song in the *rāga Belovāra* with the rhythm *Paritāla:*

*dhruṁ* ||
*karabi nāhi ākula pṛye* |
*dhari kāminīka kānu bodha die* ||
Refrain : "Oh my love, do not get agitated", and embracing the lovely woman (thus) Kānu consoled her.

*pada* ||
*ki karaba siṁhaka śūkarasaba āyā* |
*hāmāku śapata tāpa tejahu jāyā* ||
*mocala mukha priyāka pīta base* |
*kaha śaṅkara rasa keśava dāse* ||23||
Verse : "What harm all the jackals, coming in a pack, can do to the lion! Oh wife, upon my honour, let go of this misery", and (saying so), wiped off the face of His beloved with His yellow clothing; says Śaṅkara, the servant of Keśava, with pleasure.

*kathā* ||
*kṛṣṇa bola* || *āhe prāṇapṛye : hāmāku āgu : ohi rājāsaba kona pataṅga : jaice siṁhaka āgu kṣudra hariṇa : ihā jāni bhaya śoka chāḍaha : dekhaha pāpī rājāsabaka : jaice sṛkālaka : eikṣaṇe khedāvaba* ||
Dialogue: Kṛṣṇa said, "Oh my love, my life, the kings are like mere insects before me, as if a little deer in front of a lion. Knowing this, give up this fear and grief. Look, I shall chase the wicked kings away like jackals in a minute."

*ohi boli rukamiṇīka : santāpa dūra karie : svahaste tāmbula bhojana karāvala : anyo anye kautuka nirīkṣaṇa karie bolala* ||
Saying so, removing the distress of Rukmiṇī, made her chew betel nut with His own hands and observing all around with amusement, said.

*he priye : tuhu nirbhaye raha : hāmu duṣṭa rājāsabaka : yuddha karie khedāñuñ : raṅga dekhaha* ||
*ohi buli śāraṅga dhanu dharie : ṭaṅkāra kayala* ||
"Oh my love, you remain fearless. I will go and fighting with the wicked kings, chase them away. You just watch with fun."
Saying so, raising the *Śāraṅga* bow made a twanging sound.

*śloka* ||

*tataḥ śārṅga dhanurddhṛtvā ṭaṅkāramakaroddhariḥ* |
*śrutvā tacchabdamatulaṁ rājānohi cakampire* ||32||

Hymn[42]: Then, holding the *Śāraṅga* bow, Hari stretched it out, making a twanging sound, and hearing this matchless sound, all the kings started trembling with fear.

*kathā* ||

*śāraṅga dhanuka ṭaṅkārā śunie : rājāsabaka hṛdaya kampita bhela : tāhe dekhi śrīkṛṣṇa hāsi hāsi bola* ||

Dialogue: Hearing the twanging of the *Śāraṅga* bow, the hearts of all the kings trembled. Seeing that, Śrī Kṛṣṇa said laughing.

*āye duṣṭa rājāsaba : hāmāka khedi āvala : āḥ jata śakati thika : aba yuddha karaha* ||
"Oh you wicked kings, you have come chasing me. Now with whatever strength you have, come and fight with me."

*tāhe śuniye rājāsaba : śara barasiye bola* || *ae yādava anācāra : hāmāra bibāhaka kanyā : rukamiṇīka jadi nāhi chāḍaba : jata śakati thika : hāmāka yuddha dehu* ||

---

42. in *Śloka* metre, but in the 3rd foot, the 6th and 7th letters are short instead of long.

Hearing that, all the kings, showering arrows (on Him) said, "Oh you unprincipled Yādava, if you do not set Rukmiṇī, the bride of our wedding, free, fight with us with whatever strength you have."

*rājāsabaka darapa śunie : śrīkṛṣṇa jaice samara kayala : tāhe dekhaha śunaha : nirantare hari bola* ||
Hearing such proud words from the kings, as Śrī Kṛṣṇa fought with them, watch and listen to that and keep chanting the name of Hari incessantly.

*gīta* || *rāga – nāṭamallāra* || *paritāla* ||
Song in the *Rāga Nāṭamallāra* with the rhythm *Paritāla*:

*dhruṁ* ||

*yuddha dehu yādava yadurāyā* |
*garaje rājāsaba āyā re* ||
*dhari hari śāraṅga barikhala bāṇa*
*nṛpasaba bedhala kāyāre* ||

Refrain: "Come and fight with us, oh you king of the Yadus, a member of the Yadu family!", the kings coming forward, roared.
Hari, holding the *Śāraṅga* and showering arrows, pierced the bodies of the kings.

*pada* ||

*bāri bāriṣā jaca ambuda barikhala :*
*hari karu śaraka sandhāna re* |
*kāhuka bāhu kāhu uru kara kāṭi :*
*hṛdaya bidārala bāṇa re* ||1||
*bīra śiśupālaka kāṭala kirīṭi :*
*pālaṭi palāvala pāpī re* |
*saba bairī jiniye bijayī yādava :*
*śaṅkara kaha bhava tāpi re* ||2||24||

Verse: As the monsoon cloud showers rain, so Hari went on fixing arrows continuously, injuring some in their arms, cutting the thigh or the hand of some and piercing through the heart (of some others) with His arrows. (1)
Cut off the crown of powerful Śiśupāla and turning back, the sinner fled away. Having won over all the enemies, the Yādava was victorious. Śaṅkara says that the world is full of miseries. (2)

*sūtra* ||
*kṛṣṇaka sare rājāsabaka uru kara kāṭi hṛdaya bhedala : śiśupālaka kirīṭi kāṭala : dekhi mahābhaye rājāsaba : bhaṅga diye mṛta-kalapa huyā palāvala : trāse pācu cāhe nāhi : jaicana siṁhaka bhaye : śṛgāla lavaḍe tadbat : śrīkṛṣṇa kautuke kati dūre khedie : pālṭi rahala | tadanantara : rukaminī svāmīka bijaya bikrama dekhie parama ānande pradakhine : pāve praṇāma kayala : sādhu sādhu buli śire puṣpa barikhala : āñcole śramajala mucala : tāmbula bhojana karāi : sakhīsaba sahite : āñcole biñcie rahala : prathama bayasa lajjāvati : svāmīka mukha kaṭākṣe ghana ghana nirekhi : heṭha mātha kae thika | śrīkṛṣṇa pṛyāka madhura ālāpe : ānanda karāala* ||

Direction: The arrows of Kṛṣṇa cut the thighs and hands, and pierced through the hearts of the kings, and cut off the crown of Śiśupāla. Seeing that, all the kings dispersed about out of great fear and fled away looking like dead people. Being scared they did not even look back and fled, as jackals flee away hastily from the lion, greatly scared. Śrī Kṛṣṇa, with fun, chased them to a distance and then returned. Thereupon, Rukmiṇī, seeing the triumph and valour of her husband, circumambulated Him with great bliss and offered her obeisance at His feet. Saying "Well done, well done!", showered flowers on His head; wiped the sweat away with the fore-end of her clothing, feeding Him with betel nuts and remained there fanning Him with the fore-end of her clothing, along with her friends. At first, naturally shy because of her young age, (Rukmiṇī) looked at the face of her husband with sidelong glances again and again and remained with her head bowed down. Śrī Kṛṣṇa, with His sweet talk, made His beloved happy.

*śloka* ||

*toto'ti kautuko dṛṣṭaḥ priyāyāḥ parameśvaraḥ |*
*sānandalīlāgatibhirbrajan kelimakārayat* ||33||

Hymn[43]: Looking at the great happiness of His beloved the Supreme Lord started moving with much ease and amusement.

*sūtra* ||

*śrīkṛṣṇa śiśupālaka kirīṭi kāṭie : rājāsabaka kati dūra khedāi : parama kautuke juguta hayā : pṛyā rukamiṇi sahite : dvārakāpura calite : jaicana līlā gati kayala : tāhe dekhaha śunaha : nirantare hari bola* ||

Direction: Cutting off the crown of Śiśupāla and chasing away the kings to some distance with great pleasure and along with Rukmiṇī, as He started moving to the city of Dwārakā with happiness and amusement, watch and listen to that, and keep chanting the name of Hari incessantly.

*gīta* || *suhāi rāga* || *cuṭikālā māna* ||

Song in the *Rāga Suhāi* with the rhythm *Cuṭikālā*:

*dhruṁ* ||

*jagajīu ucuke calali madhāi |*
*priyā saṅge raṅge līlāi* ||

Refrain : All the people of the world looked on eagerly, as Madhāi moved on along with His beloved with great happiness and amusement.

43 . in *Śloka* metre, but in the 3rd foot, the 5th letter is long instead of short and the 6th letter is short instead of long.

*pada* ||

*hari kara dharala kāminī kaṇṭha meli :*
*keli karatahi jāi* |
*nava ramaṇī piu : paraśe bihasi :*
*cala locana mudi māi* ||*1*||
*paramānanda : magana mana rāmā :*
*daraśie hāsa bilāsā* |
*sakhīsame svāmī : sevi kautuka kara :*
*kaha śaṅkara haridāsā* ||2||25||

Verse: Extending His hands, Hari held by the neck of the lovely woman and played on amorously. The new wife smiled at the touch of her husband and moved on closing her eyes. (1)

Her mind absorbed in extreme bliss, the charming young woman expressing much pleasure and delight with smiles, enjoyed serving her husband with her friends, says Śaṅkara, the servant of Hari. (2)

*kathā* ||

*śrīkṛṣṇa parama ānande calite : pryāka kaṇṭhe hāta meli dharala : se nava taruṇī : prathama piuka paraśe : lajjita huyā : alpa hāsya karie ghana ghana ākhi mudi rahala : sakhīsaba sahita : hāsa bilāsa daraśie : kautuke svāmīka sevā karite calali : śrīkṛṣṇa jaice hastinisaba sahita : matta mātaṅga calali : tadbat* | *i kathā rahoka* | *tadanantara : rukamiṇīka jeṣṭhabhrātā : rukma nāme mandamati : rājāsabaka bhaṅga śunie : se pāpī kope parma āṭope sājie : kṛṣṇaka khedi āvala* | *rukmi ḍāki bola*||

Dialogue: Śrī Kṛṣṇa, advancing with great happiness, extended His hands and held encircling the neck of His beloved. The young girl, at the first touch of her beloved, became very shy and giggling, closed her eyes again and again. And along with her friends, showing much happiness and delight went on serving the Lord with much pleasure. Śrī Kṛṣṇa also went on along with them as an inebriated elephant moves along with the female elephants. Let this topic rest here. Thereafter, the elder brother of Rukmiṇī, Rukma by name, a fool, hearing about the fleeing of the kings, became very angry and that sinner, enraged and with great pride, came chasing after Kṛṣṇa. Rukmī called out,

*aye yādava : hāmāra bhaginīka choḍaha choḍaha : tohāka nāhi māri : rukamiṇīka nāhi choḍāi : kuṇḍine praveśa hāmu nāhi karaba : jaba bhaginīka choḍabi nāhi : taba jata śakati thika : hāmāka yuddha dehu* ||

"Oh you Yādava, leave alone, let go of my sister. Without killing you and without releasing Rukmiṇī, I shall not enter Kuṇḍina. If you do not release my sister, then fight with me with as much strength as you have."

*śloka* ||

*śrutvā kṛṣṇo vihasyāha śṛṇure kulakaṇṭaka* |
*tvāmadya niśitairbāṇairnayāmi yamamandiram* ||34||

Hymn[44]: Hearing him, Kṛṣṇa said laughing, "Listen, oh you vexation to the family, with sharp arrows I shall send you to the temple of Yama today."

*kathā* ||

*śrīkṛṣṇa bihasi bola* ||

*aye kulakaṇṭaka rukmi : tuhu hāmāka gāri desi : ohi bāṇe jampura dekhāvara : khānika raha* ||

*ohi boli śrīkṛṣṇa : rukmi sahita jaice juddha kayala : tāhe dekhaha śunaha : nirantare haribola* ||

Dialogue : Śrī Kṛṣṇa said smiling, "Oh you Rukmī, the thorn to the family, you are scolding me; with my arrows I shall show you the abode of Yama, just wait for a while."

Saying so, how Kṛṣṇa fought with Rukmī, watch and listen to that and keep chanting the name of Hari incessantly.

---

[44] . in *Śloka* metre.

*payāḍa* || *kānaḍā* || *paritāla* ||
Verse in the *Rāga Kānaḍā* with the rhythm *Paritāla:*

*kṛṣṇabākya śuni rukmi bīra* |
*hānala bāṇa kope kāmpe śira* ||

Hearing the words of Kṛṣṇa, the warrior Rukmī, with his head trembling in great anger, started attacking (Kṛṣṇa) with arrows.

*pada* ||
*kāṭala bāṇa kṛṣṇa śara māri* |
*garaje rukmi punu bāṇa prahāri* ||*1*||
*rukmi astra johi johi hāne* |
*tāheka chedala puruṣa pradhāne* ||
*bahutara bāṇe tāhe hṛdi bhedi* |
*hātaka dhanu pehlāvala chedi* ||2||
*hāte muṭhi dhari rukmi-kumāra* |
*kṛṣṇaka hṛdaye kayali prahāra* ||
*tāhe prahāre hāsi yadunāthe* |
*dharala keśa keśava bāma hate* ||3||
*ghanṭā lāḍi ghāra karaya moḍa* |
*rukmi hṛdaye mārala goḍa* ||
*pāi cota bara murucita bīra* |
*kṛṣṇa dharala khāṇḍā chedite śira* ||4||
*hāhākāra kaya rukamiṇī māi* |
*svāmīka hāte sodara badha jāi* ||
*kṛṣṇa kiṅkara ohi śaṅkara gāi* |
*bolahu rāmahari saba lokai* ||5||26||

Verse : Kṛṣṇa countered (His arrow) with a shaft and Rukmī roared and attacked with more arrows again. (1) Whatever weapons Rukmī attacked with, the Supreme Person broke them down to pieces. Attacking with many arrows, pierced through his heart and broke down his bow into pieces (2)

Forming a fist with his hand, Prince Rukmī attacked Kṛṣṇa with a blow on His chest. The king of the Yadu dynasty smiled only at his attack, and Keśava caught hold of his hair with His left hand. (3)
Shaking it (his head) like a bell, twisted his neck and kicked at his chest. Having received such heavy blows, the hero fell down fainting and Kṛṣṇa lifted up His sword to cut his head off. (4)
Rukmiṇī made a commotion with grief seeing her brother about to be killed by her husband. Śaṅkara, the servant of that same Kṛṣṇa, says, "Oh dear all the people, utter: 'Rāma and Hari!' " (5)

*sūtra* ||

*se pāpī rukmi astre nāhi pāri : kṛṣṇaka hṛdaye muṣṭi mārala* | *śrīkṛṣṇa tanikara kese dharie : hie lāṭhi mārie : kāṭite nandaka khaḍga dharala* ||

Direction: Not being able to overpower with weapons, the sinner Rukmī hit Kṛṣṇa on His chest with his fist. Śrī Kṛṣṇa, holding at his hair, kicked at his chest and held up His sword to behead him.

*śloka* ||

*dṛṣṭvā bhātṛbadhodyogaṁ govindasya suduḥkhitā*|
*karābhyāṁ gṛhya caraṇau cakāra kātaraṁ satī* ||35||

Hymn[45]: Seeing Govinda about to kill her brother, being very sad, the good woman touching His feet with both her hands entreated Him.

*kathā* ||

*tadanantara : devī rukamiṇī : tāhe dekhie : bhātṛ maraya buli : śrīkṛṣṇaka caraṇapaṅkaja dhari : kātara kaya bola* ||
*he svāmi : tohāka caraṇe lagu : bhaiyaika prāṇa dāna dehu : tuhu parama īśvara : ohi pāpī tohāka mahimā nāhi jānala :*

[45]. in *Śloka* metre, but in the 3rd foot, the 6th and 7th letters are short instead of long.

*jaice pataṅga aganita jāsa kayala : hāmāka dekhite ohi doṣa marasa svāmi* ||

Dialogue : After that, Goddess Rukmiṇī, seeing that her brother would be killed, holding onto the lotus feet of Śrī Kṛṣṇa, spoke to Him entreating earnestly.

"Oh Lord, I pray at your feet, please spare the life of my brother. You are the Supreme God, and sinner that he is, could not understand your greatness, and brought about destruction to himself as an insect burns itself down in the fire. Looking at me, oh Lord, please forgive his faults."

*ohi boli kumārī : nayanaka nīra jhurāi : jaice krandana kayala : tāhe dekhaha śunaha : nirantare hari bola* ||

Saying so, as the princess started crying, tears flowing down from her eyes, watch and listen to that and keep chanting the name of Hari incessantly.

*gīta* || *rāga – śrīgāndhāra* || *jautimāna* ||

Song in the *Rāga Śrīgāndhara* with the rhythm *Jautimāna:*

*sundarī dhari hari caraṇa bināve* |
*karahu karunā nātha māthe dharohõ tṛṇa*
*bulite nayana jhurāve* ||*dhruṁ* ||

Holding the feet of Hari the beautiful woman wails.
Please have mercy, oh Lord, here I offer you a blade of grass holding it on my head; saying so, she cried flowing tears from the eyes. Refrain.

*pada* ||

*bhāyākeri dukha: dekhiye jīu jāi:*
*rākhahu pāpīka prāṇa* |
*caraṇaku āgu: āñcola pāti māgu:*
*dehu meri sodara dāna* ||*1*||
*jabahu sodara deva: nakaraha rakṣaṇa:*
*āgahi lehu jīu moi* |

*harika pāve pari : bara bālā bilapati :*
*kaha śaṅkara rasa oi* ||2||27||

Verse: "I am loosing my life at the suffering of my brother, please save the life of this sinner. Spreading out the hanging fore-end of my upper garment in front of your feet, I seek of you, please spare the life of my brother. (1)

"If you do not save the life of my brother oh Lord, then take my life first." Thus the beautiful young girl wailed lying at the feet of Hari. Śaṅkara says about these feelings.

*kathā* ||

*aicana krandana kae : rukamiṇī hāte tṛṇa dharie bola* ||
*he svāmi : bhāyāka dukha dekhie : prāṇa phuṭi jāi : ohi adhamaka jīu rakṣā karaha : caraṇaka āgu : añcola pāti māgu* |
*he nātha : hāmāka sodara dāna dehu*||
*śrīkṛṣṇa tathāpi tanika choḍae nāhi dekhie : punu kumārī niśvāsa phokāri bola*||

Dialogue : Crying in this way, Rukmiṇī said holding a blade of grass in her hand:

"Oh Lord, seeing the suffering of my brother, my life (nearly) leaves (the body). Please save the life of that lowly person. Spreading out the hanging fore-end of my upper garment in front of your feet, I beg of you, oh Lord, please grant me the life of my brother."

Seeing Śrī Kṛṣṇa still not releasing him, leaving a sigh the princess said :

*he svāmi* || *jaba bhātṛka rakṣā nāhi karabi : taba hāmāka jīu āgu lehu* ||
*ohi bolite lotake kaṇṭha beḍhala : hā bhoyāi buli māṭi luṭi : jaice krandana kaya lāgala bālā* ||

"Oh Lord, if you do not save my brother, then take my life first."

Saying so, tears choked her voice. Uttering "Alas, alas, oh dear brother!" the young girl started crying, rolling on the ground.

*śloka* ||

*prītaḥ priyāyāḥ samprekṣya bilāpaṁ parameśvaraḥ |*
*rakṣitvā rukmiṇaḥ prāṇān kārayāmāsa muṇḍanam||36||*

Hymn[46]: Then, the Supreme God, being pleased at seeing His beloved lamenting, spared the life of Rukmī and shaved off his head.

*kathā* ||

*śrīkṛṣṇa rukamiṇīka bilāpa dekhiye : parama karunā upajala : hari bihasi bola||*

*he pṛye : tuhu bilāpa choḍaha : tohāka nimitta e pāpīka prāṇa rākhalu : kintu ihāka eka sāsti karaba : tāhe bādhā nāhi karabi ||*

Dialogue: Seeing Rukmiṇī lament, great mercy manifested in the mind of Śrī Kṛṣṇa, and Hari said smiling, "Oh my love, give up this lamentation; just for you, I have saved the life of this sinner. But I shall inflict on him a punishment, please do not oppose that."

*ohi buli śrīkṛṣṇa se rājakumāraka : gale bastra bāndhie dharala : khaḍga dharie : saba keśa muṇḍāvala : dāri gupha cakṣubhru sabāko upāḍala : mukhe kāli cūṇa ghasie ḍhaṅkā māri pehlāvala | jaice mṛtaka nava rukmi : mātite pariye rahala| āhe loka : dekhu dekhu : je harika droha karaya : hariguṇa nāma laite nindā karaya : sohi pāpīka : ohi avasthā : dekhaha : jāni haribhakataka nindā choḍi : haribola haribola ||*

Saying so, Śrī Kṛṣṇa, wrapped up the prince with a cloth in his neck, holding the sword shaved off all his hair and plucked off all the beard, moustache and eye brows and smearing black ink and lime on his face, threw him down pushing. The new Rukmī, (Rukmī with the new look) remained lying on the ground like a dead body. "Oh dear people, look, look, those who go against Hari and condemn taking the name of Hari, such sinners have to face this type of condition. Look, and understand and leave condemning the devotees of Hari and chant the name of Hari."

---

[46]. in *Śloka* metre, but in the 1st foot, the 5$^{th}$ letter is long instead of short.

*śloka* ||

*śāntvayitvā priyāṁ paścāttayā saha mahāhariḥ* |
*dvārikāpuramābiśya tāṁ priyāṁ samariramat*||37||

Hymn[47]: Having consoled His beloved, Hari, then, entering the city of Dwārakā, sported with His beloved.

*sūtra* ||

*tadanantara : śrīkṛṣṇa priyāka ākhimukha pīta bastre muci : śānta karie : parama kautuke : dvārikāpura : prabeśa karite : śrīkṛṣṇa rukamiṇī sahite : jaice ānanda kayala : tāhe dekhaha śunaha : nirantare hari bola* ||

Direction: After that, having wiped the face and eyes of His beloved with his yellow clothing, consoling His beloved, Śrī Kṛṣṇa, entered the city of Dwārakā with great happiness and how Kṛṣṇa enjoyed with Rukmiṇī, watch and listen to that and keep chanting the name of Hari incessantly.

*gīta* || *tuḍa bhāṭhiyālī rāga* || *jautimāna*||

Song in the *Rāga Tuḍa Bhāṭhiyālī* with the rhythm *Jautimāna:*

*milala kautuka kamala locani*
*calali svāmīka saṅgiyā* |
*nīla nirada jaca ujara bijurī*
*bhubana bhule bhrutaṅgiyā*[48] ||*dhruṁ*||

The lotus eyed found great happiness and (Rukmiṇī) went with her husband looking like the bright lightning on the blue cloud and making the whole world forget everything with the curve of her eye brows. Refrain.

*pada* ||

*matta mātaṅga saṅga aṅga bhaṅga*
*kariṇi kara lāsa beśayā* |
*kayala maṅgala raṅga kolāhala*
*dvārakāpura parabeśayā* ||*1*||

---

[47]. in *Śloka* metre, but in the 4th foot, the 6th letter is short instead of long.

[48]. *bhrubhaṅgiyā*

*devī daivakī* *āsie kautuki*
*dharala bara-badhu hātayā* |
*jaya jaya rava* *milala utsava*
*kahatu śaṅkara bātayā* ||2||28||

Verse: (Rukmiṇī went) like the female elephant, along with the inebriated elephant, making bodily gestures, dressing up stylishly, and skipping playfully and entered the city of Dwārakā making an auspicious uproar with great happiness. (1)
Mother Daivakī came and with great happiness held the hands of the bride and the bride-groom. "May you be victorious, may you be glorious!" With these utterances a festival took place, Śaṅkara gives (this) information. (2)

*sūtra* ||
*tadanantara : devī daivakī parama maṅgala bādyabhāṇḍe āsi kaho : bara kanyāka : hāta eka ṭhāma karikaho : mahā mahotsave gṛha parabeśa karāvala : aneka śundari strī : āyatīsaba sahite : śrīkṛṣṇa rukamiṇika māthe dūrbākṣata siñcie : tathi parama utsava milāvala* | *tadanantara : śrīkṛṣṇaka bibāha prakāra śunaha : prastutamāha* | *harika bibāha kathā jānie : jagataka jata loka : kautuke dvārakāpura bharala āsiyā* | *rājā bhīṣmaka svahaste kṛṣṇaka kanyādāna karite āvala* | *tadanantara : jagataka guru : śrīnārāyaṇa : manuṣya līlā daraśie : bibāha karite : pṛyā same āsane baiṭhala* ||
Direction: After that, mother Devakī, coming, along with the most auspicious band of musical instruments, holding together the hands of the bride and bridegroom, amidst great festivity, performed (the rites of) *gṛhapraveśa*. Along with many beautiful young girls and married women, sprinkled *dūrbā* and *akṣata* on the heads of Śrī Kṛṣṇa and Rukmiṇī and created an occasion of joy and festivity there. After that, listen to the manner of wedding of Śrī Kṛṣṇa, here I am presenting. Hearing about the wedding of Hari, all the people of the world, with great happiness and gaiety came to the city of Dwārakā and filled it up. King Bhīṣmaka

came to perform (the rites of) *kanyādāna* with his own hands. After that, the father of this world, Śrī Nārāyaṇa, exhibiting semblance of an ordinary human being, sat down, along with His beloved, on the seat, for the wedding.

*śloka* ||

*ājagāma tato brahmā kṛṣṇasyodbāha hetave* |
*sa-nārado mudāyuktaḥ sruvahasto'tikautukī* ||38||

Hymn[49]: After that, to attend the wedding ceremony of Kṛṣṇa, Brahmā, along with Nārada came happily carrying the sacrificial ladle in his hand, with great pleasure.

*sūtra* ||

*sehi samaye brahmā : nārada putra sahita : bibāhaka homa karate : jaice milala : āhe loka : tāhe dekhaha śunaha : nirantare hari bola*||

Direction: At that time, how Brahmā, along with his son Nārada, came together to perform the sacrificial rites of the wedding, watch and listen to that oh dear people and keep chanting the name of Hari incessantly.

*gīta* || *rāga-kānaḍā* || *paritāla* ||

Song in the *Rāga Kānaḍā* with the rhythm *Paritāla:*

*āvata dhātā hāte śruva dhari* |
*catura bayane ghana beda ucāri* ||*dhruṁ*||

Holding the sacrificial ladle in his hand, comes the creator, continuously pronouncing the hymns of the Veda with his four faces. Refrain.

*pada* ||

*gaurāṅga aṅga raṅga biparīta* |
*saṅgahi nārada ānanda cita* ||
*bama hāte kukha karata hāsa* |
*śaṅkara kaha ohi keśava dāsa* ||29||

Verse: Against his (Brahmā's) fair body, there was colour of happiness and along came Nārada with a very happy mind,

[49]. in *Śloka* metre.

with *kuśa* grass in his left hand and a smile on the face; he is the servant of Keśava, says Śaṅkara.

*kathā* ||

*śrīkṛṣṇa pekhi pṛyā sahita : tattakāle uṭhi kahu : praṇāma kayala : brahmā nārada āśīrbbāda kayala : śrīkṛṣṇa māthe caḍāyā kahu : karajori bola* ||

Dialogue: Seeing (him), Śrī Kṛṣṇa, along with His beloved, rising immediately, offered obeisance and Brahmā and Nārada bestowed blessings on them; Śrī Kṛṣṇa raising His head, said with folded hands.

*-he jagataka pitāmaha : tohāka daraśana devara durllabha : hāmu mānuṣa huyā : tohāka daraśana bhelu : hāmāka bhāgyaka mahimā ki kahaba : janama sāphala : āju dvārakāpura pabitra bhela* ||

"Oh grandfather of the world, your audience is difficult to be attained even by the demigods. Being human, we have had your visit. What to speak of our great fortune, our lives are fulfilled and the city of Dwārakā has become purified today!"

*brahmā bihasi bola* || *hāmu tohāka bibāha śunie : parama kautuke āvalu : svahaste āhuti karie : bibāha karāvaba* ||

Brahmā said smiling, "Hearing about your wedding, I have come with great pleasure. Offering the oblation myself, I shall perform your wedding."

*śrīkṛṣṇa tāhe śuni : āsana delaha* | *brahmā tathi baiṭhala* | *kuśaṇḍi karie homa ārambhala* ||

Hearing that, Śrī Kṛṣṇa, offered him a seat. Brahmā sat there and starting the sacrificial fire started oblation.

*śloka* ||

*tato nirīkṣya rukmiṇyāḥ rūpalāvaṇyamadbhutam* |
*vabhūva mūrcchito brahmā kāmamadana-pīrḍitaḥ* ||39||

Hymn[50]: Then seeing the extraordinary beauty and charm of Rukmiṇī, being pierced with the arrows of Madana, Brahmā fell down senseless.

*kathā* ||

*tadanantara : mukha candrikā karite : rukamiṇīka bhuvana mohana rūpa nirekhie : brahmā māṭi luṭi parala : nāradamuni dhari bodha karāvala* ||

Dialogue: Then, at the time of formally looking at the face of the bride, seeing Rukmiṇī's beauty, which mesmerises the whole world, Brahmā fell down tumbling on the ground. Nārada, holding him, brought him to senses.

*nārada bola* || *he pitā : svastha hava svastha hava : tohāra bevahāra nohe* ||

Nārada said, "Oh father, get better, be composed, this behaviour does not fit you."

*śloka* ||

*tataścetamālabhya*[51] *brahmā mantramudīrayet* |
*tadodvāhavidhau tasminnutsavaḥ sumahānabhūt* ||40||

Hymn[52]: Having regained his senses Brahmā uttered *mantra* and according to norms completed that great wedding ceremony.

*sūtra* ||

*tadanantara : brahmā cetana labhi kahu : biṣṇu biṣṇu smarie : punu śruva dhari : homa kaye lāgala* | *sohi samaye rājā bhīṣmaka : kanyā sampradāna karie : barakanyāka keśa eka ṭhāma kaye kaho : pānī dhālite : tathi jaice kautuka milala : āhe loka : tāhe dekhaha śunaha : nirantare haribola* ||

Direction: Thereafter, regaining consciousness, Brahmā, uttering "Viṣṇu, Viṣṇu!", holding up the sacrificial ladle again, started the oblation. At that time, King Bhīṣmaka, handing over his daughter, gathered together the hair of

50 . in *Śloka* metre.

51. *tataścetanamālabhya.*

52 . in *Śloka* metre.

both the bride and the bride-groom and while pouring water on it, as there took place much merriment, oh dear people, watch and listen to that and keep chanting the name of Hari incessantly.

*gīta* || *rāga- sāreṁ* || *paritāla* ||
Song in the *Rāga Sāreṁ* with the rhythm *Paritāla:*

*kahatu bidhātā bedaku bāṇī* |
*hari rukamiṇīka keśa eka karie :*
*bhīṣmaka dhāle bhṛṅgāra dhari pānī* ||*dhruṁ*||
The creator (Brahmā) uttered the words from the Veda and gathering together the hair of Hari and Rukmiṇī, Bhīṣmaka poured on water holding the pitcher.

*pada* ||
*jautuka ratana āñjuli bhari bariṣe:*
*gāve govinda guṇa surarā*|
*basuki ucuki tala ṭhuṭha thamaki:*
*nāce maheśa hāsa saba cāi* ||
*muni siddha kusuma hariṣe bariṣe:*
*kare kautuka saba loi* |
*dvārakāpura bhari milala mahotsava:*
*kaha śaṅkara gati govinda moi* ||*30*||

Verse: Showering jewels in handfuls as dowry (for the bride), the king of the gods (Indra) sang praises of Govinda.
Vāsuki with energy kept the beat with the rhythm and Maheśa danced along and everyone laughed looking at him.
The divine sages showered flowers with great happiness and all the people enjoyed.
Great festivity took place in the whole city of Dwārakā and Śaṅkara says, "Govinda is the ultimate way for me."

*sūtra* ||
*aicana parakāre : kṛṣṇaka bibāha bhela* | *tadanantara : brahmārudra : indra ādi jata devatā : pātālaka bāsuki prabhṛti*

*jata nāga : pṛthibīka jata rājā : sabāko sādare : śrīkṛṣṇa gandha candane : puṣpa tāmbula : bastra alaṅkāre : parama santuṣṭa karāvala | ataḥpare parama kautuke : trailokyara loke : jaya kṛṣṇa jaya kṛṣṇa ghuṣie : samāja bhāṅgi kāhu : svaki svaki thāne calite : anyo anye kṛṣṇaka ācarya guṇa mahimā : kīrtana kaye kahu : daśo diśe gela ||*

Direction: In this way, Kṛṣṇa's wedding took place. After that, with great hospitality for Brahmā, Rudra, Indra and all the other demigods, all the serpants including Vāsuki from Pātāla, and all the kings of this world, Śrī Kṛṣṇa, offering scented *candana*, flowers, betel nuts, clothes and jewellery, greatly satisfied them. After that, all the people from the three worlds, announcing "Glory to Kṛṣṇa, victory to Kṛṣṇa!", and breaking the assembly, went to their own places in the ten directions, narrating to one another about the surprising behaviour, qualities and greatness of Kṛṣṇa.

*śloka ||*

*tato'tikautukī kṛṣṇaḥ priyayā premarūpayā |*
*kurban kelirasotsāhan mumude ratnamandire ||41||*

Hymn[53]: Then Kṛṣṇa became very happy at the love and beauty of His wife and entering the house, decorated with gems and jewels, enjoyed sporting with great enthusiasm.

*sūtra ||*

*tadanantara : śrīkṛṣṇa parama ucuke pṛyā sahite: ratnamandire praveśie : jaice kautuke rukamiṇīka prabodhi: līlā keli kae rahala : āhe loka : tāhe dekhaha śunaha : nirantare haribola ||*

Direction: After that, Śrī Kṛṣṇa, with great eagerness entered the house studded with gems and jewels and with great happiness, satisfying Rukmiṇī, sported with her. Oh dear people, watch and listen to that and keep chanting the name of Hari incessantly.

53. in *Śloka* metre.

*gīta* || *rāga- kalyāṇa* || *kharamāna* ||
Song in the *Rāga Kalyāṇa* with the rhythm *Kharamāna:*

*karata bihāra : karata bihāra murāru* |
*kāminī kamala amala muha lambi :*
*cumbi jagata ādhāru* || *dhruṁ*||

Murāri sported with pleasure, with pleasure sported Murāru; one who is the sustenance of the whole world, kissed the whole length of the pure lotulike face of His beloved. Refrain.

*pada* ||

*ghana ghana nayana : paṅkaja muha heri :*
*heri karata kānu keli* |
*āliṅgi aṅga : anaṅga raṅga rasika :*
*ramaṇīka bhuja meli* ||*1*||
*hāsi hāsi haraṣe : haraṣe nakha paraśi :*
*kuca kāñcuri phora kāne* |
*pūrala parama : manoratha kāminī :*
*sādhu adhara madhu pāne* ||*2*||
*śrīrāma rāyā hari rasa pāyā :*
*bhakati rasika sūjānā* |
*keśava caraṇa saroruha kiṅkara :*
*śaṅkara hariguṇa gānā* ||*32*||

Verse: Looking again and again at her face with the lotuslike eyes, Kānu amused himself. Extending His hands and embracing her, found pleasure in the passions of Anaṅga (love). (1)

Laughing and smiling, Kānu pleased her and pleased her with the touch of His nails and tearing apart the covering of her breasts, and tasting the pure nectar of the lips, fulfilled the greatest desire of His beloved. (2)

Śrī Rāma Rāya, having received the blessings of Hari, is a learned person finding great pleasure in devotion. Śaṅkara, the servant, at the lotus feet of Keśava, sings this praise of Hari.

*sūtra* ||

*ohi parakāre bhakata-kṛpālu śrīkṛṣṇa : rukamiṇīka bhakati baśya hayā : bibidha bihāra madana-khelā-līlā-keli kautuke kariye : rājakumārīka parama manoratha pūrala : se nṛpanandanīka mahā mahodaya milala : jagataka parama guru nārāyaṇa : tanikara parama sobhāginī bhela | nava taruṇī padumini śata sahasra dāsī pāvala : indraka jata sampatti : nija mandire milala : śrīkṛṣṇaka caraṇa paṅkaja : paramānande paricaryā kaye sarbbathā rahala ||*

Direction: In this way, Śrī Kṛṣṇa, merciful to His devotees, conquered by the devotion of Rukmiṇī, indulged in different playful sports, recreations and amorous activities with great amusement and fulfilled the ultimate desire of the princess. That princess became extremely fortunate, became the wife of the great master of this world Nārāyaṇa. The young girl, a *padminī*, got hundreds and thousands of maids; found as much wealth as Indra in her own home; taking care of the lotus feet of Śrī Kṛṣṇa with great pleasure, remained there forever.

*śloka* ||

*rukminīharaṇaṁ nāma naṭakaṁ hariṇā kṛtam |*
*asminnimittamātro'haṁ jānantīti mahattamāḥ* ||42||

Hymn[54]: Hari has performed the play by the name *Rukmiṇī Haraṇa.* All the great souls know that I am only a means here.

*sūtra* ||

*āhe sabhāsada loka : kṛṣṇa caraṇa prasādata : rukmiṇī haraṇa nāṭa : sampūrṇa bhela : ihāta jata nyunādhika doṣa : se harika smaraṇe dūra hauka | ohi kṛṣṇaka caritrakathā : je sādhusabe śraddhāe kahe śune : se sabaka harika kṛpā miloka | āhe loka*

[54]. in *Śloka* metre.

*: dekhu dekhu bhāṭaka mukhe rukamiṇī : kṛṣṇaka guṇa śuniye : kṛṣṇara caraṇe: śraddhā mātra kayala : ataye bhakataka parama kṛpālu kṛṣṇa : tanikara baśya huyā : gṛha- gṛhiṇī kayala | aḥ hari bhakatika mahimā : ki kahaba : jāni kṛṣṇa caraṇe citta die : nirantare hari bola ||*

Direction: Oh revered audience, with the blessings of the feet of Kṛṣṇa, the drama *Rukmiṇī Haraṇa* is completed. May whatever fault is found herein, be eradicated by remembering Hari. All the good people who tell and listen to the tales of Kṛṣṇa with faith, may they receive the mercy of Hari. Oh dear people, see how, hearing about the qualities of Kṛṣṇa from the bard, Rukmiṇī maintained faith only at the feet of Kṛṣṇa and thereupon Kṛṣṇa, the greatest merciful to the devotees, being conquered by her, made her His mistress of His house. Ah what to speak of the greatness of devotion to Hari! Knowing that, concentrating on the feet of Kṛṣṇa, keep chanting the name of Hari incessantly.

*atha bhaṭṭimā || maṅgalaṁ vaktavyaṁ : muktimaṅgalam ||* Here is the eulogy – auspicious speech – for auspicious deliverance:

*jaya jaya jagata janaka yadudeva |*
*padapaṅkajaraja aja karu seva ||*
*johi harala rukamiṇī karu māna |*
*sohi karatu nitya mukuti bidhāna ||1||*
*haraṣe nācae hara jākeri āga |*
*garuḍaka pekhi palāvata nāga ||*
*khacala baghāmbara bṛṣabha ujāra |*
*sohi karatu nitya mukuti tohāra ||2||*
*johi jaladhi maha bāndhala setu |*
*rākaca rāvaṇa māraṇa hetu ||*
*bhītā bhakatā sītā karu trāṇa |*
*sohi karatu nitya mukuti bidhāna ||3||*
*agha baka keśī kaṁsa jiṭo āra |*
*duṣṭa ariṣṭaka moḍala ghāra ||*

*putanā śoṣaṇa cetana prāṇa |*
*sohi karatu nitya mukuti bidhāna ||4||*
*ṛju kubujī jo kayali ekānta |*
*kubalaya bhiri upārala dānta ||*
*kayo raṅgaśāle māla nirajāna |*
*sohi karatu nitya mukuti bidhāna ||5||*
*johi biṣa hrade bāhu āphāli |*
*karu kautuka nṛtya kāli nikāli ||*
*gokula rākhi bahni karu pāna |*
*sohi karatu nitya mukuti bidhāna ||6||*
*śrīrāma rāyā bhakati sujāna |*
*karāvata kṛṣṇa nāṭa niramāṇa ||*
*rukuni haraṇa nāma paradhāna |*
*kṛṣṇa kiṅkara ohi śaṅkara bhāṇa ||7||*
*śunā śunā sādhu sabhāsada loi |*
*murukhaka doṣa dharabi nāhi moi ||*
*hṛdi mādhava johi mati dilā |*
*sohi anurūpa karalu hari līlā ||8||*
*jāhe jāhite icā baikuṇṭha bāṭa |*
*śunā sāvadhāna kayo kṛṣṇa nāṭa ||*
*parama bandhu hari caritra bināi |*
*nāhi nāhi gati kalita lokāi ||9||*
*abahu nāhi bujhi śāstraka marma |*
*nāmata śaraṇa lela saba dharma ||*
*kalimala mocana parama hari nāma |*
*jāni sabahi nara bola rāma rāma ||10||*

Glory to the father of this world, the king from the Yadu (dynasty), the dust of whose lotuslike feet is worshipped even by Brahmā and Śiva; who abducted Rukmiṇī with due honour, may He bestow upon you eternal salvation. (1)
In front of whom, Hara dances with happiness; seeing Garuḍa, the snakes flee and his (Hara's) tiger skin clothing fall off loosening, the bull goes frantic; may He bestow upon you eternal salvation. (2)

One who built a bridge in the midst of the ocean in order to kill the demon Rāvaṇa and rescued the terrified devotee Sītā; may He bestow upon you eternal salvation. (3) One who came victorious against Agha, Baka, Keśī, Kaṁsa and all others, and twisted the neck of wicked Ariṣṭa and sucking away the consciousness and life out of Pūtanā, may He bestow upon you eternal salvation. (4)

One who made the hunch-backed (maid) absolutely straight, pressing down Kuvalayapīḍa, extracted his teeth, put the wrestlers to death in the theatre hall, may He bestow upon you eternal salvation. (5)

One who, expanding His arms in the poisonous lake, danced with great pleasure while chasing away the serpant Kāli, and saved(the residents of) Gokula drinking up the (wild) fire, may He bestow upon you eternal salvation. (6)

Śrī Rāma Rāya, a learned person in devotion, has made this play about Kṛṣṇa be composed, the best one, with the name *Rukuni Haraṇa (Rukmiṇī Haraṇa)*; thus, says Śaṅkara, the servant of Kṛṣṇa. (7)

Oh hear, hear, all the good people assembled here, please do not find fault with me, a fool. Whatever thought Mādhava revealed to my heart, I have composed about the pastime of Hari accordingly. (8)

Those who want to take the path to Vaikuṇṭha, please listen carefully to the play about Kṛṣṇa. The tales of Hari are the ultimate friends and except that, oh dear people, there is no other way of salvation in this age of Kali. (9)

(We) still do not understand the essence of the scriptures. (All the people belonging to) all different faiths, take shelter of the holy name. The name of Hari is the best and can set one free from all the evils of the age of Kali. Knowing this, all the people say "Rāma, Rāma!" (10)

*iti rukmiṇī-haraṇa nāṭa samāpta* ||

Here ends the play *Rukmiṇī Haraṇa.*

●●●

## 5.5
## *pārijāta-haraṇa nāṭa*
## The Play : Seizing of the Pārijāta (Flower)

*namaḥ śrīkṛṣṇāya*
Obeisance to Śrī Kṛṣṇa.

*śloka* ||

*namaḥ kṛṣṇaviṣṇo'cyutānantaśaktenamo*
*rāmarājīvanetraprabho te* |
*namo brahmamūrte murāre pareśa*
*namo viśvavāsa prasīda prasīda* ||1||

Hymn[1]:We offer our obeisance to Kṛṣṇa, who is firm, imperishable and all powerful Viṣṇu; we offer our obeisance to you, oh Lord, the lotus-eyed Rāma; we offer our obeisance to Brahmā incarnate, the destroyer of the demon Mura, who is the Supreme Lord Pareśa himself; we offer our obeisance to the one who is omnipresent; kindly be pleased, kindly be gracious.

*apica* ||

*khagendraṁ samāruhya nirjitya śatruṁ*
*mudā līlayā daivakīnandano yaḥ* |
*priyaṁ pārijātaṁ jahāra priyārthaṁ*
*pareśāya kṛṣṇāya tasmai namo me* ||2||

Also[2]: I offer my obeisance to that Supreme Lord Kṛṣṇa, son of Devakī, who riding on Garuḍa, the king of birds, defeating the enemy sportingly and with happiness, stole away the *pārijāta* flower for His beloved which was most liked by her.

---

1. in *Bhujaṅgaprayāta* metre.
2. in *Bhujaṅgaprayāta* metre.

*sūtra* ||

*pahilehi śrīkṛṣṇaka praṇāma kaye kahuñ :*
*sabhāsadalokaka sambodhi bola*||

Direction: At the very beginning, offering obeisance to Śrī Kṛṣṇa, said, addressing the audience:

*śloka* ||

*bho bhoḥ sāmājikā īśakṛṣṇasya jagatīpateḥ* |
*śrīpārījātaharaṇaṁ yātrāṁ samprati paśyata* ||3||

Hymn[3]: Oh dear audience, now please watch the auspicious play *Pārijātaharaṇaṁ* of Lord Kṛṣṇa, who is the master of the universe.

*atha bhatimā* ||

*jaya jaya kṛṣṇadeva nija aṁśa* |
*līlā nāsita kaṁsa sabaṁśa* ||
*jākeri caritra bhakata-avataṁśa* |
*kamalā keli kamala kalahaṁsa* ||1||
*tanu indibara-śyāmala cori* |
*tathi parakāśita pīta picori* ||
*tarita jarita jacha naya ghanakhaṇḍa* |
*makari kuṇḍala maṇḍita gaṇḍa* ||2||
*kanaka kirīṭi ratana avabhāsa* |
*kuñcita caru chikura parakāśa* ||
*ruchikara karṇa bhubana manabhula* |
*nāsā nira ratana tila phula* ||3||
*navana kamala muha-paṅkaja joḍa* |
*eku milala jacha cānda cakora* ||
*māṇika daśana hāsā tathi thora* |
*ārakata adhara bandūli ruchi cora* ||4||
*ruchira cibuka pekhi haru tāpa* |
*bhruva-yuga gāñji madanakeri cāpa* ||
*kuṭila alaka-kula tilaka kapola* |
*hṛdave hemaka hāra amola* ||5||

---

3. in *Śloka* metre, but in the 3rd foot, the 6th letter is short and not long.

*atima matima mālā lule |*
*kaustubha kambu-kaṇṭha maha ḍule ||*
*cāru udara dara hṛdaya biśāla |*
*lambita pañcabarana banamāla ||6||*
*sañcara cañcara madhukara lohe |*
*śrīśrībatsa urasthala śohe ||*
*caru caturbhuja aṅga bhuaṅga |*
*ratana keyūra ujara tacu saṅga ||7||*
*kaṅkaṇa kanaka jhanaka karu-mūla |*
*karatala rātā utapala phula ||*
*aṅguli cāru hīra hema moti |*
*nakhamaṇi nindita cāndaka jauti ||8||*
*ari*[4] *arabinda kaumudī kambupāṇi |*
*kokila-kaṇṭha amiyā jhure bāṇī ||*
*nābhi kañja kañja*[5] *anupāma |*
*bihiko janama bheli ṣohi ṭhāma ||9||*
*kaṭitaṭa kanaka kāñci parirambha |*
*uru karikarabara marakata tambha ||*
*lambi nitamba pīta ruchi cira |*
*padapaṅkaja jhure ratana mañjīra ||10||*
*nīla āṅguli jacha campaka kora |*
*nakhacaya cāru cānda ujhora ||*
*kamala padatala alakata bhānti |*
*dhvaja paṅkaja jaya*[6] *aṅkuśa kānti ||11||*
*pāśā lāṣā ceta cāmara ḍhola |*
*sañcara rājahaṁsa duho kola ||*
*māthe catra cāru śaśīkānta |*
*bariṣe sikara āmiyā nitānta ||12||*
*madhuru mūruti bhakata manapūra |*
*anamatha koṭi jāhe nahi tura ||*
*hoi jaba nīla naya ghana khaṇḍa |*
*uvare raha rabikara paracaṇḍa ||13||*
*pūrṇimāka cānda duhō duhō pāśā |*
*tathi karu indracāpa parakāśā ||*

[4]. *hari.*
[5]. *rañja.*
[6]. *java.*

*bahe duhõ dhāra surasuri nīra* |
*ujari bijurī raha tathi thira* ||14||
*abhinava sura ugata tacu mājhe* |
*tāhe lambi baka pakati birāje* ||
*tārā jhikamika karu bahu ṭhāmā* |
*taba hoi soi mūruti upāmā* ||15||
*rahu hṛdipaṅkaja sohi murāri* |
*aba soi loi dekhu bicāri* ||
*koṭi kalapataru pūraṇa kāmā* |
*aicana īśa rahaya nija ṭhāmā* ||16||
*tāhe caraṇa cinta citta lāi* |
*tanu cintāmaṇi biphalehi jāi* ||
*āve nikaṭa nita antaka garaji* |
*lehu haricaraṇa śaraṇa saba baraji* ||17||
*jo muhe rāmanāma nāhi aṁse*[7] |
*kaliyuga kāla bhujṅgama daṁse* ||
*sohi kṛṣṇaka nāṭaka upāmā* |
*pārijāta haraṇa āhe nāmā* ||18||
*bhakatika sādhi śunaha saba loi* |
*hari bine bāndhava āna nāhi koi* ||
*kṛṣṇa kiṅkara ohi śaṅkare bola* |
*kara aba narasaba hari hari rola* ||19||

Here is the eulogy: Glory to Kṛṣṇa who is part of Himself, who playfully destroyed Kaṁsa along with his whole family; whose pastimes are like ornaments for the ears of the devotees; (as if) Lakṣmī playing with her blue lotus, amongst the flamingoes, making a soft noise. (1)

The dark blue colour of the body surpasses even the blue lotus, and thereon the yellow clothing is illuminated as if lightning flashing on newly formed mass of cloud. Spider-shaped earrings hang on the cheeks. (2)

The golden crown is brightened with gems; and beautiful curly locks of hair is shining. The beautiful ears mesmerises

[7] *.āse.*

everyone in this world. The nose, as if, is sesame flower of blue gems. (3)

The lotuslike eyes, as if compete with the lotuslike face. It was as if a pair of *cakora* birds and the moon are meeting at the same place. The teeth are like pearls and there is a slight smile on them. The lips are so red that they surpass even the beautiful *banduli* flower.(4)

Looking at the charming chin, all the miseries are taken away. The eyebrows (are so beautifully curved, that they) defeat even the bow of Madana. Curly locks of hair ornaments the forehead. An invaluable gold necklace hangs on the chest.(5)

Strings of the best quality pearls hang on the chest. The conch shell shaped *kaustubha* gem hangs from the neck . The beautiful belly is deep and the chest is wide. (Thereon) hangs a long garland of wild flowers of five different colours. (6)

The restless large black bee moves about greedily and adorn the beautiful Śrībatsa. The four hands are beautiful and the (shape of the) body is like that of a serpent. Armbands made of jewels brighten them up. (7)

Gold bracelets on the wrist make jingling sound. The palms of the hands are red like lotus flower. The fingers are beautiful with diamonds, gold and pearls. The nails put to shame even the glow of the moon. (8)

He has a wheel, a lotus, a *kaumudī*, and a conch shell in his hands. From His cuckoo-like voice, words flow like nectar. The lotuslike neval is incomparably delightful; wherein took birth the creator (Brahmā). (9)

The hips and loins are encircled with a waist girdle . The thighs are like the trunks of elephants, beautiful like an emerald pillar. Glowing yellow coloured clothing hang down from the hips, and golden anklets tinkle on the lotuslike feet. (10)

The blue fingers look like the buds of *campaka* flower. The rows of nails are beautiful like the bright moon. The lotuslike feet glow in red, and (thereon) the flag, the lotus, the barley-corn, and the hook are brilliant.(11)

Moving on both the sides, the white swans slowly fan with a white *cāmara* . As an umbrella over the head, is a beautiful moon, showering very sweet, nectar-like mist. (12)

The pleasing, delightful body fulfills the minds of the devotees; even a crore of Manmathas together cannot be compared to him. It is as if a mass of blue cloud is formed and up above, the sun is shining fiercely. (13)

The two full moons (the wives) are on both the sides and thereon shines the rainbow. The divine Ganges flows in two streams; and bright lightning flashes on it. (14)

The new sun rises amidst that and there remains hanging, a row of cranes. The stars are dazzling in many places. Then, that form becomes incomparable.[8] (15)

There remains in the lotuslike heart that same Murāri; now, all the people, please consider on it. Like a crore of *kalpataru* trees, which fulfill all wishes, such a lord remains in his place. (16)

Concentrate on His feet wholeheartedly; (or else) the (human) body, which is like the *cintāmaṇi* gem, is wasted. The end (death) comes closer thundering everyday; ( hence) renouncing everything , take refuge at the feet of Hari. (17)

Whose mouth does not utter the name of Rāma in the Age of Kali, death incarnate comes (to him) and bites him like a snake. (This is) the incomparable drama about that Kṛṣṇa and *Pārijāta Haraṇa* is its name. (18)

Attaining the goal of devotion, please listen, all the people, there is no other friend but Hari; that is what the servant of Kṛṣṇa says, "All the people, please utter the name of Hari creating an uproar!" (19)

---

[8]. Bora, M., *Śaṅkardevar Nāṭ*, 2003, p. 283.

*sūtra* ||

*āhe samājikā loka : je jagataka guru : jāheri srajanā sayalā saṁsāra : brahmā maheśe bandita pādapadmañ : parama puruṣa puruṣottama śrīkṛṣṇa : rukamiṇī satyabhāmā sahita : ohi sabhā madhye prabeśi kahõ : narakāsura-badha pārijāta haraṇa : līlā yātrā : kautuke karaba : tāhe sāvadhāne dekhaha śunaha : ātapare puṇya kalita nāhi nāhi : jāni nirantare hari bola* ||

Direction: Oh dear assembled audience, one who is the master of this world, who has created this world, whose lotus-feet are worshipped by Brahmā and Maheśa, the greatest, the Supreme Personality Śrī Kṛṣṇa, along with Rukmiṇī and Satyabhāmā, entering amongst this audience, will perform with great pleasure the play *Narakāsura Badha Pārijāta Haraṇa*; watch and listen to that carefully; there is no higher pious activity (than this) in the Age of Kali; knowing that, keep chanting the name of Hari incessantly.

*tadanantara : sūtra puchata* || *āhe saṅgi : ki bādya bāje* ||
Thereafter, the Sūtradhāra asks, "Oh dear friend, what instruments are playing?"

*saṅgi bola* || *āhe devabādya bājata* ||
The companion says: "Oh, there plays the celestial instrument."

*sūtra* ||

*aḥ milala milala* ||

Direction: Ah, here He comes, here He comes.

*śloka* ||

*praveśamakaroddevo govindo garuḍāsanaḥ* |
*rukminī satyabhāmābhyāṁ saha cāruścaturbhujaḥ* ||4||

Hymn[9]: Here enters Lord Govinda, sitting on the seat of (back of) Garuḍa in a beautiful form with four hands and along with Rukmiṇī and Satyabhāmā.

*kathā* ||

*āhe loka : hāmu je kahalu : sohi parama īśvara : śrīkṛṣṇa sabhārye : yātrā nimite ethā vāata : parama sāvadhāna hayā : tāhe dekhaha śunaha : nirantare hari bola* ||

Dialogue: Oh dear people, as I have said, that Supreme Lord Śrī Kṛṣṇa comes here to perform the play; being very careful, watch and listen to that and chant the name of Hari incessantly.

*iti sūtro niṣkrāntaḥ* !
Thus the Sūtradhāra exits.

*praveśa gīta : rāga- sindhurā* || *ekatāli* ||
Here is the song of entrance, in the *Rāga Sindhurā* with the rhythm *Ekatāli:*

*dhruṁ* ||

*āve gorura-ketu kayo paraveśa* |
*madanaka lāja heri rūpa leśa* ||

Refrain: Garuḍa-ketu comes and enters and Madana becomes ashamed looking at His little beauty.

*pada* ||

*śyāma mūruti dīpita pītabāsā* |
*mukūṭa kūṇḍala maṇi mukha parakāśā* ||
*kara kaṅkaṇa banamālā ure lole* |
*caraṇaka mājhe mañjira karu role* ||1||
*koṭi madana jini ujara murāri* |
*saṅge satyabhāmā rukamiṇī bara nārī* ||
*śarīraka jauti [illegible]alaya diśa pāśā* |
*kahaya śaṅkara haridāsaku dāsā* ||2||1||

---

[9]. in *Śloka* metre.

Verse: The dark blue body is illuminated by yellow clothing; the crown, the earrings and gems brighten up the face. There are bracelets on the hands, a garland of wild flowers swings and anklets tinkle between the feet. (2)
Defeating a crore of Madana, Murāri shines up beautifully. Along with Him, there are the beautiful ladies, Satyabhāmā and Rukmiṇī; the brightness of the body illuminates all the sides; says Śaṅkara, the servant of all the servants of Hari. (1)

*sūtra* ||

*āhe sabhāsada loka : śrīkṛṣṇa patnīsaba sahita : kautuke nṛtya kaya kaho :*
*rukamiṇī sahita eka mandire rahala : satyabhāmā nija mandire rahala* ||

Direction: Oh dear audience , Śrī Kṛṣṇa, along with His wives, dancing with great pleasure with Rukmiṇī, remained in one palace while Satyabhāmā stayed in her own palace.

*śloka* ||

*paścāt purandaro devo nāradena sahāgataḥ* |
*praṇamya keśavaṁ sarbaṁ provāca bhaumaceṣṭitam* ||5||

Hymn[10]: After that, Purandara came with the divine Nārada and offering obeisance to Keśava told Him about all the actions and behaviours of the son of the earth (Naraka).

*sūtra* ||

*tadanantara : devatā indra : nārada sahita āsi kahuñ : śrīkṛṣṇaka śira paraṇāma kaya kahu : narakāsuraka biceṣṭā jaiche nibedala* | *nārada āśīrbbāda kaya : śrīkṛṣṇaka hāte jaiche pārijāta nibedala : rukamiṇīka māthe jagataka nāthe : jaiche pindhāyala : āhe loka : tāhe dekhaha śunaha : nirantare hari bole* ||

Direction: After that, Lord Indra coming along with Nārada, offering their obeisance with bowed heads to Śrī Kṛṣṇa,

[10]. in *Śloka* metre.

(as) told about the evil actions of demon Narakāsura; (as) Nārada, blessing Him, offered the *pārijāta* in the hands of Śrī Kṛṣṇa, and as the Lord of the universe decorated the head of Rukmiṇī with it. Oh dear people, watch and listen to that and keep chanting the name of Hari incessantly.

*gīta* || *rāga-āsoāri* || *paritāla* ||
Song in the *Rāga Āśovārī* with the rhythm *Paritāla*:

*dhruṁ* ||
*airāata kandhe bāsava āve* |
*āgahi nārada hariguṇa gāve* ||
Refrain: Riding on the shoulder of the Airāvata here comes Indra and preceding him comes Nārada, singing the praises of Hari.

*pada* ||
*sundarī ramaṇī sasvi*[11] *ekupāśe* |
*cale bhrubhaṅga aṅga layalāse* ||
*māthe catra bajra ekū hāte* |
*kaha śaṅkara gati gopinī nātāhe* ||2||
Verse: With the beautiful young woman Śacī on one side, (Indra) moves with curved eyebrows and his body in rhythm; with a parasol on the head and the Vajra on one hand; says Śaṅkara that the only way for salvation is (at the feet of ) Gopinīnātha.

*sūtra* ||
*tadanantara : nāradaka dekhi : śrīkṛṣṇa sabhārje uthi kahō : sapaṭe praṇāma kayala : nārada hāta toli : cirañjīva cirañjīva buli : āśīrbbāda śloka paḍhala* ||
Direction: After that, seeing Nārada, Śrī Kṛṣṇa, rising along with His wife in veil, offered obeisance. Nārada, raising his hand and saying "Long live, live long!", recited a hymn of blessings.

---
[11]. *Śaci.*

*śloka* ||

*jaya jaya yadudevo daivakīnandanantvam*
*bhuvanapati samastairarccitāṅghriḥ sadaiva* |
*nijajanabhayahārin sṛṣṭisaṁhārakārin*
*asuranarakatantān sāmpratam pāhi devān* ||6||

Hymn[12]: Glory to the honourable one from the Yadu dynasty (Śrī Kṛṣṇa), the son of Devakī, the infinite; the Lord of the universe whose feet are worshipped by everyone everyday; one who removes fear from all His own people; the creator and the destroyer, please save us from the demon Narakāsura now.

*kathā* ||

*ohi āśīrbbāda kaye : śrīkṛṣṇaka hāte pārijāta dive : nārada tāheka mahimā kahala* ||

*he kṛṣṇa : ohi pārijātaka gandha : tini prahareka patha jāi : ohi pārijāta : jāhera gṛhe rahe : dhanajana bibhaya cāḍave nāhi : ohi deva-durllabha pārijāta : jo nārī paridhāna kare : se puspaka mahimāye parama sobhāgāni haya : tāheka bāri cāri : svāmī kathāye jāye nāhi : aḥ ohi kusumaka mahimā ki kahaba* ||

Dialogue: Blessing in this way, he gave the *pārijāta* in the hands of Śrī Kṛṣṇa and told them about its greatness.

"Oh dear Kṛṣṇa, the fragrance of this *pārijāta* flower goes upto a distance of three *prahara*; whoever has this *pārijāta* flower at home, he is never in want of money, people, wealth and power. This is a rare flower, which is very difficult to attain even for the gods. Whoever woman wears it, becomes very fortunate by virtue of the power of this flower; her husband never goes anywhere leaving her behind at home. Oh, what to speak of the greatness of the flower!"

*ohi buli nārada covaḍi pāri baiṭhi maune rahala* ||

---

[12]. in *Mālinī* metre.

Saying thus, spreading a seat of the skin of the Chamara deer, Nārada sat and remained silent.

*śloka*||

*śrutvā kusuma-māhātmyaṁ rukmiṇī keśavapriyā* |
*praṇamya svāmicaraṇaṁ pārijātamayācata* ||7||

Hymn[13]: Hearing about the greatness of the flower, Rukmiṇī, the wife of Keśava, offering obeisance in the feet of her husband, asked for the flower.

*kathā* ||

*munika mukhe : kusumaka mahimā śuni rukamiṇī : parama kautuke : kṛṣṇaka gori lāgi karajuḍi bolala* ||

Dialogue: Hearing about the outstanding qualities of the flower from the sage, Rukmiṇī , with great pleasure, holding on to the feet of Kṛṣṇa and with folded hands, said:

*he svāmi : hāmi tohāra prathama patanī : jāni ohi deva-durllabha pārijāta: prāṇanātha hāmāka dehu* ||

"Oh dear husband, I am your first wife; knowing that, oh Lord of my life, please give me the *pārijāta*, which is difficult to attain even by gods."

*sūtra* ||

*ohi boli jaiche kusuma māgala : tāhe dekhaha śunaha : nirantare hari bola*||

Direction: Saying thus, as she asked for the flower, watch and listen to that and keep chanting the name of Hari incessantly.

*gīta* || *rāga-śrīgāndhāra* || *jatimāna* ||

Song in the *Rāga Śrīgāndhāra* with the rhythm *Jatimāna:*

*dhruṁ* ||

*kautuke rukumini : namive svāmīka pāye:*
*māge ājuri dhari hāta* |

---

[13]. in *Śloka* metre, but in the 3rd foot, the 6th and 7th letters are short instead of long.

*āhe piu:*
*aba prāṇanātha* *māthe milāyo mohi:*
*ohi kusuma pārijāta* ||

Refrain: Rukmiṇī, happily offering obeisance in the feet of her husband, begged joining her hands.

"Oh dear husband, oh Lord of my life, now please put this *pārijāta* flower in my hair."

*pada* ||

*āhera guṇa śuni:* *muni mukhe mādhava :*
*sādhu atave toyī māna* |
*bhakata kṛpāla:* *lāgu caraṇa teri :*
*karahu kusuma mohi dāna* ||
*tohāri prathama:* *patanī parama svāmī :*
*jāni pūraha mohi āśā* |
*dhanika bāṇī śuni :* *hāse raṣika hari :*
*kahatu śaṅkara kṛṣṇadāsā* || *dhruṁ* ||3||

Verse: "Hearing from the sage about its qualities, oh dear Mādhava, I seek as much from you; oh merciful to the devotees, I hold on to your feet, please gift me this flower. "I am your first wife , oh Supreme Lord; realising that, please fulfil my wish." Hearing the words of the woman, finding pleasure, Hari smiles; says Śaṅkara, the servant of Kṛṣṇa. Refrain.

*sūtra* ||

*tadanantara : rukamiṇīka āti kātara bāṇī śuni : śrīkṛṣṇa hāsi hāsi hāte toil : pṛyāka gaurave kole baiṭhāi : kautuke jagataka nāthe : māthe pārijāta pindhāvala* | *ramaṇīka bāñcā saphala bhela* | *tadanantare : pṛyā sahita : śrīkṛṣṇa sādare nāradata bārttā puchata* ||

Direction: After that, hearing the very earnest words of Rukmiṇī, Śrī Kṛṣṇa, laughing, raised her with His hands, making her sit on His lap with pride, the Lord of the universe dressed her hair with the *pārijāta* flower; the wish of the wife was fulfilled. After that, Śrī Kṛṣṇa, along with His beloved wife asked Nārada about his tidings.

*kṛṣṇa bola || he munirāja : tohõ kuśale āvala : aḥ tohāri āgamane : āju hāmāra dvārikāpurī pavitra bhela : tohāri darasane hāmu kṛtārtha bhelõ ||*
Kṛṣṇa said, "Oh king of the sages, are you well? With your arrival, the city of Dwārakā has become purified. Seeing you, we have become happy and satisfied."

*nārada śloka paḍha :*
Nārada recited a hymn:

*śloka ||*

*kṛṣṇasya vacanaṁ śrutvā bihasyovāca nāradaḥ |*
*nijabhṛtyastavaivāhaṁ mayi māyāṁ karoṣi kim||8||*

Hymn[14]: Hearing Kṛṣṇa's words, Nārada said smiling, "I am only your servant, are you trying to lead me to illusion?"

*kathā ||*

*he svāmikṛṣṇa : manuṣya-ceṣṭā dekhāvā sabaloka mohicha : tohāka īśvara boli jānave nāhi : hāmu tohāri bhakatikabale saba jāni : hāmāku mohite cāya : aḥ svāmi śunaha ||*

Dialogue: "Oh lord Kṛṣṇa, showing human behaviour, you are mesmerising all. They do not know that you are all powerful Supreme Lord. By virtue of my devotion to you, I know everything. Do you want to mesmerise me? Oh Lord, please listen."

*payāḍa ||*

*he parameśvara jagata-nibāsā |*
*hāmu nārada tuyā dāsakū dāsā ||*
*bharamo diśa daśa tuyā jaṣa gāyā |*
*hāmākū āgu karasi ohi māyā ||*
*jagata uddhāra jāhera caritra |*
*tāheka hāmu kayalu pavitra ||*

---
[14]. in *Śloka* metre.

*jāheri nāme mukuti-pada pāi |*
*so hari kara tuti- nati katilāi ||*
*tuhuñ jagata-guru devaka devā |*
*tohāri caraṇe rahoka seyā ||*
*mukhe janu cāḍahu tuyā guṇanāma |*
*māgu atave bara tohāri ṭhāma ||4||*

Verse: "Oh the Supreme Lord, the omnipresent, me Nārada, is your servant of servant. I move about in all the ten directions singing your glories, and you are playing this illusion with me (also).

"Delivering this whole world is whose nature, (how) have I purified Him! By whose name one can attain the state of salvation, that same Hari, why do you say such false praises!

"You are the father of the whole world and the God of all gods. Let my services remain at your feet. Lest I stop singing your praises with my mouth, I seek as much blessing as to be near you."

*kathā ||*

*nārada bola|| he kṛṣṇa : tuhuñ parama puruṣa : nārāyaṇa bhūmika bhāra haraṇa nimite avataricha : sāmprata pāpī narakāsure : devatāsabaka bahuta dukha lāgave : tannimitta śacī sahita indradevatā : tohāri caraṇe śaraṇa lelaha : he śrīkṛṣṇa dekho dekho ||*

Direction: Nārada said, "Oh dear Kṛṣṇa, you are the Supreme Personality, Nārāyaṇa; you have incarnated, to relieve this world of its burdens. At the present moment, the sinner Narakāsura is creating great distress to all the demigods. That is why Śacī, along with deity Indra, has come seeking refuse at your feet. Oh dear Śrī Kṛṣṇa, please look, look."

*sūtra ||*

*etahi buli nārada maune rahala | tadanantara : śrīkṛṣṇaka āgu paripurandara : paraṇāma kaye kahuñ : sabhārye kara-juli*[15] *tuti bolala : tāhe dekhaha śunaha : nirantare hari bola ||*

15. *joḍi.*

Direction: Saying as much, Nārada remained silent. After that, falling down in front of Śrī Kṛṣṇa, Purandara, along with his wife, started praying with folded hands. Watch and listen to that and chant the name of Hari incessantly.

*payāḍa* ||

*jaya jaya yādava deva* |
*jaya dhātā-kṛta seva* ||
*jaya bhakata-bhayahārī* |
*jaya jaya īśvara murāri* ||
*jākeri nāma ucāri* |
*pāi padāraṣa*[16] *cāri* ||
*jīva nivantā tuhuñ aja* |
*bando tuyā caraṇa-paṅkaja* ||
*aghabaka dhenuka kaṁsa* |
*mārala asura sabaṁśa* ||
*harali bhūmikeri bhāra* |
*bhakataka hetu avatāra* ||
*sāmprata gocara hāmāri* |
*bāndhava śunaha murāri* ||
*aba narakāsura pāpa* |
*kayali baḍi upatāpa*[17] ||
*ānala svargaka māri* |
*devaka atave kumārī* ||
*sarbasva narahe hāmāri* |
*tuyā pāve kayalu gohāri* ||5||

Verse: "Glory to the honourable descendant of the Yadu dynasty. Glory to the one who is served by the creator. Glory to the one who removes all the fears of His devotees. Glory to Lord Murāri, uttering whose name one can attain the four objects of life[18]. One who is the governor of all the living beings, you are the unborn one; I pray at your lotus feet. You killed all the demons like Agha, Baka, Dhenuka

---

16. *padāratha.*
17. *utapāta.*
18. i.e., *dharma, artha, kāma and mokṣa.*

and Kaṁsa, along with their families. You have incarnated for the devotees, and relieved the earth of its burdens. Now please listen to our grievances, oh dear friend Murāri. Now the sin incarnate, Narakāsura is creating great disturbance. Having defeated the heaven (planets), he has taken away many young girls. We shall be loosing everything; we make our appeal at your feet."

*kathā* ||

*he svāmi śrīkṛṣṇa : pāpī narakāsure kona nakarala : baruṇaka catra : maṇi parbbata : esaba kāḍhi ānala : he kṛṣṇa ki kahaba : mātṛ aditika kuṇḍala dohoñ rākhave nāhi pārala : āra hāmāra haite ki rahala : he kṛṣṇa : koṭi koṭi brahmāṇḍeśvara : tohāri caraṇa cori : hāmāra gati nahi : bāpa jagannātha :trāhi trāhi* ||

Dialogue: "Oh Lord Śrī Kṛṣṇa, what has the sinner Narakāsura not done! The umbrella of Varuṇa and the mountain Maṇi, he has snatched away all these! Oh Kṛṣṇa, what to tell you, even the two earrings of mother Aditi could not be saved; what remains for us now! Oh dear Kṛṣṇa, the Lord of crores of universes, leaving your feet, there is no other way (for salvation) for us; oh dear father Jagannātha, please save us, please rescue us."

*sūtra* ||

*ohi boli kṛṣṇaka āgu : kāndi kāndi pūrandara parala* ||

Direction: Saying thus, crying, Pūrandara fell down in front of Kṛṣṇa.

*śloka* ||

*dṛṣṭvā duḥkhaṁ mahendrasya śrutvā ca bhaumaceṣṭitam* |
*āśvāsya bāsavaṁ haste gṛhītvovāca keśavaḥ* ||9||

Hymn[19]: Seeing the distress of Indra, and hearing about the action and behaviour of Narakāsura, Keśava, assuring Vāsava, said holding his hands.

[19]. in *Śloka* metre.

*kathā* ||

*tadanantara : mahendraka dukha dekhive : parama kṛpāmaya nārāyaṇa : hāte dhari toli : indraka āsvāsi bolala* ||

Dialogue: After that, seeing the unhappiness of Mahendra, Keśava, the extremely merciful, raising him holding him by the hand, said consoling Indra.

*he mahendra : tohõ tāpa tejaha : tohāri bairī : pāpī narakāsura : se gatāyu bheli : tāheka māri : devatāsabaka prayojana satvare sādhaba : ohi niṣṭe jāni : tuhu āga huyā : satvare amrāvatī calaha : narakāsura badhite : hāmu āju pavāna karaba* ||

"Oh great Indra, you please give up this distress. Consider your enemy, the sinner Narakāsura, to be dead. Killing him, I shall fulfil the need of the demigods soon. Knowing it for sure, you please proceed in advance and go to Amarāvatī immediately. As for killing Narakāsura, I shall set out today itself."

*sūtra* ||

*se samaye nārada āsi kahuñ : indraka bola* ||

Direction: At that time, Nārada, coming in, said to Indra.

*kathā* ||

*he purandara : śrīkṛṣṇa jekhana aṅgīkāra kayala : tohāra śatruka tekhane kandhapāta bhela : ihāta śaṅkā nāhi : tuhuñ āgu huyā calaha : tohāka nimite: śrīkṛṣṇaka kātara kaya : hāmu pācu layā jāvaba : cintā nāhi : calaha* |

Dialogue: "Oh dear Purandara, when Śrī Kṛṣṇa has promised, your enemy is beheaded then and there itself, there is no doubt about it. You please proceed ahead, I shall entreat Śrī Kṛṣṇa for you and take him along following you. Do not worry and please proceed."

*sūtra* ||

*ohi nirbhaya bāṇī śuni bāsava : kṛṣṇaka nāradaka pradakṣiṇa kari kahuñ : pari paraṇāma kayala : bidāya laiyā airāvate cari : indra calala* ||

Direction: Hearing these reassuring words, Vāsava, circumambulating Kṛṣṇa and Nārada, offered obeisance falling down and taking leave, Indra proceeded riding on Airāvata.

*śloka* ||

*munirmādhavamāhedaṁ gantuṁ tvaraya keśava* |
*dvāravatyāḥ śriyaṁ paśyanneṣyāmi cāntikantava* ||*10*||

Hymn[20]: The sage told Mādhava thus, "Keśava, please go fast. Having a glance at the beauty of Dwārakā, I shall come to you."

*kathā* ||

*nārada bola* || *he kṛṣṇa : tuhuñ calibāka satvare sājaha : hāmu tohāri dvārakāpurīka : kautuke pekhive : eikhane āvaba* ||

Dialogue: Nārada said, please get ready quickly to go; I shall have a look at your city of Dwārakā with pleasure, and will be back right this moment.

*sūtra* ||

*ohi buli nārada hari-guṇa gāi :jaice calali : tāhe dekhaha śunaha : nirantare haribola* ||

Direction: Saying so, as Nārada went singing the glories of Hari, watch and listen to that and chant the name of Hari incessantly.

*payāḍa* || *śrīgāndhāra rāga* || *paritāla* ||

Verse in the *Rāga Śrīgāndhāra*, with the rhythm *Paritāla:*

*calali nārada hari-guṇa gāi* |
*bharame dvārikāpurī sampatti cāi* ||

---

[20]. in *Śloka* metre.

Nārada went singing praises of Hari, roaming about the city of Dwārakā, looking at its wealth.

*pada* ||

*ratane racita jata harika āvāsā* |
*aiche surapura kara parakāśā* ||
*pekhala pācu bhubana anupāmā* |
*āsane thika baiṭhi satyabhāmā* ||
*pūrṇimāka cānda badana parakāśā* |
*cirañjīva boli nārada karu hāsā* ||
*dekhi munika dhani avanata kāi* |
*pari paraṇāma kayali punu māi* ||
*jīvatu jīvatu nārada bola* |
*ḍāki karahu nara hari hari bola* ||6||

Verse: All the houses in the abode of Hari, were made of gems and jewels and that was how the city of the gods illuminated. After that, he saw an incomparably beautiful house and therein, sitting on a seat, was Satyabhāmā. Her face glowed like the full moon. "May you live long!", said Nārada, and smiled. Seeing Nārada, the young girl bowed down and falling down (at his feet), the dear young girl offered obeisance again. "Long live, live long!", said Nārada. All the people, call aloud the name of Hari repeatedly.

*sūtra* ||

*tadanantara : bāsuyā cayaḍi pārala : muni āsana bhiḍi tathi baiṭhala* ||

Direction: After that, the jester spread out a seat of the skin of the Chamara deer and the sage, spreading out the seat, sat there.

*śloka* ||

*nāradaḥ sādaraṁ devīṁ sambodhyāha haripriyāṁ* |
*kṛṣṇasya karmabiṣamaṁ satyabhāme nibodha me* ||11||

Hymn[21]: Nārada, respectfully addressing the goddess, the beloved of Hari, said, "Oh dear Satyabhāmā, listen to me, as to what great wrong Kṛṣṇa has done."

*kathā* ||

*nārada bola* || *aḥ he devī satyabhāmā : tohāri svāmī śrīkṛṣṇaka baḍi biṣama ceṣṭā dekhala : hā hā māva : tuhuñ durbhāgā bheli : hāmu ājuse jānalu* ||

Dialogue: Nārada said, "Oh dear Queen Satyabhāmā, your husband Śrī Kṛṣṇa has exhibited very unfavourable line of action. Alas, alas dear girl you have become very unfortunate! I have come to know today only."

*devī bola* || *he munirāja : tuhuñ ki kahayīcha : hāmu kicu bujhaye nāhi* ||

The queen said: "Oh great sage, what are you saying? I don't understand anything."

*munibola* || *hā hā tohāka bidhi bañcala : he māva ki kahaba : kahite baḍa dukha lāge* ||

The sage said: "Alas, alas! You have been cheated by destiny; oh dear mother, what to say? It pains me very much to tell you."

*sūtra* ||

*ohi boli heṭha māthe theṣ kaya rahala muni* ||

Direction: Saying so, with his head down, the sage remained sulking.

*śloka* ||

*satyabhāmābhavadbhītā niśamya munibhāṣitam* |
*dṛṣṭaṁ kathaya kiṁ kutra taṁ pṛcchati punaḥ punaḥ* ||12||

---

21. in *Śloka* metre, but in the 3rd foot, the 6th and 7th letters are short and not long.

Hymn[22]: Hearing the words of the sage, Satyabhāmā became greatly frightened and asked him again and again to tell her as to what he saw and where he saw.

*kathā* ||

*śuni bhīti hayā devī : karajuḍi bolala* ||

*he munirāja : hāmu jānu mohi sama sobhāginī āvari nāhi : se svāmī kṛṣṇa hāmāka cāḍi : katihu jāve nāhi : tuhu āju kona ṭhāme : ki dekhala ki śunala : hāmāka śapata : satvare svarūpa bāta kaha : citta baḍi udabega karaye : muni mauna cāḍaha* ||

Dialogue: Hearing (him), greatly scared, the lady, folding her hands said. "Oh king amongst the sages, I know, there is no one else as fortunate as I am. That husband of mine, Kṛṣṇa, goes nowhere leaving me behind; (but) today in its place(instead), what have you seen, what have you heard? On oath, tell me the truth quickly. My mind is very much agitated; oh dear sage, please stop being silent."

*śloka* ||

*dṛṣṭvā devyāḥ sunirvandhaṁ kathayāmāsa sādaram* |
*kṛṣṇasya caritaṁ sarbbaṁ rudanniva sa nāradaḥ* ||*13*||

Hymn[23]: Seeing the queen's earnest request, Nārada, with respect, told the tales of Kṛṣṇa almost crying.

*kathā* ||

*devīka nirvandha dekhi muni bola* ||

Dialogue: Seeing the earnest request of the lady, the sage said:

*hā hā he māva : ki kahaba : aisaba kathā kahite doṣa : hāmu deva –durllabha pārijāta puspa svarga hante āni : kṛṣṇaka hāte delō : se pārijāta je nārī paridhāna kare : se puspaka mahimāye : parama sobhāginī haya : ihā jāni hāmu bolalu : ohi pārijātaka yogya devī satyabhāmā : tathi kṛṣṇe kayali ki :*

---

[22]. in *Śloka* metre.

[23]. in *Śloka* metre.

*tohāka kaṭākṣa kariye : āpuna hāte pṛyā rukamiṇīka mākhe*[24]*: parama sādare se divya pārijāta pindhāala | aḥ tohāka jīvana dhika dhika : satinīka abhyudaya dekhi : ki nimite prāṇa dharaye : māya tuhuñ jiyante marala : hā hā bistara ki kahaba* ||
"Alas, alas oh dear mother! What to say! It is an offence to speak about these things. I brought the *pārijāta* flower from heaven, which is difficult to acquire even for the gods, and handed it to Kṛṣṇa. Whichever woman puts on the *pārijāta* flower, by virtue of the flower's power, becomes greatly fortunate. Knowing that, I said that queen Satyabhāmā was the most deserving for the flower. (Then), what Kṛṣṇa did with it, was that ignoring you, (He) dressed the hair of (His) wife Rukmiṇī with the divine flower with His own hands. What a pity on your life; seeing the rise in honour of your co-wife, what for do you keep on living. Oh mother, you are as good as dead while living. Alas, alas! What more shall I tell you!"

*śloka* ||

*maner*[25] *bacanamākarṇya śokakopapariplutā* |
*mūrcchitā patitā bhūmau yathā bātāhatā latā* ||*14*||

Hymn[26]: Hearing the words of the sage, overwhelmed with sorrow and anger, (Satyabhāmā) fell down unconsciousness on the ground like a creeper struck by the wind.

*sūtra* ||

*tadanantara : nārada mukhe : satinīka mahodava śuni kahuñ : kope apamāne āndhāri dekhive : devī satyabhāmā : murchita hayā paḍala : jaice layaṅga latāka bāte upārala : tadvata : keśa mukta bhela : mukhe bacana harala : nāsāta prāṇa–bāyu nāhi khele : pekhi sakhī indumatī : hā hā prāṇa-sakhī marala buli bāhu meli dhari kahuñ : śira jala siñcala : āñcale biñci : kāndi kāndi prabodha bolala* |

[24]. *māthe.*
[25]. *muner.*
[26]. in *Śloka* metre.

*indumatī bola || he prāṇasakhī : satinīka apamāne ki marite cāya : ohi kona beyahāra : aḥ se prāṇa mādhava svāmī tohāri māna sādhaba nāhi : ohi duranta cintā parihara : uṭhaha uṭhaha ||*

Direction: After that, hearing from Nārada about the good fortune of her co-wife, seeing darkness all around with feelings of anger and insult, queen Satyabhāmā fell down unconscious, as if a clove tree struck by the wind, that way. Her hair fell loose, and she became speechless; there was no air of life in her nose. Seeing that, her friend Indumatī, saying "Alas, alas! Our friend, who is dear like life, is dead!", held her with extended arms and spraying water on her head and fanning her with the fore-end of the clothing, crying a lot, said consoling.

Indumatī said, "Oh friend, dearer than life, being insulted by co-wife, should one end her life! What type of behaviour is that! Oh that dearer than life Mādhava, your husband, will not show respect to you. Abandon the wish which is unattainable. Now get up, get up."

*śloka ||*

*kathañcid cetanaṁ saṁjñāṁ labdhā devī punaḥ punaḥ |*
*viniśvasyāpamānena ruroda sakhīsannidhau ||15||*

Hymn[27]: Having regained consciousness, the queen sighing again and again for the insult she had received, cried very much near her friends.

*kathā ||*

*se devī satyabhāmā : kathañcit cetana labhive : ghana ghana nisvāśā phokāri : jaiche santāpa kayala : tāhe dekhaha śunaha : nirantare hari bola ||*

Dialogue: That respectable Satyabhāmā, somehow regaining consciousness and heaving sighs again and again, as she lamented, watch and listen to that and chant the name of Hari incessantly.

---

[27]. in *Śloka* metre, but in the 4th foot, the 5th letter is long and not short.

*gīta* || *rāga kalyāṇa* || *jatitāla* ||
Song in the *Rāga Kalyāṇa* with the rhythm *Jatitāla:*

*dhruṁ* ||

*mānani māi : nayanapaṅkaja jure bāri :*
*phokārave svāśā : hrāṣā bheli dehā :*
*ghana ghana dekho āndhiāri* ||

Refrain: Tears flow from the lotuslike eyes of the young woman offended with her husband through jealous pride. Heaving sighs, her body shrunk and she saw darkness all around again and again.

*pada* ||

*satinīka udava : hṛdaye dahe āgi :*
*adhika milaye manatāpe* |
*dhika ava jīvana : jovana mohe abhāgī :*
*rāgini karata bilāpe* ||
*hari hari piu meri : bairī adhika bheli*
*atave kayali apamānā* |
*dharaṇī luṭi luṭi : birapati*[28] *bālā*
*kṛṣṇa kiṅkare raṣabhāṇā* ||*dhruṁ* ||7||

Verse: Seeing the rise of the co-wife, the heart burns and the mental pain and anguish increases. "What a pity on my life and youth, unfortunate that I am!", the angry young woman went on lamenting, "Hari, my husband, has become more an enemy to me, he has insulted me so much!" Tossing and turning on the ground, the young girl lamented; says the servant of Kṛṣṇa about such emotion. Refrain.

*sūtra* ||

*devī satyabhāmā : ohi sakāruṇa bilāpa- apamāna kaye ṭhika: tadanantara : kalaha-prya nārada : punarbbāra kṛṣṇaka āgu giyā : je bolala : tāhe śunaha* ||

---

[28]. *bilapati.*

Direction: Lady Satyabhāmā, remained lamenting pitiably about her insults. After that, Nārada, who is fond of quarrels, went to Kṛṣṇa again, and what he said there, listen to that.

*nārada bola* || *āhe śrīkṛṣṇa : tuhuñ ethā kona sukhe rahaicha : se pṛyā satyabhāmā : pārijātaka nimite : apamāne annapāna saba cāḍala : parama tāpe marayiche : hāhā cakṣuye dekhite ki pāva ki nāhi pāya : deva : satvare jāva* ||
Nārada said: "Oh dear Śrī Kṛṣṇa, you are staying here with what pleasure! Because of the *pārijāta* flower, your wife Satyabhāmā, feeling insulted, has stopped having food and water and is dying of affliction. Alas, alas, you may be able to see her (alive) or you may not. Oh Lord, please go quickly."

*śloka* ||

*munervacanamākarṇya mādhavo bhaktavāndhavaḥ* |
*drutaṁ tasyā gṛhaṁ prāgāt priyāyāḥ premavihbalaḥ* ||*16*||

Hymn[29]: Hearing the words of the sage, Mādhava, the friend to His devotees, being afflicted with love for His beloved, reached her home immediately.

*sūtra* ||

*munika mukhe : pṛyāka dukha sūni : śrīkṛṣṇa premabihbala hayā : munika kātara kari kahuñ : bāta puchi : jaiche satyabhāmāka samīpa calala : tāhe dekhaha śunaha : nirantare hari bola* ||

Direction: Hearing from the sage about the sorrows of His wife, Śrī Kṛṣṇa, being afflicted with love, earnestly seeking information from the sage, as He went near Satyabhāmā, watch and listen to that and chant the name of Hari incessantly.

*gīta* || *rāga tuḍa* || *jatimāna* ||

Song in the *Rāga Tur* with the rhythm *Jatimāna:*

---

29. in *Śloka* metre.

*dhruṁ* ||

*e muni kahiyo kahiyo : kapaṭa parihari* |
*prāṇe ki jiyaya mora gunera sundarī* ||

Refrain: "Oh dear sage, please tell me please tell me, stop deceiving; is my virtuous and beautiful still alive?"

*pada* ||

*mānini nasahe tileko apamāna* |
*meri aparādhe kaiche dharaba parāṇa* ||
*pṛyāka santāpe tāpe dahe śoka āgi* |
*kuṣuma nā diyā bhelo tirībadha bhāgī* ||
*jhurāite nayana pṛyāka pāilā kola* |
*pekhi ākūla kṛṣṇa-kiṅkare bola* ||8||

Verse: "That woman, offended with her husband through jealous pride, does not tolerate dishonour the size of a sesame seed; how can she live on after the offence I have committed. My heart burns with misery in the fire of sorrow of my beloved. Not giving the flower to her, I have become a part of the woman-slaughter." To pacify the eyes (Śrī Kṛṣṇa) found His beloved near Him, and seeing (her), Kṛṣṇa became overwhelmed, says the servant of Kṛṣṇa.

*sūtra* ||

*śrīkṛṣṇa preme bihbala huyā : pṛyāka dekhala : lotake mukha malina : ghana ghana nisvāśā phokāri : māṭi luṭi raha : tāhe pekhi śrīkṛṣṇa : hā hā ki bheli boli : āṅkoāli dharala : nayanaka nīra jhurāve āśvāsa bolala* ||

*he pṛye : goṭa eka phula : rukamiṇīka delo : se nimitte yadi apamāna karaha : tabe uṭhaha : tohāka ekaśata pārijāta devaba: rukamiṇī jāmbavatī : tohāka sama sobhāginī have nāhi : toho hāmāka prāṇa sama priye : jāni tāpa tejaha : tohāri dukha dekhi hāmāra : hṛdave sahaye nāhi : priye hāmāka śapata : uṭhaha uṭhaha* ||

Direction: Being greatly overwhelmed with love, Śrī Kṛṣṇa looked at His beloved, her face stained with tears, heaving sighs again and again and lying on the ground. Seeing her in this way Śrī Kṛṣṇa, saying "Alas, alas, what has happened!", embraced her and with tears trickling down from th1e eyes, said reassuring her.

"Oh my dear wife, I have given one flower to Rukmiṇī; if you feel insulted because of that, then get up, I shall give you a hundred *pārijāta* flowers. Rukmiṇī and Jāmbavatī are not as fortunate as you. You are as dear as life for me; knowing that, give up this grief. My heart cannot bear to see your sorrow. Oh my beloved, upon my name, get up, get up."

*śloka* ||

*priyaṁ praṇayakopena niḥśvasyāha tataḥ satī* |
*dhurttālāpaiḥ durbhagāṁ māṁ kimarthaṁ tvambikatthase* ||17||

Hymn[30]: Then, with feigned anger towards her lover, heaving a sigh, the virtuous woman said, "With such cunning words why do you boast in front of me, the unfortunate."

*kathā sūtra* ||

*tadanantara : kṛṣṇaka bākya śuni devī satyabhāmā : svāmīka pithi dive kahõ : heṭha māthe : sakāruṇa krandana kave bolala* ||

*he svāmi : hāmi durbhāgāka : kapaṭa bākye kata kadarthanā karaha : je tohāra pṛyattamā rukmiṇī : tāheka samīpa calaha : hāmāta kona prayojana thika* ||

Dialogue and Direction: After that, hearing the words of Kṛṣṇa, Queen Satyabhāmā, showing her back to her husband, with downcast head, crying pitiably, said:

"Oh dear husband, with such cunning words how much do you torment unfortunate me! Go to Rukmiṇī, who is most dear to you; what need is there for me!"

---

30. in *Śloka* metre , but in the 3rd foot, the 5th letter is long instead of short and the 6th letter is short instead of long.

*sūtra* ||

*ohi boli bahuta bilāpa kaya : kṛṣṇaka je bolala : tāhe dekhaha śunaha : nirantare hari bola* ||

Direction: Saying so, crying a lot, what she said to Kṛṣṇa, watch and listen to that and keep chanting the name of Hari incessantly.

*gīta* || *rāga śrīgāndhāra* || *jatitāla* ||
Song in the *Rāga Śrīgāndhāra* with *Jatitāla:*

*dhruṁ* ||

*keśava he bujhalahuñ tuhu : jānalohõ toho beyahārā*
*atave cāturī cori : calahu bahuri harie :*
*jāhā pṛyā ramaṇī tohārā* ||

Refrain: "Oh Keśava, I have understood you, (I) have come to know your behaviour! Now leaving this much of your shrewdness, oh Hari, you go back there, where your beloved wife is."

*pada* ||

*tohāri kapaṭa kṛṣṇa : nābujhi mānalo hāmu :*
*nāhi sobhāginī sama moi* |
*jaichena pirīti rīti : sabahi bidita bhelire :*
*āju jānalo moti toi* ||
*ohi apamāne prāṇa : nāhi dharaba hāmu re :*
*coḍala jīvanaka āśā* |
*āgu piuka paḍi : bahu bilapati bālā re :*
*kahatu śaṅkara haridāsā* ||9||

Verse: "Oh Kṛṣṇa, not understanding your deceit, I believed that there is no one as fortunate as I am; as is your practice of love, known to all; but today only I have come to know your mind. After such dishonour, I cannot live on any more; I have given up hope for my life." Falling down in front of her husband, the young girl lamented a lot, says Śaṅkara, the servant of Hari.

*kathā* ||

*devī bola* || *he svāmi : hāmu durbhāgā : satinīka adhīna tuhu : hāmāka kataye bikarthanā karaha : ohi apamāne : hāmuprāṇa rākhaba : aḥ : taba hāmāka jīvana dhika dhika* ||

Dialogue: The queen said, "Oh dear husband, I am the unfortunate one, under (the shadow of) a co-wife, and you chastise me so much. Even after that dishonour, shall I hold on to this life? What a shame on my life then!"

*sūtra* ||

*ohi buli devī : kāndi kāndi murcchita hayā paḍala* ||

Direction: Saying so, the lady, crying a lot, fell down unconscious.

*śloka* ||

*kurbbana*[31] *hāhāravaṁ rāmāmāliṅgyākulamānasaḥ* |
*priyabākyaistataḥ sādhvīṁ sāntvayāmāsa mādhavaḥ*||*18*||

Hymn[32]: Wailing loudly, Mādhava, greatly afflicted, embracing His beloved, consoled the virtuous woman with loving words.

*kathā* ||

*tāhe dekhi śrīkṛṣṇa : hāhā boli bāhu meli dharala : pṛyāka dukha dekhive marama caḍala : kamala : nayanaka nīra jhurāve : preme prabodha bolala* ||

Dialogue: Seeing that, Śrī Kṛṣṇa, greatly lamenting, held her extending His arms; seeing the suffering of His wife, His love (for her) increased. With tears flowing down from the lotus like eyes, said, consoling her lovingly.

---

31. *kurbban.*

32. in *Śloka* metre.

*payāḍa* ||

*pṛyāka dukha dekhi nasahe śarīra* |
*kamala nayana bhari jhuri bahe nīra* ||
*ālāṅgi pṛyāka cāpi dhari kola* |
*kari āsvāśā bacana hari bola* ||1||
*he he prāṇa-pṛyā śuna bāta* |
*delahuṅ nāhi tohõ pārijāta* ||
*ata aparādha sahaba aba moi* |
*tuyā sama sobhāginī nāhi koi* ||2||
*rukamiṇīka delo goṭā eka phula* |
*tāheka lāgi tuhuṅ atave ākula* ||
*pārijāta taru samūli upāri* |
*ropaṇa kayaba āni tuyā bārī* ||3||
*jaba mohi bākya nāhi patiāyā* |
*kahalū satya satya śuna jāyā* ||
*aba tejahuṅ tāpa kumārī* |
*nasahe hṛdi dukha dekhi tohāri* ||4||
*hāmākū śapata kheḍa lahu māthe* |
*uṭhaha uṭhaha pṛyā teri dharu hāte* ||
*kara kākūti nati jagatara īśa* |
*ramaṇīka mane kicho milala hariṣa* ||5||
*parama īśvara kara kātara pṛyāka* |
*dekhu adabhuta bhakati mahimāka* ||
*brahmā maheśa jāka karu sevā* |
*māthe kheḍa moḍala sohi devā* ||6||
*kṛṣṇaka līlā bujhaye nāhi pāri* |
*punnakāma hari ki karaba nārī* ||
*bhakati kayali harika mana bhola* |
*jāni karaha nara hari hari rola*[33] ||7||10||

Verse: "My body cannot bear to see the suffering of my beloved."; tears flow down from the lotuslike eyes filled with tears. Embracing His beloved and bringing her closer, Hari said consoling words. (1)

---

33. *bola.*

"Oh my wife, dear like my life, listen to me; I have not given you the *pārijāta* flower. Please bear this much of my offence. There is no one as fortunate as you are. (2)
"I have given Rukmiṇī only one flower, and you have become so much disturbed because of that. Now uprooting the whole Pārijāta plant, we will replant it in your garden. (3)
"If you do not believe in my words, I promise to be true to my words, hear oh dear wife. Now, please stop grieving, oh dear young girl; my heart cannot bear to see your distress. (4)
"Upon my name, here I take a straw on my head; please rise, please rise, oh dear wife, I hold you by your hand." Thus, entreated the Lord of the world and the lovely young woman had some happiness. (5)
The Supreme Lord entreated His wife. See how great is the power of devotion. The one who is worshipped by even Brahmā and Maheśa, that same God is holding straw on His head. (6)
Cannot understand the pastime of Kṛṣṇa. Hari, who fulfills all the wishes, what will He do with the woman? Devotion has made His mind forget everything; knowing that, all the men, utter aloud the name of Hari again and again. (7)

*sūtra* ||

*tadanantara : sakhī indumatī bola* ||
*he prāṇasakhī : parama īśvara tohāri svāmī : māthe kheḍa dharu : ataye kātara karachai : āra kona māna sādhite rahala : sakhī tāpa tejaha : uṭhaha uṭhaha* ||
*devī svāmīka atave binaya bāṇī śuni kahu : kiñcita citta śānta bhaila : śrīkṛṣṇa tāhe dekhi : yālāṅgi toli : baiṭhāyala : pīta bastre śarīraka dhūli jhāḍala : keśa bāndhara*[34]*: nija haste kappula-tāmbula bhuñjāvala* ||

Direction: After that, friend Indumatī said:

[34]. *bāndhala.*

"Oh friend, dear like life, the Supreme Lord is your husband; holding a straw on the head, He is entreating you so much. What other way He can show you respect. Oh dear friend, give up this grief, and get up, get up."

Hearing such humble words from her husband, her mind calmed down a little; Śrī Kṛṣṇa, seeing her, raised her up embracing and made her sit; jerked off the dust from her body with His yellow clothing, tied up her hair and fed her betelnut and camphor with His own hands.

*śloka* ||

*tato devī satyabhāmā kṛṣṇabākyāmṛtena sā* |
*prītā prasannavadanā praṇamyāha priyaṁ harim* ||*19*||

Hymn[35]: Then, hearing the sweet words of Kṛṣṇa, being very pleased, Queen Satyabhāmā, offering obeisance to her husband Hari, with a happy countenance, said:

*sūtra* ||

*devī svāmīta mahāmāna labhiye : āti prasannamukhī hayā : śrīkṛṣṇaka pranami bolala* ||

Direction: Having received great honour from her husband, the Queen, offering obeisance to Śrī Kṛṣṇa with a happy countenance, said:

*he svāmi : hāmāka pārijāta taru dite : tuhu satya kavala : jāni bilamba coḍi : ei kṣaṇe āniyā deva : jāve pārijāta nāhi dekhu : tāve bāri prabeśo nāhi : hāmu satya kave bolalu* ||

"Oh dear husband, you have promised to give me the *pārijāta* tree; knowing that, avoiding delay, please bring it this very moment. As long as I do not see the *pārijāta*, I shall not enter home till then, and I speak the truth."

---

35. in *Śloka* metre , but in the 1st foot, the 5th letter is long instead of short and the 6th letter is short instead of long. Again in the 3rd foot, the 6th and 7th letters are short instead of long.

*kṛṣṇa bola || he priye : pāpī narakāsure : devatāsabaka jiniye : sarbbasva ānala : āgu tāhe māri : devakārya sādhu : pācu pārijāta āno ||*
Kṛṣṇa said, "Oh dear wife, the sinner Narakāsura, defeating the demigods has taken away everything from them. First by killing him, let me do the service to the gods and after that I shall bring the *pārijāta.*"

*devī bola || aḥ svāmi : uchita kahala : āgu devakārya sādhi : sohi yātrāye pārijāta ānaha : hāmu tohāra saṅge calaba ||*
The queen said, "Oh dear husband, well said; first finishing the service to the gods, bring the *pārijāta* in the same trip and I shall come along with you."

*kṛṣṇa bola || he priye : tuhuñ strījāti : yuddhaka samave tohāri gamana uchita nahe ||*
Kṛṣṇa said, "Oh dear wife, it is not proper for you, a woman class, to go at the time of war".

*devī bola || he svāmi : hāmāra bahuta satinī : ibāra pārijāta āni kona strīka devaba : tāhe bujhaye nāhi : hāmu kadācitu tohāri saṅga nāhi cāraba ||*
The Queen said, "Oh dear husband, I have many co-wives; bringing the *pārijāta*, which woman you will give it to this time, I do not know. (Therefore) I shall never leave your company."

*kṛṣṇa bola || he priye : tuhuñ jadi hāmāra saṅge calaba : taba satvare sājaha ||*
Kṛṣṇa said: "Oh dear wife, if you want to go with me, then get dressed quickly."

*śloka ||*

*kṛṣṇamabhyetya bhagavān jagāda nāradastadā |*
*jñātaṁ kila bhavān bhāryābhakti-sakto'si keśava ||20||*

Hymn[36]: Coming near Kṛṣṇa, Nārada, then told God, "As it is known oh Keśava, you are indeed strongly attached to your wife."

*kathā* ||

*nāradaḥ sakrodhamāha* ||

*he kṛṣṇa : jānala tuhuñ strīka lāḍikā : devakāryasaba pari rahala : tohāra bhāryāka cāṭu bulite saba dibasa gaila* ||

Dialogue: Nārada said with great anger:

"Oh Kṛṣṇa,I have come to know that you are under the control of your wife. All the services towards the gods are lying undone and the whole day is passed in coaxing your wife."

*śrīkṛṣṇa bola* || *ye munirāja : strī bujhave menā jujheka : ki karaba kūmārika hāta eḍāite pārave nāhi : he munirāja : e chalaicho : krodha nāhi karabi*||

Śrī Kṛṣṇa said: "Oh king of the sages, the womenfolk fight stubbornly without understanding. What to do, could not let go of the hand of the young girl. Oh king amongst the sages, I am going right now, please do not be angry."

*sūtra* ||

*ohi buli śrīkṛṣṇa āti satvare : yātrā kaya calala* ||

Direction: Saying so, Śrī Kṛṣṇa, started on His journey immediately.

*śloka* ||

*saharṣamakarot kṛṣṇaḥ prayāṇaṁ priyayā saha* |
*dhanuṣṭaṅkāraghoṣeṇa daśadiśaḥ prakampayan* ||21||

Hymn[37]: Shaking the ten directions with the sound of the twanging of the bow, Kṛṣṇa started on His journey happily along with His wife.

---

36. in *Śloka* metre, but in the 1st foot, the 6th and 7th letters are short instead of long.

37. in *Śloka* metre.

*kathā* ||

*śrīkṛṣṇa dhanu ṭaṅkāre daśodiśa kampāi : pṛyā sahita jaice payāna kayala : tāhe dekhaha śunaha : nirantare hari bola* ||

Dialogue: Making all the ten directions tremble with the twanging of the bow, as Śrī Kṛṣṇa along with His wife started on His journey, watch and listen to that and keep chanting the name of Hari incessantly.

*gīta* || *rāga-māura dhanaśrī* || *ekatāli* ||

Song in the *Rāga-Māhura Dhanaśrī* with the rhythm *Ekatāli*:

*dhruṁ* ||

*kayali payāna yadurāi* |
*kare śāraṅga saṅge pṛyā cali jāi* ||

Refrain: The king of Yadu dynasty started on His journey holding a bow in His hand and along went His wife.

*pada* ||

*śyāmala aṅga suraṅga pītabāsā* |
*bijurī ujala naya ghana parakāśā* ||
*aruṇa caraṇa mañjīra karu rola* |
*tāhe majoka mana śaṅkare bola* ||11||

Verse: The dark blue body with the beautiful yellow colour clothing, is shining like the lightning on newly formed dark cloud and the anklets tinkling on the red feet; let our minds be engrossed in them, says Śaṅkara.

*kathā* ||

*śrīkṛṣṇa ōhi prakāre piyā sahita : prayāne calachai : se samaye nārada āsi bola* ||

Dialogue: In this way Śrī Kṛṣṇa, along with His wife started on His journey. At that moment Nārada, coming there, said:

*he hare : tohō sama strī-jīta puruṣa : kabaho nā dekhi : yuddhaka samave strīka coraye nāhi pāra : tuhuñ jagata-guru : tohāka jaṣa gāi : tinivo lokaka beḍāñeñ : aḥ hāmāka lāja bhaila* ||

"Oh Hari, I have never seen a man won over by a woman as you; you cannot leave behind your wife even at the time of war. You are the Lord of the world; singing your praises, I wander about in the three worlds; oh, now I shall be ashamed."

*kṛṣṇa bola* || *he munirāja : ki karaba : pārijāta nimitta : satyabhāmā prāṇa cāḍaya : unikara narbandha kata sahabo* ||

Kṛṣṇa said, "Oh great sage, what to do; Satyabhāmā was giving up her life because of the *pārijāta*; how much of her persistence can I tolerate?"

*muni bola* || *he kṛṣṇa : kāmātura puruṣaka aichana avasthā : strī je ājñā kare : se avaśye karite lāge : se hoka : se kāmarūpa narakāsuraka pāṭa : ohi dvārikā hante svabhāve māsa cārika patha : strī layā jāhite basvara dui cāri pāvava : aḥ devakārya bhalla satvara sādhala : eka karmma karaha : tohāka bāhana garuḍa pakṣīrāja : tāheka ājñā karaha : tāhera kandhe caḍiye : satvara narakāsuraka māraha* ||

The sage said, "Oh Kṛṣṇa, such is the condition of a lovelorn man; whatever the woman commands, he has to do that; may it be Kāmarūpa, the city of Narakāsura, which is naturally four months way from Dvārikā; but taking along your wife, we shall reach there only after two to four years! Oh you have very well performed your duties towards the gods! Do one thing, command your vehicle, the king of the birds, Garuḍa, and riding on his shoulder kill Narakāsura immediately."

*sūtra* ||

*munika bāṇī śuni : śrīkṛṣṇa pṛyāka bolala* ||
*he pṛye : muni bhalla lahala*[38]||

Direction: Hearing the words of the sage, Śrī Kṛṣṇa said to His wife, "Oh dear wife, the sage speaks well."

*devī bola* || *he svāmi : hāmito pāve hāṭhite pārave nāhi* ||
The queen said, "Oh dear husband, I cannot walk".

*tā śuni śrīkṛṣṇa bāhanaka smarala* || *āhe gaḍura pakṣīrāja : satvare āva satvare āva* |
Hearing that Śrī Kṛṣṇa called for His vehicle, "Oh the king of the birds Garuḍa, come quickly, come quickly."

*śloka* ||

*āha cāgatya garuḍo natvā kṛṣṇaṁ kṛtāñjaliḥ* |
*mama skandhaṁ samāruhya jahi bhaumaṁ durāśayam* ||22||

Hymn[39]: Garuḍa, coming there, bowing to Kṛṣṇa and supplicating with folded hands said, "Riding on my shoulder kill the wicked son of the earth (Narakāsura)".

*kathā* ||

*garuḍa bola* || *he svāmi : hāmu thākite tohõ pāve beḍāvaba : aḥ hāmāra kandhe caḍi : pāpī narakāsura badha giyā* ||

Dialogue: Garuḍa said, "Oh master, when I am here , how can you walk on foot; riding on my shoulder, (you can) go and kill the sinner Narakāsura."

*tadanantara : śrīkṛṣṇa sabhāry gaḍura kandhe caḍi : parama līlāye calali*||
After that Śrī Kṛṣṇa, riding on the shoulder of Garuḍa along with His wife, went with pleasure.

---

38. *kahala.*

39. in *Śloka* metre , but in the 1st foot, the 6th and 7th letters are short instead of long.

*śloka* ||

*prāgjyotiṣaṁ sohati*[40] *javena jāyayā*
*suparṇamāruhya yayau janārddanaḥ* |
*kṣaṇena samprāpya puraṁ pareśo*
*mahotsavaiḥ śaṅkharavaṁ cakāra*||23||

Hymn[41]: Riding on the divine bird, Janārdana, along with His wife went to Prāgjyotiṣa very fast and reaching the city soon blowed His conch-shell with great pleasure.

*kathā* ||

*śrīkṛṣṇa gaḍurabāhane bāyubege kāmarūpa pāi : pāñcajanya dhūni kayala : tāhe śuni narakāsura khedi āvala : śrīkṛṣṇa tāheka jaiche badha kayala : tāhe dekhaha śunaha : nirantare haribola* ||

Dialogue: Śrī Kṛṣṇa, reaching Kāmrūpa with the speed of the wind by the vehicle Garuḍa, blowed on the Pāñcajanya. Hearing that, Narakāsura came chasing and how Śrī Kṛṣṇa killed him, watch and listen to that and keep chanting the name of Hari incessantly.

*payāra* || *rāga kānaḍā* ||

Verse in the *Rāga Kānaḍā:*

*calali govinda garuḍaka kandhe* |
*naraka mārite kayali prabandhe* ||
*bāyuka bege calali pakṣīrāja* |
*tileka pāyala kāmarūparāja* ||*1*||
*phuṅkala śaṅkha hari bāre bāre* |
*śuni śatruka bhaila hṛdaya bidāre* ||
*jānalu āvala mādhava dhāi* |
*garaje dānava yuddhaka lāi* ||2||
*samaraka sāji bajāvaya ḍhola* |
*dhara dhara māra māra kare bahu rola* ||

40. *so'ti*

41. in *Upajāti*, as *Vaṁśasthavila* metre, in the 1st two lines ; but in the 1st foot, the 1st letter is long instead of short. The later two lines are in the *Upendravajrā* metre.

*dhāve mura narakāsura rāgi |*
*khāṇḍā phiṅkāyava kṛṣṇaka lāgi ||3||*
*hari ṭaṅkāvala śāraṅga bhiḍi |*
*bariṣila bāṇa daityakahõ pīḍi ||*
*kāṭala kāhu kandhakara śira |*
*mārala hari saba dānava bīra ||4||*
*pekhi palāvata dānaba asura |*
*bāṇa prahārive morala mura ||*
*kope cakra khepi jaganātha |*
*kāṭala dāruṇa naraka mātha ||5||*
*dekhi devaka uruka bahula |*
*bāve dundubhi bariṣaya phula ||*
*java java yādava kare bahu rola |*
*samājika saba hari hari bola ||6||12||*

Govinda went riding on the shoulder of Garuḍa and arranged to kill Narakāsura. The bird moved with the speed of the wind and reached the kingdom of Kāmarūpa. (1)
Hari blew the conch shell again and again, and hearing that, the heart of His enemy tore apart and he knew that Mādhava had come running chasing him, the demon thundered with wrath, for war. (2)
Preparing for war, played the drum and made great uproar uttering "Catch, catch, kill, kill!". Being very angry, Mura and Narakāsura ran holding their daggers high up aiming at Kṛṣṇa. (3)
Bending and twanging the bow Śāraṅga, Hari showered the demons with arrows pressing them. Cut the shoulder, hands and head of some and killed all the great warrior demons. (4)
Seeing that, all the evil spirits and demons fled away. Striking with arrows (Kṛṣṇa) killed Mura. Searching for His disc with great anger, Jagannātha beheaded the terrible (demon) Naraka. (5)

Seeing the God all the people became very happy and played the divine drum and showered flowers, and made great uproar uttering "Glory to the descendant of Yadu!" again and again. All the assembled people, please utter the name of Hari again and again. (6)

*kathā* ||

*se mura narakaka māri kahu : śrīkṛṣṇa yaśa sādhala : dekhi devasaba ānande dundubhi bājāi : jaya kṛṣṇa jaya boli : śira kusuma barikhala : śrīkṛṣṇa sabhārye ānande rahala* ||

Dialogue: Killing those Mura and Naraka, Śrī Kṛṣṇa earned fame. Seeing that all the gods played the divine drum with great happiness and saying "Glory to Kṛṣṇa, glory to Kṛṣṇa!", showered flowers on His head and Śrī Kṛṣṇa, along with His wife, remained very happy .

*śloka* ||

*tato vasumatī pautraṁ puraḥ sthāpya hatātmajā* |
*vilapantī tadā kṛṣṇaṁ natvā provāca duḥkhitā* ||24||

Hymn[42]: Then Vasumatī, placing her grandson in the front, cried a lot losing her son. Then, offering obeisance to Kṛṣṇa, the sad woman said.

*kathā* ||

*naraka putra badha bhaila : dekhi basumatī : parama santāpe : tāheka putra bhagadatta śiśuka āga kaya kahõ : kṛṣṇa daraśana nimitta jaiche calali : āhe loka : tāhe dekhaha śunaha nirantare hari bola* ||

Dialogue: Seeing her son Naraka dead, keeping his child Bhagadatta in her front, as Vasumatī, with great distress, went to meet Kṛṣṇa, oh dear people watch and listen to that and keep chanting the name of Hari incessantly.

*gīta* || *rāga-māura dhanaśrī* || *ekatāli* ||

Song in the *Rāga-Māhura Dhanaśrī* with the rhythm *Ekatāli*:

---

[42]. in *Śloka* metre.

*dhruṁ* ||

*piuka samīpa cale māi : hari daraśana cale māi*[43] |
*śiśu same basumatī : lahu lahu gati jāi* ||

Refrain: The mother goes to her Lord, to see Hari goes the mother. Along with the child, Vasumatī moves very slowly.

*pada* ||

*sutaka santāpe tanu bheli hrāṣā* |
*lotake lepita mukha phokāre nisvāśā* ||
*svāmīka karu pāva pari paraṇāma* |
*kahatu śaṅkara gati meri rāma* ||13||

Verse: With grief for her son, her body thinned down. With her face smeared with tears, breathed out sighs falling down on the feet of her Lord, offered obeisance. "The ultimate refuge for me is Rāma.", says Śaṅkara.

*katha* ||

*aicana śiśu same basumatī āsi kahu : śrīkṛṣṇaka pari paraṇāmi : karajuḍi bolala* ||

Dialogue: In this way, coming along with the child, Vasumatī, lying down, offered obeisance to Śrī Kṛṣṇa and said with folded hands.

*he svāmi śrīkṛṣṇa : koṭi koṭi brahmāṇḍeśvara : parama puruṣa puruṣottama : tuhuñ jagata guru : tohāka droha kari : pāpī putra naraka : nija pāpe nāśa gaila : tāhāka putra : ohi śiśu bhagadatta nātika tohāra pāve samarpala āheka rakṣā karaha : hāmāra santati rahoka : tohāri caraṇa-paṅkaje kātara kaye : atave prasāda māgu gosāñi* ||

"Oh Lord Śrī Kṛṣṇa, master of crores of universe, the highest, the Supreme Personality, you are the father of the world. Rebelling against you, my sinner son Naraka has met with his destruction because of his own sin. This child is his son Bhagadatta, my grandson, and I am handing him over at

---

[43]. *lāi*.

your feet; please save him, so that our family continues. Beseeching at your lotus-feet I seek only this much blessing from you, oh God."

*sūtra* ||

*ohi boli basumatī : bahuta bilāpa śrīkṛṣṇaka āgu kayala : aichana karunā*[44] *bāṇī śuni nārāyaṇa : basumatīka āśvāsa kaya bolala* ||

Direction: Saying so, Vasumatī lamented a lot before Śrī Kṛṣṇa. Hearing such pitiful words, Nārāyaṇa said consoling Vasumatī.

*āhe basumatī : toho tāpa tejaha : tohāri putra narakāsura bhūmika bhāra bheli : se nimite ihāka māri : tohāri bhāra dūra kayala : tohāra bacane ohi bhagadatta śiśuka kāmarūpa pāṭe rājā pātaba : tuhõ chintā nāhi karabi* ||

"Oh dear Vasumatī, stop grieving. Your son Narakāsura had become burden to the earth; that is why, killing him, (I have) removed the burden from you. Upon your words, I shall make that child Bhagadatta, the King of the Kingdom of Kāmarūpa; you please do not worry."

*ohi buli śrīkṛṣṇa basumatīka ālāṅgi āsvāsive antaspura praveśi kahõ : bhagadattaka rājya abhiṣeka kayala : soḍasa hājāra kanyā tāhera bārita pāi : dvārakāpura paṭhāvala : aditika kūṇḍala : baruṇaka catra : maṇi parbbata layā : garuḍaka kandhe : satyabhāmā same svargaka kautuke calala* ||

Saying so, Śrī Kṛṣṇa embracing Vasumatī, consoled her and entering the inner apartments of the palace, performed the coronation ceremony of Bhagadatta. Finding 16,000 young girls at his home sent them to the city of Dwārakā. And taking along the ear-rings of Aditi, the umbrella of Varuṇa, and the mount Maṇi, riding on the shoulder of Garuḍa along with Satyabhāmā, went to heaven with great pleasure.

---

44. *karuṇa.*

*śloka* ||

*tataḥ svargasannikaṭaṁ dṛṣṭvā kṛṣṇo mudāyutaḥ* |
*dadhmau śaṅkhaṁ pāñcajanyaṁ harṣayandivi devatāḥ* ||25||

Hymn[45]: Then, seeing heaven very near, Kṛṣṇa with great happiness blowed the conch shell, Pāñcajanya, making the gods in heaven very happy.

*kathā* ||

*mura narakāsura māri : śrīkṛṣṇa svarga samīpa pāi : paramānande śaṅkhadhūni kayala : dhūni śuni jānala : devatāsaba : aḥ hāmāri svargaka lāgi : śrīkṛṣṇa āvala : parama hariṣe jaya jaya boli : dundubhi bājāi : śira kusuma bariṣila : tāhe pekhi satyabhāmā piuta puchata* ||

Dialogue: Killing Mura and Narakāsura, Śrī Kṛṣṇa, reaching near heaven, blowed the conch-shell with great pleasure. Hearing the sound, all the gods came to know that Śrī Kṛṣṇa had come to heaven and with great pleasure uttering "May you be glorious, may you be glorious", played the divine drum and showered flowers on His head. Seeing that, Satyabhāmā asked her husband.

*āhe svāmi : ohi kona sthāna pāvala hāmu : je dundubhi bajāi : kusuma bariṣe : esaba ke : hāmāku paricaya karāya* ||

"Oh dear husband, which place have we reached? Who are these people who are playing the divine drum and showering flowers? Please introduce me to them" .

*śloka* ||

*kṛṣṇaḥprāha priyāṁ paśya imāmamrāvatīpurīm* |
*āgatā devatā etāstvāṁ māṁ devi didṛkṣayā* ||26||

Hymn[46]: Kṛṣṇa said to His beloved wife, "Look, this is the city of Amrāvatī; these gods have come here to see me and you, oh Queen."

---

45. in *Śloka* metre, but in the 2nd foot, the 5th letter is long instead of short and the 6th letter is short instead of long.

46. in *Śloka* metre.

*kathā* ||

*(kṛṣṇaḥ bola) he devī : tuhu nāhi jānaha : ohi amrāvatī pūri : ehi devatāsaba hāmāka dekhite āvala : dekho ohi airāvata kandhe bāsava thika : unikara mahādevī ohi śacī : aisaba digapāla : siddha bidādhara* ||

Dialogue: Kṛṣṇa said, "Oh Queen, you do not know; this is the city of Amrāvatī, these gods have come to see us. See, one who is on the shoulder of Airāvata is Vāsava, and there is his Chief Queen Śacī. These are the *dik-pālas, siddhas* and *vidyādharas.*

*devī punu puchala* || *he svāmi : je bimānaka upare :prakāśa karaiche : ohi kona bṛkṣa* ||

The queen asked again, "Oh Lord, what is that tree which is shining over the palace?"

*kṛṣṇa bola* || *he priye : nāhi jānaha : jāhera nimitta mānini haichai : se pārijāta taru ohi* ||

Kṛṣṇa said, "Oh my love, don't you know? For which there is so much of turmoil, it is that same *pārijāta* tree."

*devī harṣamāha* || *aḥ hāmāra manoratha sāphala bhaila : ohi pārijāta puspa dharive : satinīsabaka māje : lāsabeśa kari beḍāvaba : he svāmi satvara karo* ||

The queen said smiling, "Oh, my wishes are fulfilled! Holding that *pārijāta* flower (in hand), I shall move about luxuriously attired among the co-wives. Oh dear husband, be quick."

*śloka* ||

*tato'ti kautukaṁ dṛṣṭvā indra āgatya sādaram* |
*dorbhyāṁ devaṁ pariṣvajya jagāda madhuraṁ vacaḥ* ||27||

Hymn[47]: Then, seeing the great eagerness, Indra approaching with respect and worshipping the God with both his arms, spoke sweet words.

---

[47]. in *Śloka* metre.

*kathā* ||

*tadanantara : indra āsi kahuñ : gaurave kṛṣṇaka dharala : śacī satyabhāmāka ālāṅgi satakāra kayala* ||

Dialogue: After that, Indra, coming there, held Kṛṣṇa with great regard; Śacī also embracing Satyabhāmā, welcomed her.

*indra bola* || *he śrīkṛṣṇa : pāpī narakāsuraka māri : hāmāka kṛtārtha kayala : bāra bāra tuhuñ uddhāra karaha : tohāka guṇa sujhave nāhi pāri* || *ohi buli premalotaka jhurave : indra maune rahala* ||

Indra said, "Oh dear Śrī Kṛṣṇa, killing the sinner Narakāsura, you have made us satisfied. You save us again and again and we can never repay your virtues." Saying so, trickling down tears of love, Indra remained silent.

*śloka* ||

*aditiṁ mātaraṁ paścāt sabhāryo jagadīśvaraḥ* |
*praṇamya devamātre'dādamṛtasrāvikuṇḍale* ||28||

Hymn[48]: After that, the lord of the world, along with His wife offered obeisance to mother Aditi and gave away the earrings which shower immortality, to the mother of Indra.

*kathā* ||

*tadanantara : śrīkṛṣṇa indra sahita : aditi mātṛka praṇāma kave kahuñ : amṛta kuṇḍala doho nibedala : śacī sahita satyabhāmā aditi svasuka jānupāri praṇāma kayala* ||

Dialogue: After that, Śrī Kṛṣṇa along with Indra, offering obeisance to mother Aditi, delivered the two earrings, which shower immortality, to her. Śacī, along with Satyabhāmā, offered obeisance to Aditi, her mother-in-law, on her knees.

*śloka* ||

*tataḥ sā devajananī kṛṣṇaṁ matvā maheśvaram* |
*baddhāñjaliḥ jagannāthaṁ stūtau devī manodadhe* ||29||

---

[48]. in *Śloka* metre.

Hymn[49]: Then the mother of Indra, understanding Kṛṣṇa to be the Supreme God, supplicating with folded hands together, concentrated on praying to Jagannātha.

*kathā* ||

*aditi śrīkṛṣṇaka parama īśvara jānive : jaice tuti ārambhala : tāhe dekhaha śunaha : nirantare hari bola* ||

Direction: Knowing Śrī Kṛṣṇa to be the Supreme God, as Aditi started praying, watch and listen to that and keep chanting the name of Hari incessantly.

*payāḍa* ||

*jaya jaya jagata-nibāsā* |
*jaya jaya asura-bināśā* ||
*jaya cedaka bhaya-pāṣā* |
*jaya tāraka nija dāsā* ||
*jaya jaya īśvara murāri* |
*jaya jaya asura-saṁhārī* ||
*jaya jaya śāraṅgadhārī* |
*jaya jaya brahma-adhikārī*[50] ||
*jaya jaya jagataka dhātā* |
*jaya jaya pāteka- ghātā* ||
*jaya jaya bhṛtaka trātā* |
*jaya jaya mukūti-dātā* ||
*jaya jaya yādava rāmā* |
*jaya jaladhara tanu-syāmā* ||
*jaya jaya pūrala manakāma* |
*jaya bhaya-tāreka nāma* ||
*karu karunā yadurāi* |
*lelõ śaraṇa tuyā pāi* ||
*parama puruṣa karu trānā* |
*tuyā bine gati nāhi ānā* ||
*bhava- bandhana coḍa meri* |
*kara ohi tuti kara yoḍi* ||

---

[49]. in *Śloka* metre, but in the 1st foot, the 6th and 7th letters are short instead of long.

[50]. *avikārī*.

*kayali pari paraṇāma* |
*sabahi bolahu rāmarāma* ||*14*||

Verse: "Glory to the one, whose abode is the whole world; glory to the one, who is the destroyer of the demons. Glory to the one, who tears away the bindings of this world; glory to the one, who protects His servants.

"Glory to the Almighty God Murāri; glory to the destroyer of the demons. Glory to the one, who bears the bow Śāraṅga; glory to the Supreme Spirit which is always constant.

"Glory to the creator of the world; glory to the destroyer of the sinners. Glory to the one, who protects His servants; glory to the one, who grants liberation.

"Glory to the member of the Yadu dynasty, who is (also) Rāma; glory to the one, whose body is dark like the cloud. Glory to the one, who fulfills all desires of the mind; glory to the one, (uttering) whose name can protect one from all the fears.

"Please have mercy, oh king of Yadus; here I take refuge at your feet. Oh you Supreme Personality, please save us; there is no way to salvation other than you.

"Please make me free from the worldly bondage; that is all I pray for with folded hands." (Thus Aditi), falling down, offered obeisance. "All of you please chant 'Rāma, Rāma!'."

*śloka* ||

*ādityā īśvarajñanaṁ niśamya madhusūdanaḥ* |
*mohanārthaṁ nijamāyāṁ tatāna janamohanīṁ* ||30||

Hymn[51]: Seeing Aditi's awareness of God, Madhusūdana, with an intention of fascinating her, spread out His enchantment which mesmerises all the people.

*kathāsūtra* ||

*tadantara : aditika īśvarajñāna dekhiye : baiṣṇabimāyā bistāri : aditika mana mohita kariye : śrīkṛṣṇa karayori : praṇāma kaya bolala* ||

[51]. in *Śloka* metre.

Dialogue and Direction: After that, seeing Aditi's knowledge of God, spreading out the illusion of Viṣṇu, fascinating the mind of Aditi, Śrī Kṛṣṇa, with folded hands, offering obeisance said:

*he mātā : tuheñ hāmāra parama devatā : āmāka sarbbathā āśīrbbāda karabi* ||
"Oh mother, you are the highest deity for me; please bless me always."

*aditi śunikahuñ parama sakāruṇa cite : kṛṣṇaka gale dhari kahuñ : bulite lāgala* ||
Hearing that, Aditi, with a very merciful mind, holding on to the neck of Kṛṣṇa, started saying.

*he putā : tuhuñ cirañjīva hava : hāmāka baradāne devatā-asure tohāka jinive nāhi pāraba* ||
"Oh dear son, may you live for ever; with my blessings, no god or demon will ever be able to defeat you."

*tadantara : śrīkṛṣṇa devīta bidāya kayala : baruṇaka chatra : maṇiparbbata : indraka hāte samappala : devatāsavata bidāva kari kahõ : nārada sahite sabhārye parivarti jaiche calala : tāhe dekhaha śunaha : nirantare hari bola* ||
After that Śrī Kṛṣṇa, took leave of the divine lady and gave back the umbrella of Varuṇa and the Maṇiparbbata in the hands of Indra. Bidding farewell to all the demigods, along with His wife and Nārada as He moved on returning, watch and listen to that and keep chanting the name of Hari.

*gīta* || *rāga-gaurī* || *jati tāla* ||
Song in the *Rāga-Gaurī* with the rhythm *Jatitāla:*

*dhruṁ* ||

*līlāgati jāi : bhubana bhulāi : madhura mūruti murāri | layalāse cale raṅge : saṅgihi bara nārī* ||

Refrain: Moving with pleasure, making the whole world forget everything, the beautiful form of Murāri moved happily with graceful manner and along went the beautiful woman.

*pada* ||

*ure banamālā : māṇika maṇi : bayana īṣata hāṣā | naya jaladhara sobhā tanu pīta ambara bhāṣā || padapaṅkaja : mañjīra jala : pallava parakāṣā | bhakati mukūti hetu : kahatu keśava dāsā* ||15||

Verse: The garland of woodflower and the string of ruby fluttered and a soft smile played on the face; the dark body like the newly formed cloud was adorned with yellow coloured clothing. The anklets on the lotuslike feet looked bright like a bud under the water. Says the servant of Keśava, for the deliverance of the devotees.

*kathā* ||

*aicana madhuru mūruti śrīkṛṣṇa : parama līlāgati : svargabāsīka mana mohi kautuke calala | tadanantara je kathā bhela : tāhe dekhaha śunaha : nirantare hari bola* ||

Dialogue: Such a sweet form was Śrī Kṛṣṇa, (who) with much grace, fascinating the minds of the dwellers of heaven, moved on happily. What happened after that, watch and listen to that and keep chanting the name of Hari incessantly.

*śloka* ||

*dhṛtvā bastre patiṁ prāha satī roṣasamānvitā* |
*kva yāsi pārijātaṁ tvaṁ nānīya madhusūdana* ||31||

Hymn[52]:

Holding on to the clothing of her husband, the chaste woman spoke with anger, "Oh Madhusūdana, where are you going without taking the *pārijāta*?".

*kathā* ||

*tadanantara : devī satyabhāmā : kṣṇaka pīta bastre dhari kahõ : mahākrodha huyā bolala* ||

Dialogue: After that, the divine lady Satyabhāmā, holding on to the yellow clothing of Kṛṣṇa, said with great anger.

*he svāmi : tuhuñ bhalla satya kayala : pārijāta nālayā : tuhuñ kāhā jāva : tohāka citta bujhave nāhi* ||

"Oh dear husband, you have very well said the truth. Without taking the *pārijāta* flower where are you going? I do not understand your mind."

*kṛṣṇa bola* || *he priye : hāmu bicorala : doṣa nāhi dharabi : śrīkṛṣṇa nāradaka bola* || *he ṛṣirāja : tuhu satvare jāva : indrata khoji : pārijāta bṛkṣa : pṛyāka nimitta satvare āna giyā* ||

Kṛṣṇa said, "Oh dear wife, I have forgotten; please do not consider me as a defaulter." Śrī Kṛṣṇa then said to Nārada, "Oh the king of the sages, please go immediately and asking from Indra, bring the *pārijāta* tree for my beloved wife."

*kṛṣṇaka bāṇī śuni nārada cali gīyā : indraka bola* ||

Hearing the words of Kṛṣṇa, Nārada went to Indra and said:

*he devarāja : śrīkṛṣṇa tohāta pārijāta khojala : satyabhāmāka nimitta : jāni satvara diā paṭhāva* ||

[52]. in *Śloka* metre.

"Oh the king of the gods, Śrī Kṛṣṇa has asked for the *pārijāta* from you for Satyabhāmā; knowing that, send it to Him immediately."

*nāradaka bāṇī śuni : parama krodha hayā : śacī uttara delaha* ||
Hearing the words of Nārada, becoming very much angry, Śacī replied:

*aḥ abhāgya kapāla : indrānī śacīka pārijāta kathāka maṇiṣī satyabhāmā : pindhite sāda gela : ṛṣirāja bola gīyā : jabe aneka puṇya kaya kahuñ : amrāvatīka adhikāriṇī haya : tebe pārijāta paridhāna karite pāve : hāmāra pārijāta indre dite pārave nāhi* ||
"Oh unfortunate, the *pārijāta*, which belongs to Śacī, the wife of Indra, is wished to be worn by Satyabhāmā, a mere nobody! Oh the king of sages, after acquiring much pious results, when one becomes the owner of Amarāvatī, then only she can wear the *pārijāta*. Indra cannot give away the *pārijāta*, which is mine."

*indra bola* || *he ṛṣirāja : devastrīka pārijāta : kimate dite pāri : strīka kathā kṛṣṇate bidita : bola giyā ṛṣirāja* ||
Indra said, "Oh the king of the sages, how can I give away the *pārijāta*, which belongs to the divine wife (Śacī). Kṛṣṇa knows the way of women; please go and tell him, oh king of the sages."

*śloka* ||

*nāradastu tato'bhyetya bhagavānāha keśavam* |
*indrānyā balgitaṁ yattat kṛṣṇe sarbbamavarṇayat* ||32||

Hymn[53]: Nārada also coming near venerable Keśava, told Kṛṣṇa everything what the wife of Indra had said boastfully.

*sūtra* ||

*tadanantara : nārada pariartti āsi kahuñ : śacī je bolala : kṛṣṇa satyabhāmāka āgu saba kahala* ||

[53]. in *Śloka* metre.

Direction: After that, Nārada, returning from there, narrated everything what Śacī had said, to Kṛṣṇa and Satyabhāmā.

*nārada bola* || *he kṛṣṇa : pārijātaka nimitta tuhu paṭhāyala: hāmu baḍi lāja bhailo : satyabhāmāka bahuta gāli pārāvala mātra : pārijātaka nāma śuni śacī krodhe bolala : aḥ kathāka maniṣī satyabhāmā : śacīka pārijāta pindhite icā kayala : abhāgya kapāla : jaba tapa japa āchari janmāntare amrāvatīka adhikārini haya : taba pārijāta pāvaba : bala gīyā* | *he kṛṣṇa : devīka dhikāra śunive hṛdava dahe : hā hā ki bheli* ||
Nārada said, "Oh Kṛṣṇa, you had sent me for the *pārijāta;* I have become greatly embarrassed; Satyabhāmā was only scolded upon greatly. Hearing the name of *pārijāta,* Śacī said in anger, 'Oh! Wherefrom is this Satyabhāmā, who wants to wear the *pārijāta* which belongs to Śacī! Oh unfortunate, when after practising much penance and after repeated prayers, taking another birth, one becomes the owner of Amarāvatī, then only one gets the *pārijāta*, go and tell her.' Hearing such rebuke from the queen, oh dear Kṛṣṇa, my heart burns. Alas, alas! What has happened!".

*tāheka śuni satyabhāmā : kope kampamāna hayā bolala* ||
Hearing him Satyabhāmā, trembling with anger, said:

*he svāmi : hāmāka kadarthite tohõ ānala : dānavaka beṭi śacī tāheka cāṭu kaya : pārijāta nevaba : aḥ taba dhikāra hoka : he prāṇanātha kāheka bhaya thika : satvare pārijāta āna giyā* ||
"Oh dear husband, you have brought me here to get me rebuked? Śacī, who is the daughter of a demon, (only after)pleasing her, you will take away the *pārijāta*! Shame on you. Oh Lord of my life, who are you so much afraid of? Go, and bring the *pārijāta* immediately."

*nārada bola* || *aḥ devī bhalla kahala : śrīkṛṣṇa satvara pārijāta ānaha* ||

Nārada said, "Well said, oh divine lady. Śrī Kṛṣṇa, bring the *pārijāta* quickly."

*śloka* ||

*niśamya satyabhāmāyā vacanaṁ kañjalocanaḥ* |
*jahāra sahasāgatya pārijātataruṁ hariḥ* ||33||

Hymn[54]: Hearing the words of Satyabhāmā, the lotus-eyed Hari, going out rashly, stole the *pārijāta.*

*kathā* ||

*tadanantara : śrīkṛṣṇa pṛyāka bākya śuniye* || *tattakāle pārijātaka samīpa cāpi : samūli upāri ānala : pekhi rakhīyāsaba kolahāla kaye bolala* ||

Dialogue: After that, hearing the words of His beloved wife, Śrī Kṛṣṇa went near the *pārijāta* in a moment, and brought it uprooting it completely. Seeing that, creating an uproar, all the watchmen said:

*he kṛṣṇa : śacīka pārijāta nite tohāri kona beyahāra* ||
"Oh Kṛṣṇa, what type of behaviour is this on your part to steal the *pārijāta* of Śacī!"

*satyabhāmā bola* || *ave rakhīyāsaba : tohāka śacīta kaha gīyā : satyabhāmā pārijāta niyā jāi : aba yata śakati thika : rākhoka āsiyā* ||
Satyabhāmā said, "Oh you watchmen, go and tell your Śacī that Satyabhāmā has taken away the *pārijāta*; now let her come and stop us with as much power as she has."

*śuni rākhiyāsaba : indraśacīka praṇāmi kahala* ||
Hearing that, the watchmen, offering obeisance to Indra and Śacī, said:

---

54. in *Śloka* metre.

*he mātā śacī : tohāri pārijāta taru satyabhāmā baḍāi karive svāmīka hāte hari niyā jāya : jāni je juyāi tā karaha* ||
"Oh mother Śacī, Satyabhāmā, with much pride, has made her husband steal your *pārijāta* tree; knowing that, do whatever you consider as proper."

*śloka* ||

*pārijātasya haraṇaṁ niśamya kupitā sacī* |
*patiṁ purandaraṁ prāha dhigastu tava vikramam* ||34||

Hymn[55]: Hearing that the *pārijāta* has been stolen, being very much angry, Śacī told her husband Purandara, "Shame on your valour!".

*kathā* ||

*pārijāta-haraṇa śuni : śacī kope purandaraka bolala* || *he svāmi toho bidyamāna thākite : hāmāka pārijāta mānuṣi niyā jāi : aḥ tohāka dhikāra thika : bajrako dhikāra hoka* ||

Dialogue: Hearing about the stealing of *pārijāta*, Śacī said to Purandara with great anger, "Oh dear husband, in your very presence my *pārijāta* has been taken away by humans. Oh shame on you and shame on your weapon *Vajra* too!".

*ohi buli indraka āge bahuta bilāpa kayala sohi* || *indra bola* || *he pṛye : dukha coḍaha : hāmāka āgu kṛṣṇa kona haya : tāheka jini pārijāta ekhane ānaba : cintā nāhi karabi* ||
Saying so, she lamented a lot in front of Indra. Indra said, "Oh dear wife, give up this grief; who is Kṛṣṇa before me! Winning him, I shall bring the *pārijāta* now itself, do not worry."

*sūtra* ||

*ohi buli : indra parama prārambhe sāji : dhanuśara dhari kahuñ: devasaba sahita : śacī samanvite airāvata kandhe : khedi āvala indra* ||

---

[55]. in *Śloka* metre.

Direction: Saying so, Indra at the very beginning, getting dressed up, held up the bow and arrow. Along with the other demigods, riding on the shoulder of Airāvata with Śacī, Indra came chasing.

*śloka* ||

*gatvā satrājitasutāṁ provāca kupitā sacī* |
*neṣyasi tvaṁ pārijātaṁ kiṁnu vajradhare sthite* ||35||

Hymn[56]: Going to the daughter of Satrājita, angry Śacī said, "Are you taking away the *pārijāta,* in the very presence of the one who is holding the *Vajra*?".

*kathā* ||

*śacī bola* || *ave satrājitaka kūmāri : tuhu mānasi huyā : hāmāra pārijāta niyā jāya : aḥ tohāka abhāgya milala : jaba bajradharaka hāte sabaṁśe nāhi māraba : taba satvare pārijāta coḍaha* ||

*ohi boli jaiche garajala : tāhe dekhaha śunaha : nirantare hari bola* ||

Dialogue: Śacī said, "Oh the daughter of Satrājita, being a human being, you are taking away my *pārijāta*; oh you will meet with misfortune now; if you do not want to be killed, along with family, by the hands of the one holding the *Vajra*, then let go of the *pārijāta* immediately."

Saying so, as she roared, watch and listen to that and keep chanting the name of Hari incessantly.

*gīta* || *rāga-āsoāri* || *kharamāna* ||

Song in the *Rāga Āśovārī*, with the rhythm *Kharamāna:*

*dhruṁ* ||

*mānasi sahāyana aichana tohāri*
*harasi kusuma hāmāri* ||

Refrain: "You have such human courage that you are stealing my flower."

[56]. in *Śloka* metre, but in the 1st foot, the 6th and 7th letters are short instead of long and in the 3rd foot, the 5th letter is long instead of short and the 6th letter is short instead of long.

*pada* ||

*svāmī purandara : bira bajradhara :*
*ācanta daitya antakārī* |
*pārijāta taru : coraha moḍā*
*rākhahu jīvana kumārī* |
*tohāri svāmī : mādhava mānuṣa :*
*kayali garaba tāhe lāyi* |
*bāsava āge : sohi kona hoi :*
*karu śacī aichana baḍāi* ||*16*||

Verse: "My husband Purandara, the brave one who holds the *Vajra*, the destroyer of demons, is coming. (So) leave my *pārijāta* tree, and oh young girl, save your life. Your husband Mādhava is a human being; and you have become proud for Him. What is He before Vāsava?", Śacī said thus proudly.

*kathā* ||

*śacī bola* || *āve satyabhāmā : tohāri svāmī mādhavaka kathā hāmu saba jāni : ohi gopi-biṭāla gopāla : unikara āgu gokūlaka strī nāhi rahala : dekho kaṁsaka dāsī kūbuji tāheka hāta eḍāla nāhi : tāheka āra ki kahaba : aicana anācārī kṛṣṇata garava kave kahõ : hāmāka pārijāta niyā jāya : aḥ bajrapāte sabaṁśe nāśa bheli : jānaba* ||

Dialogue: Śacī said, "Oh Satyabhāmā, I know everything about your husband Mādhava, that cowherd boy, the lover of the cowherd women; no woman of Gokula was spared by Him. See even Kubjī, the maid of Kaṁsa, could not get away from His hands. What more is there to speak of Him. Being proud for such a debauch as Kṛṣṇa, you are taking away my *pārijāta*. Oh you, along with all your family are sure to be destroyed with the thunderbolt, know it for sure."

*śloka* ||

*niśamya garbbavākyaṁ sā satyabhāmā haripriyā* |
*kopena kampitavatī sacīmābhāṣya balgati* ||36||

Hymn[57]: Hearing the proud words, Satyabhāmā, the beloved wife of Hari, trembling with anger, said addressing Śacī arrogantly.

*kathā* ||

*satyabhāmā bola || āve indrānī : jagataka parama guru : hāmāra svāmī : jāhera nāma sumarite : mahā mahā pāpīsaba saṁsāra nistare : tāheka atave nindā karaha : ave nilājinī : marite nājāva : tohāri svāmī indraka kathā kahite ghṛnāse upaje : dekho amrāvatīka yata beśyā : tohāka svāmīka se nāhi ānṭala : tohāri svāmī kayali ki : gautama ṛṣika bhāryā ahalyā : tāheka māyā kari kahuñ : jāti bhraṣṭa kayala: tannimite saba śarīra ḍhāki : joniḍāka bhela : ave pāmarī : aicana indraka hāmāka āgu bakhānaha ||*

*ohi boli satyabhāmā jaice balgala : tāhe dekhaha śunaha : nirantare hari bola ||*

Dialogue: Satyabhāmā said, "Oh you, wife of Indra, my husband is the master of this whole world. Remembering whose name, all the great sinners get delivered from this world. You are reproaching Him so much. Oh you shameless, why don't you go to die! I feel great disgust to speak about your husband Indra. See, all the prostitutes of Amarāvatī did not suffice him . What did your husband do! The wife of sage Gautama is Ahalyā; mesmerising her, he depraved her, and that is why covering the whole body became blemished. Oh you depraved, you are praising such Indra in front of me."

Saying so, as Satyabhāmā swaggered, watch and listen to that and keep chanting the name of Hari incessantly.

*gīta || rāga-belaāla || kharamāna ||*

Song in the *Rāga-Belovāra* with the rhythm *Kharamāna:*

---

57. in *Śloka* metre, but in the 3rd foot, the 6th and 7th letters are short instead of long.

*dhruṁ* ||

*pāmarī hariko karasi baḍāi* |
*āju caraṇapaṅkaja-raja paraśi :*
*gāri desi kati lāi* ||

Refrain: "Oh you wicked, boasting of Hari, touching the dust of the lotus-like feet just today, why are you scolding now?"

*pada* ||

*ohi jagata-guru: brahmā-rudra karu :*
*pari paraṇāma jāhāri* |
*kaice dāsī śacī : aiche svāmīka karu :*
*kandala bayana nehāri* ||
*jāhera nāma guṇa : gāi pāpī tare :*
*bhakati mukuti milāve* |
*aiche govindaka : nindaṣa pāmarī :*
*śaṅkara kaha hari-pāve* ||17||

Verse: He is the father of the world, unto whom Brahmā and Rudra offer obeisance falling down. How can that servant Śacī pick a quarrel looking into the face of such a Lord? Singing whose praises even the sinners are rescued and attain devotion and deliverance; you depraved are reproaching such Govinda!; says Śaṅkara, at the feet of Hari.

*kathā* ||

*satyabhāmā bola* || *ave dānavaka beṭi indrānī : hāmāri āgu : tohari atave baḍāi : hāmu parama darppa kave kahuñ : pārijāta ānala : dekhu aba tohāka svāmī purandaraka : yata śakati thika : yuddha kaya : hāmāra hātaka pārijāta niyā jāuka : dekhi taba saphala baḍāi kayali* ||

Dialogue: Satyabhāmā said, "Oh you wife of Indra, the daughter of a demon, you are boasting so much in front of me. I have brought the *pārijāta* with so much pride. Let us see, let your husband Purandara, fighting with all his might, take away the *pārijāta* from my hand. If I can see that, then only I will agree that you have fulfilled your boasting."

*devī satyabhāmāka : atave bikarthanā bāṇī śuni śacī : kope apamāne indraka bolala* ||
Hearing so much of reproaching words from Satyabhāmā, Śacī said to Indra with great anger and embarrassment:

*he svāmi devarāja : tohāka jīvana dhika dhika : mānuṣi strīka atave kadarthanā śuni rahaicha : chiḥ tohāta puruṣa teja kicho nāhi : aḥ devatāka indra micā bolavasi* ||
"Oh my husband, the king of the gods, shame on your life; you remain hearing so much reproach from a human woman. Fie on you, you have no male blood in you. Oh you are lying that you are the king of the gods."

*śloka* ||

*tataḥ purandaro devyāḥ pīḍito bākyasāyakaiḥ* |
*krodhena dhanurārdāya yuddhāya sammukho'bhavat* ||37||

Hymn[58]: Then, being greatly tormented by the sharp arrow-like words from his wife, Purandara, holding the bow with great anger, faced for war.

*sūtra* ||

*tadanantara : purandara bākya-sare pīḍita hayā : śacīka garihā sūni kahō : parama krodhe dhanu dhari : yuddha karite : kṛṣṇaka samukha bhelaha : pekhi śāraṅga ṭaṅkāri : śrīkṛṣṇa garuḍaka kandhe : indraka samukha huyā rahala* | *tāhe pekhi purandara darppe bolala* ||

Direction: After that, being tormented with the shaft of words, hearing the abusive words of Śacī, Purandara, holding the bow with great anger, came before Kṛṣṇa to fight. Seeing that, twanging the bow *Śāraṅga*, Kṛṣṇa, riding on the

[58]. in *Śloka* metre.

shoulder of Garuḍa, confronted Indra. Seeing that, Purandara said with pride.

*ave yādava : śacīka pārijāta : kaiche niyājāya : ohi tikhatara sare : tohāri prāṇa coḍāvaba hāmākū āgu kāhā jāvaba* ||
"Oh you, descendant of Yadu, how can you take away the *pārijāta* that belongs to Śacī. I shall make you give up your life with this sharp arrow. Where can you go in front of me?"

*aicana prakāre bahuta balgala : dibyabāṇa hāni : jaice dāmodara purandara : duhõ mahāyuddha kayala : āhe loka: tāhe dekhaha śunaha : nirantare hari bola* ||
In this way (Purandara) boasted a lot. Attacking with celestial arrows, as Dāmodara and Purandara became engaged in great fight, oh dear people watch and listen to that and keep chanting the name of Hari incessantly.

*gīta* || *rāga-tura* || *paritāla* ||
Song in the *Rāga-Tura* with the rhythm *Paritāla:*

*dhruṁ* ||
*garaji bāsava bāṇa prahāre* |
*āju jiya lehu tohāri re* ||
Refrain: Thundering, Vāsava attacked with arrows. "Oh I shall take your life today."

*pada* ||
*pekhi tāhe hari : kare śāraṅga dhari :*
*karu śara satvara murāri* |
*cedi bāṇagaṇa : harali cetana :*
*indraka hṛdave bidāri re* ||

Verse: Seeing him Hari, holding the Śāraṅga bow in His hand, Murāri, applied arrows into it immediately. The arrows piercing, tearing through his heart, made Indra lose consciousness.

*kathā* ||

*kṛṣṇaka bāṇa prahāre : murchita hoi : punaḥ cetana pāi : indra bola* ||

Dialogue: Fainting away at the blow of Kṛṣṇa's arrow, and then regaining consciousness again, Indra said:

*āve śrīkṛṣṇa : jaba pārijāta coḍaba taba coraha : nahe ohi bajra sandhāne : tohāri prāṇa coḍāñuñ* ||

"Oh you Śrī Kṛṣṇa, if you are leaving the *pārijāta,* then leave it; so that I do not fix the *Vajra* and make you leave your life."

*kṛṣṇa bola* || *ave duṣṭa devarāja : hāmāku bhīti dekhāva : yata śakati thika : prahāra dekhi* ||

Kṛṣṇa said, "Oh you wicked king of the gods, you are trying to scare me; let me see you attack with as much strength as you have."

*śuni indra bajra dhariye : punu svastha hayā : kṛṣṇaka hānala : śrīkṛṣṇa hāsi hāsi lumphi dharala : jaiche tāhe dekhaha śunaha : nirantare haribola* ||

Hearing that, Indra, holding the *Vajra*, feeling well again, attacked Kṛṣṇa. As Śrī Kṛṣṇa, laughing, snatched it jumping, watch and listen to that and keep chanting the name of Hari incessantly.

*pada* ||

*svasthakalevara : punu purandara : dharala bajra bīra toli* |
*hānala sandhāne : bāṇa aba lelahuñ : raha raha jādaba boli* ||18||

Verse: Healthy in body, brave Purandara picked up the *Vajra* again, saying "Here, now, I have picked up the arrow" and fixing it, hurled it forcefully, saying, "Wait, wait, oh you descendant of Yadu."

*sūtra* ||

*bāṇayuddhe napāri purandara : parama āṭope kope : śrīkṛṣṇaka bajra prahārala : hari hāsi hāsi bajraka lumphi dharala* ||

Direction: Not being able to stand in the arrow-war, Purandara, with great valour and anger, attacked Śrī Kṛṣṇa with the *Vajra*; Hari, laughing, snatched the *Vajra* jumping.

*śloka* ||

*tataḥ kṛṣṇo ruṣā cakraṁ śatruṁ prati gṛhītabān* |
*indro bhītyābhyadravattaṁ sa paścādbhīṣayan yayau* ||38||

Hymn[59]: Then Kṛṣṇa, with great anger took up the wheel against Indra and Indra, greatly scared, retreating, went backwards.

*kathā* ||

*śrīkṛṣṇa bola* || *ave duṣṭa devarāja : jaba tohāri prahāra hāmu sahala : aba hāmāra prahāra sambaraha* ||

Dialogue: Śrī Kṛṣṇa said, "Oh you wicked king of the gods, when I have tolerated your attack, now you receive my blow."

*sūtra* ||

*ohi buli parama prārambhe : indraka lāgi cakra toli dharala : tāheka dekhi indraka hṛdaya kampa lāgala : hāta pāva thīra nohe: mahā bhave hasti cāḍi lavaḍi palāvala tāhe pekhi śrīkṛṣṇa : hāsi hāsi pācu pācu : jaiche indraka khedala : tāhe dekhaha śunaha : nirantare haribola*||

---

59. in *Śloka* metre, but in the 3rd foot, the 6th and 7th letters are short instead of long

Direction: Saying so, with great enterprise picked up the disc for Indra. Seeing Him the heart of Indra started trembling and his hands and feet did not remain steady ; greatly scared, he fled running, leaving behind the elephant. Seeing that, as Śrī Kṛṣṇa chased Indra laughing, watch and listen to that and keep chanting the name of Hari incessantly.

*gīta* || *rāga-kānaḍā* || *paḍitāla* ||
Song in the *Rāga Kānaḍā* with the rhythm *Paritāla:*

*dhruṁ* ||

*prāṇara kātare indra palāi* |
*pācu pācu hāsi mādhave dhāi* ||

Refrain: Trembling with fear for his life, Indra fled and Mādhava ran behind him laughing.

*pada* ||

*re re purandara ḍāka murāri* |
*raha raha kāhe palāvaba bajradhārī* ||
*lavare bāsava pācu nācāi* |
*kṛṣṇaka kiṅkara śaṅkare gāi* ||19||

Verse: Murāri called, "Oh there Purandara, the one who carries the *Vajra*, wait, wait, why do you flee?". Vāsava kept on running without looking back; sings Śaṅkara, the servant of Kṛṣṇa.

*sūtra* ||

*raha raha indra boli ḍāki ḍāki : śrīkṛṣṇa pācu pācu jāi : tathāpi indra bibhaṅge palāi : rahaye nāhi : tāhe pekhi devī satyabhāmā : kadarthanā kari kahõ : hāsi bolala* ||

Direction: Calling after, "Wait, wait oh you Indra." Śrī Kṛṣṇa followed him. Yet, Indra, escaped with a stooping pose, without waiting. Seeing that, Goddess Satyabhāmā, laughing, said tormentingly.

*kathā* ||

*āhe purandara : tuhuñ ki nimite palāvala : devaka rājā huyā: mānuṣa kṛṣṇaka bhave bhaṅga delaha : uchita nahe : tohāri āgu pārijātaka mañjīra : paridhāna kariye : śacī lāsa-beśa kari beḍāve : tahuñ bajradhara bīra : aba kaice palāve lājaka piṭhi delaha | ave pāmarī śacī : ohi indraka dekhāi : atave darappa kayali : aba tohāri bhaṭāraka kaiche nāhi palāṭāyā : hāmu mānuṣi hayā : tohāri pārijāta niyā jāñuñ : ohi tāpe marite najāyaka* ||

Dialogue: "Oh you Purandara, why do you flee? Being the king of the gods, fearing the human Kṛṣṇa, you have fled away. It is not proper, that wearing bunches of *pārijāta*, Śacī should move about fancifully. You are a hero bearing the *Vajra*, how you have fled now, turning a back to your honour! Oh you mean Śacī, showing this very Indra, you have boasted so much. Now why don't you change your husband. Being a human being, here I am taking away your *pārijāta*; why don't you die out of misery for that."

*śloka* ||

*tataḥ purandaro nindāṁ devyāḥ śrutvātiduḥsahām* |
*nivartyovāca vacanaṁ satyabhāme nibodha me* ||39||

Hymn[60]: Then Purandara, hearing the abuses from the queen, which were too harsh to bear, said replying back, "Oh Satyabhāmā, listen to me."

*sūtra* ||

*tadanantara : devīka nindā śunive indra pariarti bolala* ||

Direction: Then, hearing the abuses from the Goddess, Indra said replying back:

*kathā* ||

*ave satyabhāmā : ohi śrīkṛṣṇaka yata patanī thika : tāheka madhye tuhuñ baḍi pracaṇḍa pragalbhā : ihā hāmu jānalu :*

[60]. in *Śloka* metre, but in the 3rd foot, the 6th and 7th letters are short instead of long.

*ki nimitta hāmāka atave kakarthanā karaiche : dekhu ōhi koṭi koṭi brahmāṇḍeśvara : brahmāmaheśe sebita pādapaṅkaja : jagataka parama guru nārāyaṇa śrīkṛṣṇa : tāheta hāmu yuddha hārala : ihāta kona lāja thika : tuhuñ strījāti kicho bujhave nāhi : hāmāka michā balgaha ||*
*ohi boli indra āponāka garihā kayala || hāhā hāmu pāpī : māyā mohita hayā : parama īśvaraka yuddha kayala : hāmāka dhikāra hoka || ohi boli bhave kampita tanu : trāhi trāhi boli kara jori : kṛṣṇaka āgu daṇḍavate paḍi : paraṇāmi tuti bolala ||*

Dialogue: "Oh Satyabhāmā, of the many wives that Śrī Kṛṣṇa has, you are the most talkative amongst them all, that I have known. Why are you abusing me so much? See, the master of the crores of universe, whose lotuslike feet are served even by Brahmā and Maheśa, the one who is the ultimate father of the world, the one who is Nārāyaṇa, to that Śrī Kṛṣṇa, I have lost the war. What is there to be ashamed of? You women folk do not understand anything. You are abusing me unnecessarily."
Saying so, Indra chastised himself, "Alas, alas, I am a sinner; being stupefied with illusion, I have fought with the Supreme God, shame on me!". Saying so, his body trembling with emotions and uttering "Save me, protect me!", with folded hands, offering obeisance prostrate on the ground before Kṛṣṇa, prayed to Him.

*payāḍa ||*

*jaya jaya jādava deva murāri |*
*jaya jaya kaṁsa keśī antakārī ||*
*jaya jaya giri gobarddhanadhārī |*
*jaya jaya bhakata bhīti bhaya-hārī ||1||*
*jaya jaya marddita biṣadhara kāli |*
*jaya jaya bāmana balika niskāli ||*
*jaya jaya nirjita kapibara bāli |*
*jaya jaya bāsudeva banamālī ||2||*

*jaya jaya tṛbhubana anupāma |*
*jaya jaya nija jana pūraṇa kāma ||*
*jaya jaya ariṣṭaka morana rāma |*
*jaya jaya pāteka tāreka nāma ||3||*
*tohāri māyā-mohita andha |*
*kayalu yuddha deva hāmu manda ||*
*āta aparādha sahaba hari moi |*
*caraṇe śaraṇa lelo ava toi ||4||*
*ohi indrapada āpada ghora |*
*dūra kara hari kumati mora ||*
*māgubi bhīkṣā paridhāna kaya kanthā |*
*dharabo tohāri bhakati panthā ||5||20||*

Verse: "Glory to the descendant of Yādava, oh God Murāri. Glory to the one, who has finished Kaṁsa and Keśī. Glory to the one, who held up the mountain Govardhana. Glory to the one, who removes all the fears from the minds of His devotees. (1)

"Glory to the one, who has crushed the poisonous Kāli. Glory to Vāmana who expelled Bali. Glory to the one, who has killed Bāli, the King of the monkeys. Glory to Vanamālī, the son of Vasudeva. (2)

"Glory to the one, who is incomparable in the three worlds. Glory to the one, who fulfills the wishes of His own people. Glory to Rāma who has crushed Ariṣṭa. Glory to the one, (taking) whose name alone can rescue the sinners. (3)

"I have become blind bewildered by your illusion. Evil that I am, I have fought with you, oh God! Please tolerate this much of my offence, oh my Hari. I have now taken refuge at your feet. (4)

"This position of Indra is a great botheration. Oh Hari, please remove all the evil thoughts from my mind. Wearing a torn cloth, here I beg of you. I shall take to the path of your devotion." (5)

*sūtra* ||

*ohi tuti karive purandara : parama bairāgyeḥ kṛṣṇaka āgu pari bahuta bilāpa kayala* ||

Direction: Praying in this way Purandara,with utmost aversion, lamented a lot falling down in front of Kṛṣṇa.

*śloka* ||

*dṛṣṭā kṛṣṇo bihasyāha tasya tannirmmalammanaḥ*
*santuṣysi yato deva śreṣṭhabhrātā bhabānmama* ||40||

Hymn[61]: Seeing him, Kṛṣṇa said smiling, "Your mind is pure and as you have satisfied me, oh god, you are my best brother."

*sūtra* ||

*tadanantara : indraka bhītikātara dekhiye : śrīkṛṣṇa hāsi hāsi hāte dhari kahõ : toli āśvāsa bolala* ||

Direction: After that, seeing Indra very much distressed with fear, Śrī Kṛṣṇa, smiling, raising him holding by the hand, said consoling him.

*kathā* ||

*he purandara : tuho hāmāra śreṣṭhabhrātā : tohori doṣa hāmu kicho dharave nāhi : kicho śaṅkā nāhi karabi : dharu tohoka bajra lehu : ohi pārijāta yadi sukhe nāhi deva : taba ihāka niyā jāva* ||

Dialogue: "Oh Purandara, you are my best brother; I shall not mind your faults. You please do not worry. Here, take your *Vajra* and if you do not give that *pārijāta* happily, then take it away."

*sūtra* ||

*śuni satyabhāmā : kopa kaṭākṣe nirekhi : kṛṣṇaka daśana carbbi mane garihaya* ||

---

[61]. in *Śloka* metre.

*hāhā ki bheli svāmīka mati : ohi indraka cāṭu śunala : ārabāra narakabadha nimite : kata kātara kaye āni : kāryasiddha bhaila dekhi : hāmāka bhejāvala : unikara bacane sañjāta thika : aḥ hāmāra pārijāta dite : kona adhikārī rahe ||*

*indra bola || he svāmi kṛṣṇa : ohi pārijāta tuhuñ niyā jāva : sudharmmā sabhā sohita : yata sampatti hāmāta thika : saba dvārakakāka*[62] *lāgi paṭhāñu : jāvata tuhe bhūmita rahaba : tāvata upajoga hayā rahoka ||*

Direction: Hearing that, looking with a sidelong glance with great anger and grinding her teeth, Satyabhāmā started reproaching Kṛṣṇa within her mind.

"Alas, alas! What has happened to the judgement of my husband that He has listened to the cunning words of that Indra! This time, to kill Naraka, brought us here with so much entreaty. Now, seeing that the work is completed, we are being sent away; oh, what faith is there in his words? Oh, what right he has got to give away my *pārijāta*!"

Indra said, "Oh Lord Kṛṣṇa, you please take away that *pārijāta*. Along with the Sudharmmā Sabhā, whatever wealth I have, I shall send it all to Dwārakā. As long as you are on this earth, let them be well utilized."

*śloka ||*

*indrasya vacanaṁ śrutvā prītaḥ pītāmbaro yayau ||*
*pārijātaṁ tadādāya tamanujñāpya bhāryayā ||41||*

Hymn[63]: Then hearing the words of Indra, being pleased and getting permission, taking the *pārijāta*, Pītāmbara along with His wife went happily.

*sūtra ||*

*indraka sanmāna śuni : śrīkṛṣṇa bhāryā sahita : hariṣe purandarata : anumati pāi : jaiche pārijāta laiyā : kautuke keśava calali : āhe loka : tāhe dekhaha śunaha : nirantare hari bola ||*

---

[62]. *dvārakāka.*

in *Śloka* metre.

Direction: Hearing the respectful words of Indra, as Śrī Kṛṣṇa, along with His wife, getting permission from Purandara, happily took the *pārijāta* and as Keśava went with pleasure; oh dear people, watch and listen to that and keep chanting the name of Hari incessantly.

*gīta* || *rāga belovāra* || *paritāla* ||
Song in the *Rāga Belovāra* with the rhythm *Paritāla:*

*dhruṁ* ||

*pārijāta laiyā calala lava lāse* ||
*hāse hariṣe baranārī* |
*matta gaja-gāminī : kāminī kole*
*bhole calayī murāri* ||

Refrain: Taking the *pārijāta,* moving gracefully, the beautiful woman smiled happily. Beside the proud beautiful woman with a gait like an elephant, Murāri moved on forgetting everything.

*pada* ||

*śyāma mūruti ratane ure mālā*
*maṇi mañjīra jhurāve* |
*pṛyā same cale raṅge : taruṇī karani saṅge :*
*mātaṅga jaiche līlāve* ||
*makari kuṇḍala gaṇḍa: ḍoli birājati :*
*rājība locana svāmī* |
*kṛṣṇa kiṅkara : kahai hariko*
*caraṇe pari paraṇāmi* ||21||

Verse: Bluish-black in form, the garland of gems flying the jeweled anklets dazzling, moving happily with the beloved wife, as if an elephant (moving), playfully along with the young female elephant. Spider-shaped earrings hang on the cheeks illuminating the lotus-eyed Lord. Says the servant of Kṛṣṇa, offering obeisance lying down at the feet of Hari.

*kathā* ||

*tadanantara : devī satyabhāmā sahita : līlāve kautuke keli kaya : śrīkṛṣṇa dvārakāpura prabeśa bhaila : kṛṣṇaka bijaya śunive : dvārikāta mahā mahosvava milila || ṭhāve ṭhāve jaya–bājana bajāyala : svāmī yuddha jini āvala śuni rukamiṇī : sakhīsaba sahita āsi kahuñ : sapaṭe paraṇāma kayali : kṛṣṇa ālāṅgi āśvāsala : rukamiṇī sakhī same kṛṣṇaka eka pāse rahala : satyabhāmā garbba kave kahu : rukamiṇīka bolala ||*

*he bidarbharāja-kumāri : tuhuñ svāmīka ṭhāme : goṭā eka pārijāta puspa pāvala : dekhu dekhu jāvata sohi pārijāta taru : samūle upāri : kṛṣṇaka hāte nāhi ānala : tāvata chāḍalo nāhi : hāmāra saubhāgyaka mahimā pekho ||*

Dialogue: After that, along with queen Satyabhāmā, happily, playfully sporting, Śrī Kṛṣṇa entered the city of Dwārakā. Hearing about the victory of Kṛṣṇa, there was great occasion of festivities in Dwārakā. People played the musical instrument for victory from place to place. Hearing about the return of her husband after victory in the war, Rukmiṇī, coming along with her friends, prostrated humbly with clothing(on her head). Embracing her, Kṛṣṇa consoled her. Rukmiṇī, along with her friends, remained on one side of Kṛṣṇa. Satyabhāmā, boastfully said to Rukmiṇī,

"Oh princess of the kingdom of Vidarbha, you have received from your husband only one *pārijāta* flower. Look, look, until I made Kṛṣṇa bring that same *pārijāta* tree uprooting it completely, I did not stop. Look at the glory of my good fortune."

*śloka* ||

*niśamya satyabhāmāyā bhāvaṁ bhīṣmakanandinī |*
*provāca bhaktermahimāṁ varṇayan rucirānanī ||42||*

Hymn[64]: Hearing the mind of Satyabhāmā, the beautiful faced daughter of King Bhīṣmaka, spoke describing about the greatness of *bhakti*.

*kathā* ||

*satyabhāmāka garbba-bhāva śuni : rukamiṇī hāsi bolala* ||
*ave bhaginī satyabhāmā : ki kahaicha jagataka parama guru śrīkṛṣṇa : unikara caraṇa-sevā karite : brahmāṇḍa bhitare : kona dullabha thīka : dharmma artha kāma mokṣa : cāri padāraṣa hāte milāye : tohāri pārijāta kona kathā* ||
*aicana bhakatika mahimā kahite : rukamiṇīka prema paraśala: hari-caraṇa-sevāka mahimāka jaiche bannāvala : tāhe dekhaha śunaha : nirantare hari bola*||

Dialogue: Hearing the boastful expression of Satyabhāmā, Rukmiṇī said smiling,
"Oh dear sister Satyabhāmā, what do you say! Śrī Kṛṣṇa is the ultimate father of the world. To serve in His feet is what is most difficult to attain in this universe and (thereby) one can get all the four principal objects of life - *dharmma, artha, kāma* and *mokṣa*, in hand; what to speak of your *pārijāta*."
In this way, speaking about the greatness of devotion, Rukmiṇī was touched with love. As she described the greatness of serving the feet of Hari, watch and listen to that and keep chanting the name of Hari incessantly.

*gīta* || *rāga- basanta* || *paḍitāla* ||
Song in the *Rāga-Basanta* with the rhythm *Paritāla:*

*dhruṁ* ||

*atave kaichana kahaṣi māyi* |
*harika bhakati satī kona nimilāi* ||

Refrain: "Oh dear girl how can you say so much? What the virtuous woman, who is a devotee of Hari, does not achieve!".

[64]. in *Śloka* metre, but in the 3rd foot, the 5th letter is long instead of short and the 6th letter is short instead of long.

*pada* ||

*ohi aruṇa pada-paṅkaja dhiyāi* |
*manoratha cāri padāraṣa pāi* ||
*pāpī pāteka tare nāma-guṇa gāi* |
*kaha śaṅkara hari bine gati nāi* ||22||

Verse: Meditating on those red lotuslike feet, leaving all other wishes, one can get all the four principal objects of life. Singing your name, the sinners get rid of their sins; other than Hari, there is no other refuge, says Śaṅkara.

*kathā* ||

*bhakatika mahimā kahite : kumārīka preme paraśala : nayana jhurāi rahala* ||

Dialogue: Speaking of the greatness of devotion, the young girl was touched with love, and tears flowed from her eyes.

*śloka* ||

*satyabhāmā patiṁ prāha prabho tvaṁ kinnu prekṣas* |
*pārijātatаruṁ dvāri ropaṇaṁ kuru me hare* ||43||

Hymn[65]: Satyabhāmā said to her husband, "Oh Lord, what are you looking at? Please plant the *pārijāta* tree near my door, oh Hari."

*kathā* ||

*satyabhāmā bola* || *he svāmi kṛṣṇa : ki nimitta tuhuñ apekṣā karaha : hāmāka dvāri pārijāta : satvare ropaṇa karaha* ||
*pṛyāka bāṇī śuni : śrīkṛṣṇa dvāraka bidūre : āpuna hāte pārijāta taru ropaṇa kayala : pekhi devī bola* ||
*he svāmi : aḥ ki kayala : hāmāka bahuta satinī thika pārijāta phula cori kari nite : kata kalaha kari beḍāvaba : ethā nahe : hāmāra dvāra nikaṭe niyā ropaṇa karaha* ||
*śuni śrīkṛṣṇa pṛyāka manapūri : pārijāta punarbbāra upāri : devīka dvāra samīpe ropi thāpala* || *tadanantara : satyabhāmā*

---

[65]. in *Śloka* metre.

*manoratha pūri : śrīkṛṣṇa svāmīka paraṇāmi : sakhī same praśaṁsā bahuta : kautuke kayali* ||

Dialogue: Satyabhāmā said, "Oh dear husband Kṛṣṇa, what are you waiting for? Please plant the *pārijāta* on my doorfront soon."

Hearing the words of His beloved wife, Śrī Kṛṣṇa planted the *pārijāta* tree a little away from the door with His own hands. Seeing that, the Goddess said:

"Oh dear husband, what have you done! I have many co-wives, and to steal the *pārijāta* flower how they move about quarreling. Take it and plant it near my door immediately."

Hearing that, Śrī Kṛṣṇa fulfilling the wishes of His beloved wife, uprooting the *pārijāta* again, planted it near the door of the Queen. After that, having her wishes fulfilled, Satyabhāmā, offering obeisance to her husband Śrī Kṛṣṇa, praised Him a lot happily with her friends.

*śloka* ||

*sādhitārtho'tha nātho saḥ patnībhyāṁ saha keśavaḥ* |
*kautukī krīḍayāmāsa hāsa- saṁrambha -bhāvakaiḥ* ||44||

Hymn[66]: Now, fulfilling the wishes, the Lord Keśava, along with His wives, started sporting with fun and excitement.

*kathā* ||

*tadanantara : narakāsura māri : devakārya sādhi* || *indraka jinive : pārijāta āni : pṛyāka dvāre ropi : kṛtya kṛtya hayā : śrīkṛṣṇa bhāryā duho sahita jaichana līlā-keli kautuke kayala : tāhe dekhaha śunaha : nirantare hari bola* ||

Dialogue: After that, killing Narakāsura, completing the services to the demigods, defeating Indra, bringing the *pārijāta*, planting it on the doorstep of His beloved wife, completing the task, as Śrī Kṛṣṇa, along with His two wives, sported on with pleasure, watch and listen to that and keep chanting the name of Hari incessantly.

---

[66]. in *Śloka* metre.

*gīta* || *rāga-purbbi* || *kharamāna* ||
Song in the *Rāga-Pūrabī* with the rhythm *Kharamāna:*

*dhruṁ* ||
*jaga jana-jīvana madhāi* |
*karatu kautuka keli kāminī milāi* ||

Refrain: Life of all the people of the world, Madhāi played on assembling with the beautiful women.

*pada* ||
*kuñcita cāru* : *chikaru cibuka dhar* :
*kara cumbana banamālī* |
*kāñcuri phore* : *bhore rasika guru* :
*kuca nakha ghana ghana ghāli* ||
*ramayā ramaṇī* : *milite māṇika* :
*makari kūṇḍala ḍule* |
*hīra racita maṇi* : *matima māle* :
*hemahāra ure lule* ||
*caraṇe ratana maṇi* : *mañjīra jhanake* :
*kanaka kiṅkiṇī karo role* |
*śrījagatānanda* : *bhakati raṣika nika* :
*kṛṣṇa kiṅkare ohi bole* ||

Verse: Holding onto the curling hair and chin of the beautiful women, Vanamālī kissed them. Tearing their upper garments the master connoisseur of all the emotions scratched their breasts with His nails again and again. The spider-shaped earrings with gems swayed while meeting and mixing with the beautiful women, making them happy and satisfied. Ornaments made of diamonds, necklace of pearls and golden chains hung flying. Anklets made of jewels jingled at the feet and small bells made of gold, tinkled. Śrī Jagatānanda, is the master connoisseur of the emotion of devotion, says the servant of Kṛṣṇa.

*kathā* ||

*aicana keli-kalā kautuke kaye : śrīkṛṣṇa bhakatā ramaṇī sabaka manoratha pūri : dvārikāpura prabeśi rahala | ohi pārijāta haraṇa : harika parama līlā- caritra : śraddhāve jesaba loke śune bhaṇe : kṛṣṇaka caraṇe tāheri parama bhakati baḍhāi : jāni nirantare hari bola* ||

Dialogue: Playing the art of sporting happily in this way, Śrī Kṛṣṇa, fulfilling the wishes of the devotee women, entered the city of Dwārakā. Those who listen to and speak of that *Pārijāta Haraṇa*, the tale of the great pastime of Hari, with faith, increase their great devotion to the feet of Kṛṣṇa. Knowing that, keep chanting the name of Hari.

*śloka* ||

*kṛṣṇapādaprasādena śaṅkaraḥ kṛṣṇa-kiṅkaraḥ* |
*cakāra śrīpārijātaharaṇaṁ nāma nāṭakam* ||45||

Hymn[67]: With the blessings of the feet of Kṛṣṇa, Śaṅkara, the servant of Kṛṣṇa, has composed the play by the name *Pārijāta Haraṇa.*

*tato muktimaṅgala* || *capaya chande* || *bhaṭimā* ||

Then the eulogy for auspicious deliverance in the *Capaya* metre:

*jaya jaya jaga-jīvana murāri* |
*kaṁsa-keśī-baka-agha-antakārī* ||
*so byāpaka bibhu brahmā adhikārī* |
*bhukuti mukuti nitya karatu tohāri* ||1||

Glory to Murāri, the life of all the people of the earth, the killer of Kaṁsa, Keśī, Baka and Agha, that all pervading almighty master of Brahmā; may He always bestow upon you the enjoyment of liberation.(1)

*jaya jaya jādava danuja-saṁhārī* |
*daṇḍita duṣṭaka bhakata nistāri* ||
*sohi jagata-guru gopī piyāri* |

---

[67]. in *Śloka* metre, but in the 3rd foot, the 5th letter is long instead of short and the 6th letter is short instead of long.

*bhukuti mukuti nitya karatu tohāri* ||2||

Glory to the descendant of Yadu, destroyer of the demons, one who, punishing the miscreants, protects the devotees; He is the father of the world, beloved of the cowherd women; may He always bestow upon you the enjoyment of liberation. (2)

*jaya jaya parama puruṣa devako devā* |
*brahmā maheśa karu jo padasevā* |
*sohi nārāyaṇa bhuvana ādhāri* |
*bhukuta mukuti nitya karatu tohāri* ||3||

Glory to the Supreme Personality, the God of all gods, even Brahmā and Maheśa serve whose feet, He is Nārāyaṇa, one who sustains the world; may He always bestow upon you the enjoyment of liberation. (3)

*jaya jaya mādhava dhenuka-māri* |
*ānanda birindā bipina-bihārī*||
*sohi gopāla gobarddhanadhārī*|
*bhukuti mukuti nitya karatu tohāri* ||4||

Glory to Mādhava, the one who killed Dhenuka, roaming happily in the forests of Vṛndāvana, He is Gopāla, who held up the mountain Govarddhana; may He always bestow upon you the enjoyment of liberation.(4)

*jaya jaya pitāmbara banamālī* |
*kālindri hrade jo marddala kāli* ||
*sohi govinda bhakata- bhaya-hārī* ||
*bhukuti mukuti nitya karatu tohāri* ||5||

Glory to the one, who wears yellow clothing and garland of forest flowers, one who crushed Kāli in the Lake Kālindī, He is Govinda, the one who removes all the fears of His devotees; may He always bestow upon you the enjoyment of liberation. (5)

*jaya jaya duṣṭa daitya antakārī* |
*kuvalaya moḍana danta upāri* ||
*śarata ramata johi gopinī nārī* |

*bhukuti mukuti nitya karatu tohāri* ||6||

Glory to the one who killed the wicked demons, destroyed Kuvalaya uprooting its tooth, who gratified the cowherd women in the Autumn; may He always bestow upon you the enjoyment of liberation.(6)

*śrījagatānanda dalapati jāna* |
*hariko padapaṅkaja bhajamāna* ||
*karāyata nāṭa ohi bahu chande* |
*kṛṣṇaka bhakati karite prabandhe* ||7||

Śrī Jagatānanda, the leader, the wise and learned; one who sings prayers at the feet of Hari, persuading a lot he has made this play composed, to arrange for devotion to Kṛṣṇa. (7)

*pārijāta-haraṇa āheri nāma* |
*śuna budhajana hariguṇa anupāma* ||
*kaliyuga madhye dharama ohi sāra* |
*nāhi nāhi gati hari bine āra* ||8||

*Pārijāta Haraṇa* is its name, hear oh wise people, uttering the glories of Hari is incomparable. In the Kaliyuga (Kali era), it is the essence of all religions. There is no other way to salvation but Hari. (8)

*kayali kali dekhu ekākāra* |
*pāpa-puṇya kicho nāhi bicāra* ||
*malamati loka abahu nāhi jāni* |
*nāhi nāhi gati bine śāraṅgapāṇi* ||9||

See, in the Kali era, everything has been made the same, not considering anything about sin and virtue. Oh you dirty minded people, even now you do not realise, there is no way to salvation other than Śāraṅgapāṇi. (9)

*bhaja hari caraṇe coḍahu saba āśa* |
*harināme karu sudṛḍha bichoāsa* ||
*dharamaka upari rājā nāma* |
*jāni sabahu nare bola rāma rāma* ||10||

Leaving all other hope, pray at the feet of Hari. Have firm faith in the name of Hari. Above all the ritualistic religion, the (chanting of His) name is the King. Knowing that, all the people, utter "Rāma, Rāma!". (10)

*iti jeṭha māsa : somabāra : caturthī tithi* ||
*deva 1730 iti saka : 1218 iti rāja saka* || *samāpta* ||
Here ends in the month of *Jyeṣṭha*, on Monday, *Caturthī Tithi*.
Here ends in the *Śaka Deva 1730*, end of *Rāja Śaka 1218.*

●●●

## 5.6
## *śrīrāmabijaya nāṭa*
## The Play : Victory of Śrī Rāma

*namo bhagavate śrīkṛṣṇāya* |
Obeisance to the most revered Śrī Kṛṣṇa.

*prathama śloka* ||
*yannāmākhila lokaśokaśamanaṁ yannāma premāspadam*
*pāpāpārapayodhitāraṇabidhau yannāmapīnaplavaḥ* |
*yannāmaśravaṇāt punāti svapacaḥ*[1] *prāpnoti mokṣaṁ kṣitau*
*taṁ śrīrāmamahaṁ maheśabaradaṁ vande sadā sādaram*||*1*||

The first hymn[2]: That name which can soothe the sorrows of all the people of the world, that name which is lovable, which can rescue one from the boundless ocean of sins, that name, which makes one float in profusion, hearing the name even the *caṇḍāla* is purified and attains *mokṣa* in this world itself. I respectfully offer my prayers everyday to that Śrī Rāma, who granted boon (even) to Maheśa.

*apica* ||
*yenābhāaji dhanuḥ śivasya sahasā sītā samāśvāsitā*
*yenākāri parābhavo bhṛgupatervyāsakta rāmasya ca* |
*baidehyā vidhivadvivāhamakarot nirjitya yaḥ pārthivān*
*yuṣmākaṁ vitanotu śaṁ hi bhagavān śrīrāmacandraściram* ||2||

Also[3]:By whom the bow of Śiva was broken and Sītā was reassured at once, who defeated Bhṛgupati and freed him from attachment and winning the kings, lawfully married

1. *śvapacaḥ*.
2. in *Śārdūlavikrīḍita* metre.
3. in *Śārdūlavikrīḍita* metre.

Vaidehī; may (that) Śrī Rāmacandra, the divine, bless you with peace and growth.

*nāndī || gīta || rāga –suvai || ekatāli ||*

Benedictory song in the *Rāga Suvai* with the rhythm *Ekatāli:*

*jaya jaya jagajīva rāma |*
*kayalo payori paraṇāma ||*

Glory to Rāma, who is like the life for (the living entities) the world, I offer my prayers falling down at your feet.

*pada ||*

*jāhe guṇanāma muhe gāyi |*
*pāpī parama pada pāyī ||*
*ōhi bhavatāpa āpārā |*
*jāhe smaraṇe karu pārā ||1||*
*ayagava bhañjanakārī |*
*pāvala janaka kumārī ||*
*nṛpagaṇa chedala bāṇe |*
*kṛṣṇa kiṅkara ehu bhāṇe ||2||1||*

Verse: Singing whose name with praises even the sinners achieve the final beatitude. Remembering whom, one can get across the limitless misery of this world. (1)
Breaking the *Ajagava*, attained the daughter of Janaka and dissipated the (other) kings with His arrows; says thus, the servant of Kṛṣṇa. (2)

*nāndyantare sūtradhāraḥ || alamati bistareṇa :*

At the end of the *nāndī*, here is the *sūtradhāra;* no need to go into details.

*prathamaṁ mādhavo mādhava ityuktvā śrīrāmacandraṁ praṇamya sabhāsadaḥ sambodhyāha ||*

At first, pronouncing the name of Mādhava repeatedly, offering obeisance to Śrī Rāmacandra, said addressing the assembled audience.

*śloka* ||

*bho bhoḥ sāmājikā yuyaṁ*[4] *śṛṇudhvamadhunā budhāḥ* |
*śrīrāmabijayannāma nāṭakaṁ muktisādhakam* ||3||

Hymn:[5]Oh revered audience, all of you wise men, now please listen; this play, by the name *Śrīrāmavijaya* is the means to emancipation.

*atha bhaṭimā* ||

*jaya jaya raghukula: kamala prakāśaka:*
*dāsaka nāśaka bhīti* |
*jaya jaya nija yana: jātana ghātana:*
*pātana pātaka rīti* ||
*haraka śarāsana: nāśana śāsana:*
*nṛpaguṇa bāṇa sandhāne* |
*chedala bhedala: khedala dāpe:*
*tāpe palāyata prāṇe* ||1||
*bhṛgubara rāmaka: rāmaka kāmaka:*
*kayali darppa upānta* |
*bhava-bhaya-bhañjana: rañjana sajjana:*
*jīvana jānakī-kānta* ||
*yohī banamālī: bāli ghāli:*
*rājā karu sugṛñeñ* |
*jāheri kopa: kaṭākṣa nirekṣi:*
*kampīta yaladhika jīva* ||2||
*samaraka nāgara: nāgara sāgara:*
*silā setu kaya bandha* |
*bhakataka bhītā: sītā nītā:*
*yuddhe badhie daśakandha* ||
*sāphalala bāṇī: jāni āni:*
*thāpi bibhīṣaṇa pāṭa* |

4. *yūyaṁ* is correct grammaticly and also metrically.

5. in *Śloka* metre.

*jatayā taṅkā: laṅkā śaṅkā:*
*kayali punu utapāṭa ||3||*
*jagataka antaka: santaka santaka:*
*pūrala parama kāma |*
*bhūmika bhāra: uddhārala tārala:*
*śura nara rājā rāma ||*
*brahmā maheśvara: kiṅkara jākara:*
*pari pari karatu seva |*
*tṛbhubana kāraṇa: tāraṇa māraṇa:*
*johi devaka deva ||4||*
*sohī maheśvara: rāmaka nāṭaka:*
*śuna mana kaya bichaāsa |*
*āhera kathane: mathane karai:*
*kalimala sakala bināśa ||*
*asārata sārata: kārata bhārata:*
*naratanu biphalahī jāi |*
*pada arabinda: uninda gobinda:*
*hṛdi paṅkaja dharu bhāi ||5||*
*dhanajana jīvana: jaubana biyuri:*
*ujuri dekha nedekha |*
*jānaba keśava: deyāse seyā:*
*sohī silā karu rekha ||*
*saba aparādhaka: bādhaka sādhaka:*
*siddhi karu harināma |*
*kaha kṛṣṇa-kīṅkara: loka nirantara:*
*ḍāki bolahu rāma rāma ||6||*

Here is the eulogy: Glory to the one, who shines as the lotus of the Raghu family and destroys the fear of His servants. Glory to the one, who killed the tormentor, destroying the practise of evil. One who broke the bow of Śiva and punished the kings fixing arrows (to His bow); cut, pierced and chased (them) with pride and with agony they fled saving their lives. (1)

(One who) eradicated the pride of the great Bhṛgu, who had wished for Rāma. One who destroys all the fears of this world and pleases the virtuous men; one who is the life, the most beloved husband of Jānakī. One who is Vanamālī, (who) killing Bāli enthroned Sugrīva; seeing whose sidelong glance of anger, all the animals of the ocean tremble.(2)

One who is clever in war, bound the vile ocean, building a bridge. Killed Daśakandha in the war, who was terror to the devotees and who took away Sītā. Knowing his words to be fulfilled, rescuing his wife, installed Bibhīṣaṇa on the throne and eradicated all the anguish and apprehension for Laṅkā again. (3)

One who, as the Death to the lowest of the world, fulfilled the ultimate wishes of the good and virtuous and King Rāma, delivering the world from its burden, rescued the humans and gods alike. I offer obeisance falling down on the ground repeatedly (to Him), even Brahmā and Maheśvara are whose servants; one who is the God of all gods, the origin, saviour and destroyer of the three worlds. (4)

Listen oh mind, with full faith to this play about that Supreme God Rāma; Remembering and discussing about Him, like churning destroys all the evils of the Age of Kali. Taking birth in Bhārata makes the meaningless (life in this world) meaningful; (yet) the human form goes in vain; (so) hold the flawless lotus-feet of Govinda in the lotuslike heart, oh brother. (5)

All the wealth, life and youth are very transient like the flashes of lightening, seen and unseen (in a moment) and all these are the gifts of Keśava, know it (for certain) like the mark on a stone. Preventing all the offences, uttering the name of Hari helps achieving accomplishments; says the servant of Kṛṣṇa, "Oh dear people, please utter aloud 'Rāma-Rāma!' incessantly." (6)

*kathā* ||

*bho bho sabhāsada : sādhujana : je jagataka parama īśvara nārāyaṇa : bhubika bhāra haraṇa nimitta daśaratha gṛhe avatarala : sohi bhagaanta śrīrāmarūpe : ohi sabhāmaidhye : prabeśa kaya kahuñ : sītā bibāha bihāra nṛtya : parama kautuke karaba : tāhe sāvadhāne dekhaha śunaha* || *prathame lakṣmaṇa sahīta : śrīrāmaka prabeśa : tadanantara sakhīsaba sahīta : sītāka prabeśa : iti jñātvā sarbbe sāvadhāne sthīyatām* ||

Dialogue: Oh revered audience, oh you learned people, one who is the Supreme God Nārāyaṇa, to remove the burden of this world, incarnated into the family of Daśaratha. That same God, in the form of Śrī Rāma, entering this assembly, will perform the pastime of wedding with Sītā, in the form of a play with great pleasure; watch and listen to that carefully. At first, enters Śrī Rāma along with Lakṣmaṇa; after that, enters Sītā along with her friends; knowing that, all of you please remain carefully.

*punaḥ :*

*sūtra bola* || *āhe saṅgi : ki bādya śuniye* ||
*saṅgī bola)* || *sakhi deva dundubhi bājata* || *:*
*āhe deva dundubhi bājata* ||
*-aḥ : śrīrāma candra milala* ||

Again : Says *sūtradhāra*, "Oh dear mate, what musical instrument do we hear?". The companion says, "Oh friend, there plays the divine *dundubhi*. Ah! There plays the divine *dundubhi*. Ah! Here comes Śrī Rāmacandra."

*śloka* ||

*praveśamakarot kāmaṁ rāmo rājīvalocanaḥ* |
*sasodaro dhanuṣpāṇi rūpenāpratimo bhūvi* ||4||

Hymn[6]: Here enters the lotus-eyed Rāma, who is incomparable in beauty and charm in this earth, joyfully along with His brother and holding the bow in His hand.

[6]. in *Śloka* metre.

*kathā* ||

*āhe sabhāsada : hāmu jākara kathā kahīci : se śrīrāma lakṣmaṇa sahīta eāvata*||

Dialogue : Oh dear audience, here enters that Śrī Rāma, whom I am speaking of, along with Lakṣmaṇa.

*iti sūtraḥ niṣkrāntaḥ* ||

Saying so, the *sūtradhāra* exits.

*gīta* || *sīndhuḍā rā : ekatāli*

Song in the *Rāga Sīndhuḍā* with the rhythm *Ekatāli:*

*dhruṁ* ||

*bheli parabeśa : pareśa raghunāthaḥ :*
*saṅge sodara śara dhanu dhari hāta* ||

Refrain : Here enters Pareśa Raghunātha. Along comes His brother holding bow and arrow in his hand.

*pada* ||

*śyāma ruchira cira pīta parakāśa* |
*paṅkaja nayana bayana manda hāsa* ||
*maṇimaya mukuṭa kuṇḍala gaṇḍaḍule* |
*heri müruti mana manamatha bhule* ||*1*||
*māṇika mauti jauti hemahārā* |
*gagana ujora jaicena ruchi tārā* ||
*caraṇaka rañji mañjīra maṇi rola* |
*kṛṣṇa kīṅkara ohi śaṅkara bola* ||2||2||

Verse : The charming dark body brightened with yellow clothing; the eyes are lotuslike and a slight smile appeared on the face. The crown is with gems and jewelled earrings swing on the cheeks. Looking at His form, the mind forgets (the beauty of) Manmatha. (1)

Gems, pearls and gold necklace brighten up the form as the beautiful stars brighten up the sky. The feet are brightened up with tinkling jewelled anklets; says thus, Śaṅkara, the servant of Kṛṣṇa. (2)

*sūtra* ||

*ohi parakāre : śrīrāmacandra prabeśa kaya : eka pāśa hayā rahala : tadanantara sītāka prabeśa śunaha* ||

Direction: In this way, entering, Śrī Rāmacandra remained on one side. After that, listen to the entrance of Sītā.

*sūtra* ||

*āhe saṅgi : kī bādya bāje* ||

Direction: Oh dear mate, what musical instrument plays?

*aye devabādya bāje* ||

Oh, there plays the divine instrument.

*āḥ : janakanandnī sītā : sakhīsaba sahīta milala*||35||

Ah! Here comes Sītā, the daughter of Janaka, along with her friends.

*śloka* ||

*cakāra jānakī kāmaṁ praveśaṁ sakhīsaṅgatā*[7] |
*cintayantī rāmacandracaraṇau rucirānanā* ||5||

Hymn[8]: Jānakī, the beautiful faced, entered joyfully along with her friends, meditating on the feet of Rāmacandra.

*kathā* ||

*he sāmājika : sakhī madanamantharā : kanakāvatī sahīta se janakanandanī sītā : rāmaka caraṇa cinti prabeśa kaya āve : tā dekhaha śunaha* || *nirantare hari bola* ||

Dialogue : Oh revered audience, here enters Sītā, the daughter of Janaka, along with her friends Madanamantharā and Kanakāvatī, meditating on the feet of Rāma; watch and listen to that and utter the name of Hari incessantly.

---

[7]. *sakhisaṅgatā.*

[8]. in *Śloka* metre, but in the 3rd foot, the 5th letter is long instead of short and the 6th letter is short instead of long.

*gīta* || *suhai rāṁ* || *ekatāli* ||
Song in the *Rāga Suhāi* with the rhythm *Ekatāli:*

*dhruṁ* ||
*āve janakasutā kaya parabeśa* |
*pekhiye badana madana mana kleśa* ||
Refrain: Here comes the daughter of Janaka entering; looking at her face even the mind of Madana is distressed.

*pada* ||
*māṇika mukuṭa kuṇḍala karu kānti* |
*daśana ōtima nava matima pānti* ||
*isita hāsi cāndaka ruci chora* |
*nīla alaka locana cakora* ||*1*||
*kanaka keyūra jhanakaka kāi* |
*rāmaka cāna*[9] *cintiye cita lāi* ||
*padapaṅkaja maṇi mañjīra rola* |
*rūpe bhubana bhule śaṅkare bola* ||2||3||

Verse: The crown and the earrings made of jewels brighten up; rows of teeth look like the best new pearls; the slight smile (on the face) surpasses even the charm of the moon; (she is) with blue clothing, locks of hair on the forehead and the eyes (look) like those of the *cakora* bird. (1)
The gold armlets jingle in the body and (Sītā) meditate on the feet of Rāma within her heart; on the lotuslike feet, jewelled anklets tinkle; looking at her beauty, one forgets the whole world; says Śaṅkara.(2)

*kathā* ||
*he sāmājika loka : se janaka-nandanī sītā : sakhīsaba sahita nṛtya kariye : se jātismara kanyā : purbba janmaka kathā cītte parala : tāhe sumari : pari krandana kaya rahala : tāhe pekhi : sakhī madana-mantharā : sakhī kanakāvatī : bāhu meli dhari puccata* ||

[9]. *caraṇa.*

*āhe sakhī : tuhuñ rājanandanī : kona sampati nāhī thika : kī nimite bārambāra bilāpa karaha : prāṇasakhī : hāmāka śapata : tohāra pāvare lāgu : hāmāta sattara kathā kaha* ||

Dialogue: Oh revered audience, that Sītā, the daughter of Janaka, as she could remember the condition in the former life, dancing alongwith her friends, tales of her past life came to her mind, and remembering them, lying down she remained crying. Seeing that, her friends, Madanamantharā and Kanakāvatī, embracing her with arms spreading, asked: "Oh dear friend, you are a princess and what wealth you do not have? Why are you lamenting again and again? Oh friend, as dear as life, we hold on to your feet, upon our word, talk to us immediately."

*śloka* ||

*tataḥ sītā vaniḥsvasya*[10] *caritaṁ pūrbbajanmanaḥ* |
*sakhībhyāṁ varṇayāmāsa rudatī sudatī satī* ||6||

Hymn[11]: Then Sītā, the good woman, releasing a sigh, crying, very sadly described the tales of her earlier life to her friends.

*kathā* ||

*sītā kati beri svastha hayā : āñcore ākhimukha muci : nīśvāsa phokāri : sakhīsabaka sambodhi bacana bolaye lāgala* ||

*āhe sakhīsaba : parama abhāginīka kī pucaha : hāmu puruba janama : īśvara nārāyaṇaka svāmī icā kaya : aneka janama kāya kleśa karie : bahuta bariṣa tapasyā kayalo : tadanantara ākāśī bāṇī śunala : āhe kainyā : tohō ohī janame svāmīka bheṭa nāpāaba : āra janama : śrīrāmarūpe : tohāka bibāha karāvaba : ihā jāni hāmu agaṇi praveśi : prāṇa cārala : āhe sakhīsaba : se daivabāṇīye biphala bhela : se śrīrāma svāmīka caraṇa ōhī janama bheṭa nāhī pālo* ||

*ohī bulite sītāka parama tāpa upajala : hā rāma svāmi boli moha hayā : māṭi loṭi jaiche bilāpa kayala : tā dekhaha śunaha : nirantare hari bola* ||

---

10. *vaniḥśvasya.*

11. in *Śloka* metre.

Dialogue: Sītā, feeling better after some time, wiping out her face and eyes with the fore-end of her clothing, heaving a sigh, addressing her friends, started telling them,
"Oh dear friends, what do you ask me, the most unfortunate one! In my earlier life, wishing for Nārāyaṇa as my husband, observing austerity for many lives, I practised penance for many years. Then I heard the divine words, 'Oh you young girl, you will not meet your husband in this life; in your next life He will marry you in the form of Śrī Rāma.' Knowing that, entering the fire, I gave up my life. Oh dear friends, those divine words went in vain; I could not meet those feet of Lord Śrī Rāma in this life."

*gīta || suhāi rāṁ || cuṭikālā ||*
Song in the *Rāga Suhāi* with the rhythm *Cuṭikālā:*

*dhruṁ||*
*bilapati maithilī māi |*
*nīra nayana jhurāyī ||*
*ghana ghana svāsa : phokārata :*
*tanu cetana nāi ||*

Refrain: Dear Maithilī lamented on flowing tears from her eyes, sighing again and again and with no vitality in the body.

*pada ||*
*cira birahe dahe dehā :*
*diśa dekhu āndhiāri |*
*ramayā bine : mana jhāmaru :*
*parama kuchi kumārī ||1||*
*hā hari hā hari jampaya :*
*jīva jaicana jāi ||*
*rāma caraṇe lāgu :*
*gati āvari nāi ||2||4||*

Verse: The body suffered out of long separation and saw only darkness all around. The mind of that young girl became

completely damp and (the body) very much shrunken without Śrī Rāma. (1)
Chant "Oh Hari, oh Hari!", as if life leaves; stick to the feet of Rāma, (as) there is no other way. (2)

*kathā* ||

*aicana sītāka bilāpa dekhiye : sakhīsaba prabodha kaya bolala* ||
*āhe prāṇasakhī : se bhakataka bāndhava mādhava : tohāka dukha dūra karaba : puruba janamaka : tohoka svāmī : avaśyaka pāvaba : he sakhī tāpa cāraha* ||
*he sāmājika loka : janakanandanī sītā : kiñcita svastha hayā : sakhīsaba sahīta : ekapāśa hayā rahala : rāmaka caraṇa cinti : bayane hāta carāi : adhomukha huyā rahala : tadanantara rājāka prabeśa pekhaha* ||

Dialogue: Seeing Sītā lamenting in this way, the friends, consoling her said:
"Oh friend, as dear as life, Mādhava, that friend to all His devotees, will remove your distress; you will definitely meet the husband of your past life; oh dear friend, give up this grief."
Oh dear people, Sītā, the daughter of Janaka, feeling slightly better, remained on one side along with her friends. Meditating on the feet of Rāma, keeping her hand on the face,(she) remained with downcast face. After that, watch the king entering.

*śloka* ||

*praveśamakarot kṛṣṇadāso daśarathastadā* |
*chatracāmarasaṁyukto dhanuṣpāṇi nṛpottamaḥ* ||7||

Hymn[12]:Then entered Daśaratha, the servant of Kṛṣṇa, the best of the kings, furnished with an umbrella and *cāmara* and carrying the bow in his hand.

*gīta* || *kānārā* || *ekatāli* ||

Song in the *Rāga Kānāḍā* with the rhythm *Ekatāli*:

[12]. in *Śloka* metre.

*dhruṁ* ||

*āve daśaratha pṛthibīnātha* |
*ḍhole cāmara chatra dharu mātha* ||

Refrain: Here comes Daśaratha, the Lord of the world (with) *dhola, cāmara* and holding the *chatra* on the head.

*pada* ||

*duryaya bīra dhariye śara cāpe* |
*kāmpe ṛpugaṇaka jāhe pratāpe* ||
*tṛbhubana īśvara rāmaka rāpa* |
*jāhe nehāri dūra haya tāpa* ||5||

Verse: The invincible champion holds the bow and arrow, whose radiance makes the enemies tremble; one who is the father of Rāma, the Lord of the three worlds, looking at whom all the sorrows are removed.

*kathā* ||

*aicana prabeśa kaya rājā daśaratha : parama harakhe baiṭhi rahala* ||

Dialogue : Entering in this way, King Daśaratha, remained seated with great happiness.

*śloka* ||

*śiṣyena sākamāgatya biśvāmitro mahāmuniḥ* |
*āśīrbbādaṁ dadau tasmai rājñe mantramudirayan* ||8||

Hymn[13]: The great sage Viśvāmitra, coming along with his pupils, uttering aloud hymns, blessed the King.

*kathā* ||

*tadanantara : ṛṣirāja kauṣīka : śiṣya sahīta : āsi kahu : rājā daśarathaka : āśīrbbāda kaya : je kahala : tā dekhaha śunaha : nirantare hari bola* ||

---

[13]. in *Śloka* metre, but in the 4[th] foot, the 6[th] letter is short instead of long.

Dialogue: After that, coming along with his pupil, blessing King Daśaratha, what the great sage Kauśika, said, watch and listen to that and keep chanting the name of Hari.

*gīta* || *rāga-kānāḍā* || *paḍitāla*
Song in the *Rāga Kānāḍā* with the rhythm *Paritāla:*

*dhruṁ* ||
*āve kautuke kauśika caṇḍa* |
*mālā māthe hāte dharu daṇḍa* ||
Refrain: The angry Kauśika comes happily with a wreath on the head and holding a staff in his hand.

*pada* ||
*lāraya bāhu hariguṇa gāve* |
*sacakita bhāve caudiśe cāve* ||
*śohe sulalita tilaka kapāla* |
*herata kope jaice jamakāla* ||6||
Verse: Shaking the shoulders singing the name of Hari, looking all around timidly, his forehead adorned with beautiful *tilaka*, looking on with anger as if Yama, the death personified.

*kathā* ||
*aicana prabeśa diye : se ṛṣirāja : bibhatsa bhāvanā kaya : jaice rājāka āśīrbbāda delaha : tāhe dekhaha śunaha* ||
Dialogue: Entering in this way, as that king of the sages blessed the King with a mischievous idea, watch and listen to that.

*śloka* ||
*cirañjīva cirañjīva cirañjīva janādhipa* |
*putrapatnīyuto nityaṁ bhaktimān bhava mādhave* ||9||
Hymn[14]: "May you live for ever, may you live for ever, may you live for ever, oh you King, accompanied with son and wife, may you always be devoted towards Mādhava."

[14]. in *Śloka* metre.

*kathā* ||

*he rājā daśaratha : saparibāre : ciranjīva bhava / rājā ṛṣika āsane baiṭhāyā : pari paraṇāma kaya : karajore bola* ||

*he muni : tohāra padaparaśe : āju ayodhyā pavitra bhela : tuva darasane : hāmāra janama sāphala : muni aba kona prayojana sādho ājñā karaha : sabhāmaidhye satya aṅgīkāra kayalo: āyu je dāna māgaha : tāheka satye satye devaba* | *ṛṣi : rājāka satyabāṇī śuni : hāsi hāsi kautuke uṭhi kahu : nṛtya kayala: āḥ manoratha sāphala bhela : rājāka āśīrbbāda kaya bolala*||

*he nṛpate : toho pṛthivīka kalpataru : tohora ṭhāi : prārthaka kabahu bimukha nāhī haya : ihāka jāno : kīntu hāmāra prayojana śunaha : hāmu siddhāśramata : yajña ārambhala: tāheka mārīca subāhu : duhu rākaca : bahuta bighini ācaraya: se yajña rakṣā nimite tohāra rāma- lakṣmaṇa : duhu kumāraka: hāmāra saṅge paṭhāva : tabe hāmāra prayojana siddhi haya* ||

Dialogue: "Oh King Daśaratha, may you along with your family live for ever." The King made the sage sit down and offering obeisance falling down, said with folded hands:

"Oh sage, with the touch of your feet, Ayodhyā is purified today, and seeing you, my life has become fulfilled; oh sage, please order me now, what can I do for you; in the presence of this assembly, I give you my word; whatever gift you ask for, I shall surely give it to you today." Hearing the true words of the king, laughing with great happiness, rising, started dancing, saying, "Oh my wishes are fulfilled today!" and blessing the king said:

"Oh dear King, you are the *kalpataru* in this world; no one is turned away from your place (without his wishes fulfilled), that I know; but now please listen to my need. I had started *yajña* at the Siddhāśrama. The two demons, Mārīca and Subāhu bring much hindrance there. To protect that *yajña*, please send your two princes Rāma and Lakṣmaṇa with me; then my needs will be fulfilled."

*śloka* ||

*tanniśamyābhavadbhīto papāta murcchito bhūvi* |
*karoti kātaraṁ rājā nigṛhya caraṇau muneḥ* ||*10*||

Hymn[15]: Hearing those words, the King, being greatly scared, fell down senseless on the ground and holding onto the feet of the sage entreated earnestly.

*kathā* ||

*rājā kauṣīkaka : aicana bāṇī śuniye : duranta cintāye pīḍala : murcchita hayā paḍala : tadanantara svastha hayā kauṣika-caraṇata dhari kahu : kātara kaya bolala* |

*āhe munirāja : hāmāra putra rāmalakṣmaṇa : se bālaka : tāheka rākacaka dite cāva : ohī kona beahāra : hā hā ṛsirāja : yajña – rakṣā nimita hāmāka liyā jāva* ||

Dialogue: Hearing such words from sage Kauśika, the King became greatly afflicted with worry and fell down senseless. Then feeling a little better, holding onto the feet of the sage Kauśika, said with earnest entreaty.

"Oh king of the sages, my sons Rāma and Lakṣmaṇa are mere boys and you want to give them away to the demons; what type of behaviour is this! Alas, alas, oh great sage, to protect the *yajña*, please take me along (instead)."

*rājāka bacana śuniye : kauṣika parama kope tarachaya* ||
*aye : pāpī asatyabādī : rāmalakṣmaṇaka nāhī paṭhāvata* ||
*ohī boli : kope kampamāna hayā bege calala : bāhu lāriye : kope daśana charppaya : rājā āgu hayā : ṛṣika caraṇa dhari kahu : jaiche bilāpa kayala : tā dekhaha śunaha : nirantare hari bola* ||

Hearing the words of the King, sage Kauśika started abusing him with great anger. "Oh you liar, you sinner, you are not sending Rāma and Lakṣmaṇa."

Saying so, trembling with anger, went out fast and shaking his arms grated his teeth in anger. Then, coming in the

15. in *Śloka* metre.

front, holding onto the feet of the sage, how the King lamented, watch and listen to that and keep chanting the name of Hari incessantly.

*gīta* || *suhai rāṁ* || *jati māna* ||
Song in the *Rāga Suhāi* with the rhythm *Jati māna:*

*dhruṁ* ||

*kariyo karuṇā ṛṣi sutadāna dehu* |
*kona muhe kahaba rāmaka tuhu lehu* ||

Refrain: "Oh great sage, please have mercy and give me (back) my sons; how can I say that you take away Rāma."

*pada* ||

*nehabi rāma rākaca lāgi māgī* |
*āhe adhika hṛdaya dahe āgi* ||*1*||
*bālaka rāma kicoye nāhī jāne* |
*tāhe neheri rahabi nāhi prāṇe* ||2||7||

Verse: "Please do not look at Rāma, seeking him for the demons; oh the heart burns more as if in the fire.
The young boy Rāma does not know anything, and without seeing him I cannot live on."

*kathā* ||

*ṛṣirāja : bālaka rāmaka : kaice rākacaka hāte dite cāva: hāhā ucita nahe : bāpa rāmaka cāri hāmāka niyā jāva* ||

Dialogue: "Oh king of the sages, how can you give away Rāma in the hands of the demons! Alas, alas, this is not proper. Oh dear father, leaving Rāma, take me along."

*ṛṣi bola* || *aye daśaratha : tuhu rāmaka caritra kichu jānaye nāhī : jogabale hāmu saba jāno : ohi rāmacandra parama īśvara : mahā harika aṁśa avatāra : asura rākaca : saba saṁhārī : bhūvika bhāra uttāraba : ihā jāni kicu cintā nāhi karabi : satya rākhi satvara rāmalakṣmaṇaka hāmāra saṅge paṭhāva* ||

The sage said, "Oh dear Daśaratha, you do not know anything about the character of Rāma. With the power of meditation I know everything. That Rāmacandra is the Supreme God, and has incarnated as a part of the great Hari. Destroying all the devils and demons, He will relieve the earth of its burdens. Knowing all this, please do not worry at all. Keeping your word, please send Rāma and Lakṣmaṇa with me immediately."

*rājā ṛṣika bāṇī śuni kahu : kiñcita svastha hayā : ṛṣika hāte rāmalakṣmaṇaka : samarppi delaha : kauṣika kautuke rāmakumāra duhu : saṅge laiyā calala jaice : tā dekhaha śunaha : nirantare hari bola* ||

Hearing the words of the sage, the King, feeling a little better, delivered Rāma and Lakṣmaṇa in the hands of the sage and as the sage Kauśika, taking along the two princes, went away happily, watch and listen to that and keep chanting the name of Hari incessantly.

*payāḍa* || *kānaḍā* || *māna jati* ||

Verse in the *Rāga Kānaḍā* with the rhythm *Jatimāna:*

*calala kauṣika sādhive kāma* |
*pācu pācu cala lakṣmaṇa rāma* ||
*delaha dhanuka- beda dibyamāna* |
*lakṣmaṇa rāma pathahī sabe jāna* ||*1*||
*āśrama jāite ṛṣika ucāṭa* |
*pekhiye tāḍakā beḍhala bāṭa* ||
*milala bhakṣya piśācinī hāse* |
*kāmpe kauṣika pariye tarāse* ||2||
*rākasī khāi rākha raghunāthe* |
*śuniye rāma dharala dhanu hāte* ||

*boli nirbhaya yorala bāṇa* |
*tāḍakā hṛdaye kari sandhāna* ||3||
*parala piśācī teji āṭāsa* |
*bajrapāte jaice loka tarāsa* ||
*hṛdaye ānanda milala adhika* |
*sādhu sādhu rāma kahaya kauṣika* ||4||
*hariṣe sihare dehaka lom* |
*āśrama pāi ārambhala homa* ||
*pekhiye dhuma mārīca subāhu* |
*cānda gilite jaca āvala rāhu* ||5||
*trāse kauśika kahaya ārāve* |
*dekhu dekhu duhuñ rākaca āve* ||
*aba raghunātha karahu mohe trāṇa* |
*śuniye rāma dharala dhanu bāṇa* ||6||
*bedhala hṛdaya saraka sandhāne* |
*urala rākaca rāmaka bāṇe* ||
*bheli sūbāhu sāgara pāta* |
*mārīca parala prāṇe laṅkāta* ||7||
*nāśa gela aba duhu piśāce* |
*kautuke uṭhi kahu kauśika nāce* ||
*rāmaka raṅge sādhu sādhu bola* |
*jaya jaya rāma kara ghana rola* ||8||8||

Sage Kauśika went having his wish fulfilled and following him went Rāma and Lakṣmaṇa. Gave them the knowledge of *dhanurveda* and Rāma and Lakṣmaṇa learnt everything on the way itself. (1)

The sage was in a hurry to go to the hermitage, and seeing that, Tāḍakā obstructed their way. The fiend laughed seeing that she had found food; and being greatly scared Kauśika trembled. (2)

"The fiend is going to eat us, please save us oh Raghunātha!" Hearing that, Rāma held up the bow and arrow in His hands and uttering reassuring words, Rāma fixed up an arrow aiming at the chest of Tāḍakā. (3)

The fiend fell down uttering a shriek, as people get scared of thunderbolt. Being very happy in his heart Kauśika said, "Well done Rāma!". (4)
His body was thrilled with happiness and having reached the hermitage he started the sacrifice. Seeing smoke, Mārīca and Subāhu came as if Rāhu coming to engulf the moon. (5)
Being greatly scared, Kauśika said shouting, "Look, look, here come two demons. Now, oh Raghunātha, please save me!" Hearing that, Rāma picked up the bow and arrow. (6)
And fixing an arrow pierced through the chest (of the demons) and the demons were flung into the air with the arrows of Rāma. Subāhu fell into the sea and was destroyed and Mārīca, saving his life, fell in Laṅkā. (7)
Two demons were destroyed and rising, Kauśika danced with happiness and made Rāma pleased, saying "Well done, well done!", and created an uproar uttering "Glory to Rāma!" repeatedly. (8)

*kathā* ||

*parama santoṣe kauśika : rāmaka āśīrbbāda kayala* ||

Dialogue : Kauśika, with great satisfaction, blessed Rāma.

*śloka* ||

*jaya jaya raghunātha prārthaka trāṇaheto*
*raghukula-kamalālī sūryabaryaḥ sadaiva* |
*haratu duritameṣāṁ nāma saṁkīrttanena*
*suhṛdasutakalatraiḥ jīvatāt tvaṁ cirāyuḥ* ||*11*||

Hymn[16]: "Glory to Raghunātha, who is the protector of all who beg for; who is like the most excellent sun making the lotus of the Raghu dynasty shine forever; chanting whose name all the misfortunes are averted, may you, along with friend, son and wife live long."

---

[16]. in *Mālinī* metre.

*kathā* ||

*raghukula-kamala prakāśaka sūrya rāmacandra : hāmāra āsirbbāde : patnīputra sahīta : ciranjīva bhava* ||

Dialogue: "Rāmacandra, who, like the sun, made the lotus of the Raghukula bloom, with my blessings, may you, along with your wife and son, live forever."

*ohī buli āśīrbbāda tulasī delaha : śrīrāma māthā pāti lelaha* ||
Saying so, blessed Him with *tulasī* and Śrī Rāma accepted it stooping His head.

*ṛṣibola* || *he bāpa rāmacandra : tuhu hāmāra parama upakārī : mārīca- subāhu : rākaca māri : hāmāra yajña siddha kayala : tohoka guṇa sujhaye nāhī pāri* | *samprati pratyupakāra : tohoka kā karaba* ||
The sage said, "Oh dear Rāmacandra, you have been of great assistance to us; killing the demons Mārīca and Subāhu, you have helped us complete our *yajña*. We can never repay you back for your virtues. Now, how can I help you back in return!".

*ohi boli : ṛṣi mane bimariṣa kaya : punu bolala* ||
Saying so, the sage deliberated in his mind and said again :

*āḥ sādhuprayojana milala : he raghunātha : āju jānekī sītāka sayambara miliche: hāmu jānala maheśaka dhanu : je guṇa dite pāraya : se kanyā sehi pāve : se bhubana mohanī bhāgyavatī: jaba (taba) gṛhiṇī haya : tabe hāmāra parama ānanda milaya : hāmu jogabale saba jāno : sohi sītā purbba janamata : bahuta tapa ācari : tohāka svāmī pāvala : tāheka smariye : ohi janama : tohāra caraṇa cinti sarbbathā thika : parama birahātura hayā : tohoka lāgi rahaice : se sundarīka rūpasampati kico kahaba : tāhe śunaha* ||
"Ah, here is a good occasion. Oh dear Raghunātha, today it is the *svayamvara* of Sītā, the daughter of Janaka. I have

learnt that whoever can fix the bow-string in the bow of Maheśa, he will get the maiden. When that fortunate girl, who mesmerises the whole world, becomes your wife, then I shall be very happy. With the power of meditation, I know everything. In the earlier life, that Sītā, practising much penance, had you as her husband. Remembering that, in this life also, she remains, always meditating on your feet and greatly suffering from separation, she is waiting for you only. I shall say something about the wealth of beauty of that beautiful young girl, please listen to that."

*bhaṭimā* ||

*ki kahaba rūpa kumārīka rāma* |
*kanaka putali tula tanu anupāma* ||
*ratana tīlaka lola alaka kapola* |
*heriye bhrubhaṅga tṛbhubana bhola* ||1||
*dekhiye badana cānda bheli lāja* |
*nayana nirekhi kamala jala-mājha* ||
*heriye bhujayuga milala ucchaṅka* |
*lalita mṛnāla majala jala paṅka* ||2||
*ārakata karatala munimana mohā* |
*kanaka salakā āṅguli karu sohā* ||
*banduli nindi adhara karu kānti* |
*ḍālimba nibira bīja danta pānti* ||3||
*īṣata hāsita madana moha jāi* |
*nāsā tilaphula kamalinī māyī* ||
*nava yaubana tana badarī pramāṇa* |
*uru karikara kaṭi ḍambaruka ṭhāna* ||4||
*padapaṅkaja nava pallava pānti* |
*campaka pākari āṅguli karu kānti* ||
*nakha caya cāru cānda parakāśa* |
*lahu lahu mattagaja-gamana bilāsa* ||5||
*kata lāvanu bihi niramala jāni* |
*kokila-nāda āmiyā jhure bāṇī* ||
*toho sukumāra rūpa nohe hīna* |
*rājakumārīka bayasa nabīna* ||6||

*sehī baḍa ramaṇī gharaṇī jabahoi* |
*aba gṛhabāsa saphala taba toi* ||
*kahalo svarūpa bacana śrīrāma* |
*cala abilamba janakara ṭhāma* ||7||
*bhāṅgaha ayagava dhanuka līlāve* |
*sītā bholi bhajoka tuyā pāve* ||
*jāni hāmu satya bāṇī bola* |
*ḍāki karahu nara hari hari bola* ||8||

Eulogy: "Oh Rāma, what to speak of the beauty of the young girl; her body, like a doll made of gold, is incomparable. A jewelled *tilaka* is on the forehead and a lock of hair hung thereon. Looking at the frown of her eyebrows one forgets the three worlds. (1)

"Seeing her face, the moon becomes ashamed and looking at her eyes the lotus hides itself into the water. Looking at the pair of her arms even the soft lotus-stalk immerses quickly in the mud under the water.(2)

"The palms, which are tinged red, infatuate even the minds of the sages. Gold pins beautify the fingers; the lovely lips radiate lustre reproaching the *banduli* flower. The rows of teeth are like the dense seeds of the pomegranate. (3)

"Even Madana is stupified at the slight smile and the nose of that *padminī* woman is like the sesame flower. The new young body is like the jujube tree. The thighs are like the trunks of elephants and the hips look like the *ḍambaru*.(4)

"The lotuslike feet are like newly sprung leaves and the fingers look beautiful like the buds of *campaka* flower. The nails glow beautifully like the bright moon and she moves slowly and gracefully like an inebriated elephant. (5)

"How charming the creator has created her! Her words flow like the cuckoo cooing. You are young and youthful and your beauty is not inferior; and the princess too is young in age. (6)

"When that excellent woman becomes your wife, then your family life will become successful. Here I am speaking the wise words, oh Śrī Rāma; let us go to the place of Janaka without any delay. (7)

"Break the bow *Ajagava* easily and may Sītā feel attracted and devote herself to your feet. Knowing it all, I have spoken the truth." Now, all the people, please utter aloud the name of Hari repeatedly. (8)

*śloka* ||

*sītāyāṁ rūpalāvaṇyaṁ śrutvā niḥśvasya rāghavaḥ* |
*ṛṣimābhāṣya bhagabān jagāma mithilāmprati* ||*10*||[17]

Hymn[18]: Hearing about the beauty and charm of Sītā, heaving a sigh, talking to the sage, Rāghava, the most venerable, went to Mithilā.

*kathā* ||

*sītāka rūpasampatti śunive : rāmaka mane kiñcita madana-bigāra upajala : jānakī biyoga nimitta niśvāsa phokāri : ṛṣika samboddhi bola* ||

*śrīrāma bola* || *he mahāmunirāja : se maheśaka dhanu : bajrādhika kaṭhina : hāmu bālaka : tāheka guṇa dite : hāmāra jogyatā kaicana hai : tathāpi tohāri ājñā pālite lāgaya : ṛṣirāja : jāni satvara calaha* ||

Dialogue: Hearing about the wealth of beauty of Sītā, Rāma, under the influence of Madana, had a little excitement; being separated from Jānakī, heaving a sigh, addressing the sage said:

Śrī Rāma said, "Oh king of the sages, that bow of Maheśa is harder than even *Vajra*. I am a young boy; how am I able to fix the bow-string to it. Yet I have to obey your command; knowing that, oh great sage, let us go quickly."

*sūtra* ||

*ohi buli sodara sahita ṛṣika pācu : śrīrāma jaice mithilāka payāna karala : tāhe dekhaha śunaha : nirantare hari bola* ||

---

17. ||12||.

18. in *Śloka* metre, but in the 3rd foot, the 6th and 7th letters are short instead of long.

Direction: Saying so, as Śrī Rāma, along with His brother, following the sage, went to Mithilā, watch and listen to that and keep chanting the name of Hari incessantly.

*gīta || māura rāṁ || māna jati ||*
Song in the *Rāga Māhura* with the rhythm *Jati māna:*

*dhruṁ ||*

*ramayā cale mithilāku lāi ||*
*rājīva locana: śyāma sundara:*
*sodara saṅgahi jāi ||*

Refrain: Rāma moves towards Mithilā; the lotus-eyed, dark and beautiful one, goes along with His brother.

*pada ||*

*śuni ramaṇīka nikalika*[19] *kāhāni:*
*milala moha murāri |*
*bhāva bhina rita: bheli kiñcita:*
*citta madana bigāri ||1||*
*badana indū madana jhāmara:*
*kāma pahila prabeśa |*
*calatu rāghava: kāma kautuka :*
*haratu keśava kleśa ||2||9||*

Verse: Hearing the spotless story of the lovely young woman, Murāri had fascination; His emotions changed a little and His mind was excited by Madana. (1)
The moon-like face is withered by Madana at the first entry of love; Rāghava went happily with love and may Keśava remove all the sufferings. (2)

*kathā ||*

*tadanantara : mithilāpura pāi : ṛṣi- sodara sahita : śrīrāmacandra : rājasabhā prabeśa kayala : janaka kara joḍi uṭhi kahu : rāmalakṣmaṇa sahita biśvāmitraka āsane baiṭhāi: ṛṣika praṇāmi tuti bolala ||*

---

[19]. *niṣkalaṅka.*

*rājā bola* || *he ṛṣirāja : tohāra āgamane : āju hāmāra mithilāpura pavitra bhela : meri mahābhāgya milala* || *ṛṣi āśīrbbāda śloka paḍhala* ||

Dialogue: After that, reaching the city of Mithilā along with His brother and the sage, Śrī Rāmacandra entered the court of the King Janaka. Rising with folded hands, making Viśvāmitra, along with Rāma and Lakṣmaṇa take their seats, offering obeisance to the sage, (King Janaka) started eulogy. The King said, "Oh king of the sages, with your coming here today, our city of Mithilā has become purified. I have become very fortunate," and the sage recited a hymn blessing him.

*cirañjīva cirañjīva rājan sajjana-rañjana* |
*gajavājīmahaiścaryabhāryātmajayutaḥ sadā* ||6||[20]

"May you live forever, may you live forever, oh dear king, who pleases the virtuous people. May you always be endowed with elephants, horses, great wealth, wife and son!"[21]

*kathā* ||

*he mahārājā janaka : patnī putra sahita : tuhu cirakāle sukhībhava : tohāri satkāre parama tuṣṭa bhelo* || *janaka rājā rāmalakṣmaṇaka rūpa nirekhi parama ācarya hayā : munita puchata* ||

Dialogue : "Oh dear King Janaka, may you remain happy forever, along with your wife and son. I have become very much pleased with your hospitality." Looking at the beauty and charm of Rāma and Lakṣmaṇa, being greatly surprised, King Janaka asked the sage.

*he ṛṣirāja : ohi bālaka duhu : adabhuta madhura mūruti : dekhi parama ānanda bhelo : kāhera kumāra : kibā deva :*

---

[20]. ||13||.

[21]. in *Śloka* metre.

*kibā manuṣya : hāmu bujhāye nāpāri : ohi sukumāra : kumāra duhu : dekhite hṛdaya santoṣa bhela* ||
"Oh great sage, these two young boys have such incredibly sweet forms; I have become greatly pleased to see them. Whose sons are they, whether God or human, I do not understand. Looking at these two young beautiful young boys, my mind is very satisfied."

*tāhe śuni ṛṣi śloka paḍhala* ||
Hearing that, the sage recited a hymn.

*sutau daśarathasyaitāvāgatau rāmalakṣmaṇau* |
*duhitustava sītāyāḥ svayambaradidṛkṣayā* ||*14*||
"Those two are Rāma and Lakṣmaṇa, the sons of Daśaratha, and they have come here to watch the *svayamvara* of your daughter Sītā."[22]

*kathā* ||
*he mahārājā : tohāri paricaya nāhi : je daśaratha rājā : tohāra parama mitra : tāhāra kumāra duhu : hāmāra parama śiṣya : ārā sabāra nāma rāmalakṣmaṇa : tohāra duhitā sītāra sayambara dekhite ihā āvala thika : iha jāni : satvara samāja patāi : maheśaka dhanu ānaha* ||
Dialogue: "Oh your majesty, you do not know one another; these two are the sons of King Daśaratha, who is your great friend; they are the best pupils of me and their names are Rāma and Lakṣmaṇa and they have come here to watch the *svayamvara* of your daughter Sītā. Knowing that, assembling the society immediately, bring the bow of Maheśa."

*janakarājā mahā harṣe : rāmalakṣmaṇaka āliṅgi bolala* ||
King Janaka, embracing Rāma and Lakṣmaṇa with great happiness, said:

---

22. in *Śloka* metre.

*āḥ dhanya dhanya daśaratha rājā : aicana parama sukumāra kumāra jāhera gṛhe : tāhera bhāgyaka mahimā ki kahaba* ||
"Oh, King Daśaratha is very fortunate, very blessed man indeed! What to say of the good furtune of those, in whose family such beautiful young men are there!"

*ohi boli rājā parama ucave : pañcama sabade sambāda nāda bahuta bajāvala : maṇimanta mantrīka ādeśa kayala* ||
Saying so, the King with great jubilance created great sound in the fifth note, indicating information and ordered his minister Maṇimanta.

*aye maṇimanta : ye nṛpasaba bāsā kari rahice : āheka āni sattara samāja milāva* ||
"Oh dear Maṇimanta, please bring those kings who are residing here, and get them assembled immediately."

*iti śrutvā maṇimanto niṣkrāntaḥ* ||
Hearing this, Maṇimanta went out.

*śloka* ||

*niśamya paramā rāmā rāmāgamana-kautukam* |
*sakhīṁ sampreṣayāmāsa jānakī kanakāvatīm* ||15||

Hymn[23]: Hearing the great rejoicing for the visit of Rāma, Jānakī, the most beautiful, sent her friend Kanakāvatī.

*kathā* ||

*tadanantara : ḍhola ḍhakkāśaṅkhagomukha : mṛdu mṛdaṅga : tāla karatāla : kāhāla kolāhala : mahotsavarava śuniye : jānakī sakhīka sambodhi bolala* ||
*hā hā sakhī kanakāvatī : ki nimitta sabhāta mahā hariṣa bājana śuniye : kona rājā āvala : satvare jāna giyā : hāmāka bāma aṅga phānde : kona kuśala sādhe : jānaye nāhi* ||

---

23. in *Śloka* metre.

Dialogue: After that, hearing the festive sounds of the *ḍhola, ḍhakkā, śaṅkha, gomukha, mṛdaṅga, tāla, karatāla* and *kāhāla,* addressing her friend, Jānakī said,
"Ah dear Kanakāvatī, what for do we hear music of joy and delight at the king's court? Go and learn immediately, which king has come. My left limbs are throbbing; what good will be accomplished, I do not know."

*śloka* ||

*tasyāḥ kathamathākarṇya kautukāt kaṇakāvatī* |
*yayau rājasabhāṁ sāddhī sītāṁ natvātisatvaram* ||*16*||

Hymn[24]: Hearing her words, bowing to Sītā, the good woman Kanakāvatī happily went to the king's court immediately.

*kathā* ||

*sītāka aicana ādeśa śuni kahu : kanakāvatī : sītā pāye paraṇāma karive jaice calali : tā dekhaha śunaha : nirantare hari bola* ||

Dialogue: Hearing such command from Sītā, bowing in her feet, as Kanakāvatī went, watch and listen to that and keep chanting the name of Hari incessantly.

*gīta* || *dhanaśrī rāṁ* || *ekatāli* ||
Song in the *Rāga Dhanaśrī* with the rhythm *Ekatāli:*

*dhruṁ* ||

*katuhale cale māyī : rāma paricaya lāi* |
*kāminī kanakāvatī : jāya rājahaṁsagati* ||

Refrain :The young girl Kanakāvatī went, moving (gracefully) like the flamingo, with eagerness to know and have acquaintance with Rāma.

*pada* ||

*pāve sabhāka satī : dekhala raghupati* |

---

[24]. in *Śloka* metre.

*jaicana gagana mājha : udita naikṣatrarāja* ||*1*||
*pekhi rūpa lāanu : bheli pulakita tanu* |
*jhure nayanaka nīra : tanu mana mohe*[25] *thira* ||2||*1*||

Verse : Reaching the court, the good woman saw Raghupati, as the king of the stars (the sun) shines in the middle of the sky. Seeing his beauty and charm, her body shivered with excitement and flowing tears from her eyes and her body and mind were not steady (anymore).

*kathā* ||

*sabhāka madhye rāmaka rūpa-lāvaṇya dekhi : parama bismita hayā : sītāka āgu giyā : kanakāvatī pari paraṇāmi bolala* ||

Dialogue: Seeing the beauty and charm of Rāma in the king's court, being greatly amazed, going to Sītā, Kanakāvatī, offering obeisance falling down on the ground, said.

*āhe prāṇasakhī : tohāra mahodaya milala* ||
"Oh friend as dear as life, you have become very fortunate!"

*sītā bola* || *he prāṇasakhī : tuhu ki dekhala : ki śunala : sattara kaha* |
*kanakāvatī bola* || *āhe janakanandanī : tuhu jāhera birahe prāṇa cāraha : sohi daśaratha rājāra kumāra : kauṭi kandarppadarppadalana rūpa : śrīrāmacandra : tohāri : sayambara śunie āvala : tāhe dekhi rājā janaka ānanda dundubhi bajāala : he sakhī : rāmaka ki ācarya mānuṣa rūpa ki kahaba : eku aṅgaka lāanu śata bariṣa kahite napāri : sakhī tathāpi kico kahaci : tā śunaha* ||
Sītā said, "Oh friend as dear as life, what have you seen and heard, tell me quickly."
Kanakāvatī said, "Oh dear daughter of Janaka, being separated from whom you are leaving your life, that same son of King Daśaratha, whose beauty crushes the vanity of a crore of Kandarpa, that Śrī Rāmacandra has come hearing

---

25. *nohe.*

about your *svayamvara*. Seeing Him, out of happiness, King Janaka has played the *dundubhi*. Oh dear friend, what to speak of the wonderful human form of Rāma! (I) cannot finish describing the charm of even one part of Him in a hundred years. Yet, here I am telling you some of it, listen to that."

*bhaṭimā* ||

*śuna sakhī bacana svarūpa* | *kī kahaba rāmaka rūpa* ||
*śyāma mūruti pītabāsa* | *ghana jaca bijurī bikāśa* ||1||
*mastaka chatraka beśa* | *nīla kuñcita keśa* ||
*rucikara karṇa atula* | *nāsā nīla tila phula* ||2||
*badana indu parakāśa* | *aruṇa adhara manda hāsa* ||
*otima daśana pānti* | *māṇika jhikamika kānti* ||3||
*madanaka dhanu bhruba bhaṅga*| *bhujayuga balita bhujavaṅga* ||
*nayana paṅkaja nava pātā* | *karatala utapala rātā* ||4||
*āṅguli lalita amola* | *nakhacaya cāndaka tula* ||
*sundara udara kaṭibandha* | *śohe siṁha bandha kandha* ||5||
*uru karikara nirupama* | *caraṇa kamala koṣa śyāma* ||
*padatala rātula kānti* | *dhvaja yava paṅkaja pānti*||6||
*mānuṣaka aicana rūpa* | *nāhi śuni kahalo svarūpa* ||
*nabīna bayasa sukumāra* | *nārāyaṇa avatāra* ||7||
*kino bhaila bhāgya tohāri* | *tuhu nava taruṇa kumārī* ||
*bidhi milāvala āni* | *teri manoratha jāni* ||8||
*aba saba pūrala āśa* | *biraha dukha gela nāśa* ||
*pāvaba svāmīka kola* | *kara nara hari hari bola* ||9||

Eulogy : "Oh dear friend, listen to these pleasing words; what to speak of the beauty of Rāma. The dark body with yellow clothing looks like lightning flashing brightly on the cloud. (1)

"The head with blue curly hair is like an umbrella; the charming ears are incomparable and the nose is like blue sesame flower.(2)

"The face shines like the moon and in the ruddy lips there is a soft smile. The best row of teeth dazzle brightly like ruby.(3)

"The curved eye-brows look like the bow of Madana and the pair of arms is like long snakes. The eyes are like the fresh petels of lotus and the palms are red like the water-lilies. (4)

"The fingers are beautiful and excellent and the beautiful rows of nails are bright like the moon. Beautiful are the belly and the girdle and the shoulders are handsome like that of a lion in form. (5)

"The thighs are like the trunk of an elephant and the feet are dark like a lotus bud. The feet are lovely red and thereon, in a row, are the (signs of) the flag, the barley and the lotus. (6)

"I have never heard of such beauty in human form, I am telling you the truth. He is fresh and youthful young man and is Nārāyaṇa incarnate.(7)

"What good fortune you have, you fresh young girl; the God has brought you together knowing your desire. (8)

"Now all your wishes are fulfilled; all the sorrows of separation are destroyed and you will be by the side of your Lord." All the people utter aloud the name of Hari repeatedly. (9)

*kathā* ||

*āhe sakhī : jaicana mahāpuruṣa-lakṣaṇa dekhala : jānala : ohi īśvara nārāyaṇa : śrīrāma rūpe tohāra bibāha hetu āvala : ihāta kico śaṅkā nāhi karabi : sakhī tohāra manoratha sāphala bhela* ||

Dialogue : "Oh dear friend, (I) saw such signs of *mahāpuruṣa*, that I knew that He is the Lord Nārāyaṇa, and has come in the form of Śrī Rāma for your wedding; do not keep any doubt in this regard. Oh dear friend, your wishes are fulfilled."

*śloka* ||

*śrutvā sakhīmukhādrāmacandrasya caritāmṛtam* |
*murcchitā patitā sītā sumahāharṣa-dharṣitā* ||17||

Hymn[26]: Hearing from her friend, the charming tales about Rāmacandra, Sītā, overcome with extreme happiness, fell down fainting.

*kathā* ||

*rāmaka parama caritra śuni : sītā mahā hariṣābeśe murcchita hayā parala : jaice premarase mahā ākula kailā*[27] *tā dekhaha śunaha : nirantare hari bola hari bola* ||

Dialogue: Hearing the excellent account of Rāma, Sītā, overcome with extreme happiness, fell down unconscious and as she was greatly restless with the feeling of love, watch and listen to that and keep chanting the name of Hari incessantly.

*gīta* || *rāga dhanaśrī* || *ekatāli* ||

Song in the *Rāga Dhanaśrī* with the rhythm *Ekatāli:*

*svāmīka caritra: śunie kumārī*
*bheli pulakita tanu: cetana ākula:*
*kula kāminī jhure bāri* ||

Hearing the account of her Lord, the body of the young girl shivered with excitement and her mind became greatly restless and the beautiful woman from the noble family flowed tears.

*pada* ||

*rāmaka caraṇa: citta cira cintie:*
*nayanā mudi rahu māi* |
*prema- paraśa rasa: rāja-nandanī jaca:*
*mānasa amiyā jhurāi* ||*1*||
*jāhe birahe dahe: rahala nāhi jīva:*
*so pṛya pāvala kola* |
*ānanda sindhu: magana kāminī:*
*kṛṣṇa kiṅkara ohi bola* ||2||*11*||

---

26. in *Śloka* metre.

27. *bhela.*

Verse: Meditating on the feet of Rāma for a long time, the young girl remained closing her eyes. Sensing the touch of love, as if the mind of the princess flowed with nectar. (1) Finding that beloved near her, in whose separation it burns and life stops, the beautiful woman plunged in the sea of happiness; says the servant of Kṛṣṇa. (2)

*sūtra* ||

*kanakāvatī : madana-mantharā : sītāka dhari kahu : āñcole aṅga muci : prabodha bolaya* |

*he prāṇa sakhī : tuhu jāhera caraṇa cinti : cirakāla rahaicha : se rāmacandraka bidhi hāte milāvala : ānanda samae tuhu ki nimita : ākula bhelaha he mātā svastha hava* ||

Direction: Supporting Sītā, Kanakāvatī and Madanamantharā, wiping her body with the fore-end of their clothing, consoled her,

"Oh friend, as dear as life, meditating on whose feet you have remained forever, destiny has brought that same Rāmacandra near you. At such time of happiness, why are you being so restless? Please calm down."

*sūtra* ||

*sakhīsabaka bāṇī śuni sītā ākula teji : rāmaka caraṇa cinti : eka pāśa hayā rahala* ||

Direction: Hearing the words of her friends, setting aside her restlessness, meditating on the feet of Rāma, Sītā remained in a side.

*śloka* ||

*tato nṛpān samānīya maṇimanto nṛpājñayā* |

*kārayāmāsa mahatīṁ sabhāmutsava –śobhitām* ||*18*||

Hymn[28]: Then, as ordered by the King, Maṇimanta, assembling the kings, held a beautiful huge festive meeting.

---

[28]. in *Śloka* metre, but in the 3rd foot, the 6th and 7th letters are short instead of long.

*kathā* ||

*tadanantara : maṇimanta mantrī rājāsabaka ānie : jaice sabhāmaidhye milāvala : tā dekhaha śunaha : nirantare hari bola* ||

Dialogue : After that, as minister Maṇimanta, bringing the kings assembled them in the hall, watch and listen to that and keep chanting the name of Hari incessantly.

*gīta* || *rāga-kānaḍā* || *paritāla* ||

Song in the *Rāga Kānaḍā* with the rhythm *Paritāla:*

*āve nṛpasaba dhari śara cāpe* |
*kāmpe dharaṇī parama pratāpe* ||

The kings came holding bows and arrows and the world trembled with their vigour.

*pada* ||

*kāhu kāṇḍa khāṇḍā uri hāta* |
*daśana kāmuri jhaṅkāre mātha* ||
*darape karaya māra dhara rola* |
*pāvala rājasabhākeri kola* ||2||12||

Verse: Some came holding up the arrows and the daggers, grating their teeth and shaking their heads and creating an uproar shouting "Beat him, catch him!", and reached near the king's court.

*kathā* ||

*se rājāsaba : aicana bibhatsa bhāvanā kaya : ekapāśa hayā baiṭhi sabhāta rahala* ||

Dialogue : Expressing such depraved thoughts, those kings remained sitting on one side of the assembly.

*śloka* ||

*sakhībhiḥ sākamabhedyaṁ jānakīṁ janako'nayat* |
*maheśadhanuḥ svaskandhe nidhāya śobhitāṁ sabhām* ||19||

Hymn[29]: Bearing the bow of Maheśa, which was difficult to break, on his own shoulders, Janaka brought Jānakī, adorned beautifully, along with her friends, to the assembly.

*kathā* ||

*tadanantara : rājājanaka abhyantara praveśiye : maheśaka ajagava dhanu kandhe karie : duhitā sītāka bastre alaṅkāre sumaṇḍita karie : suvarṇṇa-paṅkajamālā hāte die kahu : sakhīsava sahita : jaicana utsava utsuke : sabhā prabeśa karāala : tāhe ityādi ||*

Dialogue : After that, King Janaka entering inside, bearing *Ajagava*, the bow of Maheśa, on his shoulder, escorted his daughter Sītā along with her friends, having her well-adorned with clothes and jewellery and having her hold in her hands a garland of golden lotus, into the assembly, eagerly waiting for the festive occasion; all that and others etc.

*gīta || rāga –suhāi || cuṭikālā ||*

Song in the *Rāga Suhāi* with the rhythm *Cuṭikālā:*

*jānakī kāminī : kautuke calali lāi*[30]
*sakhīsaba saṅge : raṅge karata keli :*
*meli āñcola dulāi ||*

The beautiful woman Jānakī, went on happily with grace, having mirth and sporting happily with her friends and spreading out and waving the fore-end of her clothing.

*pada ||*

*nava piu paraśa : rasika karu bālā :*
*mālā karatale lole |*
*caraṇa rañjita manī : mañjīra jhānakita :*
*kaṅkaṇa kiṅkiṇī role ||1||*

---

29. in *Śloka* metre, but in the 1st foot, the 6th letter is short instead of long and in the 3rd foot, the 5th letter is long instead of short.
30. *cala līlāi.*

*mattagajagāminī : kāminī māi :*
*jāi nijapiu pāśā |*
*herie nṛpasaba : madane dahatu mana :*
*kahatu kṛṣṇaka dāsā ||2||13||*

Verse: The (thought of) touch from her new beloved made the young girl delighted and a garland hung from her hands. The feet glowed with jewels, the anklets jingled and the bracelets made tinkling sound.(1)
Walking like an inebriated elephant, the lovely woman went near her Lord and looking at her, the minds of the kings were tormented by Madana; says the servant of Kṛṣṇa. (2)

*kathā ||*
*rājanandanīka nava jaubanī rūpa lāvaṇya nirekhi : rājāsabaka kāmabāṇe pīḍala : acetane murccita hayā parala : punu cetana labhie : uṭhi kahu : parama ākula bhāe : sītāka kātara kaya bolala ||*

Dialogue: Looking at the newly youthful beauty and charm of the princess, the kings became tormented with the arrow of love and fell down unconscious. Again, rising, regaining consciousness, greatly agitated, spoke to Sītā entreating earnestly.

*rājāsaba bola || he prāṇeśvarī : kāmasāgare magana bhelo : nistāra karaha ||*
*kāhu āṅguli mukhe laiyā bolala || he rājanandanī : madane hāmāra mana marddaya : priye hāmāka haste parakha ||*
*daśane khera kāmuri kāhu binaya bolaye || he sundarī : madana bāṇe phuṭi : hāmāra prāṇa phuṭi churi jāi : bacana āmiyā rakha barakhi hāmāka jīvāva ||*
*kāhu kāme bhuli bolaya || hāmāra gṛhe jata mahādei thika : saba tomāka dāsī kari devaba : hāmu tohāra caraṇaka dāsa bhelo : hāmāra āge khānika tambhie : kaṭākṣa nirekhi : prāṇadāna deha ||*

The kings said, "Oh beloved, we have plunged in the sea of desire, please rescue us."
Some said holding their fingers in the mouth, "Oh Princess, our minds are crushed by Madana; oh beloved, please touch us with your hand."
Biting a blade of grass with their teeth, some said politely, "Oh beautiful, being pierced with the shaft of Madana, our lives have become pierced and cut; showering the nectar of your words, please revive us again."
Some, being absorbed in love, said, "As many queens are there at home, we will make them all your slaves. We have become slaves in your feet; stopping awhile in front of us and giving a sidelong glance at us, please save our lives."

*sūtra* ||
*aicana kāme matta hayā rājāsaba : nānā bidha bibhatsa bhāvanā karaya : pekhi sītāka sakhī : kanakāvatī : madanamantharā : candramatī : sūryaprabhā : kāhu rājāka gora māri bharacaya : kāho hāte pāe ṭheṅganā māraya : kāhu bastragale bāndhie : dui tini sakhīe dharie ghasāve : sesaba dukhako nagaṇaya : tathāpi nṛpakumārīka kātara kaya thika* ||
*aye loka : haribhakati hīna : kāmātura puruṣara dukha dekhaha : jagataka mātā janaka nandanī : tāheka jānave nāhi : iha jāni nirantare hari bola* ||

Direction : Seeing them being excited with love in this way, expressing many different depraved thoughts, the friends of Sītā, Kanakāvatī, Madanamantharā, Candramatī and Sūryaprabhā abused some with kicks, pushed away some by their hands and feet, tied up some by the neck with cloth and holding them, two or three friends together, pounded them. But the kings did not care for those sufferings and kept on entreating the princess.
Oh dear people, look at the sufferings of the love-sick men without devotion to Hari. They do not know that the

daughter of Janaka is the mother of this whole world; knowing it, keep chanting the name of Hari incessantly.

*śloka* ||

*jagāda janako vākyaṁ paśyatainaṁ dhunurnṛpāḥ*[31]|
*idaṁ sajyaṁ karoti yaḥ tasmai sītāṁ samarpaye*||20||

Hymn[32]: Janaka said the words, "Look at this bow, oh kings! I shall give away Sītā to him, who strings the bow."

*kathā* ||

*janakarājā rājasabhāka svastha kaya bolala*|| *āhe rājāsaba : hāmu satya bāṇī kahaice : tā śunaha : sītāka bibāha nimitta : cintate*[33] *: õhi maheśaka dhanu : gagana hante parala : tadanantara : ākāśī bāṇī śunala : ohī dhanuta je guṇa dite pāraya : tāheka māthe : kusuma mālā die : sītā svāmī baraba : iha satya jāni jatna karaha*||

Dialogue: Comforting the assembly at court, King Janaka said, "Oh dear kings, here I am speaking the truth, listen to it. While (I was) thinking about Sītā's wedding, that bow of Maheśa fell down from the sky. After that, I heard a voice from the heaven, 'Whoever can string that bow, offering garland of flowers on his head, Sītā will choose him as her husband.'; knowing it to be the truth, try hard."

*ohi bākya śuniye : śatadhanu nāma rāyā : parama āḍambare : kāchi giyā : pahilehi dhanuka dharala : daśana kāmuri ; guṇa dite chita hayā parala | tadanantara candra ketu : dhanu dhari kahõ : kathaṁkathamapi : ullāsi dhanu sahite parala : tā dekhi rājā purañjaya : parama āṭope : dhanu dhari kahu : śarīraka bale lāḍite nāpāri : uphari parala : tadanantara rājā kumudākṣa : kaṭi bastra kāchikahu : adhara kāmuri : dhanuka doṅga die : tulite mahāprayāsa pāi : bikhepa karala : lāja hui samajyātapari hātapāva ācaraya*||

---

31. *dhanurnṛpāḥ.*

32. in *Śloka* metre, but in the 3rd foot, the 7th letter is short instead of long.

33. *cintite.*

Hearing those words, a king by the name Śatadhanu, with great arrogance, smartly picked up the bow at first. Grating his teeth, trying to string the bow, he fell down supine. After that, Candraketu holding the bow up with great effort, became greatly delighted but fell down along with the bow. Seeing that, King Purañjaya, holding the bow with great pride, being unable to move it with all his strength, he fell down flung away. After that, King Kumudākṣa, tightening up his girdle, biting his lips, lifting the bow up with a push, found it very difficult and threw it down. Being ashamed, finding himself in trouble, flapped his hands and feet.

*śloka* ||

*rāmamāha munirbatsa kinnirīkṣyeha tiṣṭhasi* |
*kauśalyānandanottiṣṭha tvaṁ sajyaṁ kuru kārmukam* ||21||

Hymn[34]: The sage said to Rāma, "My dear son, what are you watching? Oh dear son of Kauśalyā, rise and string the bow."

*sūtra* ||

*he sāmājika : rājā sabaka parama bibhatsa dekhie : muni rāmaka bola* ||
*he kauśalyānandana : tuhu ki nimita āpekhi rahaiche uṭhaha : ohi dhanuta sattara guṇa lagāva* ||

Direction: Oh dear audience, finding the kings so disgusting, the sage said to Rāma, "Oh dear son of Kauśalyā, what are you waiting for? Rise and string that bow immediately."

*rāmacandra ṛṣika praṇāmi bolala* ||
Rāmacandra said offering obeisance to the sage:

*he munirāja : hāmu bālaka : ohi dhanu bajrādhika kaṭhina : ihāta guṇa dite : hāmāra sāmartha kaicana hai tathāpi tohāra*

[34]. in *Śloka* metre.

*ājñā pāli jatna karaba : je dhanuta guṇa dite mahārājāsaba : nāhi pārala : ihāta hāmāra kona lāja nāhi* ||

"Oh king of the sages, I am a young boy; how am I able to string that bow which is harder even than the *Vajra*. Yet, obeying your command, I shall try. There is no shame for me trying (if I fail to string the bow) the bow, which even the great kings could not string."

*ōhi buli rāmacandra : pīta bastra kācani kāci : līlāe calala : pekhi rājāsaba bihasi bolaya* ||

Saying so, Rāmacandra, smartly tying up His yellow clothing, went with pleasure and seeing Him the kings said smiling,

*rājā bola* || *ōhi kāheka cayāla : ki upālambha bheli* ||

The kings said, "Wherefrom comes that boy? What an insult to us!".

*sūtra* ||

*śrīrāma ajagava dhanuka bāmahāte dhari kahu : jaice kusuma mālāka urddhaka khepi : punrbbāra lumphi dharala : pekhi rājāsabaka mukha malina bhela* ||

Direction: The faces of the kings became clouded as they saw Śrī Rāma, holding the bow *Ajagava* in His left hand, throwing it high up as if a garland of flowers and catching it back jumping again.

*śloka* ||

*dhṛte cāpe śrīrāmena*[35] *sītā śaṅkitamānasā* |
*anantaṁ kacchapaṁ pṛthvīṁ yācamānā jagāda sā* ||22||

Hymn[36]: Seeing the bow being held up by Rāma, Sītā became greatly worried and praying to Ananta, the tortoise and the earth, she said,

*sūtra* ||

*he sāmājika loka : jenakhana rāmacandra ajagava dhanu dharala : sītā parama śaṅkita bhāve : mane cintita bheli : hā*

[35]. *śrīrāmeṇa*.

[36]. in *Śloka* metre, but in the 1st foot, the 5th letter is long instead of short.

*hā hāmāra svāmī parama sukumāra : navina bayasa : bajrādhika kaṭhora maheśaka dhanu : ihāta guṇa dite svāmī junu pāraya nāhi : hā hā pitā ki dāruṇa karmma kayali : ohi cinti pṛthibīka kātara kaya bolala ||*

Direction : Oh dear assembled people, when Rāmacandra held the bow *Ajagava*, Sītā, greatly scared, became very much worried. "Alas, alas, my Lord is very inexperienced and young in age; lest my Lord is unable to string the bow of Maheśa, which is even harder than the *Vajra!* Alas, alas, oh dear father, what a terrible thing you have done!" Thinking thus, said to the earth eantreating earnestly.

*sītā bola || he māva basumatī : tuhu thira huyā rahaba : he pitā ananta : tuhu bhalla kaya pṛthibīka dharaba : he īśvara kurmmarāja : tuhu anantaka pṛthibīka sanvadhe dharaba : torāsabaka prasāde svāmī jadi guṇa dite pāraya : tabe hāmu agatira gati haya ||*

Sītā said, "Oh mother Vasumatī, please remain steady; oh father Ananta, please hold the earth well; oh Lord Kūrmmarāja, please hold Ananta and the earth bound together. With your blessings, if my Lord can string (the bow), then helpless that I am, will have a recourse."

*ohi buli : sītā svāmīka mukha nirekhi rahala ||*

Saying thus, Sītā remained looking at her the face of her Lord.

*śloka ||*

*rāmastu śaṅkitāṁ sītāṁ nirīkṣya kṛpayā prabhuḥ |*
*prasajya sajyamakarot līlayājagavaṁ dhanuḥ ||32||*[37]

Hymn[38]: Seeing Sītā being scared, Lord Rāma also mercifully, getting ready with the string, strung the bow *Ajagava* at ease.

---

37. ||23||.

38. in *Śloka* metre, but in the 3rd foot, the 6th and the 7th letters are short instead of long.

*kathā* ||

*se kṛpāmaya rāmacandra : sītāka sakāruṇa bhāva pekhi : tatkāle līlāye dhanuta guṇa lagāala : se īśvara puruṣa rāmacandra : hasi hasi aprayāse : karṇamāne ṭāni : dhanuta ṭaṅkāra karala : ṭhātkāra sabade madhya sthāne : dhanu bhāgi pacāro ciḍala : jaicana bajrapāta bhela tadvat : rāmaka mahā mahimā dekhi : rājāsaba sacakita bhelaha : sītā bhanubhaṅga*[39] *dekhi : ānande magana hayā : jaice śrīrāmaka māthe kusumaka mālā die : svāmī buli barala : tā dekhaha śunaha : nirantare hari bola hari*||

Dialogue: That merciful Rāmacandra, seeing Sītā with sorrowful disposition, immediately fixed the string to the bow playfully, that Personality of Godhead Rāmacandra, smilingly stretched the string without effort almost to His ear and twanged the bow and in the blink of the eye, the bow broke in the middle with a loud thudding sound like the stroke of a thunderbolt. Seeing the power of Rāma, the kings became startled. Seeing the bow broken, as Sīta, being absorbed in happiness, bestowing the garland of flowers on the head of Śrī Rāma accepting Him as her husband, watch and listen to that and keep chanting the name of Hari incessantly.

*gīta* || *rāga- māura* || *paritāla* ||

Song in the *Rāga Māhura* with the rhythm *Paritāla:*

*ānande rājanandanī hāse* |
*rāmaka pāśa calaya layalāse* ||

The Princess laughed with happiness and moved with grace to Rāma.

*pada* ||

*svāmīka māthe mālā parujāi* |
*karu paraṇāma pāve pari māi* ||
*dhari kahu ramaṇī rāma hāsi tola* |
*svāmīka kāminī āñcole ḍhola* ||*14*||

[39]. *dhanubhaṅga.*

Verse : Offering the garland on the head of her husband, the dear young girl, falling at His feet, prostrated to Him. Holding her, Rāma raised the beautiful woman smiling and the lovely woman fanned her husband with the fore-end of her clothing.

*sūtra* ||

*he samājika : sītā rāmaka svāmī bhāye baḍie : karppūra-tāmbula jogāi : ānande rahala : tāhe dekhi rājāsaba : śoke kope mohita hayā : dhanubāṇa dharie : rāmaka parama darppa karie garaje* ||

Direction: Oh dear audience, accepting Rāma as her husband, Sītā, supplying Him with betel-nut and camphor, remained happily. Seeing that, the kings being bewildered with sorrow and anger, holding the bows and arrows, with great haughtiness, thundered to Rāma.

*aye kāheka cayāla : āḥ hāmāra kainyā ohi laiyā jāi : hāmusaba rājāka jīvana dhika* ||

*ohi buli : dharamāra rola āndola bahuta karala* |

"Oh, wherefrom has He come! And He is taking away our bride! Shame on the lives of all of us kings!" Saying so, created great commotion shouting, "Hold him, kill him!".

*śloka* ||

*śrutvā sītā bhavadbhītā bhūpālavīravalkalam* |
*ruroda vepitavatī patiṁ pratyanuśocati* ||24||

Hymn[40]: Hearing the noise of the brave kings, Sītā being scared, cried trembling lamenting for her husband.

*kathā* ||

*rājāsabaka parama āndola rola śunie : rāja-nandanī : bhae parama ākula bheli : jānakī jaicana : svāmīka lāgi bilāpa kae bola : tāhe dekhaha śunaha* ||

---

[40]. in *Śloka* metre, but in the 3rd foot, the 6th and the 7th letters are short instead of long.

Dialogue: Hearing the disturbing words of the kings, the Princess became greatly agitated with fear. As Jānakī said lamenting for her husband, watch and listen to that.

*hā hā bidhi : hāmāra ki kapāla milala : hari hari rāma svāmi : parama sukumāra : nabīna bayasa : saṅge sodara mātra sahāya : ohī parama nikāruṇa dāruṇa : rājāsabaka kaiche juddhe jinava : hā hā daiva : kona aparādhe : hāmāka bañcala* ||
"Alas, alas, oh destiny! What fate I have met with! Hari, Hari, oh Lord Rāma! Very youthful and inexperienced and having only His brother with Him as companion, how can He conquer those greatly merciless and expert kings! Alas, alas, destiny, for what fault of mine I am deprived!"

*ohī buli jānekī : jaice svāmīka lāgi bilāpa kayala* || *āhe ityādi* ||
Saying so, as Jānakī lamented for her husband in this manner and so on.

*gīta* || *rāga-gaurī* || *biṣama tāla* ||
Song in the *Rāga Gaurī* with the rhythm *Biṣamatāla:*

*nāi nāi cetanu nayana jhurāi bāri* |
*bilapati māi : piuka lāi :*
*tāpe pari kumārī* ||

The dear young girl not in her senses and tears flowing from the eyes, the maiden, lamented, lying down suffering for her beloved.

*pada* ||

*puruba janama : puṇya parama :*
*pāvala pahu ohi* |
*baṅkima bidhi : hātaka nidhi :*
*hare abhāgīka mohi* ||1||
*durllabha balabha : lāgi ākula :*
*karatu e bara nārī* |

*hari hari smare: niśvāsa phokāre:*
*pahuka muha nehāri* ||2||*15*||

Verse : With the great virtues of her earlier life, she has found Him as her Lord and the evasive cruel fate is taking away the wealth from the hands just in front of the unfortunate. (1) The beautiful woman became greatly agitated for her beloved, who is very difficult to attain, and she remembered the name of Hari repeatedly, heaving sighs looking at the face of her Lord. (2)

*śloka* ||

*bhītāṁ sītāntato rāmo nirīkṣya kṛpayā prabhuḥ* |
*prāha prayāṁ*[41] *samāśvāsya mābhai sīte sthite mayi* ||25||

Hymn[42]: Then looking at Sītā, who was terrified, the Lord mercifully said consoling His beloved, "Oh dear Sītā, please do not worry when I am here."

*kathā* ||

*pṛyāka parama santāpa tāpa nirekhi : rāmacandra bāhumeli : pṛyāka dhari kahu : āśvāsa kaya bolala* ||
*he prāṇapriye : tuhu kāheka bhaya karaha : ohi rājāsaba hāmāka āgu kona haya : jaice siṁhaka āgu bāleka hariṇa : hāmāka bāṇa prahāre : eikṣaṇe palāaba : tuhu āju kautuke dekhaha* ||

Dialogue: Seeing His wife suffering from great distress, Rāmacandra, holding her with outstretched arms, said consoling her, "Oh my love, as dear as life, why are you scared? What are those kings in front of me, like fawns before the lion! Against my attack with arrows, they will flee in a moment; you just watch with delight today."

*ohi āśvāsa karie rāmacandra : dhanuka ṭaṅkāra karie : rājāsabaka bolala* ||

41. *priyāṁ*.
42. in *Śloka* metre.

*rāmabola* || *aye pāpī rājāsaba : hāmu dhanubhaṅga kaya : jānekī pāala : tuhu ki nimita ihāta bipakṣa ācaraha : jata śakati thika : hāmāra śakati bujhaha* ||

Consoling thus, Rāmacandra, twanging the bow, said to the kings.

Rāma said, "Oh you wicked kings, breaking the bow, I have achieved Jānakī; why do you oppose to it! (Now) with all your strength know my strength (fight with me)."

*rāmaka bāṇī śuni : nṛpasaba parama āṭope ṭaṅkāra kaya : bāṇa barikhala : rāmacandra sohi śara saba cedie : rājāsabaka gāve gāe bāṇa prahāri : hṛdaya bhedala : kāhu kāhu rājāka uru kara kaṭi kāṭi pelāala : kāhuka bāhu karṇa cedala : apara nṛpabara parama bhae : samara curi palāala* ||

Hearing the words of Rāma, the kings, with great anger, twanging the bows, started showering arrows. Rāmacandra, breaking down all those arrows, attacking each of the kings with arrows, pierced their hearts and cut the thighs, hips and hands of some of them. Cut the arms and ears of some of them and the other kings, with great fear, fled away from the battle.

*śloka* ||

*nirīkṣya sākṣādrāmasya vijayaṁ janako mudā* |
*vivāhavidhinā dhīro rāghavāya sūtāmadāt*[43] ||26||

Hymn[44]: Seeing the victory of Rāma in person, the steadfast Janaka, following proper rites of wedding, happily gave away his daughter in marriage to brave Rāghava.

*kathā* ||

*tadanantara : rāmacandraka parama bikrama dekhie : janaka rājāka mane parama ānanda bhelaha : dūta paṭhāi rājā daśarathaka ati sattare anāala* | *rājā daśaratha : putraka bikrama : sītāka prāpti śunie : āsi kahu janakaka : parama kautuke āliṅgi dharala : jaice nācaye lāgala*| *rājā janaka*

---

[43]. *sutāmadāt.*

[44]. in *Śloka* metre, but in the 1st foot , the 5th letter is long instead of short.

*bibāhaka sambhāra milāala : biśvāmitra kuśaṇḍi karie : homa ārambhala ||*

Dialogue: After that, seeing the great valour of Rāmacandra, King Janaka became very happy. Sending a messanger brought King Daśaratha there immediately. Hearing about the heroism of his son and His achieving of Sītā, King Daśaratha coming there, embraced King Janaka with great happiness and as it were, started dancing. King Janaka brought the requisites for the wedding and starting the sacrificial fire started oblation.

*śloka ||*

*ṛṣirnirīkṣya sītāyāḥ rūpalāvaṇyamadbhutam |*
*pulakāṅgaḥ papātorbbyāṁ kāmārto mūrcchito yathā ||27||*

Hymn[45]: Seeing the wonderful beauty and charm of Sītā, the sage became enraptured, and lovelorn, fell down on the ground as if senseless.

*kathā ||*

*mukhacandrikā karite : sītāka bhubana mohana rūpa nirekhi : ṛṣi kāme ātura bhelaha : hātaka śruvacuca khasi parala : śarīra kampi muruci parala : tāhe pekhi śiṣya gālave prabodha bolala ||*

*he guru : tohāra kona bevahāra : svastha hava ||*

Dialogue: While formally looking at the moonlike face, seeing the beauty of Sītā, which mesmerises the whole world, the sage became lovelorn and the sacrificial ladle fell down from his hand and his body trembled and fell down unconscious. Seeing that, his pupil Gālava said consoling:
"Oh honourable preceptor, what type of behaviour is this; please be composed!"

*śloka ||*

*tataścetanamālabhya munirmantramudirayet |*
*tadodvāhabidhau tasmin utsavaḥ sumahānabhūt ||28||*

[45]. in *Śloka* metre.

Hymn[46]: Then regaining senses, the sage recited hymns and the rituals of that great wedding ceremony took place.

*kathā* ||

*tadanantara : muni cetana labhie : biṣṇu biṣṇu smari : hāte śruva dharie : bibāhaka homa karāite lāgala : sohi samae : bara- kanyāka keśa eka ṭhāma karie : pānī ḍhālite brahmārudraindrādi devatāsaba : jaicana ānanda milāvala : tā dekhaha śunaha : nirantare haribola haribola* ||

Dialogue: After that, the sage, gaining consciousness, remembering the name of Viṣṇu again and again, holding the ladle in his hand, started making the sacrifice for the wedding. At that time, putting the hair of the bride and the bride-groom together and pouring down water on it, how Brahmā, Rudra, Indra and other deities became so delighted, watch and listen to that and keep chanting the name of Hari incessantly.

*gīta* || *rāga-suhāi* || *jatimāna* ||

Song in the *Rāga Suhāi* with the rhythm *Jatimāna:*

*raghunātha : kautuke karatu bibāha* |
*surapura milala ucchāha* ||

Raghunātha married happily and the city of the gods became excited.

*pada* ||

*sambhu sayambhu guṇa gāe* |
*indra mṛdaṅga raṅge bāe* ||1||
*bariṣe kusuma surarāmā* |
*pūrala saba manakāmā* ||2||16||

Verse : Śambhu and Svayambhū sang praises and Indra played on the *mṛdaṅga*. (1)
The celestial women showered flowers and all their wishes were fulfilled. (2)

---

46. in *Śloka* metre, but in the 2nd foot, the 6th letter is short instead of long.

*sūtra* ||

*aicana parama maṅgala : ānande : sītāka bibāha die : rājājanaka yata sarbbasva pāvala : saba rāmaka jautaka*[47] *dilaha : daśaratha rājāko : bahuta sanmāna kaya : ayodhyāka lāgi barakanyā paṭhāala* ||

Direction: In this way, marrying off Sītā among felicity and happiness, whatever King Janaka received, gave them all to Rāma as dowry; and showing much honour to King Daśaratha sent the bride and the groom to Ayodhyā.

*śloka* ||

*tato'ti kautuko rāmaḥ priyayā saha sītayā* |
*sasodaro mudābhrājadayodhyāmprayayau purim* ||29||

Hymn[48]: Then overjoyed Rāma, along with His beloved wife Sītā and His brother, gleaming happily, went to the city of Ayodhyā.

*kathā* ||

*tadanantara : pṛyā sītā sasodara sahite : śrīrāmacandra jaice ajodhyā calala : he loka : tā dekhaha śunaha : nirantare hari bola hari bola* ||

Dialogue: After that, along with His wife Sītā and His brother, as Śrī Rāmacandra went to Ayodhyā, oh dear people, watch and listen to that and keep chanting the name of Hari incessantly.

*gīta* || *rāga-tura bhāṭhiāli* || *jatimāna* ||

Song in the *Rāga Tura bhāṭhiālī* with the rhythm *Jatimāna:*

*karatu kautuka : calatu ramayā : ramaṇī saṅgahi jāi* |
*nīla ghana jaca : bijurī urṣara : kuñjara-gamanī māi*||

Rāmacandra went with happiness and His wife went along, as if bright lightning on the blue cloud and the dear young girl walked like an elephant.

---

47. *jautuka*.

48. in *Śloka* metre.

*pada* ||

*kanaka kaṅkaṇa : jhanake jhamake : ṭhamake kaya layalāsa* |
*piuka pekhimukha : ākhi mudi rahu : lajita īṣata hāsa* ||*1*||
*matta mātaṅga : saṅge jaicana : taruṇī kārani āve* |
*jaya jaya bara*[49] *: caudiśe uccava : kṛṣṇa kiṅkara gāve* ||2||*17*||

Verse: The gold bracelets tinkled and jingled slowly with grace; looking at the face of her husband, remained closing her eyes with a bashful smile. (1)
As if a young female elephant came along an inebriated elephant. There was merriment all around with cries wishing glory; says the servant of Kṛṣṇa. (2)

*śloka* ||

*tataḥ āgatya tarasā bhārgavo bhrukuṭimukhaḥ* |
*skandhe nidhāya kaṭhinaṁ kuṭhāraṁ rāmamabravīt* ||*30*||

Hymn[50]: Then, coming energetically with a frown on his face, Bhārgava, bearing a sharp axe on his shoulder, said to Rāma.

*kathā* ||

*aicana mahotsave : rāmacandra sītāye sahita chalaice* | *tadanantara : maheśaguruka dhanubhaṅga śabada śunie : parama krodhe : paraśurāma : pracaṇḍa mūrti hayā : kandhe kuṭhāra dhari kahu : raha raha boli : rāmacandraka āgabeḍhala* ||

Dialogue: Amid such festivity, Rāmacandra went with Sītā. After that, hearing the sound of the bow of his preceptor Maheśa being broken, with great anger Paraśurāma, in a terrible form, bearing an axe on his shoulder, crying "Wait, wait!", obstructed Rāmacandra.

*parśurāma bola* || *aye beṇḍasika putra : merāguruka dhanubhaṅga kaya : toho kāhe jāva : paraśurāmaka kathā*

---

[49]. *rava.*

[50]. in *Śloka* metre, but in the 1st foot, the 6th and 7th letters are short instead of long ; in the 2nd foot, the 6th letter is short instead of long and in the 3rd foot, the 6th and 7th letters are short instead of long.

*toho jānae nāhi : hāmu eka biṁśati bāra bhūmi bhramie : saba kṣatrika muṇḍa mārala : se śoṇite kuṭhāra malina bhela : āḥ āju tohāra kandha – rudhire : punu nikā karaba* ||
Paraśurāma said, "Oh the son of a *candāla*, how can you go breaking the bow of my master. You do not know about Paraśurāma; wandering about the world for 21 times, I have beheaded all the *kṣatriyas* and with that blood the axe has become stained. Ah, today with the blood from your shoulder it will be cleaned again."

*ohi buli bāhu kāmuri : parama caṭi carppaṭi karie thika* ||
Saying so, biting his arm, boastfully bragged on.

*śloka* ||

*tanniśamyābhavadbhīto bhayāddaśaratho nṛpaḥ* |
*svaskandhe basanaṁ baddhvā bhārgavasya pade'patat* ||31||

Hymn[51]: Hearing him, being terrified, King Daśaratha, wrapping up his clothing around his shoulder, fell down (praying) at the feet of Bhārgava.

*kathā* ||

*paraśurāmaka : aicana krodhabhāvanā pekhi : rājā daśaratha : prāṇa antarikṣa bhela : hā hā sarbbanāśa bhelo buli : gale kāpara bāndhi : bhārgavaka pāe parie : aneka kātara kayala* ||

Dialogue: Seeing such angry feeling of Paraśurāma, King Daśaratha's heart became blank, and saying "Oh alas, alas, we are to meet the ultimate destruction!", wrapping up his clothing around his neck, falling down at the feet of Bhārgava, entreated him a lot.

*he paraśurāma prabhu : hāmāra putra rāmacandra : bālakamati : ihāka doṣa marasa gosāi : tohāri caraṇaka dāsa bhelo : māthe khera dharo : hāmāka putradāna dehu : jaba nāhi kṣemā karaba : taba putraka cori : hāmāra māthā lehu* ||

---

[51]. in *Śloka* metre.

"Oh lord Paraśurāma, our son Rāmacandra is like a child; please forgive His faults, oh God! I become a servant in your feet and here I hold a straw (in begging) on my head, please give me (back) my son as gift. If you do not forgive Him, then leaving my son, please take my head instead."

*aicana aneka kātara kayala : tabahu bhārgae krodhe bahuta bolaya : tāhe pekhi daśaratha rājā : hṛdaye muṭhi hāni : bahuri rāmacandraka gale bāndhi dhari kahu bolala* ||
*hā putra : antakaka hāte parala : tohāri daraśana āju paricedā bhela* ||
In this way, (Daśaratha) entreated him a lot. But even then, Bhārgava kept on babbling a lot with great anger. Seeing that, King Daśaratha, thumping his chest, embracing Rāmacandra by the neck again, said, "Alas, oh dear son, you have fallen in the hands of the death; (opportunities of) seeing you has become limited today!".

*ohi buli daśaratha : bahuta bilāpa kayala* ||
Saying so, Daśaratha lamented a lot.

*śloka* ||
*bilokya bhārgavaṁ bhītā sītā bepitamānasā* |
*ruroda patimāliṅgya hā hato'smītibādinī* ||32||
Hymn[52]: Seeing Bhārgava, terrified Sītā, with her mind trembling, embracing her husband cried saying, "Oh I am lost!".

*kathā* ||
*tadanantara : kālāntaka prāya paraśurāmaka nirekhi : sītāka śarīra kampe : hā hā sakala guṇabhājana : svāmi hāmāra : āju kāheka delahu : bidhi birambana ki bhela* ||

---

[52]. in *Śloka* metre.

Dialogue: Then, seeing Paraśurāma, as if death personified, the whole body of Sītā trembled, "Alas, alas, oh my dear husband, who have all the virtues, whom have we given you to today! How fate has become adverse!"

*ohi buli svāmīka āliṅgi dhari kahu : jaice bilāpa karala : tāhe dekhaha śunaha* ||

Saying so, embracing her husband as she lamented, watch and listen to that.

*gīta* || *rāga – gaurī* || *jatimāna* ||

Song in the *Rāga Gaurī* with the rhythm *Jatimāna:*

*hari hari ramaṇī karaya pari māi* |
*pekhi parama piu jīva jaca jāi* ||

Seeing her most beloved nearly loosing His life, the lovely woman, falling down on the ground, uttered the name of Hari again and again.

*pada* ||

*pāvala katanu puṇye pahu hāmi* |
*hāte haraya bidhi nava nidhi svāmī* ||*1*||
*nīra jhuraya phukaraya ghana svāśā* |
*baṅka bidhātā kayala saba nāsā* ||2||*18*||

Verse: After so much of moral and religious virtues I have found you, oh Lord! And now the fate is taking away the new wealth, my husband, from my hand. (1)
Flowing tears and heaving quick sighs, (said) "The evasive fate is destroying everything."(2)

*śloka* ||

*santāpaṁ prekṣya sītāyāḥ bhaktāyā bhaktabatsalaḥ* |
*priyāṁ provāca paramāṁ pāṇinā mārjayanmukham* ||33||

Hymn[53]: Seeing the suffering of His devotee Sītā, one who is so kind to His devotees, wiping the face of His most beloved wife with His hand spoke to her in pleasing manner.

*kathā* ||

*bhaktā sītāka : aicana parama santāpa pekhie : śrīrāmacandra : hāte pṛyāka mukha mocala : saprema bākya buli āśvāsa kayala ||*

*rāma bola || he priye : ohi banabāsī : ṛṣika darppa dekhiye tohāri tarāsa milala : ohi hāmāka āgu kona pataṅga : dekhu aikhane duṣṭa dvijaka darppa cūra karaba : he prāṇa priye : āju kautuke dekhaha : ṛṣira muṇḍa muṇḍaho ||*

Dialogue : Seeing the great suffering of devotee Sītā, Śrī Rāmacandra, wiped the face of His beloved wife and consoled her with loving words.

Rāma said, "Oh my love, seeing the insolence of that hermit you have become scared. He is only an insignificant insect before me. Just watch, I shall humiliate that wicked *brāhmaṇa* in a moment. Oh my love, dear like life, watch with fun, how I behead the sage."

*tadanantara : punarbbāra daśaratha : daśane tṛṇa dharie : paraśurāmaka āge parala ||*

*he ṛṣirāja : hāmāka putra-dāna dehu : tohāri pāvare lāgu ||*

After that, Daśaratha again, holding a blade of grass within his teeth, fell down (praying) before Paraśurāma.

"Oh great sage, please give me back my son in gift, here I hold on to your feet."

*tathāpi paraśurāma : daśana carppie : rājāka : tarjaya āpuna kuṭhārake dhikkāra kaya bolala ||*

*parśurāma bola || aye kuṭhāra : reṇukā māvaka kandha chedīte tuhu pārala : āju daśaratha kumāraka prati : tuhu āti*

---

[53]. in *Śloka* metre, but in the 3rd foot, the 6th and 7th letters are short instead of long.

*śānta bheli : āḥ āju taba tohāra dhikkāra : hāmāra dhikkāra thika* ||

Even then, Paraśurāma, grating his teeth, threatened the King and reproaching his axe said,

Paraśurāma said, "Oh you axe, you could cut the neck of mother Reṇukā; and today you have become very tranquil towards the son of Daśaratha. Today you are sure to be condemned, and I am sure to be condemned too."

*ohi buli kuṭhāra tuli śrīrāmaka nirekhi : bāhuta kāmara delaha: mathā jhaṅkāri : kuṭhāra urddhaka khepie : punu lumphi dhari dhari kahu : kuṭhāraka nirekhi : bāhuta kāmora delaha : śarīra kampe* ||

Saying so, raising the axe, looking at Śrī Rāma, bit his arm; jerking the head, throwing the axe up and holding it with a jump again and again, looking at the axe, bit the arm and his body trembled.

*śloka* ||

*viśvāmitrastadāgatya bhārgavaṁ prāha kopataḥ* |
*are dvijakulāṅgāra matśiṣyaṁ hantumicchasi* ||34||

Hymn[54]: Then coming there, Viśvāmitra said to Bhārgava with anger, "Oh, you disgrace to the whole race of *brāhmaṇas*, you want to kill my disciple!".

*kathā* ||

*biśvāmitra bola* || *ae duṣṭa dvijādhama : hāmāra parama śiṣya : rāmacandra : āheka badhodyama tuhu bheli : aye jata śakati thika : āju hāmāka yuddha dehu : tohora darppacūra karaba* ||

Dialogue: Viśvāmitra said, "Oh you wicked, meanest of the *brāhmaṇas*, Rāmacandra is the best amongst my pupils and you have become ready to kill Him. Oh you, come and fight

[54]. in *Śloka* metre.

with me with as much strength as you have; I shall crush your pride into dust."

*parśurāma mahā kope ḍaṇḍa dharala : biśvāmitra ḍaṇḍa dharī dhāvala : duhu ḍaṇḍa prahāraka coṭe cūra bhela || tadanantara : cayaḍi dharie judha kayala : prahāra coṭe duhu cayaḍi ciri parala : tadantara : bāhujuddha kayala : duhu dohāka dharie : pari bāgaraya : duhu ṛsika paridhāna carmma khasi parala : biṣṇuka aṁśa ajaya bīrya paraśurāma : tāhera parākrama : sahite nāpāri : biśvāmitra bhaṅga māni : prāṇa rakṣā kari palāvala : paraśurāma punarbbāra kuṭhāra tuli śrīrāmaka garjjaya ||*

Paraśurāma, with great anger, held the staff; Viśvāmitra also ran holding his staff. With the force of the attack, both the staffs broke into pieces. After that, they fought holding the chowrie and with the force of the attack both the chowries also tore into pieces. After that, they fought hand to hand; holding one another, they fell down rolling on the ground and their clothings of animal-skin slipped down. Not being able to defend the prowess of Paraśurāma, who is a part of Viṣṇu and is unconquerable in strength and courage, Viśvāmitra fled accepting defeat and saving his life. Paraśurāma, holding up the axe again, thundered against Śrī Rāma.

*śloka ||*

*lakṣmaṇaḥ prekṣya taṁ darpaṁ rāmamāha sakopataḥ |*
*ājñāpaya badhe [55]cāsya durjanasyātatāyinaḥ ||35||*

Hymn[56]: Seeing his pride, Lakṣmaṇa, with anger, said to Rāma, "Command me to kill this reckless criminal."

*kathā ||*

*ṛṣika parama darpa dekhie : lakṣmaṇa kope bastra kāci kahu : rāmaka praṇāma kaya bolala ||*

---

[55].*vadhe.*

[56]. in *Śloka* metre.

*he raghunātha : ohi ātāitāi duṣṭa dvijaka badhe kona doṣa thika : hāmāka ājñā karaha : āheka prāṇa coḍāñõ* ||

Dialogue: Seeing such extreme pride of the sage, Lakṣmaṇa, with great anger, smartly tying up his clothing, said offering obeisance to Rāma:

"Oh Raghunātha, what is the harm in killing that desperate, wicked *brāhmaṇa*? Command me and I shall kill him."

*ohi buli dhanuka ṭaṅkāri ṛṣika samukha hoi : lakṣmaṇa : daśarathaka bola*||

*he pitā : ohi kṣatrivaghātakī : parama pātakīka : kata kātara karaice : sattara antara hava : āhera muṇḍa māro*||

Saying so, twanging the bow, facing the sage, Lakṣmaṇa said to Daśaratha, "Oh dear father, how much you are entreating that great sinner, the killer of the *kṣatriyas*! Please stand aside immediately and I shall behead him."

*tāhe pekhi : rāma hasi hasi lakṣmaṇaka : pācu kaya bolala* ||

*aye bhayāi : tuhu bālaka : raha raha : ohi duṣṭa dvijaka hāmu ḍaṇḍa karaba : tuhu sukhe yuddha dekhaha*||

Seeing him, Rāma, pulling Lakṣmaṇa back laughing, said to him, "Oh brother, you are a child; wait, wait, I shall punish that wicked *brāhmaṇa*, you just watch the fight with pleasure."

*śloka*||

*dhanuḥ ṭaṅkāramakarodbhārgavaṁ bhīṣayamprabhuḥ* |
*tiṣṭha tiṣṭheti tamprāha neṣyāmyadya yamālayam* ||36||

Hymn[57]: Intimidating Bhārgava, the Lord twanged the bow and said to him, "Wait, wait, I shall take you to the place of Yama today."

*kathā*||

*śāraṅga ṭaṅkāra kaya kahu : śrīrāmacandra : paraśurāmaka samukha hayā bolala* ||

[57]. in *Śloka* metre, but in the 1st foot, the 6th and 7th letters are short instead of long.

*rāmabola* || *ae duṣṭa dvijādhama : kṣatriya saba māri tuhu garaba karaice : tohāra mātā reṇukāka kāṭi : pāpa ācarala : sohi kathā kahiyā : ki hāmāka bhīti dekhāa raha raha : āju tuhu yamapura dekhaba : yata śakati thika : hāmāka samukha hayā raha* ||

Dialogue: Twanging the Śāraṅga, Śrī Rāmacandra, confronting Paraśurāma, said:

Rāma said, "Oh you wicked vilest of the *brāhmaṇas*, you are boasting of killing the *kṣatriyas;* killing your mother Reṇukā, you have behaved sinfully. Mentioning that, why do you scare me. Wait, wait, you will see the city of Yama today; face me with as much strength as you have."

*sūtra* ||

*āhe samājika : śrīrāmaka dhanuka ṭaṅkāre : paraśurāmaka : hṛdaya bidārala : parama tarāse saba śarīra kāmpe : hātara kuṭhāra khasi parala : prāṇaka kātare jaice palāvala : āhe ityādi* ||

Direction: Oh dear audience, at the twanging of bow by Śrī Rāma, the heart of Paraśurāma wrenched and his entire body trembled. The axe fell down from his hand and as he fled fearing for his life, here is all about it.

*gīta* || *rāga – kānārā* || *jatimāna* ||

Song in the *Rāga Kānāḍā* with the rhythm *Jatimāna:*

*dhābe dhari śāraṅga raghunātha* |
*tarāse ṛṣika kāmprae pāva hāta* ||

Raghunātha runs holding the Śāraṅga and the hands and feet of the sage trembled with fear.

*pada* ||

*paraśu khasala dūra gela rāga* |
*parala ḍaṇḍaate rāmaka āga* ||*1*||

*rākhuhu tohori aṁśa hāmu rāma |*
*daśana dharu khera pari paraṇāma ||2||19||*

Verse: Paraśurāma fell down, his anger gone and he offered obeisance to Rāma falling down prostrate on the ground before Him.(1)
(And said), "Please protect me oh Rāma, I am a part of you only; here I pray you holding a blade of grass in my teeth and offering obeisance falling down on the ground." (2)

*kathā ||*

*paraśurāma : śrīrāmaka āge parie : bahuta kātara kaya bolala || he prabhu śrīrāma : tuhu parama īśvara : hāmu tohāri aṁśa : i najāni darppa kayalo : hāmāra doṣa marasa gosāi ||*

Dialogue: Paraśurāma, falling down before Śrī Rāma, entreating Him a lot, and said, "Oh Lord Śrī Rāma, you are the Supreme God and I am only a part of you; not knowing that, I have boasted; please forgive my faults, oh Lord."

*bhārgavaka kātara pekhi : lakṣmaṇa-sītā duhu bahuta hāsya kayala : śrīrāma bīhari*[58] *bola ||*
*he bhṛgupati rāma : hāmāra parama amogha bāṇa : tohāri baddha nimita udyama*[59] *bhela : ihāka sambaraṇa karite napāri ||*

Seeing Bhārgava distressed, both Lakṣmaṇa and Sītā laughed a lot and Śrī Rāma said smiling, "Oh Bhṛgupati Rāma, the most unfailing arrow of mine was drawn to kill you and it cannot be restrained now."

*ahi buli bāṇa ākarṇa pūrala : paraśurāma daśane khera laiyā : tarāse pari kāmpe || (paraśurāma bola ||) he svāmi : tohāra dharmmaka putra bhelo : hāmāka prāṇa-dāna dehu ||*

Saying so, Rāma, stretched the arrow till His ear and Paraśurāma, taking a blade of straw in His teeth trembled

58. *bihasi.*
59. *udyata.*

greatly scared. (Paraśurāma said) "Oh Lord, I have become your lawful son; please give me back my life as gift."

*śrīrāma bihari*[60] *bola* || *ae bhārgava : tuhu nirbhae rahu : tohāri jīva rākhala : kintu hāmāra bāṇa bertha nohe : tohāri svargapatha ceda karahõ* ||

*ohī buli śrīrāma gaganaka lāgi bāṇa kṣepala* ||
Śrī Rāma said smiling, "Oh you Bhārgava, you remain fearless. I have saved your life. But my arrow cannot go in vain, (so) I shall pierce your path to the heaven (instead)." Saying so, Śrī Rāma, directed the arrow to the sky.

*sūtra* ||
*paraśurāma : śrīrāmaka āliṅgi bolala* ||
*he bāpa : tohāri prasāde ājuprāṇa rahala : āḥ : punarbbāra upajala* ||
*ohī buli paraśurāma tapobane prabeśala* ||
Direction: Embracing Śrī Rāma, Paraśurāma said, "Oh father, with your kindness my life has been saved today and I am reborn.", saying so, Paraśurāma entered the *tapovana*.

*śloka* ||
*nirjītya bhārgavaṁ rāmampriyayā saha rāghavaḥ* |
*purimayodhyāmāviśya mātṛbhiḥ sampraveśitaḥ* ||37||
Hymn[61]: Conquering Bhārgava Rāma, Rāghava, coming to the city of Ayodhyā along with His wife, entered with His mothers.

*kathā* ||
*he samājika : bhārgavaka jinive : śrīrāmacandra pṛyāe sahīta ajodhyāpura prabeśala* | *rāmaka mātā kośalyā : śrīrāmaka bijaya-bāta śunie : aneka strīsaba sahita : parama maṅgala*

---
60. *bihasi.*
61. in *Śloka* metre, but in the 3rd foot, the 5th letter is long instead of short.

*gīta ānande bājanā bajāi : barakainyāka hāta eka ṭhāma dhari kahu : mahotsave : gṛha -prabeśa karāvala : āsane baiṭhāi rāmaka sītāka māthe dūrbākṣata siñcāri : āśīrbbāda kaya kaho : parama utsuke kośalyā –ānande nṛtya kayala : rāmaka aicana bibāha : mahotsava sampūrṇa bhela* ||

Dialogue : Oh dear audience, winning over Bhārgava, Śrī Rāmacandra, along with His wife, entered the city of Ayodhyā. Hearing about the victory of Rāma, Kauśalyā, the mother of Rāma, along with many other women, singing the most excellent auspicious songs and playing instruments with great happiness, putting the hands of the bride and the bridegroom together, performed the rites of *gṛhapraveśa* amidst much festivity. Making them sit on the seat, sprinkling *dūrbbā* and *akṣata* on the heads of Rāma and Sītā, blessing them, with great enthusiasm Kauśalyā danced with happiness and in this way, the celebration for the wedding of Rāma was completed.

*śloka* ||

*bhṛśaṁ hṛṣṭamanā rāmaḥ samprāpya paramāṁpriyām* |
*tayā kurbban kāmakeliṁ reme maṇimaye gṛhe* ||38||

Hymn[62]: Having achieved the most excellent wife, greatly pleased at heart, Rāma, entering the house adorned with jewels, engaged happily in amorous sports with her.

*kathā* ||

*tṛbhubana mohanī : padumanī : jānekī sītāka labhi kahu : śrīrāmacandra ānande magana hayā : manimaya mandire prabeśie : sītāye sahita : jaicana parama sakāma keli kaya rahala : tā dekhaha śunaha : nirantare haribola* ||

Dialogue: Achieving the one who fascinates the three worlds, a *padminī* woman, Jānakī, Sītā, as Śrī Rāmacandra, absorbed in happiness, entering the jewelled palace, became engaged

---

[62]. in *Śloka* metre, but in the 3rd foot, the 5th letter is long instead of short and the 6th letter is short instead of long.

in amorous sports along with Sītā, watch and listen to that and keep chanting the name of Hari incessantly .

*gīta* || *rāga- kalyāṇa* || *kharamāna* ||
Song in the *Rāga Kalyāṇa* with the rhythm *Kharamāna:*

*e karu ramayā rasa keli* |
*kāñcorā cora phora kuca cucuñka:*
*rati kautuka karāali* ||

Here Rāma gets engaged in amorous sport tearing away the clothing and smashing the breasts and nipples and happily satisfied.

*pada* ||
*navadhara dharie : adhara madhu dhañcala :*
*locana mudi rahu māi* |
*karata sūrata matta -: mātaṅgagāminī :*
*kāminī yāminī jāi* ||*1*||
*cañcara cikura : nikara kara kaṅkaṇa :*
*jhalakita ratanaku mālā* |
*śramajala bindu : indu moha soho :*
*mohe parala baḍa bālā* ||2||
*parama rasika guru : śrīśukladhvaja :*
*rājā nṛpati pradhānā* |
*jayatu jayatu nitya : īśvara kṛṣṇaka :*
*keli līlā rasa jānā* ||3||20||

Verse: Holding the new bride assaulted the honey from her lips and the dear girl remained closing her eyes. Made the lovely woman, who moved with the grace of an elephant, intoxicated with amorous pleasure and the night passed by. (1)

The wavy locks of hair flowed down and all the bunch of bracelets on the hands and the jewelled necklace tinkled.

Drops of sweat adorned the moon-like face and the beautiful woman became fascinating. (2)
The most respectable, who is the most appreciative, honourable Śrī Śukladhvaja, the Chief Minister of the King, knows that appreciation of the pastime of Lord Kṛṣṇa leads to victory forever. (3)

*kathā* ||
*aicana parama kāmaratna*[63] *keli kaya : sītāka manoratha pūri : rāmacandra anudine : ānanda mandire rahala* ||
Dialogue: In this way, playing amorous sports and fulfilling the wishes of Sītā, Rāmacandra remained in the palace of happiness day after day.

*śloka* ||
*śrīrāmabijayannāma nāṭakaṁ pūrṇatāṅgatam* |
*śrīkṛṣṇapādapadmasya prasādena suniścitam* ||39||
Hymn[64]: The play by the name *Śrīrāmavijaya* is completed, definitely with the blessings of the lotus feet of Śrī Kṛṣṇa.

*kathā* ||
*śrīkṛṣṇapādapadma prasādata rāmabijaya nāma nāṭaka sampūrṇa bhela*||
Dialogue: With the blessings of the lotus feet of Śrī Kṛṣṇa, the play by the name *Rāmavijaya* is completed.

*muktimaṅgala baktabyaṁ* || *bhaṭimā* ||
Auspicious speech for deliverance, here is the eulogy:

*jaya jaya īśvara rāghava rāma* |
*pūrala jo jānekī mana kāma* ||
*jagajana jīvana sohi murāri* |
*mukuti maṅgala karatu tohāri* ||*1*||
*johi pāli pitākeri āśa* |
*sītā sahite khapala banabāsa* ||

[63]. *kāmarasa.*
[64]. in *Śloka* metre.

*sādhala jaya jo rākaca māri |*
*sohi karatu nitya mukuti tohāri ||2||*
*bāli jo ghāli sugṛñaka pāṭa |*
*lailaha je laya bāṇaraka ṭhāṭha ||*
*bāndhala setu payodhika bāri |*
*sohi karatu nitya mukuti tohāri ||3||*
*ṭhāṭhe caudiśe beḍhala laṅkā |*
*rākaca loka milāali śaṅkā ||*
*cedala jo rākaca rāvaṇakeri mātha |*
*mukuti karu sohi raghunātha ||4||*
*āala saṅge bānaraka ṭhāṭha |*
*rājā bheli ajodhyāka pāṭa ||*
*jo jānekī-mana pūrala murāri |*
*mukuti maṅgala karatu tohāri ||5||*
*rāmaka parama bhakati rasa jāna |*
*śrīśukladhvaja nṛpati pradhāna ||*
*rāmaka bijaya jo karāali nāṭa |*
*milahu tāheka baikuṇṭhaka bāṭa ||6||*
*rāmaka caraṇa śaraṇa lehu jāni |*
*saba aparādhaka marakha tuhu svāmi ||*
*kṛṣṇaka kiṅkara śaṅkara bola |*
*kara nara aba saba hari hari bola ||7||*

Glory to the Lord Rāghava Rāma, who has fulfilled the wishes of Jānakī.

Who is like the life of the people, He is Murāri; may He bestow salvation and well-being upon you. (1)

Keeping the expectations of His father, who, along with Sītā, endured the life of a hermit. One who achieved victory killing the demon, may He always bestow salvation upon you. (2)

Killing Bāli who bestowed the throne to Sugrīva; taking the pack of monkeys along, built a bridge on the water of the ocean; may He always bestow salvation upon you. (3)

The pack of monkeys sieged Laṅkā and terrified the demons; one who beheaded the demon Rāvaṇa, may that Raghunātha always bestow salvation upon you. (4)

Along with Him came the pack of monkeys and He became the king in the throne of Ayodhyā; one who is Murāri and who fulfilled the wishes of Jānakī, may He bestow salvation and wellbeing upon you. (5)

One who is extremely devoted to Rāma, Śrī Śukladhvaja, the Chief Minister of the King, made me compose the play *Rāmavijaya*. May he find the way to Vaikuṇṭha. (6)

Knowing all this, take shelter in the feet of Rāma; and oh Lord, please forgive all the sins. And now all of you people, utter the name of Hari repeatedly, says Śaṅkara, the servant of Kṛṣṇa. (7)

*śloka* ||

*śrīgopālapadacchatracchāyālālasa mānasaḥ* |
*(śrī) śukladhvajo nṛpaśreṣṭhaḥ kārayāmāsa nāṭakam* ||40||

Hymn[65]: Wishing for the protection under the feet of Śrī Gopāla like the shadow of an umbrella, the best of the kings, honourable Śrī Śukladhvaja, made this play composed.

*śloka* ||

*bindurandhrabedacandra śāke śaṅkara saṁjñake* |
*śrīrāmabijayaṁ nāma nāṭakaṁ vidadheadhunā* ||41||

Hymn[66]: The play by the name *Śrīrāmavijaya* which has been performed now, was composed by one whose name was Śaṅkara, in zero, nine, four and one Śaka (i.e. in the Śaka 1490).

*śrīviṣṇupada hastākṣara pustaka sampūrṇa* ||
This book with the handwriting of Śrī Viṣṇupada is completed.

●●●

[65]. in *Śloka* metre.

[66]. in *Śloka* metre, but in the 1st foot, the 5th letter is long instead of short and the 6th letter is short instead of long.

# APPENDIX I
## A LIST OF THE RĀGAS AND TĀLAS

*Rāga Āśovārī* with the rhythm *Kharamāna, Jautimāna, Ekatāla, Paritāla*
*Rāga Ahira* with the rhythm *Jautimāna*
*Rāga Basanta* with the rhythm *Paritāla*
*Rāga Belovāra* with the rhythm *Kharamāna, Paritāla, Rūpakatāla*
*Rāga Bhāṭhiālī*
*Rāga Dhanaśrī* in the rhythm *Ekatāla*
*Rāga Gaurī* with the rhythm *Ekatāli, Viṣama, Rūpakatāla, Jautimāna, Jyotirmāna, Domāni Paritāla Jatimāna*
*Rāga Kalyāṇa* with the rhythm *Kharamāna, Jauti*
*Rāga Kānaḍā* with the rhythm *Jatimāna, Cuṭā*
*Rāga Kānāḍā* with the rhythm *Ekatāli, Paritāla*
*Rāga Kau* with the rhythm *Jatimāna, Paritāla*
*Rāga Kedāra* with the rhythm *Jyoti*
*Rāga Māhura* with the rhythm *Paritāla*
*Rāga Māhura Dhanaśrī* with the rhythm *Ekatāli, Domāni Jatitāla, Paritāla*
*Rāga Māura* with the rhythm *Jauti Māna*
*Rāga Nāṭa*, with the rhythm *Ekatāli*
*Rāga Nāṭamallāra* with the rhythm *Paritāla*
*Rāga Pūrbī* with the rhythm *Kharamāna*
*Rāga Sāreṁ* with the rhythm *Paritāla*
*Rāga Sindhurā* with the rhythm *Ekatāli*
*Rāga Suhāi* with the rhythm *Cuṭikālā, Paritāla, Ekatāli, Jatimāna*
*Rāga Suvai* with the rhythm *Ekatāli*
*Rāga Śrī* with the rhythm *Paritāla*
*Rāga Śrīgāndhāra* with *Jatitāla, Jautimāna, Ekatāli, Paritāla*
*Rāga Śrīgaurī* with the rhythm *Paritāla*
*Rāga Śyāma*, with the rhythm *Paritāla*
*Rāga Tathā* with the rhythm *Ekatāli*
*Rāga Tuḍa Bhāṭhiyālī* with the rhythm *Jautimāna*
*Rāga Tur* with the rhythm *Paritāla, Jatimāna*

●●●

# APPENDIX II

## Map of Koc-Behār, Kāmarūpa, Asama

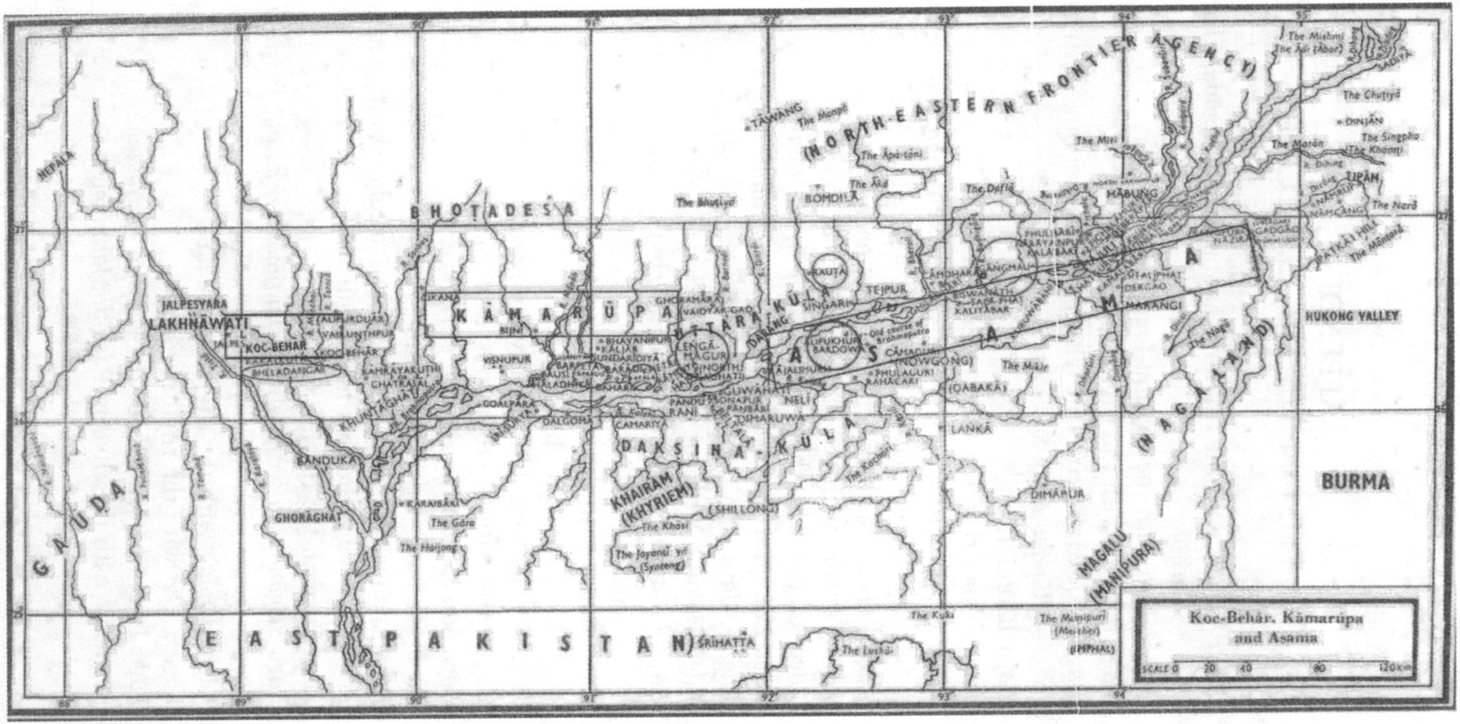

Places of importance relevant to the life of Śaṅkaradeva

Developed based on Neog. M.: Sankaradeva and His Times.

# APPENDIX III
## Glimpses of the *Satrīyā* Culture

Fig. 1. A scene from *Bhāonā*

Fig. 2. A scene from *Bhāonā*

Fig. 3. *Gāyan-bāyan*

Fig. 4. *Sutradhāri* Dance

Fig. 5. *Satrīyā* Dance

Fig. 6. *Korāpāt*- the welcome gate

Fig. 7. Dakhinpat Satra *Nāmghar* and *Maṇikuṭ*

Fig. 8. *Siṁhāsana*

Fig. 9. *Nām Prasaṅga* (Community Prayer)

Fig. 10. Learning Tradition

Fig. 11. Learning Tradition

Fig. 12. Learning Tradition

Fig. 13. Manuscript of the *Guṇamālā*, Beṅgnā-āti Satra

Fig. 14. Making of mask (by Hem Chandra Goswami)

Fig. 15. Making of mask (by Hem Chandra Goswami)

Fig. 16. A page from a manuscript- *Kurukṣetra Yuddha*

Fig. 17. Traditional Assamese Jewellary used in *Bhāonā*

# GLOSSARY

## A

**Acyuta** : a name of Viṣṇu; meaning the imperishable, permanent one.

*adhibāsa* : consecration of the bride/groom with perfumes and fragrant cosmetics etc. before the commencement of wedding rites.

**Aditi** : the mother of the gods; the mother of Indra.

**Ahalyā** : the chaste wife of sage Gautama, who was seduced by Indra in the form of her husband.

**Airāvata** : Indra's carrier elephant.

*Ajagava* : the bow of Lord Śiva.

*akṣata* : unhusked whole grain, washed with water and used as an article of worship in all religious and sacred ceremonies.

**Ambikā** : another name of Pārvatī, the wife of Lord Śiva.

**Amrāvatī** : the abode of the gods; the residence of Indra.

**Anaṅga** : a name of the Love God Kāmadeva.

**Ananta** : a name of Viṣṇu; also of Viṣṇu's couch, the serpent Śeṣa.

**Aniruddha** : one of the four *viṣṇu-tattvas* or planary expansions of Viṣṇu, appearing as a son of the Lord; meaning the unobstructed one.

**Ariṣṭa** : a demon who wanted to kill Kṛṣṇa and Balarāma, and thus assumed the form of a huge bull with sharp horns.

*aśoka* : a tree with red flowers, sacred for the Hindus (Scientific name- *Saraca indica Linn.* Family- *Caesalpiniaceae).*

**Ayodhyā** : the capital of Lord Rāma's kingdom, situated on the river Sarayū.

*āgar* : a tree from which perfume is extracted; also the barks were used for writing manuscripts (Scientific name- *Aquilaria agallocha Roxb.* Family- *Thymelaeaceae).*

### B

**Baka** : a demon, in the form of a crane, killed by Kṛṣṇa; a small tree with white flowers (Scientific name- *Sesbania grandiflora Pers.* Family- *Papilionaceae).*

***bakula*** : a big tree with small and fragrant flowers (Scientific name- *Minusops elengi Linn.* Family- *Sapotaceae).*

**Bala** : another name of Balarāma.

**Balabhadra** : another name of Balarāma.

**Balarāma** : the elder brother of Kṛṣṇa, the seventh son of Vasudeva and Devakī but born from the womb of Rohiṇī.

***banduli*** : a tree with red flowers.

**Bhagadatta** : the son of demon Narakāsura.

**Bhavānī** : another name of Pārvatī, the wife of Lord Śiva.

**Bhārata** : India, the country of Bharata, the son of King Ṛṣabhadeva.

**Bhāratavarṣa** : the kingdom of Bharata, the son of King Ṛṣabhadeva.

**Bhārgava** : another name of Paraśurāma.

**Bhārgava Rāma** : another name of Paraśurāma.

**Bhīṣmka** : the king of the Vidarbhas; the father of Queen Rukmiṇī.

**Bhṛgupati** : another name of Paraśurāma.

**Bibhīṣaṇa** : one of the brothers of Rāvaṇa, who was installed on the throne of Laṅkā by Lord Rāma after defeating Rāvaṇa.

**Brahmā** : name of the first God of the sacred Hindu Trinity, the creator of the material universe; mythologically represented as being born in a lotus which sprang from the naval of Viṣṇu.

***brāhmaṇa*** : a man belonging to learned or first of the four original castes (*brāhmaṇa, kṣatriya, vaiśya* and *śūdra*) of the Hindus.

**Buddha** : meaning the wise, the enlightened; name of Śākya siṁha, the celebrated founder of the Buddhist religion; he is said to have been born at Kapilavastu (in present day Nepal) and to have died in 543 B.C.; he is also regarded as the ninth incarnation of Viṣṇu.

## C

***cakora*** : a bird, the ruddy goose, subsists only upon moonlight.

***campaka*** : a tree bearing yellow fragrant flowers used for making garlands (Scientific name- *Plumeria rubra Linn.* Family- *Apcynaceae*).

***candana*** : Sandal, (the tree, the wood or any unctuous preparation of the wood, held in high estimation as perfume and refrigerant application) (Scientific name- *Pterocarpus santalinus Linn.* Family- *Papilionaceae*).

**Candraketu** : one of the kings who came as suitors of Sītā-devī.

**Candramatī** : a friend of Sītā-devī.

***caṇḍāla*** : a general name for the lowest of the mixed castes; an outcaste.

***Caturthī Tithi*** : the fourth day of a lunar fortnight.

***cāmara*** : a *chowrie* or bushy tail of the Chamara –i.e. Bos grunniens, used as a fan and reckoned as one of the insignia of royalty.

***capaya*** : a prayer to Viṣṇu composed in a metre of four feet.

***cintāmaṇi*** : a fabulous gem supposed to yield to its possessor all desires, the philosopher's stone.

***cūta*** : mango tree,( Scientific name- *Magnifera indica Linn.* Family- *Anacardiaceae*).

## D

*daṇḍa* : a measure of length equal to four *hastas*, each measuring about eighteen inches, being the distance between the elbow and the tip of the middle finger.

**Daśakandha** : an epithet of Rāvaṇa; meaning ten-headed.

**Daśaratha** : a celebrated king of Ayodhyā, the father of Lord Rāma.

**Dāmodara** : an epithet of Kṛṣṇa; meaning, the one who was tied around the abdomen by a rope (by mother Yaśodā).

**Dāruka** : name of Kṛṣṇa's charioteer.

**Devakī** : a daughter of Devaka, sister of Kaṁsa, wife of Vasudeva and the mother of Kṛṣṇa.

***dhanurveda*** : knowledge in the art of manipulating bow and arrows; military science as an attached part of *Yajur Veda*.

***dharma-putra*** : a lawful son.

**Dhenuka** : a demon who wanted to kill Kṛṣṇa and Balarāma, and thus assumed the form of a jackass living in the Tālavana forest of Vṛndāvana.

***dhoti*** : clothing, which is worn by men around the waist.

***digpālas*** : refers to the eight regents of the cardinal points- Indra, Vāyu, Yama, Arka, Agni, Varuṇa, Candra, Kuvera [Manusmṛti 7.4].

***dik-pālas*** : same as *digpāla*.

***dundubhi*** : a sort of large kettle drum.

***dūrbā*** : a type of grass with medicinal property, used as an article of worship in all religious and sacred ceremonies,( Scientific name- *Cynodon dactylon Pers.* Family- *Poaceae*).

**Dvividha** : a demon in the form of a monkey, a friend of Narakāsura; he was killed by Balarāma in the Revataka mountain near Dwārakā.

**Dwārakā** : the capital of the kingdom of Kṛṣṇa on the western point of present day Gujarat.

*ḍambaru* : a sort of small drum, shaped like an hour-glass and generally used by the *kapālikas*.

*ḍhakkā* : a large or double drum.

*ḍhola* : a large drum or tabor.

G

*gandharvas* : celestial musicians, a class of demigods regarded as the singers or musicians of gods and said to give good and agreeable voice to girls.

**Gaṅgā** : the river Ganges, the most sacred river in India.

**Garuḍa** : the king of birds; he is represented as the vehicle of Viṣṇu and as having a white face, an aquiline nose, red wings and a golden body.

**Garuḍa-ketu** : an epithet of Viṣṇu; meaning the one who has Garuḍa as his banner.

**Gautama** : a renowned sage.

**Gālava** : a pupil of sage Viśvāmitra.

**Gokula** : name of the village where Kṛṣṇa was brought up.

*gomukha* : a kind of musical instrument.

**Gopāla** : an epithet of Kṛṣṇa; meaning a cowherd.

*gopī* : cowherd women of Vṛndāvana.

**Gopīnātha** : an epithet of the Kṛṣṇa; meaning the lord of the cowherd women.

**Govardhana** : a celebrated hill in Vṛndāvana which was lifted by Kṛṣṇa to protect the residents of Vṛndāvana from the wrath of Indra in the form of furious rain-storm lasting for seven days.

**Govinda** : a name of Kṛṣṇa; a chief herdsman; meaning one who gives pleasure to the cows.

*gṛhapraveśa* : a solemn entrance into a house according to prescribed rites.

*guñjā* : small bright red and black seeds or conchshells of a creeper found in Vraja, which are used as ornaments.

## H

**Hara** : an epithet of Śiva,

**Hari** : a name of Kṛṣṇa; meaning one who steals.

**Hiraṇyakaśipu** : celebrated king of demons; he subjected his son Prahlāda to untold cruelties for acknowledging Viṣṇu as the Supreme Deity, but he was eventually torn apart by Lord Viṣṇu in his incarnation as Lord Nṛsiṁha.

**Hiraṇyākṣa** : brother of Hiraṇyakaśipu who was killed by Lord Viṣṇu in his incarnation as Varāha in the form of a boar.

## I

**Indra** : the lord of gods and the God of rain; the God of the firmament; he sends the lightning, uses the thunderbolt and sends down rain; he is frequently at war with the demons and by whom he is sometimes defeated; he is famous in mythology for his incontinence and adultery, one prominent instance is his seduction of Ahalyā.

**Indumatī** : friend of Satyabhāmā; meaning, a night of full moon.

## J

**Jagannātha** : an epithet of Kṛṣṇa; meaning the lord of the universe.

**Janaka** : a famous king of Videha or Mithilā, foster father of Sītā.

**Janārdana** : an epithet of Kṛṣṇa; meaning the maintainer of all living entities.

**Jarāsandha** : a celebrated king of Magadha and Chedi; when he heard that Kṛṣṇa had slain his son-in-law Kaṁsa, he gathered a large army and besieged Mathuā eighteen times but was as often repulsed and later on killed by Bhīma.

**Jānakī** : a name of Sītā; meaning the daughter of King Janaka.

***Jyeṣṭha*** : name of a lunar month.

## K

***kadamba*** : a big tree with very fragrant, beautiful, solid, round flowers, especially grown in Vṛndāvana (Scientific name- *Anthocephalus cadamba Mig.* Family- *Rubiaceae*).

**Kali** : the fourth age of the world, the Iron Age (consisting of 432,000 years of men and beginning of the 8th February, 3102 B.C.)

**Kalki** : the tenth and last incarnation of Viṣṇu in his capacity of the destroyer of the wicked and liberator of the world from its enemies.

***kalpa*** : A day of Brahmā or 1000 *Yuga*s being a period of 432 million years of mortals and measuring the duration of the world.

***kalpataru*** : one of the trees of heaven or Indra's paradise; supposed to grant all desires; wish yielding tree.

**Kamalāpati** : an epither of Viṣṇu; meaning the Lord of Kamalā, i.e. Lakṣmī.

**Kaṁsa** : the maternal uncle of Kṛṣṇa; after hearing an omen that he would be killed by the eighth child of his sister Devakī and Vasudeva, he held them captive in his prison and killed all their children; he sent many demons to kill Kṛṣṇa in Vṛndāvana and was later on killed by Kṛṣṇa himself in a wrestling match.

**Kanakāvatī** : a friend of Sītā-devī.

**Kandarpa** : another name of the Love God, Kāmadeva.

***kanyādāna*** : giving away a girl in marriage according to rites.

***karatāla*** : a kind of musical instrument; a cymbal.

***karma*** : fate; certain consequence of actions done in a previous existence.

***Kaumudī*** : the mace of Viṣṇu.

***kaustubha*** : a celebrated gem obtained with thirteen other jewels at the churning of the ocean and worn by Viṣṇu on his breast.

**Kauśalyā** : the eldest wife of Daśaratha; the mother of Lord Rāma.

**Kauśika** : another name of Viśvāmitra.

***kāhāla*** : a large drum.

**Kāli** : a tremendously large multi-headed water serpent who dwelt at the bottom of the Yamunā, a ground forbidden to Garuḍa; he was banished from Vṛndāvana by Lord Kṛṣṇa because he had poisoned the Yamunā.

**Kālindī** : a lake connected with or coming from the mountain Kalinda or the river Yamunā.

**Kāmadeva** : another name of the Love God; Cupid.

***kāmadhenu*** : wish-fulfilling cows.

**Kāmarūpa** : the kingdom of Narakāsura, on the western portion of present day Assam.

**Kānā** : an intimate nickname of Kṛṣṇa.

**Kānu** : an intimate nickname of Kṛṣṇa.

***keli kadama*** : big wood-producing, medicinal tree with fragrant flowers, (Scientific name- *Adina cordifolia Hook. f.* Family- *Rubiaceae*).

**Keśava** : an epithet of Kṛṣṇa; meaning the killer of the Keśī demon.

**Kṛṣṇa** : the eighth incarnation of Viṣṇu born as the son of Vasudeva and Devakī; the most celebrated hero of Indian mythology and most popular of all the deities; brought up by his foster parents Nanda and Yaśodā in Vṛndāvana where he killed many demons and his chief companions were the cowherds of Gokula and their wives; he is dark-bluish-black in complexion.

***kṣatriya*** : a man belonging to military or second of the four original castes (*brāhmaṇa, kṣatriya, vaiśya* and *śūdra)* of the Hindus.

**Kubjī** : the hunchbacked maid of Kaṁsa; Kṛṣṇa and Balarāma, while proceeding to Mathurā, saw her carrying fruit to Kaṁsa and asked her for some of them. She gave as much as they wanted. Kṛṣṇa being very much pleased with her kindness, made her perfectly straight and she began to appear a very beautiful woman.

**Kumudākṣa** : one of the kings who came as suitors of Sītā-devī.

***kuṁkum*** *:* a red-coloured cosmetic.

**Kuṇḍina** : the capital of the Vidarbhas.

***kuśa*** *:* a kind of grass considered holy and forming an essential requisite of several religious ceremonies (Scientific name- *Eragrostis cynosuroides Beauv.* = *Desmostachya bipinnata Stapf.* Family- *Poaceae*).

**Kuvalayapīḍa** : the celebrated elephant of Kaṁsa; he tried to kill Kṛṣṇa and Balarāma as ordered by Kaṁsa and was later on killed by Kṛṣṇa himself.

**Kuvera** : the God of riches and treasure and the regent of the northern quarters.

**Kūrmmarāja** : Viṣṇu in the form of a tortoise in his second incarnation.

## L

**Lakṣmaṇa** : a son of Daśaratha and younger brother of Rāma; he was very much attached to his elder brother Rāma and accompanied him during his travels and even during his fourteen year exile.

**Lakṣmī** : the goddess of fortune, prosperity and beauty; she is regarded as the wife of Viṣṇu.

**Līlāvatī** : a friend of Princess Rukmiṇī.

## M

**Madana** : another name of the Love God, Kāmadeva.

**Madana Mañjarī** : a friend of Princess Rukmiṇī.

**Madanamantharā** : a friend of Sītā-devī.

**Madhāi** : an intimate nickname of Kṛṣṇa.

**Madhusūdana** : an epithet of Kṛṣṇa; meaning the killer of the demon Madhu.

*mahāpuruṣa* : a great man; an eminent and distinguished person; the Supreme Spirit.

**Mahendra** : the great Indra.

**Maheśa** : a name of Śiva; meaning the Great Lord.

**Maheśvara** : a name of Śiva; meaning the Great Lord.

**Maithilī** : a name of Sītā; meaning the Princess of the kingdom of Mithilā.

**Manasija** : another name of the Love God Kāmadeva.

**Mandara** : name of a mountain used by the gods and demons as the churning stick for churning the ocean for nectar.

**Maṇi** : a mountain.

**Maṇimanta** : a minister of King Janaka.

**Manmatha** : another name of the Love God Kāmadeva.

*mantra* : a Vedic hymn or sacred prayer addressed to any deity.

**Mādhava** : a name of Kṛṣṇa; meaning the husband of Lakṣmī.

**Mithilā** : capital of a country named Videha, the kingdom of King Janaka.

**Mohana** : an intimate nickname of Kṛṣṇa; meaning the one who fascinates.

*mokṣa* : liberation; deliverance; final emancipation of the soul from recurring births or transmigration; the last of the four ends of human existence (*dharma*, *artha*, *kāma*, *mokṣa*).

*mṛdaṅga* : a kind of drum or tabor.

**Mura** : a demon slain by Kṛṣṇa.

**Murāri** : an epithet of Kṛṣṇa; meaning the enemy of the demon Mura.

**Murāru** : an intimate nickname of Kṛṣṇa; meaning the enemy of the demon Mura.

**Muṣṭika** : a demon.

## N

**Nanda** : the foster father of Kṛṣṇa; chief of the cowherds of Vṛndāvana.

**Narakāsura** : name of a demon; king of Prāgjyotiṣa; he was born of earth; he carried away the earrings of Aditi and seized the daughters of Gandharvas, gods, men and the nymphs and collected more than sixteen thousand damsels in his harem; Kṛṣṇa killed him at the request of the gods and rescued everything.

**Narasiṁha** : the fourth incarnation of Viṣṇu in the form of half lion and half man; he tore apart the king of demons Hiraṇyakaśipu.

***nāma-guṇa*** : the name and attributes of Kṛṣṇa.

**Nārāyaṇa** : an epithet of Viṣṇu.

## P

***padminī*** : a woman of the first of the four classes into which writers on erotical science divide women.

***pañcāmṛta*** : the collection of five sweet things (yogurt, milk, clarified butter, honey and sugar) used in auspicious occasions.

**Paraśurāma** : name of a celebrated *brāhmaṇa* warrior; the sixth incarnation of Viṣṇu; while young he cut off the head of his mother Reṇukā with his axe at the command of his father; he made a vow to exterminate the whole *kṣatriya* race and travelled around the earth thrice seven times for the purpose, (as *kṣatriya* princes killed his father when he was alone in his hermitage); he was later on defeated by Lord Rāma.

**Pareśa** : another name of Brahmā.

**Pāñcajanya** : Lord Kṛṣṇa's conchshell.

***pārijāta*** : name of one of the five trees of paradise, said to have been produced at the churning of the ocean and come into the possession of Indra, from whom it was wrested by Kṛṣṇa and planted in the garden of his beloved Satyabhāmā (Scientifc name- *Canna indica, Linn.* = *C. orientalis Rose.* Family- *Cannaceae).*

**Pātāla** : the last of the seven regents (Atala, Bitala, Sutala, Rasātala, Talātala, Mahātala, and Pātāla) or worlds under the earth said to be peopled by *nāgas.*

**Pītāmbara** : a name of Kṛṣṇa; meaning the one who wears yellow clothing.

**Prahara** : the eighth part of a whole day, a period roughly reckoned at three hours.

**Prāgjyotiṣa** : the kingdom of Narakāsura, on the western portion of present day Assam.

**Purandara** : another name of Indra.

**Purañjaya** : one of the kings who came as suitors of Sītā-devī.

**Pūtanā** : a female demon who, while attempting to kill Kṛṣṇa when but an infant, was herself crushed to death by him.

## R

**Raghu** : name of a celebrated king of the solar race; an ancestor of Lord Rāma.

**Raghunātha** : an epithet of Rāma; meaning the Lord of the Raghu dynasty.

**Ramaṇaka** : an island where the serpent Kāliya resided formerly, but he left the place for fear of Garuḍa and went to the Yamunā.

**Rādhā** : name of a celebrated *gopī* or cowherdess loved by Kṛṣṇa.

***Rāga*** : musical mode or order of sound; there are six primary *rāgas* and each *rāga* has six *rāginīs* regarded as its consorts and their union gives rise to several musical modes.

**Rāghava** : a name of Rāma; meaning a descendent of Raghu.

**Rāhu** : a demon, supposed to be a planet, that devours the Sun and the Moon on particular days, as is the common belief.

**Rāma** : the seventh incarnation of Viṣṇu; name of a celebrated King of Ayodhyā; meaning, pleasing, delighting beautiful, lovely, obscure, dark-coloured, black; the son of King Daśaratha; he went with sage Viśvāmitra to protect his sacrifice from the disturbing demons; he married Sītā, the daughter of King Janaka, by breaking the bow of Śiva; he later on killed the demon Rāvaṇa who had kidnapped and held his wife Sītā captive in his kingdom of Laṅkā; three personalities are named as Rāma: Paraśurāma, Raghupati Rāma and Balarāma.

***rāsa*** : a kind of sportive circular dance practised by Kṛṣṇa along with the cowherd women of Vraja.

**Rāvaṇa** : name of a celebrated King of Laṅkā and the chief of the demons; he had ten heads; he carried off Sītā and hence Rāma, assisted by his monkey troops, invaded Laṅkā and annihilated Rāvaṇa's troops and the demon himself.

**Reṇukā** : the mother of Paraśurāma.

**Rudra** : another name of Śiva.

***rudrākṣa*** : a tree whose berries are used for rosaries (Scientific name- *Eleocarpus ganitrus Roxb. -= E. Sphaericus K. Schum.* Family- *Tiliaceae*).

**Rukmiṇī** : the daughter of King Bhīṣmka of Vidarbha; she secretly loved Kṛṣṇa and sent him a letter praying to take her away, Kṛṣṇa came and snatched her off having defeated her brother and Śiśupāla and made her his queen.

**Rukmī** : the eldest son of Bhīṣmka; the brother of Rukmiṇī.

## S

**Satrājit** : the father of Satyabhāmā.

**Satyabhāmā** : the daughter of Satrājit; the wife of Kṛṣṇa; it was for her that Kṛṣṇa fought with Indra and brought the *pārijāta* tree from the garden of Indra and planted it in her garden.

***Śāraṅga*** : the bow of Kṛṣṇa.

**Śāraṅgapāṇi** : a name of Kṛṣṇa; meaning one who holds the bow *Śāraṅga* in his hand.

***siddhas*** : a semi-divine being said to be of great purity and holiness, and said to be particularly characterised by eight supernatural faculties called *siddhis*.

**Sītā** : the daughter of King Janaka and wife of Rāma; she was kidnapped by Rāvaṇa and was rescued by Rāma after killing Rāvaṇa.

**Sudharmmā Sabhā** : the assembly of gods.

***surabhi*** : a breed of cows generally found on the Vaikuṇṭha planets; the *surabhi* cow can yield milk unlimitedly, one can take as much milk as one needs, and one may milk these cows as many times as he desires.

**Sūryaprabhā** : a friend of Sītā-devī.

***sūtradhāra*** : the most important character who plays the role of director, narrator actor, singer and also the stage manager in the plays of Śaṅkaradeva.

**Svapas** : a sage.

**Svayambhū** : a name of Lord Brahmā.

***svayamvara*** : self choice or self selection of a husband by the bride herself.

**Śacī** : the wife of Indra.

***Śaka*** : an epoch, an era; the term is especially applied to the era Sālivāhana which commences 78 years after the Christian era.

**Śambhu** : a name of Lord Śiva.

**Śaṅkara** : a name of Lord Śiva; also implies Śaṅkaradeva, the preacher of *neo-Vaiṣṇavism* in Assam.

***śaṅkha*** : conschell.

**Śaṅkhacūḍa** : a demon who stole away *gopīs* from the *rāsa* dance and was thus killed by Kṛṣṇa.

**Śaśīprabhā** : the queen consort of King Bhīṣmka.

**Śatadhanu** : one of the kings who came as suitors of Sītā-devī.

*śāl* : a very tall and stately tree, producing wood of the best quality; (Scientific name- *Shorea robusta Gaertn.* Family- *Dipterocarpacaea*).

*śiriṣa* : a wood producing big tree with flowers regarded as a type of delicacy (Scientific name- *Albizzia lebbeck Benth.* Family- *Mimosaceae*).

**Śiśupāla** : king of the Chedis; According to the *Viṣṇu-Purāṇa,* this monarch was in a previous existence, the unrighteous Hiraṇyakaśipu, king of the demons killed by Viṣṇu in his incarnation of Nṛsiṁha. Next he was born as Rāvaṇa who was killed by Rāma and then being born as Śiśupāla, he continued his enmity to Kṛṣṇa, and finally his head was cut off by Kṛṣṇa with his disc.

**Śiva** : name of the third God of the sacred Hindu Trinity, who is entrusted with the work of destruction, as Brahmā and Viṣṇu are entrusted with the creation and preservation of the world.

*śloka* : a hymn

**Śrī** : an honorific prefix to the names of deities and eminent persons.

**Śrī Batsa** : an epithet of Viṣṇu; a mark or curl of hair on the breast of Viṣṇu.

**Śrī Rāma Rāyā** : an epithet of Jagatānanda-dalai, given by the Āhom king; he was a kinsmen of Śaṅkaradeva and enjoyed some favour from the Āhom kingdom; Śaṅkaradeva acknowledges patronage of Rāma Rāyā in four of his plays.

**Śyāma** : a name of Kṛṣṇa; meaning the black, dark-blue, dark coloured one.

## T

*tapovana* : the penance-groove, a sacred groove in which ascetics practise penance.

**Tāḍakā** : a female fiend; she was killed by Rāma when she began to distu[illegible] the sacrificial rites of Viśvāmitra.

***tāla*** : a musical instrument made of bell metal; a kind of cymbal.
***tulasī*** : the holy basil held in veneration by the Hindus especially the worshippers of Viṣṇu.

## V

**Vaidehī** : another name of Sītā; meaning the Princess of Videha.
**Vaikuṇṭha** : the spiritual world consisting of many planets associated with Lord Viṣṇu; meaning the world where there is no anxiety.
*Vajra* : a thunderbolt, the weapon of Indra, said to have been formed out of the bones of the sage Dadhīci.
***vanamālā*** : a garland of wood flowers.
**Vanamālī** : a name of Kṛṣṇa; meaning the one wearing *vanamālā*.
**Varuṇa** : regent of the ocean and of the western quarter, representated with a noose in hand.
**Vasumatī** : the earth; the mother of Narakāsura.
**Vatsa** : a demon who came to kill Kṛṣṇa and Balarāma in the shape of a calf while they were playing on the bank of the Yamunā and was killed eventually by Kṛṣṇa.
**Vāmana** : the fifth incarnation of Viṣṇu in the form of a dwarf to humble the demon Bali.
**Vāsava** : another name of Indra.
**Vāsudeva** : an epithet of Kṛṣṇa; meaning the son of Vasudeva.
**Vāsuki** : name of a celebrated serpent, the king of the snakes.
*Veda* : knowledge; sacred knowledge; the scriptures of the Hindus; there are four *Vedas,* (i.e.,*Ṛg-veda, Yajur-veda, Sāma-veda* and *Atharva-veda*).
*Veda-śāstras* : the Vedic scriptures.
**Vedanidhi** : a *brāhmaṇa* friend of Rukmiṇī.
**Vidarbha** : the kingdom of Bhīṣmka.
*vidyādharas* : a class of demigods or semi-divine beings.
**Viṣṇu** : name of the second God of the sacred Hindu Trinity entrusted with the preservation of the world, which duty

he is represented to have duly discharged by his various incarnations; his vehicle is Garuḍa.

**Viśvāmitra** : name of a celebrated sage who was originally a *kṣatriya* but attained the rank of *brahmarṣi* by virtue of his rigorous austerities; he was the companion and counselor of young Rāma to whom he gave several miraculous missiles.

**Vraja** : name of a district near Mathurā; meaning a station of cowherds, a cow-shed.

**Vṛndāvana** : name of a forest near Gokula in present day Uttar Pradesh where Kṛṣṇa spent his childhood as a cowherd boy under the care of Nanda and Yaśodā.

## Y

**Yadu** : name of an ancient king descending from Soma, the god in the moon planet.

**Yadunātha** : a name of Kṛṣṇa; meaning the Lord of the Yadu dynasty.

***yakṣa*** : name of a class of demigods who are described as attendents of Kuvera, the God of riches, who are employed in guarding the garden and treasures of Kuvera.

**Yama** : the God of death; death personified; regarded as a son of the Sun.

**Yamunā** : a celebrated river of India flowing through Vṛndāvana, on whose banks Kṛṣṇa performed many pastimes along with his cowherd friends.

**Yaśodā** : the wife of Nanda, the foster mother of Kṛṣṇa.

**Yaśomati** : another name of Yaśodā.

**Yādava** : a descendent of Yadu.

●●●

# BIBLIOGRAPHY

(A) Assamese :

Barman, Sivanath, ed., *Asamīyā Sāhityar Burañjī, Dvitīya Khaṇḍa*, Anundoram Borooah Institute of Language, Art and Culture, Guwahati, 1997.

Barua, Birinchikumar, ed., *Aṅkīyā Nāṭ*, Department of Historical and Antiquarian Studies, Govt. of Assam, Guwahati, 4th edn., Feb. 2012.

Baruah, Navakanta, *Asamīyā Chanda Silpar Bhūmikā*, Assam Book Dipo, Guwahati, 5th edn.

Bhagavati, Kamakhya Caraṇ, ed., *Rām Bijay Nāṭ*, New Book Stall, Guwahati.

Bharali, Sailen, *Mādhav Kandalir Para Māmoṇi Goswāmīloi*, Chandra Prakash, Guwahati, 2004.

Bora, Mahim, ed., *Śaṅkardevar Nāṭ*, Publication Board, Assam, Guwahati, 2nd edn., 2003.

Chutia, Dharmeswar, ed., *Mahāpuruṣa Śrīmanta Śaṅkaradeva Vākyāmṛta*, Srimanta Sankaradeva Sangha, Nagaon, 1998.

Das, Narayan, *Brajabuli Bhāṣā Āru Sāhitya*, Bina Library, Guwahati, 2nd edn., 2001.

Goswami, Jatindra Nath and Das, Muraricharan, ed., *Kaliram Medhi Rachanabali*, Asam Sahitya Sabha, Jorhat, 1979.

Goswami, Kesavananda dev, ed., *Aṅkamālā*, Banalata, New Market, Dibrugarh, 3rd edn., 1999.

Goswami, Kesavananda dev, *Aṅkīyā Bhāonā*, Banalata, New Market, Dibrugarh, 3rd edn., 2000.

Goswami, Suren, *Asamīyā Gadya Sāhitya*, Devjani Prakashan, Mirja, 1995.

Hazarika, Karabi Deka, *Asamīyā Sāhityar Rūp-Ras*, Banalata, Dibrugarh, 1985.

Hazarika, Manasmrita Hazarika, ed., *Rāmbijay Nāṭ*, Bani Mandir, Guwahati, 2004.

Lekharu, Upendrachandra, ed., *Kathā Gurucarita*, Dutta Baruah & Co., Guwahati, 15th edn., 1987.

Mahanta Bap Chandra, *Aitihāsik Paṭabhūmit Mahāpuruṣ Śaṅkaradev*, Banalata, Dibrugarh, 1999.

Mahanta, Bapchandra, *Yugāntarat Śaṅkardev*, Mahanta Prakashan, Jorhat, Assam, 1991.

Mahanta, Golap, Śaṅkarī Saṅgītar Ādhār Grantha,( Sādhāraṇ Ālocanā Āru Rāgar Biśleṣaṇ), Śrīmanta Śaṅkardeva Saṅgha, Guwahati, 2002.

Mahanta, Lakshmikanta, Asamīyā Sāhitya Adhyayan, Banalata, Natun Bazar, Dibrugarh, 2nd edn., 1993.

Mahanta, Pona, *Nāṭak Āru Nāṭyakār*, Banalata, New Market, Dibrugarh,2nd edn.,1992.

Mahanta, Pona, *Nāṭakar Kathā*, Banalata, New Market, Dibrugarh, 1st edn., Feb.2004.

Mahanta, Pradip Jyoti, ed., *Śrīmanta Śaṅkaradeva Samāj Āru Sanshriti*, Puberun Prakash, Ambari,Guwahati, 2000.

Mazumdar, Uttam Kumar, ed. *Rukmiṇī Haraṇ Nāṭ*, Saha Book Stall, Abhayāpurī, 1st edn., 2005.

Medhi, Kaliram, ed., *Mahāpuruṣ Śaṅkardevar Bāṇī*, Kaliram Medhi Trust, Lawyer's Book Stall, Guwahati, 1997.

Medhi, Kaliram, ed.,*Aṅkāvalī*, Kaliram Medhi Trust, Lawyer's Book Stall, Guwahati, 1997.

Neog, Dimbeswar, *Natun Poharat Asamīyā Sāhityar Burañjī*, Suwani Prakash, Guwahati, 1999.

Neog, Maheswar, *Asamīyā Sāhityar Rūprekhā*, Chandra Prakash, 9th edn., 2000.

Neog, Maheswar and Changkakati, Keshav, Vādya-viśārad, *Sattrīā Nṛtya Aru Sattrīā Nṛtyar Tāl*, Publication Board, Assam, 2nd edn., 1975.

Neog, Maheswar, *Śrī Śrī Śaṅkaradeva*, Dr. Maheswar Neog Publication Trust, Chandra Prakash, Tihu, Assam, 7th edn., 1987.

Neog, Maheswar, ed., *Banikanta Rachanavali*, Publication Board of Assam, Guwahati, 2nd edn., 2003.

Sarma, Baladev, *Udbhīd Jñānkoṣ*, Bani Mandir, Guwahati, 1st edn.,2002.

Sarma, Hemanta Kumar, *Assamīyā Sāhityat Dṛṣṭipāt*, Bina Library, Guwahati, 10th edn., 2005.

Sarma, Nabin Chandra, ed., *Kāliya Daman Nāṭ*, New Book Stall, Guwahati, 3rd edn.,1989.

Sarma, Nabin Chandra, ed., *Rukmiṇī Haraṇ Nāṭ*, Bani Prakash Pvt. Ltd.,Guwahati, 2nd edn., 1998.

Sarma, Rajaikanta Dev, ed., *Rukmiṇī Haraṇ Nāṭ*, New Book Stall, Guwahati,8th edn., 1993.

Sarma, Satyendra Nath, *Asamīyā Nāṭya Sāhitya*, Saumar Prakash, Guwahati, 8th edn.,2002.

Sarma, Satyendra Nath, *Asamīyā Sāhityar Samīkṣātmak itibṛtta*, Saumar Prakash, Guwahati, 9th edn.,2006.

Sarma, Satyendra Nath, ed., *Pārijāt Haraṇ Nāṭ*, New Book Stall, Guwahati, 3rd edn.,2002.

Sarma, Tirtha Nath, Sāhitya Vidyā Parikramā, Bani Prakash Pvt. Ltd.,Guwahati,10th edn., 2008.

Sarmadalai, Harinath, ed., *Rāmbijay Nāṭ*, Alok Prakashan Griha, Nalbari, Assam, 2nd edn., 1992.

Sharma, Mukunda Madhava, *Dhvani Āru Rasatattva*, Bani Prakash Pvt. Ltd., Guwahati, 2nd edn., 1991.

(B) English :

Anderson, Janathan, ed., *Thesis and Assignment Writing*, Wiley Eastern Limited, New Delhi.

Barua, Birinchi Kumar, *A Cultural History of Assam(Early Period)*, Bina Library, Guwahati, 3rd edn.,1986.

Brockington, J. L., *A Sacred Thread, A Short History of Hinduism*, Oxford University Press, New Delhi, 2nd edn., 2000.

Chakravarty, Shrutidhara, *Studies in Sanskrit Literature, Culture and Art*, Pratibha Prakashan, Delhi, 2011.

Crill R., 'Vrindavani Vastra : Figured Silks from Assam' (Retrieved from: https://docs.google.com/file/d/0B94xiNEdazrMNDE3MzNhMTkt N2Y0ZS00ODYyLTllYzQtYmRkZWZlNTc1NzY3/edit?hl=en_US).

Dasgupta, R.K., 'Sankaradeva : The Founder of Assamese Vaisnavism', (Retrieved October 10, 2012, from http://www.atributetosankaradeva.org/Sankaradeva_%20Founder_of_Assamese_Vaisnavism.pdf.).

Gait, Sir Edward, *A History of Assam*, Surjeet Publication, Delhi, 3rd edn., 2006.

Goswami, Kesavananda Dev, *Mahāpuruṣa Śaṅkaradeva*, Publication Board of Assam, Guwahati, 2007.

Haque Md. Z., 'Translating Literary Prose: Problems and Solutions', *In International Journal of English Linguistics*, Vol. 2, No. 6; 2012, p. 99. (Retrieved on 2013-01-12 from: http://www.ccsenet.org/journal/index.php/ijel/issue/view/702).

Kasparek C., 'The Translator's Endless Toil', The Polish Review, Vol. 28, No. 2 (1983), p. 84 (Available at: http://www.jstor.org/stable/25777966).

Long, W.J., *English Literature, its History and its Significance*, Kalyani Publishers, 1989.

Mahanta, P., *Scholar Critic Mukunda Madhava Sharma*, Anundoram Barooah Institute of Language, Art &Culture, Assam, North Guwahati, 2001.

Neog, Maheswar, *Śaṅkaradeva and His Times Early History of the Vaiṣṇava Faith and Movement in Assam*, Lawyer's Book Stall, Guwahati, 3rd edn.,1998.

Neog, Maheswar, *Sankaradeva*, National Book Trust, India, New Delhi, 2006.

Prabhupāda, A.C. Bhaktivedanta Swami, *Bhagavad-Gītā As It Is*, Bhaktivedanta Book Trust, Juhu, Mumbai, 2nd ed., 2007.

Rajkhowa, Jyoti Prasad, *Generalissimo Chilarai and His Times*, Vikram Publishers, Guwahati, 2001.

Saikia, Purnananda, *Śrīmanta Śaṅkaradeva's The Kīrtana-Ghoṣā*, Śrīmanta Śaṅkaradeva Sangha, 2005.

Sarma, Satyendra Nath, *Madhavadeva*, Sahitya Akademi, New Delhi, 1985.

Sarma, Satyendra Nath, *The Neo-Vaiṣṇavite Movement and the Satra Institution of Assam*, Lawyer's Book Stall, Guwahati, 1999.

William L. Smith, 'The Translation of Shankaradeva's Parijata Haraṇa Nata', *In* Bryant, E. F. (ed.), *Krishna. A Source Book*, Oxford University Press, 2007 (Longer summary available at: http://www.atributetosankaradeva.org/parijata.pdf).

Zakhir M., 'The History of Translation'. *In* Zainurrahman (ed.), *The Theories of Translation: From History to Procedures*, p. 3. (Retrieved February 20, 2013 from http://zainurrahmans.wordpress.com/2009/05/27/the-theories-of translation-download-e-book/).

(C) Dictionaries and Lexicons :

Apte, Vaman Shivram, *The Student's Sanskrit-English Dictionary*, Motilal Banarsidass Publishers Private Limited, Delhi, 2nd edn., Reprint 2005.

Barua, Hem Chandra, *Hem-Koṣ*, (the Assamese-English Dictionary), Devananda Barua, 6th edn., 1985.

Bhattacharya, Śrīmadgurunath Vidyanidhi, ed.and translated(to Bengali), *Amarkoṣ*, Sanskrit Pustak Bhandar, Kolkata, 1988.

Goswami, Narayan Chandra, *Brajāvalī Bhāṣār Vyākaraṇ Aru Abhidhān*,(Assamese) Lawyer's Book Stall, Guwahati, 2nd edn., 2000.

Pathak, R.C., ed.,*Bhargav's Standard Illustrated Dictionary* (Hindi-English), Bhargava Book Depot, Varanasi,5th edn., 1995.

Thompson, Della, ed., *The Pocket Oxford Dictionary of Current English*, Oxford University Press, New Delhi, 8th Indian edn., 1996.

(D) Websites :

http://www.vedabase.net
http://zainurrahmans.wordpress.com
http://www.thehindu.com
http://www.jstor.org
http://www.ccsenet.org
http://www.atributetosankaradeva.org
http://articles.timesofindia.indiatimes.com

'Majuli monks to perform unique dance drama in France, Switzerland'. *The Hindu*, Guwahati: June 12, 2012 (Retrieved from: http://www.thehindu.com/news/national/other-states/majuli-monks-to-perform-unique-dance-drama-in-france-switzerland/article3516444.ece).

'Rare Manuscript, textile from Northeast holed up in museums abroad'. *The Times of India,* Guwahati: September 25, 2007 (Retrieved from: http://articles.timesofindia.indiatimes.com/2007-09-25/india/27982679_1_manuscript-british-museum-silks).

(E) Computer Searchable Database :

Bhaktivedanta Vedabase 2003.1 : created by Folio Views, Bhaktivedanta Archives.

●●●

# GENERAL INDEX

●●●

# PERSON INDEX